AMERICAN INDIANS AND THE LAW

Edited by
Lawrence Rosen

Transaction Books
New Brunswick, New Jersey

Copyright © 1976 by Duke University.

Library of Congress Catalog Number: 77-80868
ISBN: 0-87855-266-9 (cloth)
Printed in the United States of America

Published 1978 by Transaction, Inc., New Brunswick, New Jersey 08903.

Library of Congress Cataloging in Publication Data
Main entry under title:

American Indians and the law.

   Reprint of the 1976 ed. published by School of Law, Duke University, Durham, N.C., which was issued as v. 40, no. 1 of Law and contemporary problems.
   Includes bibliographical references.
   1. Indians of North America—Legal status, laws, etc.—Addresses, essays, lectures.
I. Rosen, Lawrence, 1941-   II. Series: Law and contemporary problems; v. 40, no. 1.
[KF8205.A2A47]   342'.73'087   77-80868
ISBN 0-87855-266-9

CONTENTS

AMERICAN INDIANS AND THE LAW

FOREWORD

The American Indian occupies a unique position in American society and law. Although United States citizens, reservation Indians are not subject to the Federal Constitution or to the taxes and regulatory controls of the states in which they live and vote. Although many tribes have formulated their own constitutions and established their own courts, reservation governments are not recognized as fully sovereign entities. And although reservation Indians are characterized at times as wards of the federal government, no consistent standard of responsibility has been established to define and delimit the plenary power of Congress over the entire range of Indian affairs. As the contributors to this symposium indicate, the unique position of the American Indian is deeply affected by the social, economic, and historical context in which the relations between Indians and white America have developed.

At present Indians are among the poorest members of American society. A few statistics help to portray the bare outlines of their situation. Of the 763,000 people who identified themselves as Indians in the 1970 census,[1] 38 per cent had incomes below the poverty line. In the poorest areas of Arizona and Utah this figure reached upwards of 65 per cent, while unemployment for reservation men, which averaged 18 per cent nationwide, climbed well above the 30 per cent mark in many areas. Death from tuberculosis, dysentery, and accidents occurs four times more frequently among Indians than among the rest of the population. And although educational levels have been rising, the average number of years of schooling for Indians is still from one to three years less than for whites.

The social and economic problems of the Indian do not result only from the greed and duplicity of those who invaded the continent and forced or

---

1. The census data cited here is derived from U.S. BUREAU OF THE CENSUS, DEP'T OF COMMERCE, 1970 CENSUS OF THE POPULATION: AMERICAN INDIANS, at PC(2)-1F (1972). The overall population figure does not include the 34,000 Eskimo and Aleut peoples. Since the census survey does not include figures for over half of the more than 280 Indian reservations, the statistics cited here should not be regarded as comprehensive. For a general compilation of Indian survey data see S. LEVITAN & W. JOHNSTON, INDIAN GIVING: FEDERAL PROGRAMS FOR NATIVE AMERICANS (1975). The data on Indian health are drawn from U.S. DEP'T OF HEALTH, EDUCATION, AND WELFARE, INDIAN HEALTH SERVICE, INDIAN HEALTH TRENDS AND SERVICES (1974).

cajoled its original inhabitants to occupy ever more marginal lands. These problems also result from a long history of inconsistent laws and regulations, ill-conceived policies and contradictory reforms. Initially, federal policy recognized the limited autonomy of Indian tribes while actively encouraging them to adopt white technology and culture. Thomas Jefferson believed that the Indian was uniquely adaptable, and that with the aid of advanced technology, he would create the basis for an indigenous American yeomanry.[2] Whatever its theoretical merits, Jefferson's conception was undermined by a series of social and economic forces. The sudden introduction of modern technology among the tribes created pressures that struck at the bases of Indian social organization: their own society was being destroyed at the same time that the Indians were given no distinct place in American society at large.

In the period from 1830 to 1870, American policy was nominally directed toward the protection of tribal communities, but actually consisted of removing most tribes from the eastern half of the nation and isolating them in enclaves where missionaries and government officers could pursue their goal of "civilizing" the Indian. The establishment of reservations neither abated pioneer intrusion nor government aversion to the existence of separate entities within the body politic. The General Allotment Act of 1887 aimed at breaking up the communal land base of tribal existence by individualizing property holdings. By 1928, when it was evident that allotment had failed as a vehicle for assimilation and economic development, a new federal policy was adopted. Through the Indian Reorganization Act of 1934, the New Deal administration sought to support tribal organization and collective landholding by restricting the alienation of individual allotments, permitting tribes to organize their own governments, and increasing the level of federal support programs. Subsequent programs were directed toward the termination of the special status of tribal communities and the relocation of individual Indians away from their reservations, but these programs have in turn been denounced and partly rescinded by subsequent administrations.

In short, as Wilcomb Washburn points out, Indian legal history has been characterized by a series of ad hoc policies arising from momentary exigencies and grounded in no clearly articulated set of general principles. American Indian policy thus gives the appearance of a series of geologic strata, each successive layer being supported by but not completely effacing those of an earlier time. The allotment policy may have been overlaid by the Indian Reorganization Act, but allotments that were already formed have continued to exist, subject to federal trust supervision. Tribes whose federal services were terminated have remained subject to the effects of the discredited Ter-

---

2. B. SHEEHAN, SEEDS OF EXTINCTION: JEFFERSONIAN PHILANTHROPY AND THE AMERICAN INDIAN (1974).

mination Policy even as they seek to be reinstated to their former position. Neither Congress nor the courts have thus far succeeded in reducing the ambiguities and inconsistencies of Indian legal status.

It is, however, well within the power of Congress to alter the legal position of Indian tribes. Courts have consistently recognized that the power granted Congress under the Constitution is extensive in the field of Indian affairs, and wholesale legislative reform has been a preferred instrument for altering federal Indian policy. Recognizing the confused state of current programs and statutes, Congress has established the Indian Policy Review Commission and authorized it to formulate recommendations for possible legislative action. As Congressman Lloyd Meeds, Vice-Chairman of the Commission, points out, the investigations conducted by the Commission's numerous task forces should help to clarify the implications that would stem from the enactment of any federal Indian policies.

Any reconsideration of Indian policy will, of course, have to take into account the contending interests of the basic triad of powers involved in Indian affairs—the federal, state, and tribal governments. New policies must also consider those judicial doctrines on which the participants have come to rely; the conflicting interests of white farmers, ranchers, and environmentalists; and the aims of private corporations and public utilities seeking to utilize reservation resources. No less important is the choice of rationales used by courts to interpret the scope of federal power. The limitations on the power of the federal government vary as the source of that power is seen to rest on the initial right of discovery or conquest, the nature and terms of individual treaties, or the constitutional grant of control over trade and intercourse with the Indian tribes. If the precise range of federal, state, and tribal powers is not clearly articulated for all situations, new legislative programs affecting American Indians will only be as good as their judicial interpretations.

In exploring some of the critical areas of concern in Indian law, the contributors to this symposium focus on several major issues: the exercise of jurisdiction, the control of water and mineral resources, compensation for lost properties, taxation, and education. Several additional issues on which task forces of the Indian Policy Review Commission have worked must also be mentioned: the status of non-reservation and non-treaty tribes, the applicability of the Federal Constitution to tribal proceedings, and the reconsideration of Indian treaties.

Few political groupings in the United States have felt the implications of Mr. Justice Holmes's assertion that "jurisdiction is power" more forcefully than the American Indians. Although tribes had long been denominated "domestic dependent nations" and "semi-sovereign entities," Congress and the courts have been reluctant to recognize too broad a scope of jurisdiction in the councils and tribunals of the reservation groupings. State governments, moreover, asserted that where the federal government failed to act, state courts were free to move into the legal vacuum. However, in 1958, the Supreme Court, in *Williams v. Lee*, argued that states could exercise jurisdiction over those matters the federal government had left untended only if the state's action did not infringe on the right of the tribes "to make their own laws and be ruled by them."[3] Although the Court initially narrowed its own doctrine by arguing that Congress's power was absolute only where Congress had acted to retain exclusive control,[4] the later holding in *Warren Trading Post Company v. Arizona Tax Commission*[5] reasserted that the field of Indian law was preempted by the federal government as against the states, especially where state control of reservation activities would interfere with federal policies intended to benefit the Indians. These two doctrines—the federal preemption and the furtherance of Indian self-government—have not, however, been fully or consistently explored. The uncertainties about what is meant by tribal sovereignty and the precise bounds of federal, state, and tribal power are most evident in the areas of jurisdiction and resource control.

It is axiomatic that sovereignty implies the power to interpret and enforce the laws made by one's own form of government. The federal government has recognized this power in the Indian tribes as often as it has sought to regulate it. The Indian Reorganization Act afforded tribes the opportunity to adopt constitutions and establish their own governmental machinery. But as Russell Barsh and James Youngblood Henderson indicate, the primary concern in federal approval of tribal governments has always been the maintenance, through tribal police and courts, of those cultural precepts and organizational controls that have served the goals of the dominant force. Indeed, as Steve Nickeson's analysis of the Bureau of Indian Affairs demonstrates, the political in-fighting of the federal agency most directly charged with administering federal Indian policy is incomprehensible without an understanding of how the organization of that agency is largely divorced from the interests of those it affects. Given the underlying bureaucratic structure of the agency, Nickeson suggests, the administration of any Indian policy may stray far from its stated goals and procedures.

Although many tribes adopted constitutions—which received the requisite approval of the Secretary of Interior most readily when they followed the form suggested by the Bureau of Indian Affairs—issues such as jurisdictional scope have remained open-ended. Increasingly various state and federal courts have recognized that tribes may not only exercise jurisdiction over civil matters such as contracts,[6] torts,[7] and child custody,[8] but also may enforce

---

3. 358 U.S. 217, 220 (1958).
4. Organized Village of Kake v. Egan, 369 U.S. 60 (1962).
5. 380 U.S. 685 (1965).
6. *See* Cowan v. Rosebud Sioux Tribal Court, 404 F. Supp. 1338 (D.S.D. 1975).
7. *See* Schwartz v. White Lightning, 502 F.2d 67 (8th Cir. 1974).
8. *See* Fisher v. District Court of the Sixteenth Judicial Dist. of Mont., Civil No. 75-5366 (U.S.

their own statutes against non-Indians who are present on the reservation.[9] Even where a similar statute might not be upheld if applied by state or federal authorities outside a reservation, courts have recognized that such laws might have a legitimate scope and meaning within the context of tribal culture.[10] Indeed, the laws of an Indian tribe have, in some instances, been granted full faith and credit in state court in accordance with the same principles applied to the judgments of territories and states.[11] Such a trend is, however, based on judicial constructions of ambiguous statutes and the courts' own sense of their underlying rationales, rather than on clear legislative precepts that could be given more consistent and uniform application.

To many non-Indians the fact that Indian tribunals might apply different procedures and criteria of liability than white courts—and might even apply these alien standards to non-Indians within their domain—is antithetical to both their sense of justice and their belief in the universal applicability of the standards prescribed by the Federal Constitution. In fact, the Constitution does not apply to reservation Indians.[12] Recognizing that Indians, as American citizens, should be entitled to certain guarantees similar to those embodied in the Constitution, Congress did, however, enact the Indian Civil Rights Act in 1968.[13] This Act repeats many of the provisions of the Federal Bill of Rights and applies them to the proceedings of Indian tribal governments and courts, although it does not make the Federal Constitution and all of its judicial interpretations directly applicable to the tribes.[14] To many Indians the Act is an assault on tribal sovereignty, for it allows an action to be brought in federal court for matters that, in the eyes of its detractors, are solely the concern of the Indians. In fact, the courts have tended to apply full constitutional safeguards to Indian procedures only where the Indians themselves have adopted electoral rules or judicial forms that are identical to those used in state or federal situations.[15] Where a sufficiently high interest exists in

---

Sup. Ct., Mar. 1, 1976), in 3 INDIAN L. REP. a-6 (1976); Wakefield v. Little Light, 276 Md. 333, 347 A.2d 228 (1975).

9. *See* Wakefield v. Little Light, 276 Md. 333, 347 A.2d 228 (1975); Long v. Quinault Tribe, Civil No. C75-67T (W.D. Wash., Sept. 2, 1975), in 3 INDIAN L. REP. g-13 (1976); Belgarde v. Morton, Civil No. C74-6835 (W.D. Wash., Aug. 18, 1975).

10. *See* Big Eagle v. Andera, 508 F.2d 1293 (8th Cir. 1975). *But see* State of Nevada v. Jones, Civil No. 8416 (Nev. Sup. Ct., Feb. 20, 1976), in 3 INDIAN L. REP. h-27 (1976).

11. *See* Jim v. C.I.T. Financial Services Corp., 533 P.2d 751, 87 N.M. 362 (1975).

12. *See* Talton v. Mayes, 163 U.S. 376 (1896); McCurdy v. Steele, 506 F.2d 653 (10th Cir. 1974); Tom v. Sutton, Civil No. 75-1551 (9th Cir., Mar. 10, 1976), in 3 INDIAN L. REP. e-21 (1976).

13. Pub. L. No. 90-284, tit. II, §§ 201-03, 82 Stat. 77 (codified at 25 U.S.C. §§ 1301-03 (1970)).

14. *See* Jacobson v. Forest County Potawatomi Community, 389 F. Supp. 994 (E.D. Wis. 1974); Tom v. Sutton, Civil No. 75-1551 (9th Cir., Mar. 10, 1976).

15. Rosebud Sioux Tribe v. Driving Hawk, Civil No. 76-1077 (8th Cir., Mar. 5, 1976), in 3 INDIAN L. REP. d-1 (1976); Means v. Wilson, 522 F.2d 833 (8th Cir. 1975), *cert. denied*, 96 S. Ct. 1436 (1976); White Eagle v. One Feather, 478 F.2d 1311 (8th Cir. 1973).

furthering Indian culture, the courts have not deemed the case proper for the application of strict constitutional requirements.[16] Further litigation may, therefore, establish the Act as a primary vehicle for the preservation of tribal laws and procedures. But the ever-present possibility that federal courts may override tribal decisions when they appear too foreign stands as a constant check on the full development of practices the Indians regard as authentically their own.

Like jurisdiction, control of reservation resources is permeated by ambiguous legal implications and conflicting interests. Rivers that traverse reservation lands are also used for non-Indian irrigation and power projects; fish that live their mature lives in one part of a watercourse must have access to another part if they are to propagate themselves; coal and oil that lie buried beneath tribal domains become important elements of national and international economics. Legitimate interests may exist on both sides of an issue, and often moral arguments of equal weight come into direct conflict with one another.

Control of water resources in particular brings to the fore contending interests and policies. William Veeder forcefully argues that the waters in the Yellowstone River Basin, which have been sought by energy companies for use in the extraction of reservation coal deposits, belong exclusively to the tribes whose legal rights the federal government must not fail to preserve. Monroe Price and Gary Weatherford, in their analysis of Navajo water rights, demonstrate that a tribe nevertheless may be forced to bargain away its asserted resource rights because of the need for short-term benefits that could be lost in the course of lengthy and expensive litigation over their full legal rights. Even where legislation has been passed to compensate Native Americans for land and minerals, constant pressures may exist to reduce the ostensible gain. Arthur Lazarus, Jr. and Richard West, Jr. detail the complexities of the largest such compensation program undertaken by Congress, the Alaska Native Claims Settlement Act of 1971.[17]

The role of state governments in Indian affairs takes on special importance in disputes over taxation and regulatory controls. Reservation Indians are required to pay federal income taxes, but state governments have tried various tactics to subject them to state revenue laws as well. If, as Chief Justice Marshall once said, the power to tax is the power to destroy,[18] the power to subject tribes to state taxation may be the power to destroy absolutely. Given

---

16. *See* Howlett v. Salish and Kootenai Tribes, Civil No. 75-1478 (9th Cir., Jan. 22, 1976), in 3 INDIAN L. REP. 3-10 (1976); Crowe v. Eastern Band of Cherokee Indians, 506 F.2d 1231 (4th Cir. 1974); McCurdy v. Steele, 506 F.2d 653 (10th Cir. 1974); Daly v. United States, 483 F.2d 700 (8th Cir. 1973); O'Neal v. Cheyenne River Sioux Tribe, 482 F.2d 1140 (8th Cir. 1973); Yellow Bird v. Oglala Sioux Tribe, 380 F. Supp. 438 (D.S.D. 1974). *But see* Martinez v. Santa Clara Pueblo, Civil No. 75-1615 (10th Cir., Aug. 16, 1976).

17. 43 U.S.C. §§ 1601-24 (Supp. III, 1973).

18. McCulloch v. Maryland, 17 U.S. (4 Wheat.) 316, 427 (1819).

their poor economic status and uncertain legal rights, reservation Indians might be hard put to maintain their societies and governments in the face of additional tax burdens. But if taxation by the states threatens organized reservation life, tribal taxation of non-Indian businesses operating on reservation lands may, as Carole Goldberg suggests, constitute a legitimate vehicle for developing tribal revenues. As in the case of water rights, however, the need to balance Indian taxing efforts with more immediate economic and political exigencies takes on as much importance as the question of the overall legality of an Indian taxing program. Similar problems also emerge when state and county governments attempt to apply construction, zoning, and other regulations to reservations, thereby threatening the competitive edge and governmental autonomy tribes need in order to attract capital and jobs to areas where Indians will have an opportunity to benefit from them.

Most of American Indian law has grown out of questions relating to the status of reservation tribes and property. But a substantial number of Indians no longer live on reservations, and many tribal groupings have never received federal recognition. Between 1960 and 1970 the number of Indians living in urban areas doubled, and nearly half of all Indians now live in metropolitan regions.[19] Large numbers of Indians, including most of those who live in the eastern United States and possess no treaties with the federal government, remain ineligible for federal benefits. Non-reservation Indians pose two distinct legal problems: how are such concepts as "tribe" and "Indian" to be defined for various federal purposes, and to what extent are those Indians who live off-reservation entitled to participate in benefits primarily accorded reservation dwellers? The former question has raised complex issues concerning the circumstances under which reservations cease to exist, the status of plaintiffs seeking compensation before the Indian Claims Commission, the nature of federal responsibility to a non-recognized tribe, and eligibility for preferential federal hiring based on percentage of Indian blood. Non-reservation Indians have been ruled eligible for the same welfare benefits accorded reservation residents as long as they live "near their native reservation, and . . . maintain close economic and social ties with that reservation."[20] Unresolved are the definition of "near" and the precise rights of urban Indians. Congress and the courts are faced with resolving the status of tribes that, for whatever reason, never signed treaties with the federal government, yet retain some tribal identity, and the status of individual Indians who have left their reservations to seek a livelihood elsewhere.

Indeed, the very nature of the treaties that were signed with Indian tribes

---

19. U.S. Bureau of the Census, *supra* note 1. On urban Indians generally see E. Neils, Reservation to City: Indian Migration and Federal Relocation (1971); The American Indian in Urban Society (J. Waddell & O. Watson eds. 1971).
20. Morton v. Ruiz, 415 U.S. 199, 238 (1974).

remains open to question. Courts have generally deferred to the power of Congress on the issue of treaties, even refusing to invalidate those that were clearly obtained by fraud or duress.[21] Some commentors, including Vine Deloria, Jr., argue that tribes should be regarded as "contractual sovereignties" whose autonomy for many functions is guaranteed by their original treaties.[22] Others argue that revitalizing the treaty form will complicate issues more readily handled by direct legislation. One point, however, is clear: without greater clarification of the status of existing treaties and federal willingness to honor the terms of prior agreements, it will be impossible to establish a climate of mutual trust in Indian-white relations.

Finally, programs designed to increase the availability and quality of Indian education raise important legal problems. As Daniel Rosenfelt indicates, the financing of Indian schools is often tied up with federal programs that also benefit nearby white schools. In the past, monies intended for Indian schools have been siphoned off to support school districts with few Indian students. More precise regulations and more carefully guarded administration will be necessary to ensure that benefits actually reach their intended recipients.

There has been an uneven trend toward greater self-determination by Indian tribes in recent years, but the conceptual and political bases of federal Indian policy remain clouded, confused, and contradictory. Where once whites coveted the yellow gold of the Black Hills, now they covet the black gold of the Yellowstone Basin. And as always, the simple imposition of statutory remedies is complicated by a unique history that brings the problems of necessity, fairness, and legal constancy sharply to the fore. The purpose of this symposium is to clarify the implications that might follow in the wake of any attempt to restructure federal Indian policy, and to help establish criteria on the basis of which Indians and whites can reach greater accord on their common legal problems.

LAWRENCE ROSEN

---

21. *See, e.g.*, Lone Wolf v. Hitchcock, 187 U.S. 553 (1903); Cherokee Nation v. Hitchcock, 187 U.S. 294 (1902). *See also* Wilkinson & Volkman, *Judicial Review of Indian Treaty Abrogation*, 63 CALIF. L. REV. 601 (1975).
22. V. DELORIA, JR., BEHIND THE TRAIL OF BROKEN TREATIES: AN INDIAN DECLARATION OF INDEPENDENCE 141-86 (1974).

THE INDIAN POLICY REVIEW
COMMISSION

LLOYD MEEDS*

"Congress declares that it is timely and essential to conduct a comprehensive review of the historical and legal developments underlying the Indians' unique relationship with the Federal Government in order to determine the nature and scope of necessary revisions in the formulation of policies and programs for the benefit of Indians."[1] With these profound words, the American Indian Policy Review Commission was born in the Ninety-third Congress. All of us in the field of Indian affairs in Congress have realized for some time that an organized study must be initiated and plausible legislation must be enacted to bring order and aid to the chaotic world of Indian affairs. It is clear that Congress has plenary power in Indian affairs. This power enables Congress to legislate, clarify, define, and create policy.

The unique relationship which exists between the United States and Indian tribes pre-dates the ratification of the Constitution. In 1754 the Albany Congress placed Indian affairs under auspices of the Congress. In 1775 the Continental Congress directed that three departments be established to exert a collective influence over the Indians. The Articles of Confederation, which became effective in 1781, gave "[t]he United States in Congress . . . the sole and exclusive right and power of . . . regulating the trade and managing all affairs with the Indians . . . provided that the legislative right of any State within its own limits be not infringed or violated."[2] From the earliest history of our country the federal government has had authority over Indians and Indian tribes. The relationship established from the inception of this country, however, has no exact counterpart in the history of international or domestic law. This unique relationship has never been exactly defined. Therefore, the inconsistent history of governmental relations and the vague body of law related to the Indian field has made it impossible to find justice for Indians and non-Indians alike. Solomon would have wept had he to decide justice in present-day Indian affairs.

The federal policy implementing this relationship has shifted and changed with different administrations and passing years. These policies have included peacemaking diplomacy, armed conflict, tribal removal, subjugation, extermination, concentration, assimilation, termination, and self-determination—not

* United States Representative from Washington; Vice-chairman, American Indian Policy Review Commission.
1. Act of Jan. 2, 1975, Pub. L. No. 93-580, 88 Stat. 1910.
2. ARTICLES OF CONFEDERATION art. IX.

necessarily in that order. Laws were piled upon laws without regard to the effect of the one upon the other. Programs have been initiated, terminated, replaced, and reinstituted without apparent rational design. In short, there exists a unique relationship between the United States and Indian tribes which has never admitted of an exact definition and which has never been implemented by a coherent, consistent policy.

Two major studies of Indian affairs were conducted during this century, primarily directed at the operations of the Bureau of Indian Affairs rather than at the totality of the relationship. In 1926, the Department of the Interior invited the Institute for Government Research to make a survey of the social and economic conditions of the Indians. In 1928, the Institute made a comprehensive report, known as the Meriam Report.[3] The insights of this report were basically responsible for the major reform in Indian affairs in the early 1930s, including the Indian Reorganization Act of 1934.[4]

In the Eighty-second Congress, the Committee on Interior and Insular Affairs submitted House Resolution 698, which passed the House on July 1, 1952.[5] The resolution directed and authorized the committee to make a full and complete investigation and report of the activities and operations of the Bureau of Indian Affairs. On December 15, 1952, the committee submitted its report to the House.[6] The bitter fruit of this report was the termination era of the 1950s, which has been repudiated by the Ninety-third Congress, particularly in the Menominee Restoration Act of 1973.[7]

The end result has been that the federal programs to benefit Indians and the many dollars poured into them have been a comparative failure in eliminating basic Indian problems and placing Indian people on the road to self-sufficiency.

Admittedly, the United States owes a trust responsibility to Indian tribes, but no one can define that responsibility exactly or even agree on whether or not it should be given an exact definition. And although it is admitted that Indians and Indian tribes have certain rights, the morass of conflicting or duplicating laws makes it nearly impossible to render them the necessary protection.

Congress is now in a position to assess the role of history in Indian affairs, to view its own responsibility, and to be aware of the possible consequences of suggested legislative change. Through the American Indian Policy Review Commission it is hoped that a thorough study can be made and that new legislation can be recommended to a waiting Congress.

3. L. MERIAM, THE PROBLEMS OF INDIAN ADMINISTRATION (1928).
4. Indian Reorganization Act of 1934, ch. 576, § 16, 48 Stat. 987.
5. H.R. Res. 698, 82d Cong., 2d Sess. (1952).
6. H.R. REP. No. 2503, 82d Cong., 2d Sess. (1952).
7. Menominee Restoration Act of 1973, Pub. L. No. 93-197, 87 Stat. 770.

Eleven task force study areas have been identified and three professionals have been assigned to each task force in order to perform the major functions of the Commission.[8] The actual work of the task forces began in early August 1975. Other problem areas, such as housing, have been placed specifically within the jurisdictional confines of existing task forces. Although dependent on the individual capabilities, intellectual professionalism, and tenacity of the members of each task force, Congress hopes that the recommendations provided by each task force will clarify the congressional responsibility and will precipitate organized change.

The eleven task force study areas are:

1. Trust responsibility, and federal Indian relationship
2. Tribal government
3. Federal administration and structure of Indian affairs
4. Federal, state, and tribal jurisdiction
5. Indian education
6. Indian health
7. Reservation development
8. Urban, rural nonreservation
9. Indian law revision, consolidation, and codification
10. Terminated and nonfederally recognized Indians
11. Alcoholism and drug abuse

Fortunately, very fine candidates were nominated and excellent professionals have been appointed to these task forces. The Commissioners are anxious that this Commission receive national Indian support and have been most encouraged by the acceptance of well qualified people. Each Commissioner seems keenly aware of his or her responsibility to appoint the best qualified person to the task forces.

The structure of the Commission, the caliber of the Commission members and task force personnel, and the broad spectrum of the study all present the Congress with a unique opportunity to base American Indian policy squarely on solidly-based, factual conclusions.

---

8. S. 2073, 94th Cong., 1st Sess. (1975) permits voluntary services to be contributed to the work of the Commission. Act of Aug. 9, 1975, Pub. L. No. 94-80, 89 Stat. 415.

THE HISTORICAL CONTEXT OF AMERICAN INDIAN LEGAL PROBLEMS

Wilcomb E. Washburn*

Few people realize that American Indians comprise the only minority group which possesses a special legal status within the United States. Although they are citizens like everybody else, they are also, by virtue of their tribal affiliations, possessed of special rights. This special status has puzzled and sometimes irritated white Americans. Indeed, so august a body as the Supreme Court of the State of Washington, in *Makah Indian Tribe v. Clallam County* observed:[1]

> Although the natural dignity of the American Indian as a person and a citizen, his valor as a warrior, and his contributions to this country, military and civil, cannot and ought not be denied, one wonders, as he reads the case law on Indian matters, whether the law has not conferred upon tribal Indians and their descendants what amounts to titles of nobility, with all that entails, in contravention of Article 1, § 9, of the United States Constitution prohibiting such titles. But this is a question beyond our jurisdiction.

While strong support for this special legal status of the American Indian is not immutable, Indian tribes presently enjoy what can be described as "internal sovereignty" or "local autonomy" in their respective jurisdictions. This paper will attempt to show how this status derives directly from the peculiar historical experiences of Indians and whites in the New World.

The experience of Indian-white relations in the United States has always differed from that in other parts of this hemisphere. In Latin America, for example, the relationship between Europeans and natives did not allow tribal autonomy to persist as it has in the present area of the United States. Physical destruction of large portions of the massive native populations was more overwhelming; physical integration of those who survived was more complete. Spanish and Portuguese policy did not allow the same degree of native legal existence apart from the institutions of the dominant society.

In British America, on the other hand, the colonists treated many of the Indian groups as independent nations with whom formal treaties and agreements were made. This policy was followed despite the fact that the Crown claimed ultimate sovereignty in all lands discovered and to be discovered when it granted royal charters and letters patent to those exploring or settling in the New World. The assertion of sovereignty over the lands of the New

---

* Director, Office of American Studies, Smithsonian Institution.
1.   73 Wash. 2d 677, 687, 440 P.2d 442, 448 (1968).

World was directed primarily at competing European states, who denied each other's pretensions to sovereignty over lands casually explored or lightly settled. Occupation rather than discovery increasingly became the only proof of sovereignty recognized by Europeans in their dealings with one another. Against the Indians the claim to European sovereignty was not pressed until much later, after Indian nations had lost their original power and could not contest the assertion of European title.[2]

The ambiguities inherent in the European policy were gradually clarified. In North America, the doctrine of the right of preemption was developed to stem the confusion. By this doctrine, most effectively articulated by Secretary of State Thomas Jefferson and Secretary of War Henry Knox in the 1790s, the Indian nations maintained full possession of their lands, but the United States retained the exclusive right to purchase any Indian land when the Indians chose to sell. In addition, of course, conquest of land in a just war was a valid method of acquisition. Although the concept of a just war is associated primarily with medieval theorists, in fact the doctrine, without ecclesiastical sanction or interpretation, continued to inform legislatures in British America before and after the Revolution.[3]

Why were Indian nations allowed to retain their separate and distinct status? First, English settlements did not result from a single impulse; nor were they under unified control. Charter colonies, proprietary colonies, and royal colonies, each with separate links and responsibilities to the mother country, found themselves dealing with local Indian nations of varying power and uncertain disposition. Each colony, separated from England by a vast ocean, had to determine how best to deal with the native inhabitants they encountered. Second, there was no agreement on what law applied to Englishmen who went abroad: indeed, it took a revolution to determine what rights the colonists had in the New World. Third, there was no coherent system of law spelling out the relationship that was to be established with Indians. The English had no compilation similar to the Spanish Laws of the Indies to guide them in their relations with the Indians.[4] As a result, Indian nations in North America were able to deal with the English (and their

---

2. See generally W. WASHBURN, RED MAN'S LAND/WHITE MAN'S LAW: A STUDY OF THE PAST AND PRESENT STATUS OF THE AMERICAN INDIAN (1971).

3. The Northwest Ordinance of 1787, for example, assured the Indians of the Old Northwest that they would "never be invaded or disturbed, unless in just and lawful wars authorized by Congress . . . ." SOURCES AND DOCUMENTS ILLUSTRATING THE AMERICAN REVOLUTION, 1763-1788, AND THE FORMATION OF THE FEDERAL CONSTITUTION 231 (S. Morrison ed. 1951). For an informative account of the origins of the Ordinance and its predecessor Ordinance of 1784 see Berkhofer, Jefferson, the Ordinance of 1784, and the Origins of the American Territorial System, 29 WM. & MARY Q. 231 (1972).

4. For a discussion of the Spanish law see W. WASHBURN, supra note 2, at 6-8. See also THE NEW LAWS FOR THE GOVERNMENT OF THE INDIES AND FOR THE PRESERVATION OF THE INDIANS, 1542-1543 (1968); Washburn, Law and Authority in Colonial Virginia, in LAW AND AUTHORITY IN COLONIAL AMERICA: SELECTED ESSAYS 116 (G. Billias ed. 1965).

American successors) largely in terms of ad hoc problems, since the English tended to base their decisions on expediency rather than abstract theory.

Many of the Puritan divines and colonial governors sought to justify their claims to Indian lands by arguing that European farmers had a right to settle in areas that were incompletely possessed by nomadic hunters or insufficiently utilized by native agriculturalists. In such Puritan writings as John Cotton's *God's Promise to his Plantation*,[5] this claim was grounded in divine sanction. In later years, stripped of its theological overtones, it would reappear in Theodore Roosevelt's assertion: "This great continent could not have been kept as nothing but a game preserve for squalid savages."[6]

Despite such theologically tinged arguments most of the colonists' dealings with the American Indian were effected through a variety of practical agreements. These agreements accepted the right of the Indian to possess the land to which he laid claim, although such lands were subject to transfer to whites by virtue of war, sale, or the disappearance or departure of the original inhabitants. Purchase was probably the principal means by which Indians transferred the land title of the present area of the United States to whites. Felix Cohen, the great authority on Indian law, noted that up to 1947 some $800 million of federal funds had been appropriated for the purchase of Indian lands. The federal government had not always honored the principle of respect for Indian possessory rights, Cohen pointed out, but few other countries could boast a better record.[7] To compensate for the many instances of the government's failure to deal honorably with the Indian, Congress, in 1946, created the Indian Claims Commission. The Commission continues to hear claims in law and equity arising under the Constitution, laws, treaties, and executive orders, as well as claims that would result if the treaties, contracts, and agreements between the claimant and the United States were revised on the ground of fraud, duress, unconscionable consideration, mutual or unilateral mistake, whether of law or fact. Indeed, the powers of the Commission extend to hearing claims based upon "fair and honorable dealings that are not recognized by any existing rule of law or equity."[8]

Although direct purchase of land by English colonists was not uncommon, most of the agreements between whites and Indians took the form of a treaty. Treaties could be either oral or written, and it was with great solemnity and formality that the colonists entered into them. For example, the negotiations between Plymouth colony and the Wampanoags commenced, in the spring of 1621 when, as a Pilgrim chronicler noted, Massasoit, the Wampanoag chief, was ushered[9]

---

5. *See* J. COTTON, GOD'S PROMISE TO HIS PLANTATION (1630).
6. 1 T. ROOSEVELT, THE WINNING OF THE WEST 90 (1889).
7. Cohen, *Original Indian Title*, 32 MINN. L. REV. 28, 45-46 (1947).
8. 60 Stat. 1049 (1946) (codified in 25 U.S.C. § 70(a) (1970)).
9. Quoted from *Mourt's Relation*, in W. BRADFORD, OF PLYMOUTH PLANTATION, 1620-1647, at

. . . to an house then in building, where we placed a green rug and three or four cushions. Then instantly came our Governor, [John Carver, who died shortly after] with drum and trumpet after him, and some few musketeers. After salutations, our Governor kissing his hand, the King kissed him; and so they sat down. The Governor called for some strong water and drunk to him; and he drunk a great draught, that made him sweat all the while after.

Squanto, an Indian who had learned English in England after being kidnapped by an English ship captain, served as interpreter. Carver's successor, William Bradford, later recorded the terms of the peace:[10]

1. That neither he nor any of his should injure or do hurt to any of their people.
2. That if any of his did hurt to any of theirs he should send the offender, that they might punish him.
3. That if anything were taken away from any of theirs, he should cause it to be restored; and they should do the like to his.
4. If any did unjustly war against him, they would aid him; if any did war against them, he should aid them.
5. He should send to his neighbours confederates to certify them of this, that they might not wrong them, but might be likewise comprised in the conditions of peace.
6. That when their men came to them, they should leave their bows and arrows behind them.

The peace concluded in the treaty of 1621 was faithfully kept throughout the lives of Massasoit and Governor Bradford. The peace began to unravel, however, after the Englishman's death in 1657 and the Indian's in 1660. Relations between the colony and Philip, the successor to Wamsutta (who had succeeded Massasoit), deteriorated as misunderstanding was piled upon insult. In 1671 the treaty relationship between the Indians and Plymouth was renegotiated, as a result of which the Wampanoags became virtual subjects or pawns of the colony.[11] Our knowledge of the Indian reaction to the Pilgrim moves is clouded, but there seems no doubt that the resulting "conspiracy" and war which ravaged New England derived from a desperate feeling on the part of the Indians that the autonomy they had enjoyed in earlier years had been destroyed, and that their only hope of honorable survival lay in war.[12]

The treaty form of negotiating differences between Indians and whites has frequently been the object of ridicule or shame. Too often laymen and historians alike have assumed that such negotiations were either a farce or a fraud, in the course of which scheming white men imposed their terms upon simple-minded Indians. The classic example, hallowed in the annals of popular culture (whose influence on our understanding of the subject should not

80 (S. MORISON ed. 1952). *See also* G. LANGDON, PILGRIM COLONY: A HISTORY OF NEW PLYMOUTH, 1620-1691, at 152 (1966); A. VAUGHAN, NEW ENGLAND FRONTIER: PURITANS AND INDIANS, 1620-1675, at 71-73 (1965).

10. W. BRADFORD, *supra* note 9, at 80-81.
11. G. LANGDON, *supra* note 9, at 160-61.
12. Washburn, Book Review, 82 PA. MAGAZINE HIST. & BIOG. 473-74 (1958).

be overlooked) is the purchase of Manhattan Island by the Dutch for twenty-four dollars from the local Indians. While instances of fraud and deceit in treaty making are not lacking, it must be remembered, particularly for this formative period in American history, that the treaty process was one in which whites and Indians, bargaining from varying positions of strength and weakness, sought agreements or concessions each regarded as desirable or necessary. Often the Indians placed greater value on trade items, such as guns and beads, than on marginally used lands.[13] Thus, agreements reflected different values and interests as well as differences of power.[14]

With the achievement of national independence the government of the United States was faced with the question of how seriously treaties with the Indians should be regarded. The Constitution granted the President the power "by and with the Advice and Consent of the Senate to make Treaties."[15] No distinction was made between treaties with Indian nations and those with foreign powers. In a communication to the Senate, dated September 17, 1789, President George Washington wrote: "It doubtless is important that all treaties and compacts, formed by the United States with other nations, whether civilized or not, should be made with caution, and executed with fidelity."[16] Washington and his early successors attempted to execute Indian treaties faithfully, although they were often frustrated by the inability of the federal government to prevent state or local action against Indian groups in violation of earlier treaties.

The fact that not all Americans agreed with George Washington is implicit in the way in which the President's communication was phrased. A steady undercurrent of disagreement with the treaty process surfaced in the nineteenth century, particularly among individuals like General Andrew Jackson, who, as an army officer and territorial governor in the years following the War of 1812, had frequently been called upon to negotiate Indian treaties. Jackson increasingly came to feel that dealing with Indians in formal treaties was "an absurdity" and an anachronism.[17] It is true that as Indian power

---

13. Washburn, *Symbol, Utility, and Aesthetics in the Indian Fur Trade*, 40 MINN. HIST. no. 4, at 198-202 (1966).

14. It is noteworthy that treaty negotiations were conducted in the Indian style of address and tended to proceed at an Indian pace. This was not, I would assert, an expression of condescension on the part of the whites. It was rather the necessary pre-condition to successful negotiations with the Indians who continued in a powerful position throughout the early centuries of contact with the whites. Indeed, the whites' willingness to utilize the Indian form of negotiation rather than to insist on European forms suggests a grudging admiration for the eloquence and dignity of the Indian adversaries they faced. Benjamin Franklin was so impressed with the eloquence of the native inhabitants that he published the text of a number of the early Pennsylvania Indian treaties. *See, e.g.*, INDIAN TREATIES PRINTED BY BENJAMIN FRANKLIN, 1736-1762 (J. Boyd ed. 1938). *See generally* W. WASHBURN, THE INDIAN IN AMERICA 99-100 (1975).

15. U.S. CONST. art. II, § 2.

16. 1 AMERICAN STATE PAPERS, CLASS II, INDIAN AFFAIRS 58 (1832). *See generally* W. WASHBURN, THE AMERICAN INDIAN AND THE UNITED STATES (1973).

17. R. SATZ, AMERICAN INDIAN POLICY IN THE JACKSONIAN ERA 10 (1975).

declined and white power increased the consequences of breaking or ignoring earlier Indian treaties became less serious. Nevertheless treaties continued to be made in good faith until 1871, when a rider to a House of Representatives appropriation bill ended the process for the future even while acknowledging the validity of treaties made in the past.[18]

In the mid-nineteenth century, as white settlers rapidly moved westward, the autonomy of the western Indian nations suffered a series of blows. Implicit in the concept of the autonomy of the western Indian nations was the idea of an "Indian Barrier," fixed at the western boundary of the existing white settlements, beyond which all Indians would live free from white control. As white settlers penetrated this barrier, the federal government trailed behind, trying to provide a viable and stable relationship between the white newcomers—whether trappers, traders, miners, ranchers, missionaries, or agriculturists—and the affected Indian tribes.

The expedient seized upon by the government in the 1840s and 1850s to meet the new situation was the creation, by treaty, of a series of reservations which would serve to concentrate the various Indian nations away from the major paths of white westward movement. Isolation would also make it easier for government officials and missionaries to implement programs for "civilizing" the native populations. Once again American policy in this period was hastily improvised in response to a series of specific problems. Although framed in theoretical terms, the policy was not an expression of a coherent political or philosophical doctrine but a practical response to white pressure on the "permanent Indian barrier."[19]

The destruction of many of the reservations at the end of the nineteenth century resulted from a similar expedient response to the pressure of white settlers on the reservations created in the 1840s. The crisis came to a head in the 1870s with the continuing rapid expansion of white population. The new weapon in the white arsenal was the railroad, which provided a physical presence of white power in the heart of the Indian country and guaranteed rapid movement of white military power wherever needed. Indian lands, though seemingly protected by the treaties negotiated in the 1840s and 1850s, were increasingly subject to invasion by undisciplined and unregulated frontiers-

---

18. The end of the treaty making process was, interestingly enough, largely the result of the insistence of Henry L. Dawes. When chairman of the Appropriations Committee of the House of Representatives, Dawes stipulated that the Senate do away with the treaty system as the price for obtaining appropriations from the House for carrying out the government's obligations to the Indians. Dawes's purpose, it has been argued, was to break up the treaty system as the first step toward general allotment of Indian lands, a goal reached in the Dawes Act of 1887, passed when Dawes was a member of the United States Senate. W. WASHBURN, THE ASSAULT ON INDIAN TRIBALISM: THE GENERAL ALLOTMENT LAW (DAWES ACT) OF 1887, at 25 (1975), quoting from F. Nicklason, The Early Career of Henry L. Dawes, 1816-1871, at 369 (unpublished thesis at Yale University 1967).

19. See R. TRENNERT, ALTERNATIVE TO EXTINCTION: FEDERAL INDIAN POLICY AND THE BEGINNINGS OF THE RESERVATION SYSTEM, 1846-1851 chs. 1-4 & epilogue (1975).

men. Miners rushed into the Black Hills of the Sioux Reservation in search of gold. Stockmen and settlers invaded the homelands of the Utes of Wyoming and the Nez Perce of Washington and Idaho. Even the Indian Territory, inhabited by Indians who had been coerced or induced into moving west to form the prototype of a separate Indian state or territory, was under constant threat of invasion by white ruffians perched on its borders. The outcome of this pressure was occasionally war. Chief Joseph and his Nez Perce were humbled and defeated in 1877. Even the Sioux, though they destroyed George Custer's Seventh Cavalry Regiment, gained only temporary satisfaction before being crushed by larger forces. These military confrontations were the outward expressions of a crisis that seemed to men of both good and ill will to require radical solutions.

The solution proposed was to break up the reservations by dividing the communally held lands into individualized parcels. Tribal members would be given enough land to allow them to become farmers. The surplus remaining after individual allotments were made would be sold to whites, the proceeds going to assist in the educational and "civilizational" process by which Indians would be integrated into white society. The proposal received wide support, not only from those who were eager to obtain Indian lands but from white people of good will, frightened by the invasion of Indian lands, who formed Indian rights organizations and agitated for a solution to the dilemma. Viewed in the most favorable light, the "friends of the Indians" sought to save the Indians from destruction by authorizing the government to take from them some of their lands in exchange for a stronger title to the remainder. The surplus land would be sold to appease the land-hungry white settlers who, it was argued, might otherwise overrun the reservations and completely dispossess the Indians. Profits from the sale of the lands would go to support the adjustment of the Indians to their new condition in life.[20]

The proposal was enacted into law with the passage of the General Allotment Act of 1887, popularly known as the Dawes Act, after its champion in the Senate, Henry L. Dawes of Massachusetts.[21] Historians still debate the motivations behind the Dawes Act. To some, the threat to the Indian land base and tribal integrity was not sufficient to warrant a wholesale retreat from the system by which Indian-white relations had been conducted in the past. Others argue that the friends of the Indians acted just in time to save them from being totally deprived of their remaining lands. Scholars have attempted to find evidence of selfish interests steering the legislation to enactment, but so far no one has been able to demonstrate that the act was the result of the improper influence of railroads, miners, settlers, or others who stood to profit from the results of allotment. The principal force behind the law was the vast

---

20. *See* W. WASHBURN, *supra* note 18.
21. Ch. 119, § 1, 24 Stat. 288, *as amended*, 25 U.S.C. § 331 (1970).

corps of Indian rights organizations who convinced themselves that allotment and assimilation were the only solutions to the Indian "problem."

The Dawes Act was addressed not only to the issue of collective landholding but to the issues of tribal organization and the legal status of individual Indians. Increasingly during this period, the movement was toward the exercise of federal, as opposed to tribal, jurisdiction over individual Indians and toward inclusion of the Indians within the body politic as full citizens. In these issues, as in those concerning land tenure, policy and circumstance deeply influenced one another.

From the earliest period of American colonial history, individual Indians had entered into a wide range of associations with whites. For the most part these relationships were characterized by inequality and political separation. Even the Indian converts in the "Praying Towns" of seventeenth-century Massachusetts lived not as fully equal citizens within the Puritan Commonwealth but as carefully controlled associates.[22] In later years, some Indians became members of white communities by virtue of the allotment provisions of early treaties, or by individual choice. However, the legal status of such individuals was rarely subject to thoughtful analysis as long as their numbers were small and the Indian nations continued to exist as separate and isolated enclaves.

But as pressures mounted for the breakup of tribal lands and whites came to live in greater proximity to western Indian settlements, some clarification of the legal status of the individual Indian became necessary. Legislation affecting the Indian's legal status was stimulated by two dramatic cases occurring in 1883 and 1884, in the midst of the debate over the breakup of the reservations and the destruction of tribal authority. The decision in *Elk v. Wilkins*[23] played a significant role in shaping the Dawes Act, while the case of Ex Parte *Crow Dog*[24] inspired legislation concerning criminal jurisdiction over individual Indians.

In the case of *Elk v. Wilkins*, the plaintiff, an Indian who had voluntarily separated himself from his tribe and taken up residence among the white citizens of Omaha, Nebraska, was denied the right to register to vote by Wilkins, the local registrar, on the grounds that he was not a citizen of the United States. The decision was upheld by the Supreme Court, though two justices dissented. The decision in *Elk* acutely embarrassed the proponents of severalty legislation. Their argument that tribalism had to be destroyed in order to allow the individual Indian to assume his rightful place in white society seemed, in the light of the Supreme Court's decision, either false, hypocritical, or both. If the Indian were to lose his tribal affiliation and to move into white

---

22. *See, e.g.*, Kawashima, *Legal Origins of the Indian Reservation in Colonial Massachusetts*, 13 Am. J. Legal Hist. 42 (1969); Kawashima, *Jurisdiction of the Colonial Courts Over the Indians in Massachusetts, 1689-1763*, 42 New England Q. no. 4, at 532-55 (1969).

23. 112 U.S. 94 (1884).

24. 109 U.S. 556 (1883).

society, he would be left in limbo. Friends of the Indian protested vigorously against the *Elk* decision. At the same time they encouraged Senator Dawes to write into the severalty legislation the provision that every Indian born within the territorial limits of the United States,[25]

> ... to whom allotments shall have been made under the provisions of this act, or under any law or treaty, and every Indian born within the territorial limits of the United States who has voluntarily taken up, within said limits, his residence separate and apart from any tribe of Indians therein, and has adopted the habits of civilized life, is hereby declared to be a citizen of the United States ....

The Dawes Act did not fully resolve the "problem" of reconciling the Indian's status as an Indian with his status as a citizen of the United States. It took another historical event (rather than logic or theory) to stimulate Congress to clarify the status of the individual Indian. In 1924 the Congress declared citizens all Indians not already so designated.[26] The remarkable role played by Indians in World War I, both on the battlefield and in the domestic war effort, made their exclusion from full participation in the political process seem arbitrary and unjust. From the white point of view, the bravery and dedication of Indians in World War I—whether based on the warrior values of Indian culture or other motivations—compounded the injustice of their exclusion from the country's politics, particularly at a time when America welcomed to full political equality millions of immigrants from Europe.[27] Just as *Elk v. Wilkins* stimulated further consideration of the citizenship status of Indians, Ex Parte *Crow Dog* raised the issue of criminal jurisdiction over individual Indians.

Crow Dog had killed Spotted Tail, a fellow Sioux, within the reservation boundaries in retaliation for the latter's appropriating the wife of Crow Dog's friend. Although the Sioux had imposed their own justice, federal agents arrested Crow Dog and charged him with murder. He appealed for a writ of habeas corpus on the grounds that federal courts lacked jurisdiction over crimes committed by one Indian against another in Indian country. The Supreme Court agreed with Crow Dog's argument and set him free, noting that any prosecution must be pressed within the judicial system of the tribe. The

---

25. Indian General Allotment Act of 1887, ch. 119, § 6, 24 Stat. 390.

26. Act of June 2, 1924, ch. 233, 43 Stat. 253 (codified in 8 U.S.C. § 140(a)(2) (1970).

27. *See* W. WASHBURN, *supra* note 14, at 252. The 1924 declaration of Indian citizenship did not, however, clarify all confusion concerning the rights and duties of Indian citizens. It did not, for example, clarify the issue of eligibility to vote in state elections. Thus, as late as the 1950s, some states, particularly in the southwest, refused to recognize Indians living on reservations as "residents" for voting purposes. *See, e.g.,* Allen v. Merrell, 6 Utah 2d 32, 305 P.2d 490 (1956); Rothfels v. Southworth, 11 Utah 2d 169, 356 P.2d 612 (1960). The Utah statute was later repealed. The fact that reservation Indians are exempt from state and local taxes but are eligible to stand for office and vote in those areas continues to disturb neighboring whites. *Navajos Who Pay No₂ Tax Seek County Role in Arizona,* N.Y. Times, Feb. 11, 1974, at 24, col. 3; Shirley v. Superior Court, 109 Ariz. 510, 513 P.2d 939 (1973).

response of Congress, outraged at the latitude thus conceded to the tribes, was to pass the Major Crimes Act of 1885, which extended federal criminal jurisdiction to the seven major crimes of murder, manslaughter, rape, assault with intent to kill, arson, burglary, and larceny.[28]

Congress did not, however, move to assert full jurisdiction over all reservation activities. Owing, in part, to successful experiments by local agents with tribal police and tribal judges, bureaucrats and legislators gave support to tribal institutions which contributed to the reduction in Indian-white tensions. Because there was no comprehensive theory of federal-Indian relations guiding policy in every domain of Indian life, indigenous institutions were able to survive even in the face of the dominant, if loosely articulated, program of individualized allotment and status contained in the Dawes Act.[29]

The General Allotment Act of 1887 reflected the rampant individualism and economic laissez-faire philosophy of America at the end of the nineteenth century. Whatever the effects of that philosophy in other areas of American economic life its particular form of application to the Indians proved totally unsuccessful. Already by the 1920s it was clear that Indians were not developing into prototypical American farmers: the inadequate size and quality of allotments, the poor facilities for health and education, and the positive attachment of Indians to their tribal identities contributed to this situation. When Lewis Merriam's famous report to the Secretary of the Interior was published in 1928, recognition of the failure of American Indian policy was required. Just as the philosophy of laissez-faire economics influenced the formulation of the Dawes Act, so too the next major piece of legislation, the Indian Reorganization Act of 1934, was influenced by the reconsideration of the ethic during the Great Depression.

For many Americans during the years of the Depression collectivism, whether of the Soviet variety or of the traditional native American variety, suddenly had new appeal. John Collier, who was selected as Commissioner of Indian Affairs by President Franklin D. Roosevelt and Secretary of the Interior Harold Ickes, had been deeply influenced in his earlier years by the communal values he had observed in Indian societies of the southwest. In devising a new policy for the Indian as part of the general restructuring of American society in the period of the New Deal, Collier sought to reestablish these values throughout the Indian segment of American society.[30]

---

28. 23 Stat. 385, The Major Crimes Act has been amended on numerous occasions since. The present version covers thirteen crimes, 18 U.S.C. § 1153 (1970). There is, however, some question whether the act confers exclusive or concurrent jurisdiction on the federal courts. Cf. 1 INDIAN L. REP. no. 3, at 52 (1974). The Criminal Justice Reform Act, S. 1, 94th Cong., 1st Sess. § 203 (1975), would also affect the existing jurisdictional scheme. Cf. 2 INDIAN L. REP. no. 5, at 30 (1975).

29. See, e.g., W. HAGAN, INDIAN POLICE AND JUDGES: EXPERIMENTS IN ACCULTURATION AND CONTROL 34-43 (1966).

30. Collier even believed that the communal values of the Indians could help shape a similar orientation of white society. See Failure to Create a Red Atlantis: John Collier and the Con-

Collier's dream of a "red Atlantis"—as one scholar has termed it—came near to realization.[31] But the program ran up against the very individualism which Collier's predecessors had successfully fostered in many American Indian tribes. Collier's attempt to ban the inheritance of lands already allotted to individual Indians (coupled with his proposed ban on further allotments and the return to communal ownership of all surplus Indian lands) was met by bitter opposition in areas like Oklahoma, where many Indians thought more of their newly gained individual property than of tribal integrity. The aim of the nineteenth-century reformers—to encourage individualistic values —had, Collier recognized to his sorrow, been partially realized. The new cultural climate in many Indian communities caused Collier to modify his plan to return individual land holdings to communal ownership. Instead he made particular efforts to maintain as fully communal societies those tribes the aridity of whose lands had made application of the acreage provisions of the General Allotment Act patently impractical. Collier also sought authorization for the purchase on the open market of individual land holdings that could then be returned to tribal control.[32]

As part of his scheme for strengthening Indian communal societies, Collier encouraged the revitalization of tribal governments, hitherto the object of direct assault by all government policies. The Indian Reorganization Act gave legal recognition to tribal governments as distinct from federal, state, and local governments. At the same time the Act maintained and strengthened prior recognition of the trust responsibilities of the federal government to the Indians. In order to win approval for the new structure in a white dominated legislature, Collier prescribed certain organizational procedures and forms intended to reassure Congress that responsible democratic government—as white Americans defined it—would be established. Thus tribal leaders were to be elected by ballot, each adult Indian man and woman having an equal vote. Traditional methods of selection by consensus, heredity, or appointment by a smaller element of the tribe were ignored or prohibited. Moreover, each tribe was to draw up a constitution and a set of by-laws for the organization and operation of tribal affairs. Not insignificantly, the Secretary of the Interior was made the reviewing officer for many of the processes by which tribal governments would function.

The provisions of the Indian Reorganization Act have been the source of sharp conflicts within many reservation groups. For example, spokesmen for the American Indian Movement at Pine Ridge in 1972 demanded the ouster of the elected tribal government, the discontinuance of electoral procedures

troversy Over the Wheeler-Howard Bill of 1934, address by Kenneth R. Philp, National Archives Conference on Research in the History of Indian-White Relations, Washington, D.C., June 16, 1972. See also W. WASHBURN, supra note 14, at 254-57.

31. Philp, supra note 30.
32. Id.

authorized under the Act, and the return to "traditional" forms of leadership selection. Other segments of the tribe argued that a one man/one vote system was a more equitable method of determining leadership. The Indian Reorganization Act may or may not have contributed to internal tribal factionalism by stressing proportion of Indian parentage for tribal membership or highlighting degrees of assimilation to white values. But what is certain is that the Act has, during a crucial period in American Indian history, preserved and strengthened the concept of tribal authority. "As a reform measure," writes Vine Deloria, Jr., "Collier's original draft of the Indian Reorganization Act was so thoughtful, philosophical, and ahead of its time that it had a hard time gaining credibility."[33] Indeed, says Deloria, "Collier had more faith in Indians than they had in themselves."[34] He concludes: "The present contention of Indian activists and others that the Indian Reorganization Act was a step away from the traditional right of Indians to govern themselves is inaccurate if they mean that the scope of legal powers was reduced by the adoption of the act."[35]

The Indian Reorganization Act remains the guiding expression of federal Indian policy. Although Congress acted in 1953 to terminate federal services and jurisdiction over Indians as rapidly as possible, the economic hardship accompanying that policy has led to its subsequent rejection.[36] And the Indian Civil Rights Act of 1968,[37] which extended most of the constitutional requirements of the Bill of Rights to reservation groups, has raised difficult issues of the relations between organized tribal governments and their individual members. Throughout, the Supreme Court has reaffirmed the concept of tribal authority, even though its precise boundaries and implications have been the subject of extensive litigation.[38]

American Indian policy has, therefore, been an amalgam of insight and greed, implicit bias and practical concern. At its best, it has developed in response to mutual understanding rather than blind adherence to abstract doctrine. Internal disputes will continue within Indian communities, but the fact that the Indian tribe has survived as a viable legal entity in our day is a tribute to the good will and dedication of men like Governor William Bradford of Plymouth Colony in the seventeenth century and John Collier in the twen-

---

33. V. DELORIA, JR., BEHIND THE TRAIL OF BROKEN TREATIES 196 (1974).
34. *Id.* at 199.
35. *Id.* at 204.
36. H.R. Con. Res. 108, 67 Stat. B132 (1953). This led to termination statutes such as 25 U.S.C. §§ 891-902 (1954). The Menominee Restoration Act, 25 U.S.C. § 903 (Supp. III, 1974) has since repealed this termination statute. *See generally* Orfield, *A Study of the Termination Policy,* in 4 SUBCOMM. ON INDIAN EDUCATION, THE EDUCATION OF AMERICAN INDIANS, THE ORGANIZATION QUESTION 673 (1970). *See also* FREEDOM WITH RESERVATION: THE MENOMINEE STRUGGLE TO SAVE THEIR LAND AND PEOPLE (D. Shames ed. 1972).
37. 25 U.S.C. §§ 132-03 (1970).
38. *See, e.g.,* McClanahan v. Arizona State Tax Comm'n, 411 U.S. 164 (1973).

tieth; and to the practical, non-theoretical ideology of the English settlers and officials who established the American nation. The legal relations of the United States with the American Indians reinforces Justice Oliver Wendell Holmes's dictum that "[t]he life of law has not been logic: it has been experience."[39]

---

39.   O.W. HOLMES, THE COMMON LAW 5 (M. Howe ed. 1963).

TRIBAL COURTS, THE MODEL CODE, AND THE POLICE IDEA IN AMERICAN INDIAN POLICY

RUSSEL LAWRENCE BARSH*

J. YOUNGBLOOD HENDERSON†

Acting under congressional authority granted eight years ago, the Indian Civil Rights Task Force is at last circulating a draft "Model Code for the Administration of Justice by Courts of Indian Offenses."[1] These courts, originally established under the auspices of the Bureau of Indian Affairs, have been replaced on virtually all reservations by "tribal courts," which are free from Bureau control.[2] However, tribal courts usually follow procedural codes derived from, if not identical to, those governing Courts of Indian Offenses because the latter are readily available without developmental costs and are assured of the requisite approval of the Secretary of Interior.

The Model Code authorization was enacted as part of the so-called "Indian Bill of Rights," which enumerates those constitutional requirements that Congress, in 1968, deemed it necessary to extend to Indian tribes.[3] In fact, at that time, Congress had before it evidence that approximately half of all reservation courts were already substantially in compliance with Indian Bill of Rights limitations, and that the perceived "abuses" of reservation courts —absence of the right to counsel, self-incrimination, jury trial, and appeal —were aggravated if not caused by the inadequacy of tribal law and order budgets.[4] With the passage of the Indian Bill of Rights, tribes instantly experienced increased costs—without any commensurate increase in budgetary assistance—in bringing their procedures up to standard and defending civil rights challenges in the federal courts.[5] Moreover, a special task force was

---

* Assistant Professor of Business, Government and Society, University of Washington School of Business Administration.

† Assistant Professor of Native American Studies, University of California, Berkeley.

1. 25 C.F.R. § 11 (1975).

2. *Hearings on Constitutional Rights of the American Indian Before the Subcomm. on Constitutional Rights of the Senate Comm. on the Judiciary*, 89th Cong., 1st Sess. 50-51, 54-55 (1965). Authority for substituting "tribal courts" for "courts of Indian offenses" is found in 25 C.F.R. § 11.1(4) (1975).

3. Act of April 11, 1968, Pub. L. No. 90-284, tit. II, § 201, 82 Stat. 77. *See generally* Burnette, *Indian Civil Rights Act*, 9 HARV. J. LEGIS. 557, 595 (1972).

4. *Id.* at 579, 581-83. But the Bureau denied this charge, *Hearings on Constitutional Rights of the American Indian, supra* note 2, at 50-51.

5. Between 1966 and 1970, the Bureau of Indian Affairs law and order budget increased rather uniformly from $2,925,000 to $4,952,000, or 69 per cent. During the same period, reported reservation crimes increased from 63,366 to 106,397, or 68 per cent. This does not suggest that any substantial investment in upgraded administration was made. BUDGET OF THE U.S. GOVERNMENT, FISCAL YEAR 1968, SPECIAL ANALYSES app. 577 (1967); FISCAL YEAR 1969 app. 575

established within the Justice Department to investigate individual complaints against tribes, thus assuring that the cost to a private citizen of prosecuting tribes would be nearly zero. The ultimate result has been extreme reluctance on the part of tribes to engage in aggressive law reform, and a tendency to avoid additional costs by dropping charges against anyone who appears willing and able to bring a civil rights attack on the proceedings. If the tribes follow the Model Code, however, there can be no conceivable challenge in the federal courts, whereas if an independent code is drafted it will be a sure target for federally-subsidized attacks on every section. Congress could not have chosen a better way to neutralize tribal government, *or to assure widespread adoption of the Model Code*.

An examination of the Model proves that it is nothing more than a redraft of the old Bureau regulations, harmonized with the Indian Bill of Rights largely through borrowings from the American Law Institute's Model Code for Pre-Arraignment Procedure.[6] No procedural innovations especially suited to tribal needs have been suggested, no substantive improvements in the notoriously antiquated Bureau penal code made, nor necessary expansions of tribal civil jurisdiction provided. But the real significance of the Model Code is that in seeking to cure alleged constitutional errors in the administration of justice it perpetuates errors of a more fundamental nature—historical errors of policy. For three centuries, as an analysis of the Code's historical context shows, the policy of the federal government has been to employ tribal government to defeat tribalism by lodging civil jurisdiction in non-Indian courts while requiring Indians to support and maintain police institutions among themselves.

I
CRIMINALITY AND THE WHOLE LAW

Throughout modern times the development of the criminal law has been intimately linked to the definition and allocation of property rights. According to John Locke, "[t]he great end of men's entering into society being the enjoyment of their properties in peace and safety, and the great instrument and means of that being the laws established in that society, the first and fundamental positive law of all commonwealths is the establishing of the legislative power."[7] John Stuart Mill wrote a century and a half later that the "first" of the duties of government[8]

(1968); FISCAL YEAR 1970 app. 560 (1969); FISCAL YEAR 1971 app. 543 (1970); FISCAL YEAR 1972 app. 561 (1971).

6. Apparently the subcommittee that reviewed the Model Code legislation had this in mind as a modus operandi. *Hearings on Constitutional Rights of the American Indian, supra* note 2, at 28.

7. J. LOCKE, THE SECOND TREATISE OF GOVERNMENT ch. 11, § 134, at 75 (T. Peardon ed. 1952).

8. J.S. MILL, PRINCIPLES OF POLITICAL ECONOMY 239, 243 (D. Winch ed. 1970). *See also* 5 A.

is the protection of person and property. There is no need to expatiate on the influence exercised over the economical interests of society by the degree of completeness with which this duty of government is performed. Insecurity of person and property, is as much as to say, uncertainty of the connexion between all human exertion or sacrifice, and the attainment of the ends for the sake of which they are undergone. It means, uncertainty whether they who sow shall reap, whether they who produce shall consume, and they who spare to-day shall enjoy to-morrow.

Has the criminal law ever fulfilled the purposes to which Locke, Mill, and the other progenitors of our republican institutions attributed the duties of government? Reasoning after the fact, Blackstone concluded that crimes had become separately dealt with by the state because they "strike at the very being of society"—the threat to social cohesion exceeds the damage to any individual.[9] Apart from any skepticism that may justifiably attach to this characterization of the great majority of offenses actually before the courts, there is no historical basis for what may be referred to as the conventional theory of criminalization. The separate administration of criminal justice arose as an exercise of royal prerogative, principally to increase crown revenue and displace the autonomy of local, baronial, trade, and merchant courts.[10]

The great wellspring of English law was tort—private actions for damage, principally in the form of trespass. In the diversity of local customs and traditions, tort was prosecuted differently depending upon the jurisdiction invoked by the plaintiff. One of the earliest triumphs, then, of the Crown and common law was the extension to private parties of a royal action of trespass that could be taken in the same form from any jurisdiction, through royal officers, to the royal justices. The sheer military power of the King and his ability to ignore local jurisdictional boundaries made royal writs frequently more attractive to suitors than local suits. Gradually, the authority of the local courts and the applicability of local laws was thereby undermined. The growth of the common law reflects the unification of England under the authority of the King, and the centralization of virtually all rules of policy and morality in London.

One of the chief attractions of the royal writ of trespass was the option of imprisonment of recalcitrant defendants at the King's pleasure, or until they "made fine with the King," which is to say they ransomed themselves. This was the origin both of our concept of the criminal "fine" and the misdemeanor jurisdiction of criminal courts. Gradually the requirement of private

---

SMITH, AN INQUIRY INTO THE NATURE AND CAUSES OF THE WEALTH OF NATIONS ch. 1, pt. 2 (1776).

9. 5 W. BLACKSTONE, COMMENTARIES *5.

10. See G. KEETON, THE NORMAN CONQUEST AND THE COMMON LAW ch. 15 (1966); S. MILSON, HISTORICAL FOUNDATIONS OF THE COMMON LAW 353 (1969); M. POLLACK & F. MAITLAND, THE HISTORY OF ENGLISH LAW BEFORE THE TIME OF EDWARD I ch. 8 (1968).

prosecution disappeared. Today the same activity may be privately prosecuted in tort *or* publicly prosecuted as a misdemeanor for a fine or imprisonment; indeed we have gone so far as to dispense entirely with the element of private injury, as in so-called "victimless crimes." Sadly, extensive poverty and progress in our regard for the health and safety of prisoners has ceased to make misdemeanor jurisdiction profitable for the state.[11]

Felony jurisdiction had its origins in the Pleas of the Crown, a relatively limited enumeration of very serious matters of which at an early date the King took an exclusive cognizance. Here the Crown enjoyed a forfeiture of the accused's property upon conviction and execution. The reforms that followed our revolution abolished forfeiture as an abhorrent cruelty, but preserved the enumeration and the execution of convicts without modification.

The King's profit on felony was only one of many abuses of criminal justice that helped to precipitate the American Revolution. Most of the colonies were granted original charters that empowered them to exercise exclusive criminal jurisdiction over their subjects. Significantly, a key point in the Crown's program of reasserting its waning authority, years before the Townshend Acts, was the revocation of that exclusive jurisdiction and the requirement that American felons be tried before English courts or before royal appointees under English procedure. Since the list of felonies was then cancerously consuming the misdemeanors[12]—over two hundred crimes were punishable by death—the impact of that policy was profound. As had been the case in earliest England, the assertion of royal criminal justice was manipulated as an instrument of unification and subordination. Unlike their medieval counterparts, however, Americans resisted violently and successfully. Nonetheless it was not the strategy but its application to them that Americans resisted. Preserving the skeleton of English criminal law in the several states,[13] Americans were within a century to attempt the very same stratagem on the Indians.

---

11. But even in recent times some American towns have supported themselves out of court receipts, *see, e.g.,* N. MILLER & J. SNELL, WHY THE WEST WAS WILD 13 (1963). From the inception of reservation police courts, Indians have tended to be too poor to pay any considerable fines. In 1929 virtually no fines levied by reservation courts exceeded thirty dollars. *Hearings on Law and Order on Indian Reservations of the Northwest Before the Senate Comm. on Indian Affairs,* 82d Cong., 1st Sess., pt. 26, at 14222 (1932). This was still true in our 1973 survey of the Crow Tribes's law and order system.

12. *See* W. LEE, A HISTORY OF POLICE IN ENGLAND (1901).

13. There was a general tendency to adopt or retain English forms and laws both civil and criminal. *See, e.g.,* E. BROWN, BRITISH STATUTES IN AMERICAN LAW, 1776-1836, at 24 (1964); G. WOOD, THE CREATION OF THE AMERICAN REPUBLIC (1776-1787), at 292 (1969); Morris, *Legalism versus Revolutionary Doctrine in New England,* 4 NEW ENGLAND Q. 195 (1931). Conflict over the retention of British criminal principles was limited to the area of common-law crimes—the power of judges to redefine punishable acts without legislative direction. 1 E. WARREN, THE SUPREME COURT IN UNITED STATES HISTORY 159 (1922). It is highly significant that revolutionary Americans conceived of this as the only fundamental political evil of the criminal process as received from England.

The institution of the police has a parallel and no less dramatic history. In the contemporary sense of a professional armed force, police were unknown in England or America until the early part of the last century. The earliest forms of "police" were founded on the assumptions that truly dangerous persons were few and known individually, and that citizens had a collective responsibility for maintaining public safety. In Saxon times men were grouped by tens (or tythings). Each tythingman pledged to keep his fellows in order and, failing that, to deliver up the malefactor to the local tribunal for conciliation with and restitution to the victim's family.[14] Tythingmen were jointly liable for damages and not infrequently also jointly accountable in revenge.

The Normans instituted the first national system of law officers, the sheriffes, but at first their function was merely to administer the tythings. Not until the Assize of Clarendon (1166) were the sheriffes assisted by a jury of twelve for investigation and presentment of felony to a royal court. Needless to say, the system of Norman sheriffes represented an effort at unifying and subjugating the diverse (and for many generations rebellious) communities, many with their own kings, that comprised Saxon England. Nevertheless, the system was almost wholly reliant upon the cooperation of individual citizens. The only enforcement agency at the sheriffe's command, apart from the extraordinary expedient of "summoning the array" (royal troops), was the *posse comitatus*, or committee of citizens organized to search out fugitives.

Ironically, Norman feudalism swiftly made for the undoing of this national justice system. The Saxons at peace, the invaders turned their attentions to dividing and cultivating their lands, resulting in a redivision of the countryside into essentially autonomous jurisdictions, the manors. The Assize of Northampton (1176) limited the power of the sheriffes over the new landlords, as did Magna Carta.

The evolution of urban concentrations broke down the effectiveness of the tything system and revived interest in organized law enforcement. No longer face-to-face communities, the growing cities experienced a breakdown of the motivation and ability of citizens to check and watch one another. The Statute of Winchester (1285) created the first rotated night watch and required every urban citizen to be armed and ready to be called out by the watch in pursuit of fugitives. Joint liability disappeared. In its stead, wards and parishes were authorized to elect constables on rotation. The principal value of the constabulary was in controlling those incidents of urban prosperity, drunkenness, vagrancy, and petty looting. Unfortunately, the problem in London rapidly outstripped the means appointed to suppress it, and, as the constabulary remained unpaid, its personnel declined accordingly. "In practice . . . the

---

14. T. Critchley, A History of Police in England and Wales ch. 1 (1967); R. Hunnisett, The Medieval Coroner (1961); G. Keeton, *supra* note 10 ch. 15; S. Milson, *supra* note 10; M. Pollock & F. Maitland, *supra* note 10 ch. 8.

old principles, devised for a stable, unchanging community, simply broke down."[15] The initial response was an orgy of severity in the criminal courts. "Vagrants and disorderly women . . . almost naked, with only a few filthy rags almost alive and in motion with vermin . . . unable to treat the constable even with a pot of beer to let them escape, are drove in shoals to gaols."[16] Nothing seemed to work. Lawlessness culminated in rioting that verged on insurrection. Parliament at last responded in 1829 with the creation of the "New Police" within the Home Office.

The professional police was therefore an urban concept introduced as a result of the failure of courts alone to preserve order. Traditional criminal law depended on active public cooperation in relatively small, continuous social networks. The civil law, where it provided analogous remedies, was valueless in conditions of general poverty: judgment debtors would have gone to prison anyway. Victim compensation having become virtually impossible, and reconciliation of the offender and the community meaningless, urban law enforcement took on a single direction: systematic deterrence.

When the professional police concept was still new, social theorists predicted that punishment would have a deterrent effect on human behavior.[17] The utility of the police was to ensure that punishment be swift and certain. However, the same demographic conditions that frustrated the tything and constable—concentration, transiency, and poverty—have made swiftness and certainty an increasingly distant hope. Even more to the point, there is empirical reason to doubt the efficacy of punishment as such.[18] Punishment, it has been argued, sustains and ritualizes the "solidarity" of the community by branding deviance.[19] Even if this were true, it would be the best possible indictment of any attempt to extend the criminal law to alien communities enjoying substantially different sentiments regarding order and virtue. An extension of the criminal law system under this theory can, it seems to us, be rationally supported only if it is the instrument of some objective purpose shared by both communities, not merely a symbol of one community's cultural

---

15. T. CRITCHLEY, *supra* note 14, at 21.

16. C. REITH, THE POLICE IDEA 13 (1938), quoting an eyewitness of 1776.

17. Chief among them was Bentham, who argued that punishment should be so devised as to exceed marginally the satisfaction derived from commission of the crime. J. BENTHAM, *Principles of Penal Law*, in THE WORKS OF JEREMY BENTHAM pt. 2, bk. 1, ch. 6, at 367 (J. Bowring ed. 1838); J. BENTHAM, AN INTRODUCTION TO THE PRINCIPLES OF MORALS AND LEGISLATION (J. Burns & H. Hart eds. 1970).

18. *See, e.g.,* H. PACKER, THE LIMITS OF THE CRIMINAL SANCTION (1968); Andenaes, *The General Preventive Effects of Punishment*, 114 U. PA. L. REV. 949 (1966); Cramton, *Driver Behavior and Legal Sanctions: A Study of Deterrence*, 67 MICH. L. REV. 421 (1969). *See also* PRESIDENT'S COMM. ON LAW ENFORCEMENT AND ADMINISTRATION OF JUSTICE, THE CHALLENGE OF CRIME IN A FREE SOCIETY ch. 6 (1968).

19. E. DURKHEIM, THE DIVISION OF LABOR IN SOCIETY 93 (G. Simpson transl. 1933); E. DURKHEIM, THE ELEMENTARY FORMS OF THE RELIGIOUS LIFE 237 (T. Swain ed. 1967). Some recent approbation for this view is found in P. DEVLIN, THE ENFORCEMENT OF MORALS (1965). *See also* MODEL PENAL CODE § 207.12, Comment (Tent. Draft No. 9, 1959).

vanity. Similarly, true rehabilitation[20] necessitates that the motivation or "opportunity" for crime be eliminated and that there be a genuine community for the past offender to return to and be reconciled with.

The criminal law has evolved in an impersonal social environment, the city, in which the reconciliation of disputing parties has been made insignificant by mobility or transiency.[21] Nothing is done to restore the social network because there is no network to restore. In small communities where mobility is low and disputes tend to arise among neighbors, however, reconciliation may prove a more effective deterrent than punishment. As in the business world, continuity of relationships has real value for co-operation and mutual reliance. Unfortunately, while the civil winner-takes-all rule has given way to arbitration and other conciliatory procedures in business disputes, the criminal law does not officially recognize the importance of continuity and is not structurally differentiated to reflect local patterns of transiency and stability.[22]

To some extent the final redoubt of the criminal law is the inadequacy of civil sanctions against impoverished defendants. This cannot suffice without evidence that punishment has a substantial deterrent effect, and one that is not offset, as some believe, by the alienation and criminalization of some defendants by the corrections process. In cases of poverty, as in cases of self-destructive behavior such as drug abuse and alcoholism, the question is not so much one of the adequacy of private remedies as the inadequacy of any existing institution.

We conclude, therefore, that the first objective of law should be to assure as far as possible that *private* relief is inexpensive, readily accessible, and suitable to the ends of compensation and reconciliation. In small, relatively continuous communities, reform can go a long way in this direction.

II

THE POLICE IDEA AND ASSIMILATION

Recognizing the failures of the criminal justice system and its particular inappropriateness in small communities, no pretense can be maintained that

---

20. On rehabilitation, see THE CHALLENGE OF CRIME IN A FREE SOCIETY, *supra* note 18 ch. 6; Allen, *Criminal Justice, Legal Values, and the Rehabilitative Ideal*, 59 J. CRIM. L.C. & P.S. 266 (1959). There is reason to believe that we are entering a period of reevaluation of the criminal law. Ironically, many "reform" concepts—such as decriminalization, restitution, and therapeutic confrontation of victim and accused in informal proceedings—were conventional among Indian tribal governments until suppressed by federal authority, and continue to be discouraged by agencies responsible for assisting tribal law enforcement.

21. Several recent sociological studies of urban neighborhoods strongly suggest that transiency, rather than population density, is the urban factor that most contributes to anonymity and lack of cooperation. *See, e.g.*, E. BOTT, FAMILY AND SOCIAL NETWORK (1957); H. GANS, THE URBAN VILLAGERS (1962); M. YOUNG & P. WILLMOT, FAMILY AND KINSHIP IN EAST LONDON (1957).

22. *See generally* Coons, *Approaches to Court Imposed Compromise—The Uses of Doubt and Reason*, 58 NW. U.L. REV. 750 (1964).

its imposition on Indian tribes was idealistically motivated. It is difficult not to be impressed by the persistence of the police idea in Indian policy, however, and it is challenging to understand why such an archaic institution was hailed for generations as one of the most efficacious instruments of progress.

When English adventurers first settled the East coast, they made little effort to discover the nature and substance of native laws. Young Henry Spelman, perhaps the first Englishman to live among the tideland tribes of Virginia, apologized in his memoirs that "concerninge ther lawes my years and understandinge, made me the less to looke after bycause I thought that Infidels wear lawless."[23] Spelman's preconception was shared by most of the commentators of his age. John Smith was to write of Powhatan that neither "[h]e nor any of his people vnderstand any letters wherby to write or read; the only lawes wherby he ruleth is custome."[24] Nearly a century later, Robert Beverley explained that "having no sort of Letters . . . they can have no Written Laws; nor did the Constitution in which we found them, seem to need many. Nature and their own convenience having taught them to obey one Chief, who is arbiter of all things among them."[25] Dr. Douglass criticized the lack of any "absolute compelling power" among the Indians.[26]

Governed by pure arbitrary will, as Smith and Beverley conceived it, or living in a rude democratic chaos as Douglass and Edmund Burke argued, all observers were happily agreed that the Indians lacked systematic, positive law.[27] This prompted John Locke and his disciples to reason that, since property is the creature of positive law, societies lacking positive law have no property.[28] Locke envisaged law as wholly the instrument of social policy and arising only when resources become so scarce that men must agree upon some scheme of allocating them. The absence of law therefore implied an absence of scarcity. The "fact" that Indians had no law conveniently proved

---

23. Spelman, *Relation of Virginea*, in BRADLEY'S ARBER, TRAVELS AND WORKS OF CAPTAINE JOHN SMITH, PRESIDENT OF VIRGINIA, AND ADMIRAL OF NEW ENGLAND ci, cx-cxi (1965).

24. Smith, *A Map of Virginia, With a Description of the Country, the Commodities, People, Government and Religion*, in BRADLEY'S ARBER, *id.* at 41, 81.

25. R. BEVERLEY, THE HISTORY AND PRESENT STATE OF VIRGINIA 225-26 (L. Wright ed. 1947).

26. W. DOUGLASS, A SUMMARY, HISTORICAL AND POLITICAL, OF THE FIRST PLANTING, PROGRESSIVE IMPROVEMENTS, AND PRESENT STATE OF THE BRITISH SETTLEMENTS IN NORTH-AMERICA 160 (1760). *See also* E. BURKE, AN ACCOUNT OF THE EUROPEAN SETTLEMENTS IN AMERICA 176 (1760).

27. This despite abundant evidence from their own mouths of the existence of routine, orderly, customary processes, especially in family law. *E.g.*, R. BEVERLEY, *supra* note 25, at 170-71; W. BYRD, HISTORY OF THE DIVIDING LINE BETWIXT VIRGINIA AND NORTH CAROLINA 116 (W. Boyd ed. 1967); Spelman, *supra* note 23, at cviii; *An Account of the Indians in Virginia*, 16 WM. & MARY Q. no. 3, at 288, 233-34 (1959).

28. J. LOCKE, *supra* note 7 ch. 5. A similar argument is found in C. MOLLOY, DE JURE MARITIMO ET NAVALI: OR, A TREATISE OF AFFAIRES MARITIME, AND OF COMMERCE ch. 5 (1679); A leading figure in Connecticut land speculation, John Bulkley, popularized Locke in America. J. BULKLEY, AN INQUIRY INTO THE RIGHT OF THE ABORIGINAL NATIVES TO THE LANDS IN AMERICA, AND THE TITLES DERIVED FROM THEM (1724).

that they would not mind giving up a modest portion of their lands to the English.

The idea of lawlessness had an additional implication: that Indians would "need" law once scarcity had been imposed upon them, lest they lapse into uncontrolled robbery and plunder. With some pride Englishmen looked upon their own laws as the most rational, efficacious, and perfect in the whole world, hence they were uncritical of any proposal to loan English laws to benighted pagans. But the colonial government had no illusions that the native tribes would appreciate the gratuity.

As early as 1669, the Governor of New York suggested that frontier villages appoint constables among the Indians "to keep them in ye better ord^r."[29] Two years later, settlers at Narragansett petitioned the Executive Council that[30]

> seeing ye Indians are numerous among us, Wee propose that o^r Governm^t may extend to them, & power to Sumon them to our Co^{rts}. wth respect to matt^{rs} of Trespass, Debt, & other Miscarriages, & to Try & judge them according to our Lawes, when published amongst them.

In reply, the Council cautioned[31]

> that They bee carefull to use such Moderaçon amongst them, That they be not exasperated, but by Degrees may be brought to be conformable to ye Lawes; To wch End, They are to Nominate and Appoint Constables amongst them who may have staves wth ye Kings Armes upon them, the better to keep their People in Awe, & good Ord^r. as is practiced wth good Success amongst ye Indians at ye East end of Long-Island.

The petitioners evidently were concerned first and foremost with protecting themselves in civil matters involving land acquisition and trade, rather than the good government of the Indians. The Council clearly anticipated resistance. The institution of the native constable was hardly a gesture of respect for tribal autonomy. In the process of choosing the constabulary and giving it the force of crown law, English settlers would have the opportunity to create a new tribal leadership, maintained and protected by the English, through which all commands and favors from the royal government would issue. Established in power and property, it could handily draw allegiance away from traditional tribal leaders and institutions.

Related measures were taken by Massachusetts, which organized Indian townships and appointed Indian officers and judges.[32] The native court sys-

---

29. 13 DOCUMENTS RELATIVE TO THE COLONIAL HISTORY OF THE STATE OF NEW YORK 430 (E. O'Callaghan ed. 1853-87).

30. 1 MINUTES OF THE EXECUTIVE COUNCIL OF THE PROVINCE OF NEW YORK 359 (B. Psaltis ed. 1910).

31. *Id.* at 362.

32. Kawashima, *Legal Origins of the Indian Reservation in Colonial Massachusetts*, 13 AM. J. LEGAL HIST. 42 (1969).

tem, first established in 1658, provided for trial before an Indian magistrate, appeal to a panel of Indian magistrates under the supervision of an English judge, and transfer of felony cases to the English courts. Apparently the business of the native courts was the suppression of drunkeness, which was prohibited throughout the colony. The General Court of the colony soon promulgated regulations to be enforced by the native courts and eventually replaced them altogether with English justices. To complete the transition, all native officials were subordinated to committees of "trustees" enjoying absolute authority to manage and dispose of the township's natural resources. Non-Indians were permitted to settle on Indian township land and to participate in town meetings. One town survived into the nineteenth century and the state terminated it.[33]

In Connecticut, the Assembly frequently appointed those tribal leaders with whom they would treat. Not only did these instantaneous monarchs enjoy a complete monopoly of English gifts and attentions, but any who protested their absolute rule were punishable for petty treason in the colony courts. In one colorful case, an appointive sachem incurred so much displeasure that his people ransacked and burned his house and ran him out on a rail. On his complaint, the General Court rounded up the dissidents and ordered them to pay compensation and never again question the authority of their pretended sachem. In another, the General Court appointed a committee to draft laws for the use of the Indians—the first model code.[34] Similar policies were pursued by Maryland and Virginia.[35]

The function and effect of these policies is clear: the alienation of traditional leadership and suppression of traditional law. With native government neutralized and resistance subject to penalty, the way was cleared for the safe confiscation of resources.

The police idea was revived in the west with greater vigor and many added dimensions. Plains Indians already enjoyed a paraprofessional police institution, variously known as "Police Societies" or "Camp Soldiers."[36] These

---

33. W. APES, INDIAN NULLIFICATION OF THE UNCONSTITUTIONAL LAWS OF MASSACHUSETTS *passim* (1835).

34. *See* 1 THE PUBLIC RECORDS OF THE COLONY OF CONNECTICUT 299 (C. Hoadley & J. Trumbull eds. 1850); 2 *id.* at 39, 56-57, 66, 256-57, 440, 483 (native constables "to serve warrants, publish order, and to gather the tribute"); 3 *id.* at 55; 4 *id.* at 86, 122-23, 140, 326; 5 *id.* at 518; 6 *id.* at 428-29; 7 *id.* at 517; 9 *id.* at 540. *See also* 2 *id.* at 117, a predecessor of the Major Crimes Act, 23 Stat. 385 (1885).

35. Robinson, *Tributary Indians in Colonial Virginia*, 67 VA. MAGAZINE HIST. & BIOGRAPHY 49 (1959); 1 ARCHIVES OF MARYLAND 329-331 (W. Browne ed. 1913); 3 ARCHIVES OF MARYLAND 360 (B. Steiner ed. 1916).

36. *See* K. LLEWELLYN & E. HOEBEL, THE CHEYENNE WAY (1941). Other tribes developed formal court systems without direct federal intervention, *e.g.*, the Cherokee and Iroquois. *See* J. NOON, LAW AND GOVERNMENT OF THE GRAND RIVER IROQUOIS (1949); J. REID, A LAW OF BLOOD: THE PRIMITIVE LAW OF THE CHEROKEE NATION (1970); CHEROKEE ADVOCATE, LAWS OF THE

organizations typically functioned only when the entire community was en-
camped together and, with the exception of certain direct hazards to public
welfare such as the scaring off of buffalo, offenders were pressed to make
restitution rather than suffer the penalty of destruction of their property.[37]
Because of the size and nature of these communities, identification was simple, prosecution swift, and cooperation, even of the accused, generally assured. Reconciliation was a principal objective of mediation.

Following the Civil War, individual Indian agents experimented with
paramilitary native police forces in order to wrest jurisdiction and authority
from the Army.[38] Gradually, the policy gained attention in Washington, and
in 1878 a general system of Indian Police was authorized by Congress. Four
years later, the Secretary of the Interior promulgated rules for the establishment of native courts—Courts of Indian Offenses—and in 1884 circulated a
penal code of reservation offenses.

Perhaps the best introduction to the philosophy of these institutions is
found in this advice given to agents:[39]

> The chief duty of an agent is to induce his Indians to labor in civilized
> pursuits. To attain this end every possible influence should be brought to
> bear, and in proportion as it is attained, other things being equal, an agent's
> administration is successful or unsuccessful.

In 1873, the Commissioner of Indian Affairs assailed what he called the
"fiction of sovereignty" of tribes.[40]

> The first condition of civilization is protection of life and property
> through the administration of law. As the Indians are taken out of their wild
> life, they leave behind them the force attaching to the distinctive tribal condi-
> tion. The chiefs inevitably lose their power . . . until their government be-
> comes, in most cases, a mere form, without power of coercion and restraint.
> Their authority is founded only on "the consent of the governed."

CHEROKEE NATION (1852); COMMISSIONER OF INDIAN AFFAIRS, ANNUAL REPORT 1882, at 133-34
[hereinafter cited as ANNUAL REPORT]; Humphrey, *Police and Tribal Welfare in Plains Indian Cul-
tures*, 33 J. CRIM. L. & CRIMINOLOGY 147 (1942).

37. Humphrey, *supra* note 36. Ridicule was also an important element of the "correctional"
process. W. HAGAN, INDIAN POLICE AND JUDGES 16 (1966); C. WISSLER, RED MAN RESERVATIONS
133-34 (1971). This also appears to have been true of eastern tribes. Spelman, *supra* note 23, at
cxi, reported that felonies were punishable by death as in England, but a somewhat later
narrative of the same Indians concludes that "[t]hey don't punish any crimes with death, only
they pay so much money." *An Account of the Indians in Virginia, supra* note 27, at 243. This is
supported by the frequency with which tribes offered to pay restitution to the families of
Englishmen killed by Indians, a notable and detailed example being found in S. AMES, COUNTY
COURT RECORDS OF ACCOMACK-NORTHAMPTON, VIRGINIA 1632-1640, at 57-58 (1954). There are,
in fact, instances in which Indians asked that Englishmen condemned to death for the murder of
Indians be set free, *e.g.*, H. MCILWAINE, MINUTES OF THE COUNCIL AND GENERAL COURT OF
COLONIAL VIRGINIA, 1622-1632, 1670-1676, at 483 (1924).

38. W. HAGAN, *supra* note 37, at 25-30.

39. U.S. DEP'T OF THE INTERIOR, REGULATIONS § 486, at 84 (1884).

40. ANNUAL REPORT 1873, at 4-5.

Not unlike his colonial forebears, the Commissioner's argument began with the "fact" of lawlessness and the "need" for law. He was advocating that Congress empower the Bureau to organize "suitable government" on reservations including a police force.[41] The plan contemplated an immediate transfer of civil and criminal jurisdiction to United States courts so that every Indian "will be effectively protected, by the authority and power of the Government, in his life, liberty, property, and character, as certainly as if he were a white man."[42]

A significant change of policy was made in 1877, leading to congressional approval for the scheme. Indians were no longer to have the benefit of general laws, but were to be subjected to a special code "based upon the result of the experience of those familiar with Indian life and manners."[43] Many reform groups opposed the change, arguing for example that "it would perpetuate the evil . . . of keeping Indians apart from all others, and of maintaining a hundred petty sovereignities within our borders. . . . The laws which are good enough for all other kindreds and peoples and tribes and nations are good enough for Indians."[44]

The reformers were gravely deceived if they believed the official program was anti-assimilationist. Quite the contrary, the problem was that *in reality* tribes retained their traditional governments and laws and were in no way willing as yet to accept a revolutionary reordering of their affairs. Before the Bureau could effect the absolute transfer of jurisdiction it originally proposed, it had to bring about or accelerate the deterioration of native institutions that it had so confidently assured Congress was already well underway. .

Appropriately, then, the Indian Police and Courts of Indian Offenses took on a subversive (or "educational") character.[45]

> The indirect results and ultimate influence of this system are even more important than its direct advantages. Well trained and disciplined, the police force is a perpetual educator. It is a power entirely independent of the chiefs. It weakens, and will finally destroy, the power of tribes and bands. It fosters a spirit of personal responsibility. It makes the Indian himself the representative of the power and majesty of the Government of the United States. . . . The Indians need to be taught the supremacy of law, and the necessity for strict obedience thereto . . . where the Indians themselves are the recognized agents for the enforcement of law, they will the more readily learn to be obedient to its requirements.

---

41. ANNUAL REPORT 1874, at 15.
42. ANNUAL REPORT 1876, at x.
43. ANNUAL REPORT 1877, at 1-2.
44. BOARD OF INDIAN COMM'RS, REPORT FOR 1885; W. HAGAN, *supra* note 37, at 159.
45. ANNUAL REPORT 1881, at xvii-xviii. Compare later reports which attribute the decline of tribal government entirely to *natural* causes. ANNUAL REPORT 1882, at xix; ANNUAL REPORT 1883, at x-xi.

In a word, "tribal relations should be broken up, socialism destroyed, and the family and the autonomy of the individual substituted."[46]

Where agents condescended to approve tribal elections for judge, the purpose was to undermine the traditional leadership succession process.[47] Elections were bitter and divisive, and understandably so, because of the exclusive power wielded by the winners. More typically, police and judges were appointed by the agent. Great care was taken that they be sympathetic to assimilation. According to the regulations, judges wherever possible were to be able to "read and write English readily, wear citizens' dress, and engage in civilized pursuits, and no person shall be eligible to such appointment who is a polygamist."[48] Once selected, these officers were given to understand that they were to set a good example and be absolutely obedient to the Agent.[49] An effort was made to attract the best and the brightest. Police candidates were required to "be of some influence in the tribe."[50] Several expedients were advised to strengthen their allegiance. With higher pay, enlistment would become "a road to distinction, that formerly was the reward of prowess in battle or skill in hunting."[51] Given sixshooters and "a few brass buttons by way of distinction," the Police would be "proud of being considered U.S. soldiers."[52] Travelling through Indian country towards the close of the nineteenth century, the anthropologist Clark Wissler observed that owing to its power and exploits the Police "rose to such a level of prestige, that every young Indian . . . hoped some day to be considered worthy of a place in the troop."[53]

In 1892, the Commissioner of Indian Affairs admitted that the police and judges "may be and sometimes are, merely instrumentalities in the hands of the agent for the enforcement of his power."[54] In Wissler's words, "like all good police, they merely obeyed orders."[55] But the police predictably paid a great price for their rise to glory. Although several agents reported from the start that tribes were responding warmly to the police idea,[56] just as many

---

46. ANNUAL REPORT 1889, at 3-4.
47. W. HAGAN, *supra* note 37, at 16.
48. SECRETARY OF THE INTERIOR, PUNISHMENT OF CRIMES AND MISDEMEANORS COMMITTED BY INDIANS, H. R. Exec. Doc. No. 1, 52d Cong., 2d Sess. pt. 5, at 28-31 (1892).
49. *E.g.*, ANNUAL REPORT 1882, at 170, regarding the Yakimas. Agents frequently commended the police for their obedience and loyalty.
50. U.S. DEP'T OF THE INTERIOR, *supra* note 39, at 108.
51. ANNUAL REPORT 1882, at 31.
52. ANNUAL REPORT 1877, at 3; ANNUAL REPORT 1882, at xliv. *See also* ANNUAL REPORT 1883, at 26, 76-77.
53. C. WISSLER, *supra* note 37, at 105. *See also* W. HAGAN, *supra* note 37, at 3; ANNUAL REPORT 1881, at 145.
54. ANNUAL REPORT 1892, at 23. In the same year the Board of Indian Commissioners reported that the reservation courts "practically register the decrees of the Indian agent." W. HAGAN, *supra* note 37, at 110.
55. C. WISSLER, *supra* note 37, at 99, 104, 106.
56. ANNUAL REPORT 1882, at 143, 157; ANNUAL REPORT 1883, at 2-3, 84.

observed friction and resistance. Policemen complained of the "enmity and risk" involved, and on many reservations no one could be found willing to undertake a judicial appointment.[57] Often the resistance was spearheaded by the remnants of the old police societies, as at Cheyenne and Pine Ridge, where they retained considerable authority.[58] At least at one agency, this was overcome by enlisting the traditional camp soldiers.[59] Elsewhere opposition to the police idea came from tribal leaders, who "looked upon it as an infringement of their authority" and were often appeased by permitting them to modify the regulations issued by the Secretary.[60]

The Commissioner was fully aware of the intrusive nature of the police idea:[61]

> When it is borne in mind that a great majority of the cases upon which they are called to act are offenses committed by their own race against laws made by a race with which they have not hitherto been in sympathy . . . and that many of the regulations established forbid practices which almost form a part of the very existence of the Indian, practices and customs which are to them a religion, and which, if neglected, they believe will result in disaster and death, the impartiality with which the police have performed the duties devolving upon them is creditable in the highest degree.

Some agents were so apprehensive of violent divisions resulting from the introduction of the police idea that they refused to take part in it.[62] But the aggravation of factionalism was generally understood to be a necessary element in the attack on tribal government. The Osage agent confidently predicted that the police "will gradually but surely destroy the old chieftainship and Indian form of government."[63]

Essential to an appreciation of the police idea in the West is the fact that most of the Bureau penal code actually dealt with "heathenish practices" rather than the protection of life and property. In other words, the Court of Indian Offenses code concentrated on victimless crimes. In establishing the courts, Secretary of the Interior Teller condemned ritual dancing as "calculated to stimulate the warlike passions" and lead to the "demoralization of the young, who are incited to emulate the wicked conduct of their elders."[64] Among the other "great hindrance[s] to the civilization of the Indians" was

---

57. ANNUAL REPORT 1882, at 27; ANNUAL REPORT 1884, at 84; ANNUAL REPORT 1890, at 105.
58. STANDS IN TIMBER, CHEYENNE MEMORIES 271, 273 (1972). *See also* ANNUAL REPORT 1881, at xviii; ANNUAL REPORT 1890, at 177.
59. C. WISSLER, *supra* note 37, at 102-03.
60. For example at Umatilla, Washington, ANNUAL REPORT 1882, at 143 and at Nez Perce, ANNUAL REPORT 1883, at 57-58.
61. ANNUAL REPORT 1884, at vi-xvii.
62. *E.g.*, at Grande Ronde, Oregon, ANNUAL REPORT 1882, at 135 ("would only promote discord and contention and strife"), and at Hoopa, California, ANNUAL REPORT 1883, at 13 ("mere aggravation of disorder and existing animosities").
63. ANNUAL REPORT 1882, at 73, 76, 79; ANNUAL REPORT 1883, at 57.
64. U.S. DEP'T OF THE INTERIOR, *supra* note 39, § 496, at 86-88.

the shocking fact that their marriages existed "only by the consent of both parties," and the survival of medicine men, "who are always found with the anti-progressive party" and persist in "using their conjurers' arts to prevent the people from abandoning their heathenish rites and customs." Teller also criticized destruction of the property of the dead as being a disincentive to capitalism.[65]

Consistent with his wishes, the first penal code prohibited dancing, polygamy, practicing as a medicine man, prostitution, and drunkeness.[66] *The only other crime enumerated* was stealing, but its purpose is betrayed by the provision that it would be no defense to answer that the property was *taken or destroyed* in the process of mourning the dead. Traditional inheritance and religion were outlawed in a single blow.

In 1892 the code was revised, with the addition of a catch-all provision empowering the courts to prosecute "any misdemeanor . . . defined in the laws of the State or Territory within which the reservation may be located."[67] The new code also authorized the fine or imprisonment of any Indian who "refuses or neglects to adopt habits of industry, or to engage in civilized pursuits or employments."[68] Tribal reaction was often bitter, but there is reason to believe that native officers were cautious to avoid executing its more objectionable features. At an early stage the courts came to deal more typically with drunkeness and other blessings of compulsory civilization than with resistance to civilized habits.[69] However, such was the zeal of the Bureau that it strove to make Indians even more moral and law-abiding than their neighbors.[70] The police idea in the West was more than an Indian policy; it was an experiment in the effectiveness of unlimited police power to shape society.

A.   Allotment and Reform

Reservation government in the 1880s was purely transitional. In the words of the Supreme Court, its legitimacy was no greater than its usefulness as an

---

65.   This practice survives, for example in the Navajo Nation, alongside a complex system of inheritance rules that have gradually become absorbed into the tribal courts. Shepard, *Navajo Inheritance Patterns: Random or Regular?*, 5 ETHNOLOGY 87 (1966); R. Barsh, The Formative Period of Navajo Law: Probate 1940-1972, June 1973 (unpublished manuscript at Kennedy Institute of Politics, Cambridge). In point of fact, very little *economic* property was ever destroyed, but rather tokens were distributed to all of the mourners in a subtle interplay of guilt and grief, and some personal effects, such as jewelry, were buried with the deceased. Sheep and land remained within the residential unit, descending by locality, not blood.

66.   U.S. DEP'T OF THE INTERIOR, *supra* note 39, §§ 4-6, 8, at 89-90.

67.   H.R. EXEC. DOC. NO. 1, *supra* note 48, at 30.

68.   *Id.*

69.   W. HAGAN, *supra* note 37, at 122. A spectacular exception was the thorough suppression of the Sun Dance, described both by Hagan and Wissler, *supra* note 37. Many individual agents enforced Teller morality with great zeal and in the face of considerable resistance, *e.g.*, ANNUAL REPORT 1883, at 42, 65, 86.

70.   According to some observers, it succeeded. ANNUAL REPORT 1881, at xix; ANNUAL REPORT

"educational and disciplinary instrumentalit[y]" of the United States.[71] Accordingly, the jurisdiction of the courts extended only to Indians. What civil powers they enjoyed were required to "conform as nearly as practicable" to rules of state law, and it was their duty to "advise, and inform either or both parties . . . in regard to the requirements of these rules."[72]

The reservation court system was only five years old when Congress authorized the Secretary of the Interior to allot Indian lands in severalty.[73] The plan was to reorganize simultaneously the distribution of Indian land ownership along state lines and subject the Indians themselves to state civil and criminal law. It was soon found necessary to postpone the dissolution of reservation government for the duration of the "trust" period during which allottees were incapacitated to dispose of their land.[74] This may be better understood as a political courtesy to the states unable to tax trust land for the support of services, than an admission that the period of "transition" had been terminated too hastily.

At the same time, Congress provided for federal jurisdiction of certain serious felonies committed by Indians on reservations, allegedly in response to complaints that there remained a dangerous jurisdictional vacuum—an absence of state jurisdiction generally and the limitation of the jurisdiction of Courts of Indian Offenses to misdemeanors.[75] It must be pointed out, however, that the precipitating incident involved a murderer required to pay restitution by tribal authorities.[76] Congress's action was more to suppress tribal criminal law than to provide punishment where there had been none.

Repeated extensions of the trust period gave the reservation courts a precarious reprieve for the first third of this century. In the interim, Bureau law and order policy lacked direction. The judges became reactionary and entrenched in their offices.[77] Although the "overwhelming" share of their business continued to involve drunkeness and minor, typically concensual sex offenses, the Indian courts were also developing or recreating a conciliatory style for resolving bipartisan disputes.[78] Ironically, to the extent that Indian

---

1882, at 76; C. WISSLER, *supra* note 37, at 109; *Hearings on Law and Order on Indian Reservations of the Northwest, supra* note 11, at 14208.

71.   United States v. Clapox, 35 F. 575, 577 (D. Ore. 1888).

72.   U.S. DEP'T OF THE INTERIOR, *supra* note 39, § 9, at 90-91.

73.   General Allotment Act, ch. 119, § 6, 24 Stat. 390 (1887), *as amended*, Act of May 8, 1906, ch. 2348, 34 Stat. 182.

74.   34 Stat. 182 (1906).

75.   Major Crimes Act, 23 Stat. 385 (1885).

76.   *Ex parte* Crow Dog, 109 U.S. 556 (1883). According to W. HAGAN, *supra* note 37, at 118-19, 123, traditional restitution procedures persisted for many years after the establishment of reservation courts.

77.   C. WISSLER, *supra* note 37, at 138, observed this in the 1890s. Surveys conducted in 1929 found the same to be true; *Hearings on Law and Order on Indian Reservations of the Northwest, supra* note 11, at 14215-216.

78.   "No sharp line . . . can be drawn between civil and criminal cases, and often the judgment

judges of the twenties perpetuated the moralistic fervor of Secretary Teller, they were found to be regarded by younger Indians as backward, paternalistic, and un-American.[79]

Although reservation courts remained cheaper and more readily accessible to Indians than state tribunals after allotment, there were artificial constraints on their powers that rendered them ineffective. In the absence of a systematic policy of interference with their decisions, they were free to evolve procedures for disposing of property and adjudicating commercial matters.[80] What they lacked, however, was jurisdiction over non-Indians, jurisdiction over "fee patent Indians" within the reservation, and recognition of their judgments in the state courts. Their jurisdiction was thus fragmentary and, without any basis to compel execution of their judgments elsewhere, they offered no security to Indian entrepreneurs or non-Indian creditors. The net effect of the Courts of Indian Offenses was therefore to instill respect for federal power and state law on the criminal side, while providing no meaningful civil protection for Indian property against non-Indians and no basis for the extension of credit to Indians. They maintained tribes in a state of *submissive poverty*.

Two years after the publication of his well-known survey of the social conditions of American Indians,[81] Dr. Lewis Meriam coordinated a study of northwest reservation law and order for the Senate Committee on Indian Affairs. Its major thrust was that the transitional function of the Courts of Indian Offenses had been frustrated by Bureau mismanagement, and that administrative reforms were necessary to assure complete political and legal assimilation at the earliest possible time.

The Meriam study concluded that most Indians were law-abiding and that observed patterns of law-breaking could be attributed in the main to "lack of interests, boredom, poverty, and family and community disintegration."[82] Its

---

in a single case will give relief of a civil character to the complaining party and provide for the punishment of the defendant." *Hearings on Law and Order on Indian Reservations of the Northwest, supra* note 11, at 14212.

79. *E.g.*, *id.* at 14224-225.

80. Some did just that, to judge from the records of this period in the Navajo archives. R. Barsh, *supra* note 65. Nonetheless on many reservations individual agents maintained their customary grip on the courts. *Hearings on Law and Order on Indian Reservations of the Northwest, supra* note 11, at 14213, 14224.

81. L. MERIAM, THE PROBLEM OF INDIAN ADMINISTRATION (1928).

82. *Hearings on Law and Order on Indian Reservations of the Northwest, supra* note 11, at 14142. Summarizing a major statistical study of reservation court business, the study also concluded that Indian crimes were "very rarely . . . of the type from which society must protect itself." *Id.* Virtually all fell into the category of minor victimless crimes. Roughly 50 per cent of all prosecutions were for drunkenness alone, another 16 per cent were for concensual sex offenses such as adultery and fornication. *Id.* at 14153. Altogether, felonies—larceny, robbery, burglary, arson, rape, murder, and aggravated assault—comprised only three per cent of the business of the Courts of Indian Offenses, and only 11 per cent of all prosecutions of Indians in all courts. What is even more significant is that Indian crime *rates* for these serious offenses were considerably lower than the national average. U.S. BUREAU OF THE CENSUS, 1932 STATISTICAL ABSTRACT OF

authors were in agreement with the prevalent philosophy of the Depression years that "crime is a symptom of social ill health" and that "society is a party to every offense."[83] Consistent with this view, they suspected that existing "deterrents" such as imprisonment were "essentially superficial" and ineffective.[84] "Courts and laws can, of course, punish but they are not, unsupplemented, the agencies to remove the causes."[85] The inadequacy of punishment was particularly evident on reservations where "no disgrace" was attached to punishment and where ridicule was as much or a more powerful force.[86]

The great inadequacy of reservation courts in the civil area was observed but not appreciated. For example, it was noted that stealing often merely reflected a dispute over ownership.[87] Lacking a civil remedy in the Indian court, a person aggrieved over the taking or injury of his property would seize some of his adversary's property in compensation. If this led to a criminal complaint for theft, the Court of Indian Offenses tended to resolve it by trying title, not guilt—it was a jurisdictional fiction, like the nontraversable allegation of *vis et armis* in common law trespass writs.[88] Our own study of Navajo courts of the 1920s and 1930s indicates that a large part of the assault prosecutions were in fact boundary disputes in disguise, and were dealt with by the judges accordingly.[89] The Meriam Commission study concluded, however, that since Indians had a *right* of access to state courts, the only benefit of tribal civil jurisdiction was that it cost so little to invoke it. They recommended that tribal civil jurisdiction be preserved pending complete termination. They would have limited jurisdiction to cases involving moveable goods of the value of three hundred dollars or less, making it of very little real economic importance.[90]

The central recommendations of the study showed little more progress in policy, though couched in humanistic terminology. "The causes of crime are to be found in the economic and social lives of the offenders."[91] Indians

---

THE UNITED STATES 72 (1932). (The text of the Major Crimes Act, § 9, 23 Stat. 385 (1885), made it clear that tribes retained a right of *original* prosecution even for the enumerated felonies.)

83. *Hearings on Law and Order on Indian Reservations of the Northwest, supra* note 11, at 14148, 14173.

84. *Id.* at 14165-167, 14183, 14216-217. "We have little faith in the value of punishment . . . however . . . we must more or less accept our civilization as it is." *Id.* at 14226-227.

85. *Id.* at 14142.

86. *Id.* at 14163-164, 14180 ("control through public opinion is much more effective than law enforcement").

87. *Id.* at 14150.

88. The Meriam team concluded that these "informal sentences," constituting some eight per cent of all judgments, were often "more suited to the needs of the Indians" than the sentences of non-Indian courts. *Id.* at 14164. Often the defendant was put to work for the benefit of the victim or the community. *Id.* at 14164, 14221-224.

89. R. Barsh, *supra* note 65.

90. *Hearings on Law and Order on Indian Reservations of the Northwest, supra* note 11, at 14231, 14196-197.

91. *Id.* at 14183.

committed crimes because they were poor. But while the Commission was willing to attribute some of the problem to the general agricultural depression that had plagued the country for a generation, it was certain that the real cause of poverty was Indianess. "They do not know what they are missing," the investigators lamented, "they lack the incentives to work."[92] Even where they observed high unemployment in the counties surrounding reservations, the real fault was the Indians' for having avoided migrating to the cities.[93] The point was made that the better type left the reservation, leaving behind "the less adaptable, less ambitious, and less able."

Chief among the defects in tribal society were family and community habits that discouraged competitive individualism. For example, "[t]he family is everywhere recognized as the most important of the social institutions affecting the child," and "experience has pretty well proved that the presence of 'in-laws' and other outsiders tends to weaken the bonds between members of the two-generation family and often causes family disruption."[94] Children in extended families tend to be "confused" and "lack a feeling of security and permanence in their lives."[95] This is aggravated by the continual observation of "sponging" by relatives.[96] In effect, they argued that Indian family life instilled a belief in sharing rather than saving. Recommendation: Social service agencies should do everything possible to motivate Indians to live in nuclear family households.[97]

This objective required the cooperation of law for the reform of the marriage relationship. Dismissing Indian complaints that marriage and divorce were too expensive and sexually oppressive (a very modern theme), the Meriam panel concluded that marriages solemnized under state law were necessary to the Indian economy. They reasoned that the traditional social network depended upon the fact that matriarchal clans controlled most real wealth. Men might come and go as they pleased; the children remained with the mother and her kin because that was where their support came from. But since the "general economy" prefers to make *men* the source of all wealth, they should be required by means of legal marriage to take *sole* financial responsibility for their offspring! Graciously, the study did not recommend that compulsion be employed, in the style of the Teller rules. Rather, they advo-

---

92. *Id.* at 14184. They also explained the economic failure of Indian allottees as due to a lack of "ambition." *Id.* at 14187.

93. *Id.* at 14185.

94. *Id.* at 14173.

95. *Id.* at 14174-175.

96. *Id.* at 14173, 14188-189.

97. *Id.* at 14234. The Meriam team also criticized Indians' "unearned income" from the lease or sale of trust resources as a disincentive to industriousness. *Id.* at 14189. We imagine that the coupon-clipping capitalists of the twenties would have been amused by this judgment.

cated a program of persuading them "that they would be happier living in permanent family groups."[98]

The Meriam study continued in the tradition of arguing from alleged lawlessness.[99]

> The old Indian culture has almost entirely disappeared. The old Indian form of government has gone, tribal authority has broken down, Indian customs and Indian laws are no longer effective. They cannot be restored because the economic basis upon which they rested has been largely destroyed. For these Indians the only way ahead is gradual absorption into or adjustment to the dominant white civilization.

Concededly, this had largely been the responsibility of the "dominant white civilization," but the panel was unwilling to lay the blame on any *existing* policies. They concluded that there was no racial prejudice against Indians. The frequent failure of off-reservation courts to punish Indians was largely a matter of sympathy, not indifference.[100] Discrimination was indeed present, but the study suggested that it was rational. The states *legitimately* resented supplying services to people who could not pay taxes.[101] More particularly, "we know that people who have nothing to lose constitute a danger to those with possessions; that in any community the lower standards of life tend to depress the higher."[102] There is a certain ring to this that is reminiscent of the anarchism scare in the twenties, especially where the report compares non-Indian values in privacy, acquisitiveness and private property with Indian *gregariousness* and *communalism*.

If followed that "[t]he task of helping the Indians to become adjusted is educational. In the matter of law and order the lesson they have to learn is to know, respect, and observe the laws of the State in which they reside."[103] A reorganization of the reservation court system was proposed consistent with this philosophy. To begin with, each court was to have a non-Indian chief judge, because Indian judges "alone could not well apply State law or themselves educate the Indians to prepare for the ultimate transition to State law."[104] Indian associate judges were nonetheless considered "useful." It would prove an "educational" experience for them; moreover they could be elected so that the community would "feel they had a real part in the court" and be "train[ed]" in the electoral process.

Since Indian offenders "need more help than punishment," the court system was to be integrated with Bureau social services.[105] Social workers were to

---

98. *Id.* at 14175-177.
99. *Id.* at 14142.
100. *Id.* at 14200-204, 14181.
101. *Id.* at 14182-183, 14207.
102. *Id.* at 14182, 14190.
103. *Id.* at 14138, 14139, 14142.
104. *Id.* at 14139, 14230.
105. *Id.* at 14164.

be assigned to each court, and in some cases even sit as judges.[106] This was not necessarily an effort to be progressive. There is, for example, a certain element of "behavior modification" in the suggestion made that "law enforcement does build up a certain respect for law, whether or not the law is of the group's own making."[107]

Naturally, the law of the reservation was to be state law because of its "educational value."[108] Its administration by Indian courts was to be strictly transitional, to ease the change by degrees. A special code of Indian misdemeanors was to be promulgated by the Bureau, but its function too was conceived of as transitional. "As most of the offenses committed by Indians are of the minor character usually covered by municipal and township ordinances and not by State laws, and as such organized governmental units do not exist on many reservations," the code would have to serve until such time as Indians could join with non-Indians to form their own townships under state law.[109] As for tribal government, its value had become purely "recreational."[110]

"We must popularize rather than compel" was the theme of much of the report.[111] But as Depression-era liberals, its authors must have had some doubts about the perfection of the American institutions they planned to sell. "It is true," they admitted, "that some of our traditional institutions are at present under attack. . . . It is not the province of the present investigation to enter into such debate."[112] Their object was not to give the Indians wholesome laws, but to make them the same, for better or worse, as everyone else.

These sentiments were shared by many of those who testified before Congress on behalf of the Indian Reorganization Act (IRA) of 1934.[113] Although Commissioner of Indian Affairs Collier insisted repeatedly that the critical change made by the proposed law was to abolish Bureau despotism and leave Indians free to choose their own laws, Senate Committee Chairman Wheeler of Montana noted that the bill as written provided for no such thing.[114] Title I required that tribal charters and constitutions be approved by the Secretary

---

106. *Id.* at 14139-140.

107. *Id.* at 14164. The report-writers appear to have been caught up in the wave of behaviorism that swept American social science in the late twenties. See, for example, their assertion that "[c]ustoms grow out of habits formed because the process of forming them is pleasurable." *Id.* at 14179-180. Their theory of legal change attributes everything to conditioned responses and nothing to choice or policy.

108. *Id.* at 14140-141.

109. *Id.* at 14229.

110. *Id.* at 14177.

111. *Id.* at 14179.

112. *Id.* at 14226. In all fairness, it should be pointed out that they did accede to some minor variations in reservation courts, but only perhaps for the purpose of minimizing resistance. *Id.* at 14179.

113. Act of June 18, 1934, ch. 567, § 16, 48 Stat. 987.

114. *Hearings on Readjustment of Indian Affairs Before the Senate Comm. on Indian Affairs*, 73d Cong., 2d Sess. 31-32, 64-65, 106-07, Collier; 66-67, 106-07, 163-69, Wheeler (1934).

of the Interior before taking effect, a power that could be, and has in fact been, used to hold up new governments until they comply structurally with Bureau recommendations.[115] As Collier eventually admitted in his testimony, the net effect of Title I was to protect *approved* governments from arbitrary *revocation* by an administrative agency. He assured Congress that it would retain absolute authority to terminate approved tribes. As Wheeler appropriately observed, this gave tribes little more security against the future.[116]

Neither in conception nor enactment did the Indian Reorganization Act materially alter the condition of reservation police and courts. In his presentation Collier insisted that reservation legislatures would have cognizance of only "matters of local concern." He compared it to "town government."[117] Of the courts, their "powers at the outset could not be any wider than the powers of the existing court of Indian offenses. The difference would be that it would be a court responsible to the local community."[118] Elimination of Bureau autocracy over law and order would simply assure individual Indians of "due process." Collier and his staff conceded the wisdom of permitting tribes to regulate domestic relations, school administration, and inheritance and agreed that they should be prohibited from making any law inconsistent with that of the State.[119] Generally, they appear to have been following the advice of the Meriam study, that Indian courts should remain merely as stopgaps in the absence of state municipal organizations.

This impression is reinforced by an examination of Title IV of the bill, which was never approved by Congress.[120] Title IV established a national Court of Indian Affairs consisting of seven presidentially-appointed judges. The judges were *not* to be assured that independence of the executive that life tenure provides in the federal court system. Section 14 gave the President, with the consent of the Senate, authority to remove any judge *without cause*. Thus what appeared to be a component of the judiciary was in reality an administrative agency of the executive department, just like the Bureau.

Jurisdiction of the Court of Indian Affairs was original in the case of violations of the federal criminal code, federal questions, and federal Indian law (such as heirship and allotment, and disputes to which a tribe was a party). At that time all of these matters were heard by United States district courts so

---

115. This provision of Title I, Act of June 18, 1934, ch. 567, §§ 16-17, 48 Stat. 987, is now codified at 25 U.S.C. §§ 476, 477 (1975). Collier defended this on the grounds that the discretion would be used to grant "more or less" power according to the needs of individual tribes. *Hearings on Readjustment of Indian Affairs, supra* note 114, at 32.

116. *Hearings on Readjustment of Indian Affairs, supra* note 114, at 175.

117. *Id.* at 65, 66, 71.

118. *Id.* at 69-70.

119. *Id.* at 69, 78, 94-95, 180, 199. *See also* Oliver LaFarge's comments, *id.* at 177, in which Collier apparently concurred by his silence.

120. The text of this part of the bill may be found in *Hearings on Readjustment of Indian Affairs, supra* note 114, at 11-14.

that Title IV worked a transfer of existing federal jurisdiction. The Court of Indian Affairs was also to have original jurisdiction over interracial civil disputes involving "commerce" (presumably trade, contract, credit and the like) and over all cases involving the application of tribal ordinances to non-Indians, which we must assume was intended to comprehend both civil and criminal matters. Wherever the court's jurisdiction was original it was also to have jurisdiction of appeals from tribal courts. The court was required by section 12 to apply state law in the absence of a controlling federal law or tribal ordinance; tribal custom or common law was not recognized.

From the beginning, Senator Wheeler's position was that Title IV "is out," nor did Collier present it as "indispensable."[121] The only explanation Collier could give of the proposal was that it would, in his opinion, avoid the inconvenience of taking certain matters to the district courts and possibly avoid the insensitivity of federal judges to Indian culture.[122] It would constitute "a special system of courts rather than a special system of substantive law."[123]

Senator Wheeler was unimpressed. He believed that Indians always got a "square deal" in the state courts and that the federal judiciary "lean backward" to be fair to Indian litigants.[124] The Court of Indian Affairs was therefore "expensive and unnecessary."[125] More to the point, he persuaded Collier to concede that the proposed court was entirely too small an institution to bear the workload that would be required.[126] If he was wrong, it was because the structure of the court was calculated to discourage its use. Over the course of a year it could not possibly sit for even a single day in each of the seats of a district court in the United States, nor in the vicinity of each of the nearly 250 Indian reservations existing in 1934. If it chose (as pursuant to section 2 it had discretion to do) to remain in the nation's capital, or to sit in only a dozen or so cities or towns, it would be *at least* as inconvenient as the district courts.

A more damning feature of Title IV was its potential impact on Indian

---

121. *Id*. at 136, 208.

122. *Id*. at 33, 205 ("basic reason for this is . . . convenience"). Collier also suggested that Title IV would extend judicial review to Bureau administrative actions, but this could have been accomplished much more simply by amending the general delegations of power to that agency. Act of July 9, 1932, ch. 174, § 1, 4 Stat. 564; Act of July 27, 1868, ch. 259, § 1, 155 Stat. 228, and in fact was ultimately achieved through the courts in Tooanippah v. Hickel, 397 U.S. 598 (1970).

123. Comments of Alexander Holtzoff, in *Hearings on Readjustment of Indian Affairs, supra* note 114, at 207.

124. *Id*. at 140, 208.

125. *Id*. at 146, 170.

126. *Id*. at 139, 197. On the basis of the Meriam study, *Hearings on Law and Order on Indian Reservations of the Northwest, supra* note 11, at 14153, not fewer than five thousand cases were heard in 1929 on reservations from which appeals could have gone to the proposed Court of Indian Affairs. There is no way to estimate the number of additional cases that might have been brought by virtue of the new court's original jurisdiction. Today, reservation courts probably handle over one hundred thousand criminal prosecutions alone each year, judging from federal and local statistics. *See* BUDGET OF THE U.S. GOVERNMENT, *supra* note 5, and our study of Crow law and order records.

credit and labor. The jurisdictional incapacities of the Courts of Indian Offenses and their tendency to lack civil laws made non-Indians about as unlikely to extend credit to Indians as the remoteness of state courts and their expense made Indians unable to vindicate their property rights against others. Rather than thrust all interracial cases either into the state or tribal courts to eliminate one or the other of these evils, Collier proposed to remove them all to this special court, which would be even more remote, probably overcrowded, dependent upon presidential whim, and tending to apply state civil law anyway. It could only put a further chill on the Indian economy. But it would tend to preserve the separate supervised status of Indians more surely than either immediate assimilation, which the Wheeler Committee tended to favor, or the unaugmented continuance of the Courts of Indian Offenses which had no statutory authority. Perhaps this is why Collier endorsed Title IV at the same time that he continued to plead with Congress that the lack of capital and credit was the greatest cause of Indian poverty and the most important objective of reorganization.[127]

Without Title IV, Title I of the Indian Reorganization Act merely authorized tribes to replace the Courts of Indian Offenses with courts of their own making, subject always to the same artificial jurisdictional restraints. Since it was jurisdiction and enforcement power that contributed most to the valuelessness of the old courts in civil matters, the IRA had the effect of shifting the apparent responsibility for the failures to the Indians themselves. Tribal government assumed political accountability for the court system but was not given the most essential powers necessary to make it work, nor did the Bureau provide research and drafting subsidies to tribal lawmakers except in the form of pre-packaged "tribal codes" that read conspicuously like the Courts of Indian Offenses regulations. Reorganization renewed the policy of education. Tribal courts would be required in the approval process to behave like state courts but would have no power. Instead of attacking the Bureau, dissident tribal members would attack the tribal leaders who appeared immediately responsible, hastening the discreditation of all tribal government and its eventual demise.[128]

Because of tribal poverty and the absence of a suitable tax base—precisely the "legitimate" reason for state reluctance to assume responsibility—tribal law and order would continue to have to be subsidized in large part by the Bureau. On many reservations judges continue to receive their paychecks

---

127. *Hearings on Readjustment of Indian Affairs, supra* note 114, at 73, 74.

128. We suggest that the confrontation of tribal officers and dissidents in the recent Wounded Knee incident was a manifestation of the consequences bred by this process of fostering easily discredited tribal governments. In 1883, the Nez Perce agent applauded the Commissioner of Indian Affairs for authorizing agency staff to veto tribal legislation, noting that it would deal a "severe blow" to Indian political unity. ANNUAL REPORT 1883, at 56-57. Disguised as "protective," the power of approval and review has been a keystone of federal policy ever since.

from the Bureau. More significantly, most reservation police forces are paid by the Bureau and commanded by the Superintendent pursuant to federal regulations, precisely as they have been since 1878.[129] This circumstance is probably aggravated by the separation of powers principles drafted by the Bureau into most tribal constitutions. With no direct appeal or accountability to the legislature, judges and police can tend to respond as obediently to the wishes of the Bureau as the electorate. Since the purpose of separation of powers is to permit the judiciary to defend the people against legislative or executive excess, its place in tribes with town-meeting type governments is completely unwarranted except as another educational mimicry of state government.

Simply because Congress refused to enact Title IV and did enact Title I does not mean that the IRA represents an advance in the principle of tribal sovereignty. Senator Wheeler, perhaps the single most influential supporter of the legislation, considered its use to foster separate tribal laws "a step backward."[130] "[W]hat we are seeking to do . . . is to have these Indians . . . adopt the white-man's ways and laws. . . . I do not think you ought to give them the power to set up laws which would conflict with the laws of the United States or of the States."[131] His reasoning was that real legal differentiation would lead to an intensification of interracial tensions and a further drying up of credit.[132] This of course assumed that tribal laws would be so different from state laws that it would deter commerce and travel substantially more than state boundaries do. The Committee had no reason to predict that tribes would be so foolish as to use their governmental powers to commit economic suicide, unless they were assuming that Indian leaders were "incompetent" in the strongest sense of the word. What they opposed was differentness, even prosperous differentness. Or were they opposed to the entrenchment of tax exemption and Indian resource management that went along with continued tribal existence?

B. Termination and More Reform

The Blackfeet, Klamath, Standing Rock Sioux, and Assiniboine complained to Congress that passage of the Indian Reorganization Act would

---

129. As of 1963, for example, the Sioux reservations of North and South Dakota were between 25 per cent and 100 per cent dependent on federal aid for law and order operations. *Hearings on Constitutional Rights of the American Indian, supra* note 2, at 113. The Navajo bear 93 per cent of their law and order costs, but they are able to rely on their multi-million dollar natural resource development revenue. INDIAN JUSTICE PLANNING PROJECT, THE PEOPLE WILL JUDGE (1971). *See* 25 C.F.R. §§ 11.1, 11.3 (1975), which provides for Bureau fiscal and personnel authority over the Courts of Indian Offenses, and 25 C.F.R. § 11.301 (1975) regarding police authority.

130. *Hearings on Readjustment of Indian Affairs, supra* note 114, at 169.

131. *Id.* at 177-78.

132. *Id.* at 68, 170, 177-78, 198, 199-200, 208. *See also id.* at 98, 152 (Senator Thomas remarks).

pave the way for complete termination of tribal existence.[133] They noted that the Act would subsidize and require the consolidation of reservation lands into public (tribal) ownership, minimizing the extent of private Indian ownership. Then, if the tribal charter were ever revoked by Congress, almost all of the tribe's property would instantly become public domain of the state and individual Indians would get nothing. Unfortunately, they were entirely correct.

During the war years and scarcely a decade after passage of the Indian Reorganization Act, there were already suggestions in Congress and the Interior Department that transitional tribal government had outlived its usefulness.[134] Termination did not come suddenly; it was the culmination of another decade of "transition" during which, in what might appear paradoxical, the Bureau intensified its efforts to organize tribal government and courts but froze investment in capital improvements such as roads, hospitals, and business.[135] Tribal government was, in effect, being rapidly transformed into a semblance of state government to minimize the impact of and quite probably the resistance to assumption of jurisdiction by the states. At the same time it would have been wasteful for the United States to sink its tax dollars into physical plant that the states would soon have the legal responsibility to provide!

Although termination became "official" in 1953[136] it was executed over the span of another decade on a tribe-by-tribe basis. In the meantime, the tribal court system was given *increasing* recognition by the federal judiciary.[137] The Supreme Court quite explicitly regarded it as a transitional instrumentality and, in the same spirit as nineteenth-century decisions, emphasized that this purpose and not popular sovereignty gave them their legitimacy.[138] Thus, the Court joined the Bureau in graduating Indians into state law, rather than recognizing their separate nature.

Following passage of the Indian Reorganization Act, the Bureau produced a new procedural and penal code for tribes to replace the 1892 regulations.[139] Pursuant to section 11.1(4) of this model code, a reorganized tribe may substitute its own code of law subject to secretarial approval, which, once again, can

---

133. *Id.* at 53. *See also id.* at 108 (statement of Jesse Rowlodge).

134. See the remarks in U.S. DEP'T OF THE INTERIOR, ANNUAL REPORT for each of the following years: 1946, at 375-76; 1949, at 338, 366; 1950, at 342-43; 1951, at 353; 1952, at 389-91; 1953, at 42; 1954, at 244.

135. U.S. DEP'T OF THE INTERIOR, ANNUAL REPORT 1946, at 376-77; 1951, at 377; Burnette, *supra* note 3, at 567-68.

136. 67 Stat. 588 (1953).

137. *E.g.*, Iron Crow v. Oglala Sioux Tribe, 129 F. Supp. 15 (W.D.S.D. 1955), *aff'd*, 231 F.2d 89 (8th Cir. 1956); Oglala Sioux Tribe v. Barta, 146 F. Supp. 917 (W.D.S.D. 1956); Williams v. Lee, 358 U.S. 217 (1958).

138. *See* Williams v. Lee, 358 U.S. 217. Compare the theory of reservation government here with that of United States v. Clapox, 35 F. 575 (D. Ore. 1888).

139. 25 C.F.R. § 11 (1975).

be exercised to require near conformity. Coupled with the fact that the Bureau provided little in the way of technical legislative assistance or subsidies, but trained and paid for the police and judges, there was little opportunity or incentive for tribes to expand on the model. Few did to any significant degree.[140]

A brief consideration of the model, as presently amended, that the Bureau now proposes to update is in order. Code courts have not generally been recognized as having jurisdiction over non-Indians, either civil or criminal.[141] Only recently have some courts recognized such jurisdiction as an inherent element of tribal sovereignty.[142] Even such criminal jurisdiction as they may exercise over Indians is made expressly concurrent with the state courts when the victim is not Indian.[143] However, in apparent defiance of the Meriam study and the representations made to Congress by Collier, they are authorized to recognize tribal custom, "not prohibited by federal law," as a rule of decision.[144] It must, however, be pleaded and proved as a fact if contested, and in the absence of such proof, state law must be applied. The common law development of the court is thereby stifled. The judge is not authorized to draw upon reason, history, or analogy, but can only rely on state precedents and what amounts to anthropological precedents.

The penal code is, to be sure, outdated and overreaching. It prohibits gambling, adultery, fornication, illicit cohabitation, and prostitution but offers

140.   Burnette, *supra* note 3, at 582-83. In its 1968 testimony before the Senate Committee on the Judiciary, Subcommittee on Constitutional Rights, the Bureau represented that it had fulfilled its responsibilities by training Indian police and judges. *Hearings on Constitutional Rights of the American Indian, supra* note 2, at 50-51. It also represented that most tribes had adopted substitute or modified codes, *id.* at 62, although many of them, such as Crow, with which we are familiar, had in fact merely changed the language of the old code, or made a few specific alterations, *e.g.*, popular election of judges, exclusion of undesirables from the reservation.

141.   25 C.F.R. §§ 11.2, 11.22 (1975). The latter section also provides for consent jurisdiction of non-Indians in civil causes.

142.   Oliphant v. Schlie, Civil No. 74-2154 (9th Cir., Aug. 24, 1976), held that a tribal court acting under an approved law and order code may exercise concurrent jurisdiction over an offense by a non-Indian on tribal property. *Accord*, Belgarde v. Morton, Civil No. 74-68-35 (W.D. Wash., filed Aug. 18, 1975). Thereafter, the Solicitor of the Department of the Interior issued a memorandum indicating that reconsideration was being given an earlier Solicitor's opinion holding that tribes have no jurisdiction over non-Indians. 1 INDIAN L. REP. no. 2, at 51 (1974).

143.   Concurrent jurisdiction is compatible with 18 U.S.C. § 1152 (1970). Senate Bill 1, the Criminal Justice Reform Act of 1975, would delete section 1152 and would tend to weaken the scope of tribal jurisdiction. *See* Statement of Arthur Lazarus, Jr., in *Hearings Before the Subcomm. on Criminal Laws and Procedure of the Senate Comm. on the Judiciary in Opposition to Certain Provisions in S. 1 Relating to Indian Tribes*, 94th Cong., 2d Sess., pt. 12, at 236-39 (1975). Some doubt has been expressed whether 18 U.S.C. § 13 (1970) can be interpreted as authorizing federal prosecution of state law misdemeanors within Indian reservations. Acunia v. United States, 404 F.2d 140 (9th Cir. 1968). Such application would nullify tribal self-government, rendering tribal penal laws that are inconsistent with state laws effectively unenforceable. We read section 203(a)(3) of Senate Bill 1 to resolve this doubt in favor of applying to reservations a *federal* misdemeanor identical to that which is applicable to military and park areas.

144.   25 C.F.R. § 11.23(a) (1975).

no remedy for homicide, rape or other serious felonies. As a result of this and the reluctance of federal prosecutors to conduct investigations on reservations, many tribes prosecute Indians accused of these crimes for several counts of assault and battery in order to provide some response.[145] Astonishingly, the code makes it a crime, punishable by up to three months labor, "to infect another with a venereal disease." There is no requirement of knowledge or of intent.[146]

However the most serious flaw in the old model is on the civil side. Again, in defiance of the understanding with Congress, the regulations do authorize tribes to recognize customary marriage and adoption procedures, determine paternity, punish nonsupport, and distribute non-trust property of deceased Indians.[147] But family law is only a small part of the civil sphere. What of contract, property and tort law, all of the rules that govern trade and business and regulate the economy of the community? We have two outstanding decisions of the Supreme Court that guarantee a reservation Indian defendant the absolute right to be tried civilly in tribal court.[148] But the only guidance the Bureau has ever offered to tribes is section 11.24 of the regulations. It amounts to a slim shadow of the tort law. The court is authorized to "fairly compensate" the victim of "careless" injury, penalize willful wrongdoers, and allow the victims of "accidental" damage "a reasonable part" of the loss. We can see a certain conciliatory ideal in the provision for accidental injury, which is of course at odds with the general tort law, but what is the meaning of the section as a whole except to recognize what reservation courts had been doing without interruption since 1878? It adds nothing, and fails either to remedy the defects in court powers, or to provide guidelines for a more comprehensive system of civil laws. There is no authority for enforcing contracts, recognizing or settling the affairs of business associations, or quieting title to property except as ancillary to a suit for injury or a criminal prosecution for trespass or stealing. How indeed could a non-Indian creditor have much security or an Indian entrepreneur adequate protection for his business?

Understandably few civil cases are tried in the majority of reservation courts that remain close to the regulations. On the Crow Reservation in recent

---

145. In our experience, this has been true in the Crow tribe. *See also* THE PEOPLE WILL JUDGE, *supra* note 129.

146. 25 C.F.R. § 11.63 (1975). It has been sporadically enforced even in recent years at the Crow Reservation according to the record of arraignments, probably exclusively as a means of compelling the involuntary commitment of disease carriers.

147. 25 C.F.R. §§ 11.28-.32, 11.64 (1975). One tribal court has also claimed power to adjudicate the division of trust property between parties to a divorce action. Conroy v. Tibbets (Oglala Sioux Tribal Court of Appeals, Dec. 16, 1974), 2 INDIAN L. REP. no. 2, at 54 (1975).

148. Williams v. Lee, 358 U.S. 217 (1958); Kennerly v. District Court, 400 U.S. 423 (1970). One court has also held that the laws of the Navajo Nation are entitled to full faith and credit in state courts although a forum state need not necessarily subordinate its policies to those of another jurisdiction. Jim v. C.I.T. Financial Services, Corp., 87 N.M. 362, 533 P.2d 751 (1975).

years there have been about three hundred criminal prosecutions for each civil complaint, excluding support and paternity suits.[149] At the same time, the expense of state process, combined perhaps with its lack of credibility, meant that Crows resorted to it on the average one-third less often than non-Indians in the same county, adjusted for population.[150] The IRA has changed little for this court system, although the tribe has adopted modifications on the Bureau model. As in 1929, most prosecutions were for drinking and related conduct (73 per cent), and very few for violent crimes that affected third parties (two per cent).[151] Tribal laws and ordinances are not generally known, cover little in the way of commercial matters, and appear in court in fewer than two per cent of all cases. Safety is not the problem here, nor elsewhere in our experience. Yet the present legal institution is designed, as its name implies, for "law and order"—the police idea.

Some limitations of a constitutional nature on the activities of reservation courts were first proposed as a part of Title IV of the Indian Reorganization Act, which failed to pass Congress.[152] In the course of hearings held around the country by Senator Ervin's Senate Subcommittee beginning in 1961, a pattern of complaints emerged that focused on abuses of the right to counsel, self-incrimination, jury trial, and appeal.[153] Often it was apparent that such abuses as did exist had their roots in the financial inability of tribes to foot the cost of public defenders, jurors, investigators and experts, and additional judges. Although the hearings tended to indicate that much more serious abuses were common in cases of Indians before the state courts,[154] the Committee made no recommendations in that regard, nor did it consider or provide for financial assistance to tribes for upgrading of their judiciaries. Ironically, this sets up a situation in which the standards set for tribal courts could close them down and force all Indian litigation into the state courts where the danger is even greater.

---

149. Our sample of 7600 recorded complaints, 1968-73. *Cf.* Shepardson, *Problems of the Navajo Tribal Courts in Transition*, 24 HUMAN ORGANIZATION 250 (1965) (95 per cent criminal).

150. Divorce was an exception; Crows resorted to the state courts 60 per cent more than non-Crows, adjusted for population. This may be explained by the fact that social service agencies require proof of legal divorce, whereas other civil matters may remain entirely between the immediate parties. The Crow tribe has voluntarily relinquished its power to grant divorces.

151. In 1929 some 58 per cent of Crow prosecutions were for drinking and related conduct, and 13 per cent for violent crimes. *Hearings on Law and Order on Indian Reservations of the Northwest, supra* note 11, at 14258-259. The rate of violent crimes (per ten thousand) is today comparable to the national average, whereas the rate of victimless crimes such as drunkenness, disorderly conduct, and possession of liquor is far greater. U.S. BUREAU OF THE CENSUS, 1974 STATISTICAL ABSTRACT OF THE UNITED STATES 153 (1974). The fact that Crow, like many reservations, is "dry" contributes significantly to the rates. Although official records do not indicate the degree of intoxication of those prosecuted, our observation of police operations indicated that only a small percentage would have been liable to prosecution under state public drunkenness laws.

152. *See Hearings on Readjustment of Indian Affairs, supra* note 114, §§ 9, 10.

153. Burnette, *supra* note 3, at 579, 581.

154. *Id.* at 584-86.

In 1965 Senator Ervin challenged the court regulations as "outmoded, impractical, and . . . failing to provide for an adequate administration of justice on Indian reservations."[155] His proposed legislative package included constitutional limitations, appeal to the Bureau, a model code, and new procedures for assumption of jurisdiction by the states.

The Bureau responded negatively to the model code idea, but its objection was one of technique and not goals. Representing the Bureau, Solicitor Barry advised that[156]

> tribes are widely diverse and that a code appropriate for one tribe might be wholly inappropriate for another. Further, since the long-term objective of the administration of Indian Affairs is to secure the smooth assimilation of the Indian people into our society, I think that Indian codes should conform as much as possible to the substantive and procedural laws of the States in which the Indians live. Since the codes in various States differ, a uniform code for Indian tribes would frustrate this objective.

Note that in the end Barry's objection to uniformity was that the codes should reflect the diversity of the states and not the diversity of tribes. This is a solidly transitional argument, and is reinforced by a conception of the reservation court system that has advanced little beyond the Meriam study. For example, one additional objection to the model was that "a step in the process of . . . preparation" for assimilation is "skill and experience in the formulation of legislation," therefore each tribe should draft its own code as an educational experience. "Of course," he conceded, there is the "risk that they will make mistakes," but education is everywhere understood to consist in trial and error![157]

The Bureau's objections were satisfied by the assurance of the Subcommittee that the model would not be mandatory and would serve only "as a guide."[158] Beyond that they were in complete agreement. John Baker, Minority Counsel for the Subcommittee, agreed that the function of reservation law was educational, and added his belief that the model code "would be a particularly appropriate vehicle for this education. . . . [Y]ou would serve to steer the tribal council toward existing law."[159] For his part, Barry offered the Subcommittee some advice on the technique of assimilation the Bureau would follow. Rather than take "too long a step" all at once, reservtion jurisdiction should be transferred by Congress to the states "piecemeal." "I think you would find there would be more transferred that way," he concluded.[160] It is

---

155. *Hearings on Constitutional Rights of the American Indian, supra* note 2, at 3.
156. *Id.* at 20.
157. *Id. See also id.* at 26, Barry's comment that tribes should be encouraged to "*practice* making their own rules" (emphasis added).
158. *Id.* at 28, 52-53. On behalf of the Bureau, Mr. Barry acknowledged that even without this modification the proposal was not a "disaster" but merely "unnecessary."
159. *Id.* at 51. Senator Fong remarked, *id.* at 62, that he "assumed" that this would be done.
160. *Id.* at 93-94. *See also* the remarks of Marvin Sonosky, *id.* at 131, 136.

hard to interpret this statement except to mean that the more gradual and insidious the process, the less Indians were liable to resist in Congress and the courts.

The model code issue did not meet much criticism from tribes. Arthur Lazarus, representing the American Association for Indian Affairs, endorsed the model insofar as it would be merely "an example to be set," subject to tribal modification and consent, and principally substantive. The spokesman for the United Sioux Tribes, Cato Valandra, even told the senators that his organization was going to draft its own model "comparable to the State code."[161] Apparently the concensus was that the model was to substitute for the assistance tribes had never obtained from the Bureau in order to draft their own codes.

The draft now available betrays that anticipation. In the area of pre-arraignment procedure, it serves mostly to add detail to the 1934 regulations —as for example to enumerate the contents of a complaint or warrant. Four substantive changes have been made. A procedure is established by which a court officer would screen criminal complaints "for sufficiency."[162] This is an extremely dangerous proposition, giving an administrative officer authority, in effect, to refuse to prosecute any complaint made by the victim of a crime, with no appeal being possible from his decision. Weighing this together with the fact that the model does not, as yet, provide any alternative to the old *civil* procedures, this could serve to chill further the ability of individual Indians to obtain relief from injury.

Next, a requirement that Miranda warnings be given has been inserted.[163] This is unnecessary because of the application of Miranda to tribes through the due process provisions of the Indian Bill of Rights. The provision of an alternative to arrest by warrant, the summons,[164] is a commendable step towards informality of the process, and it is in keeping with the recommendation of this procedure by the American Law Institute. Finally, warrantless searches have been authorized, a questionable matter because it actually diminishes the right of privacy of reservation Indians.[165] Of course this may have some law enforcement value, but is it really necessary? As the commentary to the A.L.I. Model Code points out, the development of warrantless search law is intimately connected with drug abuse enforcement because it was found necessary to prevent the destruction of evidence. We are not aware

---

161. *Hearings on Constitutional Rights of the American Indian, supra* note 2, at 151.
162. Proposed Model Code for Administration of Justice By Courts of Indian Offenses § 101(c), 40 Fed. Reg. 16691 (1975) [hereinafter cited as Proposed Model Code]; *cf.* commentary to sections 121 and 122.
163. Proposed Model Code § 104, 40 Fed. Reg. 16692 (1975).
164. *Id.* § 105.
165. 25 C.F.R. § 11.16 (1975) *requires* a warrant.

of that being a problem on reservations. The cost in civil rights could easily exceed any benefits.[166]

The arraignment provisions reduce the time limit on commitment without charges from thirty-six hours to the "next regularly scheduled session of the court."[167] This is also potentially an abridgement rather than expansion of rights because there is nothing to require that the court meet at least every thirty-six hours. Automatic bail was previously provided by section 11.8; the Model Code enumerates additional kinds of conditions that may be imposed on persons released on bail.[168]

Jury trial may have been limited by a redefinition of those cases in which it may be demanded of right. Old section 11.7c(a) grants jury trial in any case in which there is a "substantial question of fact," which may be broader than the minimal requirement of federal law repeated in the Model Code, *i.e.*, cases in which the penalty may be imprisonment.[169] Beyond this, the Model is a more detailed and explanatory expansion of the 1934 regulations, with purely advisory language regarding evidence, stare decisis, and trial format.

Most seriously, there is no position taken on the absolutely critical issue of jurisdiction: whether it shall continue to be fragmentary and limited to Indians or expanded to give the courts that competence and power they need to protect Indian *property*, as opposed to their *liberty*. Even to the extent that the Model Code fulfills the laudable objective of protecting Indians from arbitrary and corrupt power, it is not necessarily a break with tradition. It sets Indians against their government and leaves their property, as well as their lives and liberties in many cases, in the hands of foreign courts and legislatures effectively beyond their power to affect. The preconditions for assimilation pressure have only been renewed.

III

THE VIRTUES OF DIVERSITY

The whole course of federal reservation law and order policy has supposed that diversity of law is purely transitional, a necessary delay in the process of assimilation. There has been no hint that diversity may serve any lasting or continuing function in modern society. Yet this flies in the face of the whole structure and history of the United States. The federal system is founded on the principle that diversity can be harmonized with unity, thereby enabling us to enjoy the greatest possible liberty with the greatest possible strength. To successfully deny this constitutional position on diversity in In-

---

166. *Cf.* AMERICAN LAW IINSTITUTE, A MODEL CODE OF PRE-ARRAIGNMENT PROCEDURE §§ 120.1, 210.1 (1975).

167. Proposed Model Code § 111(b), 40 Fed. Reg. 16694 (1975).

168. Proposed Model Code §§ 115, 116, 40 Fed. Reg. 16695 (1975). Section 115 permits a police officer to release an accused in accordance with a bail schedule supplied him.

169. Proposed Model Code § 124(a), 40 Fed. Reg. 16699 (1975).

dian affairs does more than reaffirm that Indians are a people apart, deprived of the ordinary incidents of citizenship. It challenges the security of the states themselves. Little insight into recent affairs is necessary to appreciate the slow collapse of state sovereignty. The federal government has strived for centralization throughout our political system. Regarding tribes, the excuse has been that they are antiquated, inefficient, and even unjust. Of states, much the same has been said. The federal government has been more persuasive in its position on tribes, but do they merely represent the test case of the limits of federal absolutism?

Diversity of law has been with us since the beginning, and we fought at least one war to defend it. By 1750 the American colonies had evolved a dozen different variations on the English common law, variations suited to their individual economies and lifestyles. Early nineteenth-century American jurists would later advance this fact as proof that law was not divine and absolute, but human and flexible.[170] It spurred us to reshape the political economy we inherited from England because it demonstrated that law grew out of policy rather than logic. But in the years that led to the Revolution, our patchwork law was a great embarrassment to English statesmen. They complained that it threw sand in the gears of the great, uniform, transoceanic commercial empire that English power had built.[171] Left to their own devices, the colonies threatened to challenge the theory of the intellectual supremacy of British institutions. More to the point, they increasingly sought to fashion laws that would serve their own several interests rather than the King's. In 1776, diversity of law sounded in treason.

English policy was not so lacking in subtlety that it chose to address the matter directly. Rather, the argument was widely circulated that diversity of law multiplied the costs of commerce. With one law, commerce would flourish to the benefit of all subjects. Property would be protected from confusing problems of ownership and the people would be saved the danger of capricious legislatures making any laws they wished, by the existence of a single, inflexible common law. To join proof with persuasion, Parliament extended uniform laws of trade and navigation to the colonies, appointed their governors and judges to ensure uniformity, and claimed a power to disapprove the acts of their assemblies. Colonies were in some cases aggregated into larger units, and continental agencies were established to administer them.

The Revolution reaffirmed both the independence of the colonies from English supervision and their independence of one another. It vindicated diversity over centralization. The failures of the Confederation did not shake

---

170. Horwitz, *The Emergence of an Instrumental Conception of American Law 1780-1820*, 5 PERSPECTIVES AM. HIST. 287 (1971).

171. *E.g.*, T. POWNALL, THE ADMINISTRATION OF THE BRITISH COLONIES 105 & ch. 1 (5th ed. 1774).

this, so much as it taught us to optimize diversity with security, commerce, and mutual trust.

Of course, England was correct. Diversity is costly. Multiple layers of public administration, jurisdictional boundaries, conflicts of laws, protective and competitive local legislation, all add up to what may be thought of as the price of diversity. Individual liberty has its price. Personal, religious, and political habits may infringe upon the rights and interests of others, but in our constitutional framework this is an acceptable burden within certain limits. Diversity is the price of group liberty.

As long as the general public holds these principles in high regard, and as long as we respect the institution of the states and bear the costs of their differentness, what is the logic of denying the same to Indian citizens? Have we implicitly determined now that fifty is the limit of diversity and freedom in our system of government? The criterion is certainly not fiscal self-sufficiency. If that were the case, many of the nation's cities and several of the states would have, at some time or another, lost their claim to diversity and self-regulation. The distinction cannot be one of history. Tribes are about as truly self-governing today as the American colonies were in 1775; both the original states and tribes have endured a period of political alienation in the chain of their histories. Is the distinction between tribes and the recognized levels of the federal system not one of policy at all, but merely a function of power?

Diversity may actually have three economic virtues: experimental efficiency, administrative efficiency, and distributive equity. The first two tend to make up for the costs of diversity in savings on the operations of government. The last is what we associate with group liberty.

Mr. Justice Brandeis eloquently summed up the importance of experimental efficiency in 1931. Commenting on the radical economic and political controversies arising out of the Depression experience he concluded[172]

> The discoveries in physical science, the triumphs in invention, attest the value of the process of trial and error. In large measure, these advances have been due to experimentation. In those fields experimentation has, for two centuries, been not only free but encouraged. Some people assert that our present plight is due, in part, to the limitations set by courts upon experimentation in the fields of social and economic science; and to the discouragement to which proposals for betterment there have been subjected otherwise. There must be power in the States and the Nation to remould, through experimentation, our economic practices and institutions to meet changing social and economic needs. . . .
>
> To stay experimentation in things social and economic is a grave responsibility. Denial of the right to experiment may be fraught with serious consequences to the Nation. It is one of the happy incidents of the federal system that a single courageous State may, if its citizens choose, serve as a laboratory and try novel social and economic experiments without risk to the rest of the

---

172. New State Ice Co. v. Kiebmann, 285 U.S. 262, 310-11 (1931).

country. . . . If we would guide by the light of reason, we must let our mind
be bold.

Diversity accelerates the institutional progress of the nation by permitting any
number of relatively small, inexpensive innovative reforms to proceed simultaneously. It forces each political subdivision to compare its behavioral assumptions with the experience of others. In general, the system becomes
more flexible and capable of more rapid accomodation to what is becoming a
more and more rapidly changing environment.

"We suggest that tribes are not vestiges of the past, but laboratories for the
future,"[173] in the same capacity as the other political subdivisions of the nation. The depressing historical realization is that to some degree they have
always been laboratories of the future, but not by their own wishes or under
their own control. Federal autocracy and "progressive" theories of social management and control have been experimented with on Indians throughout the
nation's history. Some were disasters, such as the panacea of public education.
Many specific programs now proposed for general consumption have had a
long history in Indian country, including federal administrative regulation of
the economy and socialized medicine. We even hear talk of federal power
being used to curb state "parochialism," which is not far different from the
doctrine of Indian backwardness. Experimentation ought not to be at the expense of liberty, nor should one community entirely bear the risks and costs
of a social experiment for the benefit of another.

Diversity may also promote administrative efficiency. If in fact there are
variations in local conditions, uniform administration of general policies cannot be expected to be uniformly effective. A uniform set of guidelines for
funding tribal police programs, for example, requires that tribes adopt
guideline police systems in order to participate. The result is not to optimize
the law enforcement value of each dollar of subsidy, but to maximize conformity. Conformity is not in itself an element of social welfare. On the contrary
it may have a demoralizing effect and frustrate innovation. The explanation
for conformity in Indian affairs however may be that it is cheaper to *administer* a uniform system, and, the fewer alternatives groups have to provide for
their own needs, the more readily they will conform to some condition imposed by government rather than do without subsidy. In social management
terms, it is efficient to demand conformity of the poor but not the comparatively wealthy, from the perspective of a bureaucracy seeking to minimize its
costs.

By far the most important function of diversity is distributive equity. The
civil law best serves the economy in an allocational sense by minimizing
"transaction costs," the costs associated with the process of buying and selling.

---

173. Vine DeLoria Jr., in *Hearings on Constitutional Rights of the American Indian, supra* note 2,
at 195.

In a general sense, this entails certainty and predictability of property and contract rules, simple and inexpensive enforcement procedures, and the division of property rights into appropriate units. It may be argued with some justice that these objectives can be accomplished regardless of local conditions, because they depend upon very general attributes of economic behavior and markets. From the point of view of allocation, there is probably not much difference between the best subdivision of water rights into readily transferable bundles in Massachusetts and Nevada, although the value of those units may be considerably different on account of scarcity. We observe, for example, the near unanimous adoption of the Uniform Commercial Code, which had transactional certainty and simplicity as its goal. The fact that Louisiana has not adopted the Uniform Commercial Code, choosing instead to retain its own code, has not, however, undermined commercial transactions across its borders.

But the civil law has never been and can never be purely allocational. The most obvious examples are found in the taxing and zoning powers, which may be used to level income distribution in a community, or to skew it even further. Redistribution need not, however, be so explicit. Contract rules may tend to favor buyers or sellers, merchants or consumers. Property law, in the process of determining original title to things, benefits that class of persons deemed to be the proper owners. The history of American air and water law is replete with reversals in property rules redistributing the benefit of these resources.[174] Tort rules distribute burdens of care, investigation, and insurance. In many cases these rules have no efficiency effect. Any clear rule would do equally well.[175] The heart of the matter is that in choosing one rule over another the jurisdiction makes critical, subjective choices regarding the distribution of the enjoyment of its resources, and the nature of its quality of life.

It is because of this process that jurisdiction must always remain a prerequisite of freedom. A policy that is aimed solely at social control through uniform criminal procedures is inadequate: the power to establish and preserve distinctive concepts of material and social welfare within the federal system is equally important. The failure of American Indian policy, as contained in the Model Code, is the failure to take the principles of toleration and responsible social experimentation seriously.

---

174. *See, e.g.*, the discussion of water policy in J. HIRSHLEIFER, J. DEHAVEN, & J. MILLIMAN, WATER SUPPLY: ECONOMICS, TECHNOLOGY, AND POLICY (1960).

175. Consider, *e.g.*, Professor Calabresi's perambulations through the economics of the tort law. G. CALABRESI, THE COST OF ACCIDENTS: A LEGAL AND ECONOMIC ANALYSIS (1970); Calabresi & Melamed, *Property Rules, Liability Rules, and Inalienability: One View of the Cathedral*, 85 HARV. L. REV. 1089 (1972).

THE STRUCTURE OF THE BUREAU OF INDIAN AFFAIRS

STEVE NICKESON*

The Bureau of Indian Affairs has always had a militant disinclination toward change. It is like Mother Nature: it can be probed, occupied, undermined, or incinerated, but its essence always seems to remain immutable, its form determined more by the composite debris of passing careers than by directed action. Any efforts to encourage basic change become the feckless hobbies of frustrated men.

Like most bureaucracies, the BIA frequently gives a superficial appearance of change while moving to preserve its existing structure. An excellent illustration of this process was provided early in this decade, when the BIA agreed that the federally recognized tribes should have 20 per cent of the influence over the Bureau's budget formulating process. Tribal officials were given an approximation of how much money would be available on their reservations, and they drafted budgets that reflected local priorities from among the Bureau's five program areas: Education, Indian Services, Reservation Resource Development, Trust Responsibilities and Services, and Administration. The tribes' imput was first blended with the federal government's 80 per cent control to create the FY 1974 budget, which was not questioned. But the next year the tribal representatives compared their own priorities with the amounts the BIA had budgeted for each program area and it was clear that the two did not mesh.

The evidence was on two graphs. The first graph showed program sizes and projected growth rates of the Bureau's approved FY 1975 budget. The second one did the same for a set of figures that a computer analysis indicated would have been the 1975 budget had the Bureau honestly given the tribes 20 per cent control.

On the first graph Education was the largest, fastest growing Bureau expenditure. Indian Services was second in size and rate of growth. Reservation Resource Development was small and growing slowly. Trust Responsibilities and Services was one-tenth the size of Education and was not growing at all. Management (fixed administrative costs) was of moderate size and growth.

But on the second graph, the one that reflected 20 per cent tribal input, Education was tapering off into a slow-growing, low priority program. Indian

---

* Staff member, National Indian Youth Council, Albuquerque, New Mexico; former Senior Editor of the *Race Relations Reporter*.

Services once again followed Education's rate, but was slightly larger. Reservation Resource Development was taking a drastic jump upward to overshadow the first two areas. Trust Responsibilities and Services was climbing vertically from the bottom to become the largest Bureau expenditure. And Management was continuing its moderate way.

In short, the Bureau had thrown the tribal input away because it pointed in the direction of unrestricted trust protection and economic self-sufficiency instead of supporting the Bureau's policies of off-reservation education and the maintenance of reservations as welfare states.

When the findings were displayed and explained during a national conference,[1] the reaction was a subdued acknowledgement that business was usual at the Bureau. Chalk up another lie, another reason for loving to hate, additional proof for whatever theory one has for making reason out of what appears as federal madness. But none of these theories—the BIA as a racist conspiracy, or a colonial office, or a black hole in space—explains the budget sharing lie as well as the simple notion that the tribes had attacked the Bureau's entire organizational and policy structure. For the Bureau to have turned over to the tribes control of a significant proportion of the budget —particularly in the area of education[2]—would have been to revolutionize the entrenched bureaucracy that has grown up in support of a policy aimed at bringing Native Americans in line culturally and economically with the majority population.

The budget sharing proposal is only one of a host of programs that has sought directly or indirectly to restructure the relations between the BIA and the Indians. As the central administrative agency for federal Indian policy, the BIA has an immense impact on the daily lives of reservation Indians. To understand the possible impact of new proposals one must consider two centuries of policy structure and the power of all those who have a vested interest—professionally, personally, or ideologically—in maintaining the present system. To confront change realistically, one must consider the true structure of the Bureau; one must consider policy and the power that it generates.

The Bureau of Indian Affairs has several structures. One is visible, the rest are nonetheless real. The visible one is represented in the Bureau's mercurial organization manual and flow chart. These documents are dependable for mapping the advance of paperwork and naming offices, but beyond that they can be misleading because they show little more than a thin, single dimension of an organization that does not always work according to its schematic design. It could only do so if the Bureau were a mass of managerial theory bound by inflexible rules instead of a mass of human beings bound by

---

1. National Conference on Tribal Policy, Washington, D.C., June 5-6, 1974.
2. The education budget for FY 1976 is $230 million, while the budget for trust responsibilities is $21 million.

regulations, politics, loyalties, fears, ideals, and ambitions.

At present the flow chart shows power percolating down from the Commissioner and Deputy Commissioner through the Central Office staff and the Area Offices to the Agency Offices. The basic Central/Area/Agency structure is a generation old, and was arrived at, like many things in the Bureau, by legislation that justified and organized past practice.

Just as the aged sometimes resemble themselves in childhood, so too the Bureau's three-tiered structure resembles its early organization. At its birth in 1824 the Bureau consisted of a Commissioner linked directly to the Indian Agents in the field. For ease of administration, regional superintendents were later placed between the two. As the Bureau expanded during the Allotment period, the Indian Agent became an Agency Superintendent and the old regional superintendent network formed the basis of a new structure for administrative officers. As Indian programs proliferated at the turn of the century, separate regional systems developed for each of them. By the time Laurence Schmickebier completed his inspection of the Bureau in 1927, separate regional structures existed for health, irrigation, administration, and education, and the agency superintendents were reporting directly to the Central Office.[3] This visible structure had grown helter-skelter and did not square with the fundamental bureaucratic need for efficiency and uniformity of action. It took twenty years from the publication of Schmickebier's study to harmonize the discord into the Central/Area/Agency arrangement, a structure John Collier had proposed in the 1930s as a way of aiding the transfer of power from Washington, D.C. to the reservation. The transfer stopped, however, the instant the Area Offices realized they were not simply intermediaries, but the heads of miniature Central Offices capable of controlling communication between Central and Agency, and back again. Naturally political alliances formed along the lines of communication, and in no time the Area Offices became the frontier checkpoints for those going in or out of Indian Country.

One definition of a bureaucracy says it is "always a government of experts, of an 'experienced minority.' "[4] The Bureau makes that observation a cliché, and the Bureau's most experienced minority are the Area Office Directors. They are the only personnel who have as much daily contact with the reservations as they do with the Central Offices; they know the politics, the strengths and weaknesses, and the prices of each one. They also have the cohesion, the pay grade, the line authority, the friends in Congress, and organized pressure groups to make the system conform to their expectations. They have several distinct advantages over anyone in the Central Office, not to mention their subordinates in the Agencies.

---

3. L. Schmickebier, Structure of the BIA (1927); see especially the appendix on locations of Bureau installations.
4. H. Arendt, Origins of Totalitarianism 214 (1951).

In theory most of the Bureau's power is in the Central Office because it is delegated there broadly by Congress and specifically by the Secretary of Interior; from Central it is to be delegated on down the chart. But delegated power is controlled by those who delegate it: it is visible and the actions it precipitates are constantly monitored by the Administration, Congress, the press, and the major Indian organizations. But the Area Offices are not always subject to that kind of scrutiny and the powers delegated to them can be exercised with greater impunity. The power to play favorites, to meddle in tribal politics, to obscure issues or decide matters not covered in the manual are largely invisible powers. And the less they are seen the more arbitrary and absolute they can become. They are powers the Area Officials had successfully fought to maintain for many years, and they were secure with that power when Robert Bennett left office as Commissioner of Indian Affairs in 1969. But their past struggles were minor compared to the one that began after Bennett's departure. It is a story that provides more information on the Bureau and its structure than any organizational manual, flow chart, or anatomical exploration.[5]

The first warning of battle came in the fall of 1969 when Louis Bruce, on assuming the duties of Commissioner, announced that his administration would be opposed to the policy of terminating the special status of Indian tribes. It is ironic that such a pronouncement would bode any disastrous consequences because termination had long since been discredited and few if any in the Bureau paid it tribute. In fact termination was not the point at all. Rather, by noting his opposition to termination, Bruce was forecasting changes in policy. And in the context of the times a policy change could only mean a loss in the Bureau's regulatory abilities and a gain in the tribes' independence. In the coming months, as Bruce's intentions became clearer, the Commissioner found himself opposed by two distinct but allied factions within the Bureau, the Old Liners and the Hard Hats.

All bureaucracies need Old Liners just as all armies need career NCO's. Old Liners are the doctrinaire lifers who can recognize more faults in a bureaucratic agency than anyone on the outside, but are loyal to it nonetheless. For better or worse, they make agencies like the BIA work by applying with annoying objectivity the dictates of the Code of Federal Regulations and the Bureau's manuals of policy guidelines. They know that, in the absence of proper contacts and political dexterity, imagination can be a liability in a civil service career. Instead they prefer to take the creativity and imagination of others and make them work, provided there are complete instructions.

---

5. The progress of this three-year war within the Bureau was closely covered in the dispatches of Richard La Course and Karen Ducheneaux of the American Indian Press Association, and two writers for the *Race Relations Reporter*, Frye Gaillard and the author. Most of the following material is derived from these sources.

Old Liners shun idealism, except in the most general sense, because ideals tend to become tinged with politics and interfere with that repetition of daily tasks which passes for efficiency. If neither law nor bureaucratic precedent can be applied action stops because an Old Liner would rather not act than act in error. However, if policy conflicts with either their generalized ideals or their expectations Old Liners have the power to subvert that policy or to undermine the actions of their superiors. And like all loyalists, Old Liners can become confused or vengeful when those they serve do not share or respect their fidelity.

If there is a generalized ideal in the Bureau which Old Liners have promoted to the status of doctrine, it is the ideal of merging Indians into non-Indian society with a minimum of confusion and conflict. It is up to others to facilitate or impede the appropriation of Indian wealth into the non-Indian economy, and it is the Old Liners' perceived duty not to oppose these powers, but to find ways to make them compatible with their own conception of gradual merger. In recent years, with the Indians' emphasis on self-determination, control of resources, and tribal sovereignty, Old Liners have found it increasingly difficult to practice their ideal or maintain a sense of professional integrity based on this two-centuries-old doctrine. It is, therefore, little wonder that Old Liners became irritable in the face of Bruce's emphasis on non-assimilation, self-determination, and tribal sovereignty.

But Bureau personnel is not limited to Old Liners. The Bureau has produced or acquired employees who have combined imagination and political skill with an ability to conform or make nonconformity secretive or palatable. To make this combination work, to parlay it into power, requires time and the ability to survive. Those who survive in the Bureau are those who have inherited the doctrinal ideal of a bureaucrat's life. In other words, conservatives survive safe in the knowledge that they *are* the experts who are more capable of governing the people they serve than the people themselves. When this form of institutional arrogance is added to political acumen a Hard Hat is created.[6]

---

6. Such multi-faceted combinations are rare, but they exist and those who embody them are truly powerful. History had no better prototype of the Hard Hat than Lord Cromer, British Consul General in Egypt from 1883 to 1907. In his final summation, an essay entitled "The Government of Subject Races," published one year before his death, he stated:

Cromer started by recognizing that "personal influence" without a legal or written political treaty could be enough for "sufficiently effective supervision over public affairs" in foreign countries. This kind of informal influence was preferable to a well-defined policy because it could be altered at a moment's notice and did not necessarily involve the home government in case of difficulties. It required a highly trained, highly reliable staff whose loyalty and patriotism were not connected with personal ambition or vanity and who would even be required to renounce the human aspiration of having their name connected with their achievements. Their greatest passion would have to be for secrecy . . . for a role behind the scenes; their greatest contempt would be directed at publicity and people who love it.

Like the Old Liners, Hard Hats can be highly skilled technicians servicing the policy structure of the Bureau. But Hard Hats will always retain an undercurrent of personal amibiton, while Old Liners will always be subordinates no matter how high in the Bureau they advance. It is that personal ambition and the skills of promoting it that set the Hard Hats apart and enable them to create another dimension to the Bureau's structure, one grounded in personal power.

A Hard Hat can begin a career at the Agency level, but cannot thrive there since the potential for power is limited and the scrutiny of a tribe can be scathing. By the same token a Hard Hat cannot be master of the Bureau, because the top level of Central is too exposed to the examination of the Administration, Congress, the press, and the major Indian organizations. Although they can survive and thrive in those Central Office positions ranked just below Deputy Commissioner, they fare best in the top levels of various field operations. That is where the Hard Hats have their jealously-guarded power, and from where a handful of them can be as successful as a Bureau full of Old Liners in frustrating any policy or colleague that challenges them. Louis Bruce and his administration did exactly that.

Eight months after Bruce became Commissioner, President Nixon delivered his "self-determination without termination" policy to Congress,[7] and Bruce felt the responsibility to implement it. He assumed he had the support of the Administration, especially Secretary of Interior Walter Hickel, who began 1970 with an "executive realignment" in the Bureau's Central Office. This reshuffling upgraded Bruce's authority by abolishing the posts of Deputy Commissioner and six Assistant Commissioners and replacing them with the lower ranking positions of two Associate Commissioners and five Staff Directors. Nine months later, Hickel announced the appointment of fifteen Indians to key Bureau positions. This was the New Team who, under Bruce's guidance, was to start changing policy. However, it soon became clear that even Bruce's fervor for reform was lagging behind that of several New Teamers (a group that can be called the Insurgents), who began taking over the direction and speed of Bureau renovation. None of the New Team, particularly the Insurgents, had been made by the Bureau. Their loyalties were toward Indian self-determination, and they had been educated in the minor-

---

Cromer himself possessed all these qualities to a very high degree; his wrath was never more strongly aroused than when he was "brought out of [his] hiding place," when "the reality which before was only known to a few behind the scenes [became] patent to all the world." His pride was indeed to "remain more or less hidden [and] to pull the strings." In exchange, and in order to make his work possible at all, the bureaucrat has to feel safe from control—the praise as well as the blame, that is—of all public institutions, either Parliament . . . or the press.
H. ARENDT, *supra* note 4, at 213.
7. Nixon's Environmental Reorganization Plan, *Text of Indian Message*, 28 CONG. Q. 1820 (1970).

ity movements of the 1960s and the War on Poverty. None was old enough to have worked under the termination administrations of Commissioners Glenn Emmons or Phileo Nash, but they knew that no new policy had replaced that of termination. They also knew they were moving into a slightly derelict, caretaker Bureau that was operating from issue to issue, doing its best to prevent the worst. Reportedly, the Bureau was performing its routine task well when they arrived; it was an Old Liner's Bureau, controlled by the Area Directors, and as such it had no consolidated, structural ambition or reformist zeal. But 1969 was a time for zealots and the Bureau was an anachronism.

As the struggle for a guiding policy sharpened, all issues became political issues. Insurgents and Old Liners differed as to the means by which new policies should be implemented, with the former advocating more direct control of programs by the tribes. The Insurgents also differed from the Hard Hats, whose imagination and political acumen they shared, but whose control of the Area Offices was an obstacle to the Insurgents' own political goals. As every issue became a vehicle for political struggle each side accused the other of being secretive, power hungry, lawless, and arbitrary. In time, it became clear that Secretary Hickel was willing to back Commissioner Bruce and the Insurgents against the Hard Hats. On November 24, 1970, Bruce and Hickel announced the "Rotation Policy."[8] This policy transformed the Area Offices into "Support Service Centers," a name almost as banal as the status envisioned for them. This part of the program was designed as a policy offensive in the spirit of self-determination. But rotation affected the power structure as well with its plan to transfer Area Directors from post to post in order to break their holds on their personal constituencies. It was a program designed by the Insurgents to win the hearts and minds of the Old Liners and reservation leaders who were known to resent the independent power of the Hard Hats. The opposition itself was off guard and in retreat. But there was no time for the Insurgents to capitalize on the gain, for Hickel did not remain as Secretary of Interior for long.

In the first six weeks of Rogers Morton's administration, the new Secretary created a Management Assistance Survey Team to examine the workings of the Bureau. He also named to his personal staff Miss Wilma Victor, a conservative, politically influential charter member of the Haskell Mafia—a close-knit contingent of Indian Old Liners who had attended Haskell, a school run by the BIA, and who trace their standing in the Bureau back to the first Indian preference policies of John Collier. Her elevation from head of the education department of the Phoenix Area Office to Special Assistant to the

---

8. U.S. DEP'T OF INTERIOR, PROPOSED CHANGES IN STRUCTURE AND POLICY OF THE BUREAU OF INDIAN AFFAIRS (1971) explained the policy and had attached a letter of policy clarification from Commissioner Bruce to all tribes, Dec. 13, 1971.

Secretary for Indian Affairs was an entirely gratuitous blow for the Hard Hats.

Then in May 1971 the Management Assistance Survey Team began supplying ammunition for the Old Liners when it reported that a significant gap had developed between Central and all field offices, and that the existing administrative and organizational "turmoil" had been caused by attempting to implement self-determination by decree. It added weight to the Old Liners' charges that the Insurgents were trying to make self-determination an "event" rather than an evolutionary process and were bending laws and issuing procedural orders that conflicted with both precedent and regulation. The Insurgents responded that if they were to comply with the Nixon anti-termination policy when the regulations were designed to justify termination, they had to do things that had never been done before. During those first months of the Bruce administration, as journalist Frye Gaillard has written, the Insurgents did indeed institute some novel procedures:[9]

> [F]or a while, things happened around the BIA that had never occurred before. As acting director of economic services, Leon Cook with the help of such lieutenants as William Veeder and Phillip Corke . . . began an enthusiastic defense of Indian land and water rights. Browning Pipestem unearthed the legal justification for a broad range of policies, including an obscure 1946 solicitor's opinion that upheld preferential hiring and promotion of Indians within the Bureau. Ernest Stevens, as director of community services, began revamping the BIA's urban relocation program, and Alexander McNabb plunged into the task of negotiating self-determination contracts with various tribes and Indian groups.

But by the summer of 1971, the anti-Insurgent opposition, smarting under the effect of these innovations, regrouped for a counter-attack. They were assisted by a second conservative on the Secretary's staff, William Rogers, whose promotion on June 25 from Deputy Under-secretary for Public Land Management to Deputy Assistant Secretary for Indian Affairs was intended to heal the factionalism in the BIA staff. The first objective of the counter-attack was the alteration of contracting procedures.

For some time the Insurgents had been operating as if the Area Offices had in fact become Support Service Centers. They had been by-passing them and establishing direct links between Central and the reservations, links that meant power was being siphoned out of the Area Offices toward the reservation, and, by implication, back toward Central as well. According to Alexander McNabb, director of operating services, from April 1970 to May of the following year, they had tried to pump from $10 to $15 million directly into reservation economies. Moreover, he had rewritten Bureau contracting procedures to conform with Insurgent ideals. But on June 28 McNabb was divested of contracting authority in the wake of a Government Accounting Of-

---

9. Gaillard, *Indians Demand Bureau Reform*, 2 RACE RELATIONS REP. no. 18, at 6, 9 (1971).

fice audit of the contracting activities which concluded that the Bureau did
not have any legislative mandate to justify either the new procedures or a
number of the contracts. In the four months following McNabb's removal, not
one new contract was negotiated out of the 119 that were pending in June,
but 93 old contracts were renegotiated.[10]

One month later the counterattack produced its most substantial victory.
On July 26 Secretary Morton revived the office of Deputy Commissioner and
filled it with John O. Crow, who had held the same post under Phileo Nash
and who had the reputation of being a tough, but progressive Haskell Mafia
Old Liner. Crow was an advocate of self-determination, who respected the
drives and talents of the Insurgents, but who also realized that none of them
had the years of Bureau experience that create an intuitive understanding
and appreciation for the unique amenities and attributes of the federal way of
life: in-house statemanship, personal obscurity and loyalty to bureauacratic
efficiency. It was to be Crow's task to give the Central Office at least the
appearance of a standard bureaucracy and, because the Old Liners were already beginning to subvert and stall, to turn Insurgent expectations and
deeds into programs compatible with the Old Liners' world view.

For this Crow was given powers equal to Bruce's in administrative
areas—*i.e.*, the ability to direct Central Office manpower—which he first used
to demote Leon Cook, the most vocal and impatient of the Insurgents, from
Acting Director of Economic Development to Deputy Director under a non-
Indian Old Liner, William Freeman. Crow then removed Ernest Stevens from
the job of Acting Associate Commissioner for Education and Programs (one of
the top four jobs in the Bureau), returned him to Director of Community
Services, and suggested abolishing the Education and Program Office. Then he
ordered William Veeder transferred to Phoenix at the request of John Ar-
tichoker, the Area Director there, and ordered Phillip Corke transferred to a
subsidiary Bureau position in Denver.

To Indians, who were already complaining about the attempts to disman-
tle Bruce's Bureau reforms, the Veeder transfer was the precipitating event.
On September 21 a delegation of tribal chairmen voiced their disapproval to
White House and Interior officials at a meeting in the Interior Building at
the same time that members of the American Indian Movement and the National Indian Youth Council were marching on the Bureau headquarters in
Washington in an unsuccessful attempt to make a citizen's arrest of John O.
Crow. This combination of militant and middle-of-the-road protest did have
an impact. The Veeder and Corke transfers were rescinded and it became
obvious to everyone that another attempt would have to be made to remodel
the Central Office to make it big enough for Crow and his allies and for
Bruce and his allies.

---

10. *Id.*

The new reorganization which Bruce sent to Morton in October included the appointment of Ernest Stevens as permanent Associate Commissioner for Education and Programs and the elevation of that office to the third highest rank in the Bureau. It also called for the abolition of the Associate Commissioner for Support Services in order to enhance McNabb's position. As a compromise, Leon Cook would not be affected by the restructuring. However, Cook soon resigned and was elected president of the National Congress of American Indians where he cemented an alliance between that organization and the surviving Insurgents.

Bruce's plan, which he admitted was a compromise, was further modified by Victor, Rogers, and Morton. By the time it was announced in December it bore only slight resemblance to Bruce's original proposal, but it did contain a little of something for everyone. It abolished all associate commissioner positions and replaced them with thirteen division offices, three of which were headed by Stevens, McNabb, and their non-Indian ally Robert Gajdys. The rest were a mixture of New Teamers and Crow supporters. However, Crow's authority was expanded across the board to the point where he became Bruce's equal in everything but name. It was an unwieldy structure from a management point of view, but it was not a management-made structure—it was a political one. And while it made for a broad, symmetrical flow chart, it also created an unplotted picture of power that Gaillard described as the "multiple-sandwich, squeeze-play effect."

At the top of the stack was Secretary Morton, a neutral, who could be responsive to either side. Below Morton was Interior Under-secretary for Public Land Management, Harrison Loesch, who was no friend of Bruce or the Insurgents. But for approval of Bureau policy or programs, it was Loesch through whom Bruce worked, Bruce through whom Crow worked, Crow through whom the Insurgents worked, and the Insurgents through whom the Old Liners and Hard Hats worked. And at the base of the stack were the reservation Indians whose expectations of the Bureau had been raised by the Insurgency and who were putting more pressure on the Old Liners and Hard Hats than those two factions had ever felt from below. No one rested easy for the next eleven months and it was not the Bureau's most productive time. Everyone was trying to engineer a new offensive.

But the final initiative did not belong to either side. It was commandeered by the Trail of Broken Treaties Caravan and its six-day occupation of the Central Office.[11] When the Caravan left, it was clear that the Bureau would never be the same. During the weeks of Central Office renovation that followed the occupation, the staff was dispersed into any federal space available, communications faltered, and the work load piled high. The confusion was a propaganda coup for the Hard Hats who sought permanently to discredit

---

11. *See generally* V. DELORIA, JR., BEHIND THE TRAIL OF BROKEN TREATIES (1974).

Bruce and the Insurgents by charging that they were accessories to the takeover. Authority over the Central Office fell to the receivers; partly to Morton, but mainly to Loesch, who appointed Crow to rebuild the structure. Crow, however, was unable to make any headway. The takeover had so polarized the factions and crystallized the squeeze-play that any action was impossible. Early in December, Morton gave Crow and Bruce six weeks notice, relieved them of all authority in the Bureau and transferred the Bureau out from under Loesch's authority. Most of the more notable combatants were swept from the Central Office. Some of the New Team stayed, as did some of the Old Liners. Crow, Bruce, and Stevens left government service and McNabb and Gajdys moved into the Interior Office of Management and Budget.

On December 6, 1972 Morton put the Bureau under the temporary command of Richard Bodman, Assistant Interior Secretary for Management and Budget, who was to oversee the revival of day-to-day operations and develop the next final solution for the Central Office's structural dilemma. Six weeks later Bodman announced his plan to streamline the Bureau's operations by reducing the number of Central Office divisions from thirteen to seven and the number of Central Office positions from 1,375 to 715. It was obvious that Secretary Morton was taking control of Indian Affairs and was using Bodman, the management technician, to de-politicize the Bureau and make it conform to Interior's expectations. But Morton had not counted on the strength remaining in the factions, or the influence McNabb and Gajdys would have with Bodman and his successors in the Office of Management and Budget, or the influence the Hard Hat-Old Line axis would have with Marvin Franklin, whom Morton appointed, on February 7, 1973, as Assistant Secretary for Indian Affairs with duties as acting Commissioner.

Franklin made two notable changes in Bodman's reorganization plan. First, he reduced the number of Central divisions from seven to six. The heads of each division were, together with the Commissioner, to act as the Bureau's governing board. The Commissioner was to preside over meetings but, like the other members, had only one vote in policy decisions. Second, Franklin created, as an adjunct to the Commissioner's office, a new advisory panel, the Committee on Field and Internal Operations. It soon became apparent that through this new structure Franklin was once again placing the Bureau's reliance on the expert's experts, the conservative and politically astute Hard Hats.

Franklin appointed as acting heads of the six divisions leading Old Liners, most of whom had been detailed into the Central Office from permanent assignments as Assistant Area Directors. Next he filled the Committee on Field and Internal Operations with a majority of Area Directors, including the leading Hard Hats. In theory the Committee was merely an advisory board whose sole responsibility was to meet monthly with Franklin for consultation on policy matters. But under Franklin, as so often in the past, governing boards may not do all of the governing and the advisory board may do more than merely advise.

The actual structure became somewhat clearer on April 10 when Franklin issued his major organizational memo. Part of it was commonplace, like the admonition that "the control of power is the control of money and man-power."[12] The memo then explained that bureaucratic control would follow the line set out in the new organizational chart: from Commissioner and Deputy Commissioner to Area Directors to Agency Superintendents. How-ever, such a plan is only as plausible as the flow chart is dependable. And Franklin weakened the dependability of the flow chart by doubling back and writing: "The management concepts that are required represent changes in the roles of the Central Office staff. Those offices must carry out policy estab-lished by line authority."[13] But since the key members of the Central Office staff—the six acting division heads—were on leave from positions as *Assistant* Area Directors—and still consulted monthly with their superiors in the field—the governing board members effectively remained subordinates of the Hard Hat Area Directors. Formally and informally it made for some strange structural geometry, a circuitous and discreet way for the Area Directors, through intermediaries and superiors, to tell themselves and the Bureau what to do.

If the structure had been allowed to stand it would have been a total Hard Hat victory, but it would not have been a total return to a pre-Bruce Bureau. The Bruce Administration was the soundest evidence yet that undeniable change had occurred in Indian Country and Congress. It was obvious that the concept of self-determination, though frustrated by the war in Central, was a policy taken for granted on most reservations. It would soon be given legisla-tive effect in the Indian Self-Determination and Education Assistance Act.[14] But who would turn the relatively few pages of the Self-Determination and Education Act into regulations, and who would revise the BIA manuals to reflect the law? What remained of Insurgent strength foresaw the possibility that under Franklin those jobs would fall to the Old Liners who would act on the advice and consent of the Hard Hats. The Insurgents were fearful that such an axis could regulate self-determination to its own advantage in the same way that that axis had accused the Insurgents of using self-determination to their own advantage, and, more to the point, in the same way that the axis had subverted Collier's concept by transforming Area Of-fices from intermediate service centers into inscrutable and powerful minia-ture Central Offices.

---

12. National Congress of American Indians, Synopsis of the National Consultation on BIA Delivery Systems, Denver, Sept. 14-15, 1973 (unpublished manuscript on file with the author).
   13. *Id.*
   14. 25 U.S.C. § 450 (Supp. 1976).

But the structure was not allowed to stand, for it soon encountered opposition from two fronts. Publicly, Franklin's realignment was attacked during the summer of 1973 by the National Congress of American Indians and its closest congressional ally, Senator James Abourezk, who requested that Morton once again take charge of the Bureau. Franklin, they charged, was acting "illegally" because he had gone without Senate confirmation longer than the law allowed. At the same time, but behind the scenes, Franklin was also drawing fire from another study group created by Interior Secretary Morton called the Committee on Bureau Reorganization. This committee included Franklin, Interior Solicitor Kent Frizzell, Assistant Interior Secretary for Program Development Larry Lynn, and Assistant Interior Secretary for Management James Clark. The majority of these men wanted Franklin to stop the realignment for the ostensible reason that its field research group had not completed a report on how reservation Indians thought the Bureau should be structured. That was probably only part of their reason; when the report appeared late that fall stating that Indians wanted a Bruce-like structure, the entire matter was quietly swept under the rug. A more plausible reason for the committee's opposition was that it reflected the attitude of the Interior Department, which had expected Franklin to further the Department's own Bureau reorganization plan. Franklin, however, had listened more to the Area Directors than he had to Interior. In August, Franklin announced that he was stopping the implementation of his realignment and was withdrawing his name from consideration as Commissioner. In his written announcement to Interior Undersecretary John Whittaker, Franklin broadly implied that he had been undercut by the Administration.

Interior's plan for the Bureau was never articulated publicly, but in July 1973, an issue arose that gave the plan some definition besides adding spice and confusion to the summer's hostilities. During that month John Sidle, Deputy Assistant Secretary for Program Development, authored an "administratively confidential" memo to Undersecretary Whittaker, who was then the intermediary between Secretary Morton and the Bureau. The memo began: "During our conversation of June 15 you [Whittaker] questioned the need for and desirability of having BIA Area Directors."[15] Sidle then agreed that the question had merit and posed two alternatives to the structure: replace the directors with "new, young management" or "reorganize the Area Offices out of existence" and place their duties in Federal Regional Councils.

Sidle went on to argue against replacement on the grounds that Bruce's rotation policy had failed to shake the power of the Area Directors and cited, for additional proof, instances in which Oklahoma Representative Carl Albert and Montana Senators Metcalf and Mansfield had intervened to prevent the

---

15. American Indian Press Ass'n News Dispatch, Oct. 2, 1973, in which the Sidle Memo was printed in full.

transfer of Area Directors out of their respective states. The best option in Sidle's opinion was the abolition of the Area Offices. In this regard the memo had been heavily influenced by two of Sidle's subordinates, Insurgents McNabb and Gajdys. Sidle even reminded Whittaker that McNabb had once briefed him on the "effectiveness of the various Area Directors."

Sidle concluded with the belief that Whittaker and others in Interior could probably gather support from the National Congress of American Indians (NCAI) and the National Indian Youth Council for his "regionalization" plan. But here he was in error because he had not counted on the total distrust some Insurgents, including those closely associated with NCAI, had for Nixon's New Federalism Doctrine, of which the Federal Regional Councils were a part. They felt that any dispersal of power out of the BIA would only cripple the Bureau's integrity, and thus the integrity of the unique Indian-federal government relationship that lies at the heart of all attempts toward self-determination, sovereignty, and trust protection. NCAI lobbied this point with Franklin's Old Line division heads, who agreed. Sidle was also unaware that after leaving the Bureau the Insurgents were slightly divided over the question of Bureau integrity. One side, those who opposed Sidle, wanted all Bureau power put back into the Central Office in the hope that someday the Bureau could be transformed into a Super Bureau, an independent public corporation that could provide services to reservations and be governed by the people it served. But the other side, those who backed Sidle, wanted a gradual dispersal of Bureau service programs into those agencies of the government established specifically for service: Indian Education would follow Indian Health into HEW, Indian Housing would move into HUD, and manpower development would move into the Labor Department. In other words, the plan was to kill the Bureau through gradual evisceration. This, of course, would be contingent on the creation of the Indian Trust Council Authority, a legislative proposal that seeks to establish an independent legal commission which would protect tribal governmental sovereignty and the trust status.[16]

Regionalization, then, created a new and somewhat bewildering line-up of allies. The anti-regionalists were the Old Line-Hard Hat Axis and one faction of the Insurgency. The regionalists were the other side of the Insurgency and the top officials of the Interior Department. Each had its share of grass roots support. And each, except the Old Line-Hard Hat Axis, was opposed to Franklin on the issue of realignment. However, on the issue of regionalization, Franklin seemed to be in everybody's camp. Although he had championed the Area Director's return to power, Franklin stated in an interview in November 1973 that placing the functions of the Area Offices in Federal Regional Councils was a logical extension of the realignment policy.[17]

---

16. S. 1339, 93d Cong., 2d Sess. (1973).
17. Nickeson, *Paternalism and Its Mates*, 5 RACE RELATIONS REP. no. 5, at 22 (1974).

The hostilities suddenly ceased in December 1973 when Morris Thompson was confirmed as Indian Commissioner. There were several reasons for this cessation, but only two were apparent at the time. First, commissioners, like presidents, are given a honeymoon period with the Bureau while their staffs are selected and their intentions become clear. Thompson's honeymoon was a long one because his staff selection seemed interminable, and as his people began to fall into place no definite Central Office characteristic developed as it had in the two previous administrations. Secondly, Thompson opened the doors of the Central Office to everyone who had complained that either Bruce or Franklin had excluded them. Both of these factors had a cooling effect.

Only later did it become clear that during these initial months the present organization of the Bureau was taking shape almost unnoticed. Currently, the visible structure under Thompson is a modified version of Franklin's modifications of the Bodman plan. The only major changes have been the abolition of the Committee on Field and Internal Operations, and the removal of the Office of Public Affairs, one of the six divisions under Franklin, from what could be called the Program Line and its incorporation into the Commissioner's own staff. But more significantly, Thompson's Central Office is largely a de-politicized one, a fact that pleases Interior, which in the past two years has made inroads into policy making, primarily through the Interior Solicitor's office. There is now in Central a sprinkling of Old Liners, an Insurgency flavor here and there, and a couple of small power domains that appear to be personal and free of the partisanship that so characterized the two previous administrations. But there are no visible Hard Hats. They and their closest Old Line associates have left the Central Office and have once again entrenched themselves in the Area Offices. Although the power to decide policy formally resides in the Central Office, the actual administration of programs is largely in the hands of the Area Directors. Powers delegated by the Secretary to the Commissioner have effectively been redelegated to the Area Directors and their subordinates. The process merely institutionalizes what has existed since Franklin's organizational memo. The Area Offices have been given the responsibility of administration and control of almost all Bureau programs. Through their control of money and manpower they maintain substantial control of policy, for it would be impossible for the Central Office to ignore or slight in the least the stated expectations of those who are administering the programs for which Central is establishing policy. However, there are indications that the Area Offices have never regained their old prominance, but were also weakened during the five year war. The composite losses of the opposition were never translated directly into Area Office gains; the war had a degenerating effect on all of its participants. For example, several of the Area Offices have gone without permanent directors for months, a situation that resulted in a suit being filed recently against the Department of

Interior by tribes in the Albuquerque area.[18] In another instance, some Dakota tribes petitioned for the closure of the Aberdeen Area Office late in 1974, and Central appeared willing to follow those wishes had there been unanimity among the tribes in the area. There also have been a number of management complaints that the Area Offices have become little more than duplicate and expensive bottlenecks in the day-to-day processing of Bureau work. For this reason the Area Offices have been required to bear an unequal share in Interior's efforts to reduce its overall work force. In other words, the Area Offices and their power are no longer being taken for granted, the worst setback a sub-institution of the self-made type can suffer.

When taken as a whole, the greatest accomplishment of the entire structural war was an acceleration of entropy. When the war began all the energies were directed toward reforming the relationships between the Bureau and its constituency. But it soon became apparent that such reform was totally contingent upon a reformation within the structural sphere of the Bureau. Yet when pulled into this sphere, where the constituency is secondary, the action suddenly became almost a conflict over structure for its own sake, fought as if structure had far more causal capabilities than it can claim in reality. From this point there was no other way for the war to go except toward a degrading of energies from a concrete level to increasingly abstract ones. The final realignment/regionalization controversy was little more than a decadent parody of the action that touched off the war. The chronology of the war indicates that the deeper the action went into structure the closer it came to a dead end, because structure is an end. Structure is the cause of little, but the effect of much: It is a temporary manifestation of the interplay between policy and power. In the long run it will make little difference whether the Bureau takes on the form of Amtrac and the TVA, or dissolves into the total federal network. If the elements of policy and power remain unchanged, the Bureau will still be the Bureau (or Bureaus, as the case might be). Such has always been the case. Despite the six structural changes that the Bureau has undergone in the past six years—despite all past changes—the Bureau has remained essentially unchanged since 1824, because Indian policy and the powers that implement it have changed only in their complexity since John Cabot put Britain's Christian claim on North America in 1497.

As the Indian Policy Review Commission reexamines the formal organization of the Bureau, it might best look at it for what it is—a costume of changeable style in which the Bureau chooses to dress to go to work. Obviously, it is not enough to consider style; the effort must be placed on the substance behind it. In this light it might be best for the recommendations concerning the structure of the BIA to be the last that unfold from the Commission as it works out its own style for countering that of the status quo.

---

18.   Pueblo of Acoma v. Hathaway, Civil No. 75-419 (D.N.M., filed July 16, 1975).

WATER RIGHTS
IN THE COAL FIELDS OF
THE YELLOWSTONE RIVER BASIN

WILLIAM H. VEEDER*

> Here there was no water for the people to drink.
> 2. They quarreled therefore with Moses . . . .
> 4. So Moses cried out to the Lord, "What shall
> I do with this people? A little more and they
> will stone me!"
> — Exodus 17:1-4

There is a deadly contest being waged in and around the coal fields of the Yellowstone River Basin of southeastern Montana and northeastern Wyoming. That struggle does not relate primarily to the vast coal deposits of the region but rather to control of the insufficient water supplies of the Yellowstone River and its principal tributaries. If the thirty-four billion tons of strippable coal deposits[1] are to be used to alleviate the energy crisis, a solution must be found to the question of the distribution of water resources in the area.

Ultimately, the formidable body of law pertaining to water rights in the Yellowstone River Basin will control. At the moment, however, law and logic are being overwhelmed by politics, which mixes readily with coal and water to create a volatile combination. Montana and Wyoming have major stakes in the anticipated development.[2] It is from Montana and Wyoming that the waters primarily flow. Farmers and cattlemen in the area asserting rights in the streams pursuant to state law are gravely threatened by a possible invasion of those rights. Federal policies, agencies, and water rights are often in conflict with the policies and agencies of the states and the rights of those claiming under the states. Moreover, the fact that the Bureau of Reclamation has entered into contracts with the major energy companies for the sale of water rights[3] has sparked an interagency dispute, presaging almost unlimited con-

---

* Bureau of Indian Affairs, Department of the Interior. The views expressed herein are those of the author and do not purport to represent the policies of any governmental entity.

1. U.S. DEP'T OF THE INTERIOR, BUREAU OF RECLAMATION, APPRAISAL REPORT ON MONTANA-WYOMING AQUEDUCTS 13 (1972). *See generally* Smith, *The Wringing of the West*, Washington Post, Feb. 16, 1975, § B, at 1, col. 1; Josephy, *Ripping Coal From the Northern Plains*, Washington Star-News, July 29, 1973, § C, at 2, cols. 1-5.

2. The area involved is "one of very low population, rural population averaging 1.4 persons per square mile. Urban population accounts for almost half the total of over 68,000 persons." *See* REPORT ON MONTANA-WYOMING AQUEDUCTS, *supra* note 1.

3. *See* Memorandum from Morris Thompson, Commissioner of Indian Affairs to Rogers C.B. Morton, Secretary of the Interior, Feb. 24, 1975.

flicts among all the holders of rights to the use of water, irrespective of their source of title. Most gravely threatened by the water crisis and interagency struggles are the Indians who occupy Montana's Crow and Northern Cheyenne Indian Reservations and Wyoming's Arapahoe and Shoshone Tribes of the Wind River Reservation. In order to formulate an appropriate policy for the control of water rights in the coal fields of the Yellowstone Basin it is essential to understand the development and implications of conflicting federal, state, and Indian claims.

I
THE DEVELOPMENT OF FEDERAL AND WESTERN WATER LAW

In 1496 Henry VII of England commissioned John Cabot to discover and claim on behalf of His Majesty all lands not otherwise claimed or occupied by "Christian" princes. From Cabot's voyages stem the British, and later the American, claims to the lands and waters of this continent.[4] Confronted by powerful tribes,[5] the British Crown and other European potentates were forced to enter into treaties with the Indians. These treaties acknowledged the Indians' rights of occupancy and self-government. Among themselves the European powers recognized each other's rights to obtain the Indians' lands by purchase or conquest.[6] Similar rights were asserted by France to the lands west of the Mississippi.[7]

Following independence, the United States reaffirmed these principles[8] and coupled them with a specific division of powers between the state and

---

4. In *Johnson v. McIntosh*, Chief Justice Marshall, reviewing this nation's laws respecting the claims to Indian lands, described as an "extravagant" pretension the proposition that by sailing down the Virginia coast Cabot had claimed for the King all the lands which came within his view. "To this discovery the English trace their title." 21 U.S. (8 Wheat.) 543, 576 (1823). This claim was also recognized as preposterous by Chief Justice Story who scoffed at the idea that an alleged "discovery" of inhabited lands could serve as a basis for asserting title to it. Rather, Story recognized the claim for what it was and is—an assertion of European bias against native peoples in general. 1 J. STORY, COMMENTARIES ON THE CONSTITUTION § 152, at 106 (5th ed. 1891). And throughout the early decades of American history, as Chancellor Kent remarked, the non-Indian settlers were "penetrated with a perfect contempt of Indian rights." 3 J. KENT, COMMENTARIES 557, 558 n.(b) (13th ed. 1884).

5. As the Court stated in *Johnson v. McIntosh*, Great Britain has ascertained thorough harsh experience that the Indian nations were "too powerful and brave not to be dreaded as formidable enemies. . . ." 21 U.S. at 596.

6. The European powers regulated rights of acquisition according to the principle that "discovery gave title to the government by whose subjects, or by whose authority, it was made, against all other European governments, which title might be consummated by possession." However, they did not declare that the Indian nations and tribes were totally without right to their land. 21 U.S. at 573. It was conceded—seemingly by all Europeans—that the Indians were "the rightful occupants of the soil, with a legal as well as just claim to retain possession of it. . . ." But the discoverer-nation possessed the power to extinguish that title or to recognize the Indian rights of occupancy. 21 U.S. at 574.

7. 21 U.S. at 574-75.

8. 21 U.S. at 584-85. *See also* Tee-Hit-Ton Indians v. United States, 348 U.S. 272, 280 (1955).

federal governments under which the federal government was delegated the power to regulate commerce and to enter into treaties with the Indians.[9] Moreover, Congress could control the admission of new states to the Union,[10] pass laws regarding territories and federal properties,[11] and insure the supremacy of federal laws.[12] Despite extravagant claims based on the right of discovery, the federal goverment and its courts recognized, from the earliest years of independence, that the Indians possessed that inherent sovereign power from which stem their treaty rights—rights which the federal government in the exercise of its constitutional control over Indian affairs was bound to honor, but which it frequently violated.

The principle of federal control over new territories was extended to the Louisiana Territory following its purchase from France in 1803.[13] Although Congress did not for many years enact any laws directly relating to the waters of the Yellowstone River Basin, it was in this period that the Supreme Court, under Chief Justice Marshall, began to lay down principles of treaty interpretation that continue to affect the issue of water rights in the region. Thus, in *Worchester v. Georgia* the Court, faced with the issue of the paramount treaty rights of the Cherokee Nation vis-à-vis the laws of Georgia, held that the reference to "hunting grounds" in the Cherokee treaty could not be construed as implying "that any intention existed of restricting the full use of the lands they [the Indians] reserved."[14] The Court thus recognized that the Indians reserved to themselves that which they did not grant to the United States; hence, the particular use to which they put their lands was "a matter of no concern" to the United States.[15] The Court further rejected the assertion that Indian rights to use reserved lands were limited to the use to which they were put at the time of the treaty.[16] These early tenets of treaty construction remain extremely important when applied to the present-day reservation of water rights and the uses to which they may be put.

Almost half a century elapsed between the 1803 Louisiana Purchase and the execution of the first Indian treaty pertaining to a portion of the Yellow-

---

9. U.S. CONST. art. I, § 8.

10. U.S. CONST. art. IV, § 3.

11. *Id*. Federal Power Comm'n v. Oregon, 349 U.S. 435, 443 (1955); California Oregon Power Co. v. Portland Cement Co., 295 U.S. 142, 162 (1935).

12. U.S. CONST. art. VI. This same article asserts that "the Judges in every State shall be bound [by the Constitution of the United States, its laws and its treaties] anything in the Constitution or Laws of any State to the Contrary notwithstanding."

13. Treaty of Paris, Act of March 26, 1804, ch. 38, § 15, 2 Stat. 283.

14. Worchester v. Georgia, 31 U.S. (6 Pet.) 515, 553 (1832). One year earlier, in *Cherokee Nation v. Georgia*, Marshall first declared that the Indians were best denominated as "domestic dependent nations" bound to the federal government by a trust relationship resembling " that of a ward to his guardian." 30 U.S. (5 Pet.) 1, 17 (1831).

15. 31 U.S. at 553.

16. As the Court in *Worchester* pointed out, the use of the phrase "hunting grounds" in early treaties with the Crown did not imply "a right in the British government to take their lands, or to interfere with their internal government." *Id*.

stone River Basin. The Treaty of Fort Laramie, entered into on September 17, 1851, recognized the rights of the Cheyenne and Arapahoe to a broad stretch of land that includes part of the coal fields here under consideration.[17] A few years later, on May 30, 1854, Congress adopted "An Act to Organize the Territories of Nebraska and Kansas," which covered an area embracing the present states of Montana and Wyoming and including, of course, the Yellowstone River and all its tributaries.[18] Congress guaranteed that nothing in the Act would "impair the right of person or property now pertaining to the Indians in said Territory, so long as such rights shall remain unextinguished by treaty between the United States and such Indians." Moreover, the Indians would not have their lands included in the territory of Nebraska without their consent. The United States remained fully empowered to exercise its authority "respecting such Indians, their lands, property, or other rights, by treaty, law, or otherwise."[19]

The Territorial Act did not refer directly to any controlling law of water rights. It was in the gold fields of California and in subsequent judicial and legislative action that water laws were formulated. At the time Mexico ceded California to the United States under the 1848 Treaty of Guadalupe Hidalgo,[20] there was neither federal nor state law applicable to rights to the use of water on the vast public domain which had been acquired. To achieve order in the gold fields the miners developed their own customs, usages, and regulations, and these were to form the basis for all of western water law. In its simplest terms, these customs declared that the individual who first made use of an available water supply had a prior right over all other claimants to as much of the water as he could beneficially use. Moreover, the first user could appropriate to his own use *all* of the waters of a stream if he could apply it to beneficial uses.[21] The California legislature gave legal effect to these customs in 1851.[22] Thereafter, further support for this developing doc-

---

17. The Treaty provides that the territory of the Cheyenne and Arapahos would embrace an area commencing at a point on the north fork of the Platte River
    thence up the north fork of the Platte River to its source; thence along the main range of the Rocky Mountains to the head-waters of the Arkansas River; thence down the Arkansas River to the crossing of the Santa Fe road; thence in a northwesterly direction to the forks of the Platte River; and thence up the Platte River to the place of beginning.
11 Stat. 749 (1855); 2 C. KAPPLER, INDIAN AFFAIRS—LAWS AND TREATIES 595 (1904). Moreover, by the terms of the Treaty the nations and tribes involved did not "abandon or prejudice any rights or claims they may have to other lands. . . ." *Id*. The Treaty of October 17, 1855 with the Blackfoot Indians also takes cognizance of the provisions of the Treaty of Fort Laramie. 11 Stat. 657; C. KAPPLER, *supra* at 736.
    18. Ch. 59, 10 Stat. 277. *See also* C. PAULLIN, ATLAS OF THE HISTORICAL GEOGRAPHY OF THE UNITED STATES plate 64 (1932).
    19. Ch. 59, 10 Stat. 277, 278.
    20. Act of Feb. 2, 1848, 9 Stat. 922.
    21. *See* Jennison v. Kirk, 98 U.S. 453, 457-58 (1879).
    22. California Practice Act, CAL. STAT. ch. 5, § 249 (1851). *See also* Irwin v. Phillips, 5 Cal. 140, 146-47 (1855).

trine of prior appropriation was supplied by the federal government and by the territorial legislature.[23]

In 1866 Congress passed its first law affecting rights to the use of water on public lands, including those in the territory of Montana. The Act declared "[t]hat whenever, by priority of possession, rights to the use of water for mining, agricultural, manufacturing, or other purposes have vested and accrued, and the same are recognized and acknowledged by the local customs, laws, and the decisions of courts, the possessors and owners of such vested rights shall be maintained and protected in the same."[24] Later, in an attempt to attract settlers to the arid lands of the West, Congress passed the Desert Land Act of 1877 which authorized the appropriation of "surplus" water on the nation's public lands by those who demonstrated actual appropriation and use of such waters pursuant to state or territorial laws.[25] With reference to the Acts of 1866 and 1877, it is, however, important to note that during this period the federal government continued to accord full legal effect to treaties with the Indian tribes,[26] and to pass laws for the organization of new territories that acknowledged "the rights of persons or property now pertaining to the Indians."[27] Moreover, the courts construed and applied the term "public lands" as used by Congress to mean only those lands "unqualifiedly subject to sale and disposition"[28] by the federal government, a characterization

---

23. *See* Lux v. Haggin, 69 Cal. 255, 10 P. 674, 721 (1886).

24. Act of July 26, 1866, ch. 262, § 9, 14 Stat. 251, 253 (codified in 43 U.S.C. § 661 (1970)). *See also* Act of July 9, 1870, ch. 237, § 17, 16 Stat. 217, 218 (codified in 43 U.S.C. § 661 (1970)), which provides that, by the Act of 1866, "all patents granted, or preemption or homesteads allowed, shall be subject to any vested and accrued water rights, or right to ditches and reservoirs used in connection with such water rights, as may have been acquired under or recognized."

25. Ch. 107, § 1, 19 Stat. 377 (codified in part in 43 U.S.C. § 321 (1970)) states that one claiming water for the desert land entry must "depend upon bona fide prior appropriation: and such right shall not exceed the amount of water actually appropriated, and necessarily used for the purpose of irrigation and reclamation. . . ."

26. *See, e.g.*, Treaty With the Crow Tribe, May 7, 1868, 16 Stat. 649, which, in the words of the Supreme Court, created a large reservation in the territory of Montana for the " 'absolute and undisturbed use and occupation' of the Crow Indians, and they undertook to make thier permanent homes thereon." United States v. Powers, 305 U.S. 527, 528 (1939). *See also* Treaty With the Shoshonees and Bannocks, July 3, 1868, 15 Stat. 673, establishing the Wind River Indian Reservation in the Territory of Wyoming.

27. The Act of July 25, 1868, ch. 235, 15 Stat. 178 (reprinted in 1 Wyo. Stat. § 35 (1957)). This Organic Act established a temporary government for the territory of Wyoming. The Montana Territorial Act gave additional safeguards to the Indians by guaranteeing that the treaties, laws, and other engagements made by the United States with the Indians "inhabitating the territory embraced within the provisions of this act, shall be faithfully and ridgidly observed, anything contained in this act to the contrary notwithstanding. . . ." Act of May 26, 1864, ch. 95, § 17, 13 Stat. 85, 91 (reprinted in 1 Mont. Rev. Code § 17 (1947)).

28. Federal Power Comm'n v. Oregon, 349 U.S. 435, 448 (1955). It was provided in the Desert Land Act of 1877 that "all surplus water over and above such actual appropriation and use, together with the water of all lakes, rivers and other sources of water supply *upon the public lands and not navigable*, shall remain and be held free for the appropriation and use of the public for irrigation, mining and manufacturing purposes subject to existing rights." Ch. 107, § 1, 19 Stat. 377 (codified in part in 43 U.S.C. § 321 (1970)) (emphasis added).

which is inapplicable to lands of Indians or Indian tribes.[29] Only surplus waters on federal lands properly designated as "public lands" were open to appropriation under federal law.

As the territories of Montana and Wyoming approached statehood it was clear that water would become the basis—and the limit—of their future growth. Both territories therefore moved to assert greater control over the water resources within their boundaries and to regularize the laws governing its appropriation. Montana's Territorial Legislative Assembly enacted a primitive water code in 1865 that provided for the distribution of water "in a just and equitable proportion."[30] The territories' highest court thereafter held that with regard to the apportionment of water, "equity declares that he who is first in time is first in right,"[31] and the Territorial Legislature gave formal recognition to this principle in 1885.[32] The Montana statutes and cases did not, in this early period, explicitly reject the common law doctrine of riparian rights. That doctrine recognizes the principle that the owners of lands which abut upon natural streams or bodies of water have vested rights in those waters. The doctrine of riparian rights denies a landowner whose property does not abut upon a stream any right to water, irrespective of need or purpose. By contrast, the doctrine of prior appropriation authorizes the diversion and use of water to non-adjacent lands. Moreover, it assures a senior and better right to the appropriator based upon his date of priority. Beneficial use, therefore, is the basis, the measure, and the limit of the rights of the appropriator, with the first in time being the first in right. It was not until 1921 that the Supreme Court of Montana firmly rejected the common law rule of riparian rights in favor of the doctrine of prior appropriation.[33]

Where Montana was slow to formulate its laws respecting rights to the use of water or to establish centralized control over the administration and appropriations of rights, Wyoming reached the same goals more quickly and directly. From its inception, the territory of Wyoming declared its adherence to the doctrine of prior appropriation[34] and formulated administrative procedures to implement that doctrine.[35] The Wyoming Territorial Legislative As-

---

29. United States v. Minnesota, 270 U.S. 181, 206 (1926).

30. An Act to Protect and Regulate the Irrigation of Land in Montana Territory, [1864] Laws of Mont. Territory 367.

31. Thorpe v. Woolman, 1 Mont. 168, 171-72 (1870).

32. MONT. COMPILED STAT. ch. 74, § 1254 (1887).

33. Mettler v. Ames Realty Co., 61 Mont. 152, 201 P. 702 (1921).

34. Act to Create and Regulate Corporations, ch. 8, §§ 28, 29 [1869] Wyo. Laws 234, 244-45. *See also* Act to Develop Mining Resources in the Territory, ch. 22, §§ 15-18 [1869] Wyo. Laws 307, 310-11.

35. Act to Protect and Legislate the Irrigation of Lands in the Territory of Wyoming, WYO. COMPILED LAWS ch. 65, § 1 (1876). A later territorial statute referred to this Act as the "[r]ights of riparian owners." WYO. REV. STAT. tit. 19, § 1317 (1887)). However, when a claimant sought to assert rights as a riparian owner, the Wyoming court was quick to declare: "The common-law

sembly went further, stating that: "The water of every natural stream not heretofore appropriated within this Territory, is hereby declared to be the property of the public, and the same is dedicated to the use of the people, subject to appropriation as herein provided."[36] Montana made a similar claim in earlier statutes and has updated its practices and procedures respecting the acquisition, control, and use of the state's water resources through its revised constitutions and statutes.[37]

At the time of their admission to the Union, both Montana and Wyoming acknowledged existing Indian rights and the plenary power of Congress to control Indian affairs. The Enabling Act of 1889 that authorized statehood for Montana (as well as North Dakota, South Dakota, and Washington) provided: "That the people inhabiting said proposed States do agree and declare that they forever disclaim all right and title . . . to all lands lying within said limits owned or held by any Indian or Indian Tribes."[38] This disclaimer was repeated in the various western state constitutions,[39] including that of Wyoming.[40]

In both Montana and Wyoming, therefore, the law of water rights has reached essentially the same results. The right to the use of water is regarded as a usufructory right,[41] a vested right to the corpus of water flowing in a natural stream.[42] This right to the use of water is an interest in real property and entitled to all the dignity of a freehold interest. The date of priority is in

---

doctrine relating to the rights of a riparian proprietor in the water of a natural stream, and the use thereof is unsuited to our requirements and necessities, and never obtained in Wyoming." Moyer v. Preston, 6 Wyo. 308, 318, 71 Am. St. R. 914, 919 (1896).

36. Act to Regulate the Use of Water for Irrigation, ch. 61, § 14 [1869] Wyo. Laws 294, 299.

37. MONT. CONST. art. III, § 15 (1889). *See generally* 2A P. NICHOL, EMINENT DOMAIN § 7.621, at 626 (1975); Annot., 27 A.L.R. 519 (1923); Annot., 9 A.L.R. 583 (1920). A similar claim was made in Wyoming's constitution. "The waters of all natural streams, springs or lakes or other collections of still water, within the boundaries of the state, are hereby declared to be the property of the state." WYO. CONST. art. 8, § 1. Whereas Wyoming exercised its full power and authority over the waters within its jurisdiction at the time it was admitted to the Union, Montana did not take strict control of the acquisition, administration, and adjudication of rights to the use of water until 1972. MONT. CONST. art. 10, § 3 (1972).

38. Act of Feb. 22, 1889, ch. 180, § 4, 25 Stat. 676, 677.

39. MONT. CONST. ord. 1 (1889); MONT. CONST. art. 1 (1972).

40. WYO. CONST. art. 21, § 26.

41. *See* Lindsey v. McClure, 136 F.2d 65, 70 (10th Cir. 1943); Wright v. Best, 19 Cal. 2d 368, 121 P.2d 702 (1942); Fuller v. Swan River Placer Mining Co., 12 Colo. 12, 19 P. 836 (1888); Sowards v. Meagher, 37 Utah 212, 108 P. 1112 (1910).

42. This right is subject to extensive state regulation. *See, e.g.,* WYO. STAT. § 41-201 (1957). *See generally* 2 S. WIEL, WATER RIGHTS IN THE WESTERN STATES § 1184 (3d ed. 1911); *see* R. CLARK, WATERS AND WATER RIGHTS (1967). Failure to comply with a state regulatory scheme would not necessarily serve to divest one who had actually diverted waters prior to a claimant who did conform to the statutory scheme. *See* Murray v. Tingley, 20 Mont. 260, 50 P. 723, 724-25 (1897). The overriding importance of the doctrine of prior appropriation was stressed in Morris v. Bean, 146 F. 423 (9th Cir. 1906), *aff'd*, 221 U.S. 485 (1911), in which Justice Holmes, writing for the Court, also noted that the doctrine of prior appropriation obtained in Montana and Wyoming even prior to their organization as territories.

itself a valuable property, a component of that real property interest.[43] When courts adjudicate rights to the use of water, the suits are in the nature of a proceeding to quiet title to real property. Courts do not create the rights by adjudicating them; they merely accord to them judicial cognizance.[44] States, in the exercise of their police power, have adopted elaborate procedures for the acquisition, administration, and adjudication of rights to the use of water. Wyoming has pioneered the way for many western states in establishing strict regulation under a board of control created by statute pursuant to its constitution.[45] However, such policy regulations pertain only to matters coming within the scope of state jurisdiction. They have no application to federal rights or to the rights of Indian tribes and people.

II

THE CLASH OF FEDERAL AND STATE WATER RIGHTS

The conflict between the states and the federal government over water rights involves two basic questions. First, has the federal government conveyed or delegated to the states the power to regulate the use of water on federal and Indian lands by virtue of statutes permitting appropriations according to state laws on "public lands"? And second, absent a specific delegation, to what extent may the states nevertheless exercise regulatory control over the waters that pass through lands that lie within their jurisdictions?

Despite the claims of Wyoming and Montana to all the unappropriated waters within their territories, the courts have recognized that under the

---

43.' It is elementary that rights to the use of water are interests in real property. 2 S. WIEL, *supra* note 42, at 20, 21, 301. *See* Ashwander v. T.V.A., 297 U.S. 288, 330 (1936); United States v. Chandler-Dunbar Co., 229 U.S. 53, 73 (1913). A priority to use water out of a stream is itself a component of the interest in real property.

Property rights in water consist not alone in the amount of the appropriation, but also in the priority of the appropriation. It often happens that the chief value of an appropriation consists in its priority over other appropriations from the same natural stream. *Hence, to deprive a person of his priority is to deprive him of a most valuable property right* . . . .
Nichols v. McIntosh, 19 Colo. 22, 34 P. 278, 280 (1893) (emphasis added). *See also* Whitmore v. Murray City, 107 Utah 445, 154 P.2d 748, 751 (1944). No person may be deprived of this interest without due process of law. Nichols v. McIntosh, *supra* at 278; *see* United States v. Gerlach Livestock Co., 339 U.S. 725 (1950).

44. Proceedings to adjudicate water rights are generally equated with proceedings to quiet title to realty. Rickey Land & Cattle Co. v. Miller & Lux, 152 F. 11, 15 (9th Cir. 1907), *aff'd*, 218 U.S. 258 (1910); United States v. Ahtanum Irrigation Dist., 236 F.2d 321, 339 (9th Cir. 1956); Crippen v. XY Irrigation Co., 32 Colo. 447, 76 P. 794 (1904); Louden v. Handy Ditch Co., 22 Colo. 102, 43 P. 535 (1895). *See also* C. KINNEY, IRRIGATION AND WATER RIGHTS § 1569, at 2844 (2d ed. 1912).

45. WYO. STAT. § 41-154 (1957); WYO. CONST. art. 1, § 31. *See also* MONT. CONST. art 9, § 3. The Wyoming constitution declared that, although private property shall not be taken by eminent domain for private use, an exception would exist for private ways of necessity and for "reservoirs, drains, flumes or ditches on or across the lands of others for agricultural, mining, milling, domestic or sanitary purposes . . . ." WYO. CONST. § 32. Provision, of course, was made for just compensation for property taken under proviso.

Property and Commerce Clauses of the Federal Constitution, Congress retains control over the public domain and navigable waters, and that within this sphere the power of the federal government is supreme. It was pursuant to these powers that with the acquisition of the Louisiana Purchase there passed to the nation, subject to the rights of the Indians, title to "all lands, lakes [and] rivers"[46] in the territory. Hence, the statutory claims of Wyoming, Montana, and other states to all the unappropriated waters within their territories have been held not to vest "in the state title or ownership of the water as a proprietor."[47] Rather, as the Wyoming[48] and Colorado[49] courts have noted, these state statutes are an exercise of regulatory authority, not an exercise of proprietary rights. Moreover the United States Supreme Court has held that these regulatory powers are further circumscribed as they relate to federal title in the public domain. Pursuant to its constitiutional authority, said the Court, "the government possessed the power to dispose of land and water thereon together, or to dispose of them separately."[50] Under the Acts of 1866, 1870, and the Desert Land Act of 1877,[51] the federal government opened to appropriation and use of the public surplus waters on the public lands. The Court found that by this action Congress had vested in the states the power to affect the water rights of persons who took public lands by patent from the United States. Thus by action of these statutes a patent to "public land" did not carry with it rights to the use of water, as Congress had provided that those rights could only be separately acquired by compliance with "the customs, laws, and judicial decisions of the state of their location."[52] When the United States withdrew "public lands" and reserved them for federal purposes, the then existing surplus waters were no longer open to appropriation pursuant to state laws. Since the federal government is the source of the full title, it has the power to reserve the surplus waters for its own needs and those of Indians.[53]

Moreover, as the Supreme Court stated in *Federal Power Commission v.*

---

46. E. VATTEL, LAW OF NATIONS 120 (1883). Full import of the legal aspects of the investiture of complete title in the United States is reviewed at length by the Supreme Court in United States v. California, 332 U.S. 19 (1947).

47. Wrathall v. Johnson, 86 Utah 50, 40 P.2d 755, 777 (1935). This case, decided by the Utah Supreme Court, construed language in its own statutes virtually identical to the Montana and Wyoming laws.

48. Farm Investment Co. v. Carpenter, 9 Wyo. 110, 61 P. 258, 260 (1900).

49. Farmers' Independent Ditch Co. v. Agricultural Ditch Co., 22 Colo. 513, 45 P. 444, 449 (1896). Farmers' High Line Canal Co. v. Southworth, 13 Colo. 111, 21 P. 1028, 1031 (1889).

50. California Oregon Power Co. v. Beaver Portland Cement Co., 295 U.S. 142, 162 (1935).

51. *See* references at notes 24 and 25 *supra*.

52. California Oregon Power Co. v. Beaver Portland Cement Co., 295 U.S. at 162.

53. Howell v. Johnson, 89 F. 556 (9th Cir. 1898). The separation of the rights to the use of surplus waters from the "public lands" for the purpose of disposal by the states was applicable only to lands designated in the statutes and did not pertain to Indian lands. United States v. Minnesota, 270 U.S. 181 (1926).

Oregon, under the Acts of 1866, 1870, and the Desert Land Act of 1877, the state does not have the right to exercise its regulatory powers when a license has been granted by a federal agency for the construction of a dam on the reserved lands of the federal government or an Indian tribe, although the waters are within the state's jurisdiction. In overruling the court of appeals, the Supreme Court stated: "To allow Oregon to veto such use, by requiring the State's additional permission, would result in the very duplication of regulatory control precluded by the *First Iowa* decision. No such duplication is called for by the [Federal Power Commission Act]."[54] The Court in *First Iowa* relied on the Commerce Clause to deny state regulatory control of a navigable stream,[55] and in *Federal Power Commission* used the Property Clause to deny comparable power over public lands and reservations.[56] Similar rulings have been handed down in cases involving reclamation projects[57] and reservations created by executive order.[58] Indeed, it is recognized that where federal or Indian lands or rights to the use of water are involved, the power of Congress is absolute,[59] and states may not limit the exercise of that power vested in agents or agencies of the federal government.[60]

Another of the constitutional powers that directly affects control over water rights between the state and federal governments is the Compact Clause of article I. It declares, in part, that "[n]o state shall, without the Consent of Congress . . . enter into any Agreement or Compact with another State . . . ."[61] As the Supreme Court has noted, "the prohibition is directed to the formation of any combination tending to the increase of political power in the States, which may encroach upon or interfere with the just supremacy of the United States."[62] Thus, the Yellowstone River Compact of 1950 formed among the states of Montana, Wyoming, and North Dakota specifically provides that the sovereignty and jurisdiction of the federal government,[63] as well as the water rights of the Indian tribes,[64] shall not be affected by the Compact. The agreement, therefore, could not constitutionally restrict or change the responsibilities or powers of the United States or the Indians within the drainage system to which the Compact pertains.[65]

---

54. Federal Power Comm'n v. Oregon, 349 U.S. 435, 445 (1955).
55. First Iowa Hydro-Electric Coop. v. Federal Power Comm'n, 328 U.S. 152 (1945).
56. 349 U.S. at 442-43.
57. Ivanhoe Irrigation Dist. v. McCracken, 357 U.S. 275 (1958).
58. Arizona v. California, 373 U.S. 546 (1963).
59. United States v. San Francisco, 310 U.S. 16, 29, 30 (1940).
60. Arizona v. California, 373 U.S. at 590.
61. U.S. CONST. art. I, § 10.
62. Virginia v. Tennessee, 148 U.S. 503, 519 (1893).
63. 6 MONT. REV. CODE § 89-903, art. XVI (1947); 12 N.D. CENT. CODE § 61-23-01, art. XII (1960); 9 WYO. STAT. 41-517, art. XVI (1957).
64. 6 MONT. REV. CODE § 89-903, art. VI (1947); 12 N.D. CENT. CODE § 63-23-01, art. VI (1960); 9 WYO. STAT. § 41-511, art. VI (1957).
65. Pennsylvania v. Wheeling & Belmont Bridge Co., 59 U.S. 421, 433 (1855).

There is, then, an unbroken line of authority which holds that the federal government is exempt in its own jurisdiction from state regulatory controls. As Chief Justice Marshall said in *McCulloch v. Maryland:* "If any one proposition could command the universal assent of mankind, we might expect it would be this—that the government of the Union, though limited in its powers, is supreme within its sphere of action."[66] In denying that a state could tax a federal agency, Marshall emphasized that the "power of taxing" the agency "may be exercised so as to destroy it."[67] Similarly, if states had the power to veto this nation's will respecting its rights to the use of water, that authority would be tantamount to vesting in those subordinate quasi-sovereigns the power to destroy it, particularly in the arid and semi-arid West. This language from *McCulloch v. Maryland* leaves no doubt as to where the power resides when national interests are involved in the development of the water resources of the Yellowstone River Basin: "No trace is to be found in the constitution, of an intention to create a dependence of the government of the Union on those of the States, for the execution of the great powers assigned to it. Its means are adequate to its ends; and on those means alone was it expected to rely for the accomplishment of its ends."[68]

To allow the states of Montana or Wyoming to regulate the actions of the federal government would force the government to resort "to means which it cannot control," thus rendering "its course precarious" and its powers dependent "on other governments, which might disappoint its most important designs." Such control by the states of the nation "is incompatible with the language of the Constitution."[69] It should be emphasized, nevertheless, that where rights to the use of water have been privately acquired by compliance with the laws of the states of Montana and Wyoming they may only be taken by the federal government through the exercise of its powers of eminent domain.

III
The Nature and Extent of Indian Water Rights

Although the federal government may assert against the states its control over waters on the public domain and Indian reservations, the rights of the federal government and the Indian tribes are distinct and separate. Whereas federal water rights became vested in it by purchase or conquest and the control of those rights stems from powers granted by the Constitution, Indian water rights are vested in the Indian tribes from time immemorial. These

---

66. 17 U.S. (4 Wheat.) 315, 404 (1819).
67. 17 U.S. at 427.
68. 17 U.S. at 424.
69. *Id.* State courts may, however, exercise jurisdiction over federal water rights, including Indian water rights held in trust by the federal government, when so authorized by Congress. Colorado River Water Conservation Dist. v. United States, 96 S. Ct. 1236 (1976).

Indian rights were reserved by the tribes through the treaties signed with the federal government. The courts have drawn a clear distinction between United States and Indian water rights and have given close consideration to the scope of Indian rights. Moreover, the courts have recognized the obligation of the United States, as trustee of the Indian tribes and people, to preserve and protect the Indian rights to the use of water.

The leading case on Indian water rights is *Winters v. United States*.[70] The United States, on behalf of Montana's Fort Belknap Tribe, sought to enjoin Winters and others from diverting water from the Milk River at a point above the reservation's northern boundary. The Supreme Court was asked to determine the effect of the Treaty of 1855[71] and of a subsequent agreement entered into between the national government and the tribe, neither of which made mention of water. In affirming the final decree enjoining the defendants, the Supreme Court held that when the Fort Belknap Indians ceded to the United States their vast domain they "had command of the lands and the waters—command of all beneficial use" whether for hunting, grazing livestock, "or agriculture and the arts of civilization."[72] Noting that "the lands [retained by the Indians] were arid and, without irrigation, were practically valueless," the Court then asked: "Did they give up all this? Did they reduce the area of their occupation and give up the waters which made it valuable or adequate?"[73] Indicating its scepticism of affirmative answers to these questions and reiterating the accepted rule that ambiguous treaty provisions should be resolved from the standpoint of the Indians, the Court then held that "the Government is asserting the rights of the Indians."[74] This holding was consonant with the Court's decision one year earlier in a fishing rights case, in which the Court held that the treaty with the Yakima Indians "was not a grant of rights to the Indians, but a grant of rights from them—a reservation of those not granted."[75] This right, said the Court at that time, "was intended to be continuing against the United States and its grantees as well as against the State and its grantees."[76] In subsequent years the courts have consistently upheld and applied the *Winters* reserved rights doctrine, the Supreme Court having specifically implemented it to define the rights of the Crow Indians to

---

70.   143 F. 740, 749 (9th Cir. 1906).

71.   Treaty With the Blackfoot Indians, Oct. 17, 1855, 11 Stat. 657. The court was also called on to consider the effect of an Act of April 15, 1874, ch. 96, 18 Stat. 28, which reduced the size of the reservation, and of the Act of May 1, 1888, which established its present boundaries. Ch. 213, 25 Stat. 113.

72.   Winters v. United States, 207 U.S. 564, 575 (1908).

73.   207 U.S. at 575.

74.   *Id.* The Court also rejected the argument that the admission of Montana to the union in 1889 abrogated the federal government's convenant with the Fork Belknap Indians. 207 U.S. at 577.

75.   United States v. Winans, 198 U.S. 371, 381 (1939).

76.   198 U.S. at 381-82.

the waters of the Big Horn River, a major tributary of the Yellowstone River.[77]

In 1908, the same year that the Supreme Court rendered the hallmark decision in *Winters*, the Court of Appeals for the Ninth Circuit, in *Conrad Investment Company v. United States*, placed other users on notice that the Indians retained for themselves "whatever water . . . may be reasonably necessary, *not only for present uses, but for future requirements*."[78] *Conrad* and subsequent cases have, therefore, consistently presented a caveat to all users of water in which Indians have a valid legal interest. Moreover, the Supreme Court has recognized that *Winters* rights are equally applicable to reservations that were created not by treaty but by executive order. Although earlier courts in reported cases had considered only Indian rights involving treaty reservations, a 1939 court of appeals decision attempted to limit Indian water rights on an executive order reservation to historic uses.[79] The Supreme Court, however, in *Arizona v. California*, without distinguishing between executive order and treaty reservations, held that the federal government could and did reserve rights to the use of water to meet present and future water requirements for Indians who were placed on executive order reservations.[80]

The *Arizona v. California* Court also rejected the argument that reservation needs should be fixed according to a population projection. Instead, the Court stated: "[T]he only feasible and fair way by which reserved water for the reservations can be measured is irrigable acreage."[81] There is, however, no reason in law, logic, or equity to limit Indian rights to agriculture. Although agricultural uses predominate in the Colorado River Basin, to which the Court addressed itself in *Arizona*, in the coal fields of the Yellowstone River Basin industrial uses may ultimately be foremost. Earlier courts recognized the validity of multiple purpose use,[82] and it has more recently been held that Indian rights to water may be exercised for any beneficial use.[83]

It will be recalled, too, that in *Winters* the Court recognized that the Indians, prior to the advent of the white man, had control of their lands and waters for beneficial use. In *Winters*, the court also recognized that on the reservations the Indians could turn both "to agriculture and the arts of civilization."[84] Surely this includes industrial as well as irrigation rights. Yet, it

---

77. United States v. Powers, 305 U.S. 527 (1939).
78. 161 F. 829, 832 (9th Cir. 1908). To underscore the measure of the rights thus reserved by the Indians, the court of appeals declared that its ruling recognized the Indian rights for future requirements and *"is clearly within the terms of the treaties as construed by the Supreme Court in the* Winters *case." Id.* (emphasis added).
79. United States v. Walker River Irrigation Dist., 104 F.2d 334, 340 (9th Cir. 1939).
80. 373 U.S. 546 (1963).
81. 373 U.S. at 601.
82. United States v. Walker River Irrigation Dist., 104 F.2d at 340.
83. United States v. Ahtanum Irrigation Dist., 330 F.2d 897, 915 (9th Cir. 1964).
84. 207 U.S. at 576.

is precisely this issue (and the desperate efforts of the Reclamation bureau to denegrate Indian rights) which divides the Department of the Interior at the present time. The Bureau of Reclamation espouses the argument of the industrial giants, asserting that Indian reserved water rights are limited to agricultural purposes. If this view prevails it would free water for use by coal interests. Furthermore, it would violate one of the basic principles of property law, as stated by Wiel,[85] namely, that rights to the use of water, being property rights, may be enjoyed and utilized for any purpose, so long as the rights of others are not impaired.

In addition to arguing that Indian reserved water rights are limited by the purposes to which they may be placed, state governments—and some federal agencies—have urged other restrictions on Indian water rights. They would, for example, limit Indian rights to waters within or bordering their reservations. The courts have consistently rejected any argument that states may authorize a user to divert waters from the tributary sources of rivers in which there are vested rights that would be impaired by such diversions.[86] As the Oregon Supreme Court stated: "The rights of prior appropriators from a stream cannot be impaired by subsequent appropriations of water from its tributaries."[87] These concepts have also been applied to Indian rights. Moreover, the courts have rejected the argument that failure on the part of the federal government to assert Indian water rights means that these rights have been forfeited.[88] There are, of course, many instances in which Indians were using water on their lands prior to white settlement.[89] Unfortunately, however, in many cases the interagency disputes[90] have delayed Indian water developments. That delay, however, in the eyes of the law, does not justify a

---

85.   1 S. WIEL, *supra* note 42 § 496, at 529.

86.   *See* Nebraska v. Wyoming, 325 U.S. 589, 618 (1945); Wyoming v. Colorado, 259 U.S. 419 (1921); Bean v. Morris, 221 U.S. 485 (1911); United States v. Ahtanum Irrigation Dist., 236 F.2d 321, 340 (9th Cir. 1956); Strickler v. Colorado Springs, 16 Colo. 61, 26 P. 313, 315 (1891); Richlands Irrigation Co. v. Westview Irrigation Co., 96 Utah 403, 80 P.2d 458, 465 (1938).

87.   Dry Gulch Ditch Co. v. Hutton, 170 Ore. 656, 133 P.2d 601, 611 (1943). *See also* Richland Irrigation Co. v. Westview Irrigation Co., 96 Utah at 403, 80 P.2d at 465.

88.   United States v. Ahtanum Irrigation Dist., 236 F.2d 321, 328 (9th Cir. 1956), *cert. denied*, 352 U.S. 988 (1957).

89.   The first venture in irrigation construction in the United States was the authorization by Congress in 1867 for the construction of a project on the Colorado River Indian Reservation. Act of March 2, 1867, ch. 173, 14 Stat. 492; *see* F. COHEN, HANDBOOK ON FEDERAL INDIAN LAW 248 (1942); Arizona v. California, 373 U.S. at 598-601. The Indian General Allotment Act of 1887, ch. 119, 24 Stat. 388 (codified in scattered sections of 25 U.S.C. (1970)), also provided for irrigation projects and the distribution of water among the "Indians residing" on the reservations. 25 U.S.C. § 381 (1970). In 1885, prior to the admission of Wyoming and Montana to the union, Congress appropriated money for irrigation on the Crow Reservation. United States v. Powers, 305 U.S. 527, 531 (1939). It has also been held that Congress, under the Reclamation Act of 1902, ch. 1039, 32 Stat. 388 (codified in scattered sections of 43 U.S.C. (1970)), did not give up to the states its power to regulate the waters granted or to limit delivery of water to 160 acres in a single ownership. Nebraska v. Wyoming, 325 U.S. 589, 615 (1945); Ivanhoe Irrigation Dist. v. McCracken, 357 U.S. 275, 292 (1958).

90.   *See* 2 JOINT ECONOMIC COMM., FEDERAL ENCROACHMENT ON INDIAN WATER RIGHTS AND

loss of Indian reserved rights. A far more serious question is rapidly emerging. The power of the federal government to apply reserved water rights on lands held in trust by the federal government for the development of national energy resources cannot be seriously questioned. What may be questioned is whether federal officials will act to protect Indian rights and to assist Indians in the exercise of those rights even as they try to implement a national energy program.

IV
FEDERAL RESOURCE PROGRAMS AND INDIAN WATER RIGHTS

The present concern with developing additional energy resources for the nation has focused renewed attention on the distribution of waters in the Yellowstone River Basin. Drastic changes were, however, transpiring in regard to national and state policies in this area well in advance of the present crisis. In particular, significant alterations were occurring in the water marketing programs of the federal agencies. Careful consideration of the legality of these programs is essential to a determination of water rights within the Yellowstone system.

Beginning in 1967 the Bureau of Reclamation initiated a program for the sale to industrial users of waters from the Big Horn River. Contracts were signed which purported to effectuate the sale of approximately 625,000 acre-feet of the water from the Big Horn River and the streams impounded in Big Horn Lake, a reservoir created by the Yellowtail Dam on the Crow Indian Reservation of Montana. Two years later, a contract with Sun Oil Company purported to provide 35,000 acre-feet of Big Horn River water from the Boysen Reservoir, located on the Wind River Indian Reservation in Wyoming. (The Wind River, a major tributary of the Big Horn, rises on the Wind River Reservation.) About two-thirds of the total amount contracted for would be used by the major oil companies for the development of coal resources in Wyoming.

Authority for these contracts was sought in the Federal Reclamation Act of 1902[91] and in the Yellowstone River Compact.[92] These laws, however, deal with agricultural uses and acknowledge the rights of prior appropriators. Recognizing that reclamation projects were in furtherance of agricultural development, Congress provided in the Act of February 25, 1920[93] that the sale of water by the Bureau of Reclamation for purposes other than irrigation is conditioned on a showing that no other practicable source of water exists for

THE IMPAIRMENT OF RESERVATION DEVELOPMENT, in TOWARD ECONOMIC DEVELOPMENT FOR NATIVE AMERICAN COMMUNITIES, 91ST CONG., 1ST SESS. 460 (1970).
91. Ch. 1093, 32 Stat. 388.
92. *See* references at notes 62 and 63 *supra.*
93. 43 U.S.C. § 521 (1970).

the proposed project, that such use would not adversely affect irrigation projects, and that "no water shall be furnished" for non-agricultural purposes if it is detrimental "to the rights of any prior appropriator."[94] Moreover, the sale of project water could not be made without the consent of the water users associations that usually administer the projects.

The 1920 Act must be read in the light of subsequent legislation envisioning the multiple use of water in the entire Missouri River Basin, of which the Yellowstone and Big Horn Rivers form a part. The Reclamation Project Act of 1939[95] authorized the sale of water from reclamation projects for municipal or miscellaneous purposes. Although the requirement for approval by the water users on the project was omitted, that power survived under the earlier acts. The 1939 Act vested in the Secretary of the Interior broad discretionary power to dispose of water from irrigation projects so long as it did not impair the efficiency of those projects. Moreover, the Secretary's powers obviously could not transcend the constitutional rights of users to be free from the seizure of vested rights without due process of law and the payment of just compensation.

Another fundamental act pertaining to the waters of the Yellowstone River Basin is the Flood Control Act of 1944.[96] It combines the powers of the Bureau of Reclamation and the Corps of Engineers by authorizing the Secretary of the Army, as chief administrator of the Corps of Engineers, "to make contracts with States, municipalities, private concerns, or individuals . . . for domestic and industrial uses for surplus water that may be available at any reservoir under the control of the Department of the Army."[97] That authority, however, is subject to the condition that "no contracts for such water shall adversely affect then existing lawful uses of such water."[98] In the Water Supply Act of 1958 Congress further authorized the Corps of Engineers or the Bureau of Reclamation to "impound water for present or anticipated future demand or need for municipal or industrial water."[99]

These statutes, however, leave crucial issues unresolved. They do not propose to authorize the seizure of Indian water rights pursuant to the national power of eminent domain. There is no suggestion in any of the acts that the rights of the Indians would be subject to infringement by those broad statutory schemes in the Reclamation Laws. Despite the multiple use provisions, it is, therefore, doubtful whether these statutes empower the Bureau of Reclamation to sell water from the Big Horn River and its tributaries in contravention of treaties or any other rights of the Indian tribes. Clearly the trust re-

---

94. *Id.*
95. 43 U.S.C. § 485(h)(c) (1970).
96. Ch. 1-8, 15, 58 Stat. 887 (codified in scattered sections of 16, 33, 43 U.S.C. (1970)).
97. 33 U.S.C. § 708 (1970).
98. *Id.*
99. 43 U.S.C. § 390(b) (1970).

sponsibility of the federal government to the Indian tribes involved is not to be abrogated or diminished without specific congressional authorization to that effect and provision for just compensation for any taking of Indian rights.

This power of "taking" is rendered still more questionable by reason of the legislative history of the Boysen and Big Horn Reservoirs.[100] The authorization for the Boysen Reservoir on the Wind River Indian Reservation followed protracted negotiations with the Arapahoe and Shoshone tribes living there. A careful review of the legislative history of the project and of the memorandum of understanding entered into by the tribes, the Secretary of the Interior, the Bureau of Reclamation, and the Bureau of Indian Affairs reveals no reference to the acquisition of the tribes' rights to the use of water or the subordination of these rights to the Boysen Dam Project. By the Act of July 18, 1952,[101] Congress declared its purpose "to vest title in the United States to certain lands and interests in lands of the Shoshone and Arapahoe Indian Tribes of the Wind River Reservation and to provide compensation" totaling $458,000. However, the Act did not affect any of the Indians' water rights, and indeed specifically provided that the conveyances and relinquishments shall be in accord with the above memorandum of understanding.

Moreover, the Supreme Court has held that the vested rights of a non-Indian water user may not be seized or disposed of by any agent of the United States. In *United States v. Gerlach Live Stock Company*, the Justice Department argued that under the Commerce Clause the United States, in furtherance of a federal reclamation project, "does not have to compensate for destruction" of private rights to the use of water when exercising its "superior navigation easement."[102] The Court, however, noted that the Reclamation Act of 1902[103] required the Secretary of the Interior to give "full recognition to every vested right under" state law.[104] Moreover, the Court took note that the Bureau of Reclamation had, in fact, paid compensation for rights to the use of water destroyed or impaired by the federal reclamation project. Without denying the superior rights of the federal government to control navigable streams the Court declared: "[W]e need not ponder whether, by virtue of a highly fictional navigation purpose, the Government could destroy the flow of a navigable stream and carry away its waters for sale to private interests without compensation to those deprived of them. We have never held that or anything like it . . . ."[105] Thus a federal agency may not take such property—including rights to the use of water acquired by prior appro-

---

100. S. Doc. Nos. 199, 247, 78th Cong., 2d Sess. (1944).
101. Ch. 946, 66 Stat. 780.
102. 339 U.S. at 736.
103. 43 U.S.C. § 383 (1970).
104. United States v. Gerlach Live Stock Co., 339 U.S. at 734.
105. 339 U.S. at 737.

priation[106]—without proper authorization and compensation. Similarly, it may be argued that in the absence of any authorization to purchase their reserved water rights, the Shoshone and Arapahoe tribes have retained those rights.

Further support for the Indians' water rights is found in the Court's interpretation of the 1868 treaty rights of the Shoshone. Referring to the government's fiduciary duty to the Indians, the Supreme Court, in *Shoshone Tribe of Indians v. United States* said: "The power does not extend so far as to enable the Government 'to give the tribal lands to others, or to appropriate them to its own purposes, without rendering, or assuming an obligation to render, just compensation . . . for that would not be an exercise of guardianship, but an act of confiscation.' "[107]

Similar limitations on the exercise of federal power over Indian water rights is found in the laws and treaties bearing on the creation of the Big Horn Reservoir on the Crow Reservation of Montana. Like the Arapahoe and Shoshone, the Crow maintain that, under the *Winters* doctrine, their water rights were reserved under their 1868 treaty with the United States. But unlike the amicable settlement worked out with the Wyoming tribes, the Crows challenged the invasion of their reservation by the Bureau of Reclamation[108] and demanded reasonable compensation for the Yellowtail Dam site. Congress did enact "taking" legislation,[109] which authorized payment of just compensation for the right, title, and interest of the Crows in "lands" required for the dam. A series of subsequent court cases[110] was addressed to the government's authority for taking the site, the extent of the right allegedly acquired, and the amount of just compensation owing.

The courts denied that the government held a "dominant servitude" or had "dominant control" over the Big Horn River within the Crow Reservation. Moreover, it was held that since the seizure by eminent domain of Crow property at the dam site was "for irrigation and recreation, as well as power production"[111] an increased sum should be awarded over and above the

---

106. Nichols v. McIntosh, 19 Colo. 22, 34 P. 278, 280 (1893).

107. 299 U.S. 476, 497 (1937). Congress has explicitly acted to prohibit "the sale, disposition, lease or encumbrance of tribal lands, interests in lands, or other tribal assets without the consent of the tribe . . . ." 25 U.S.C. § 476 (1970).

108. Precipitating the controversy was the announcement on October 24, 1976 by the Reclamation Bureau's Assistant Secretary of Water and Power of an intention to sell Humble Oil and Refining Company 50,000 acre-feet of water from the Yellowtail Reservoir for industrial use. It was further proposed that a total of 500,000 acre-feet of water be similarly disposed from the Big Horn Reservoir. There was no indication that the interests or approval of the Crow Tribe would be taken into account. Memorandum Respecting Crow Indian Rights to the Use of Water in the Big Horn River and its Tributaries from William H. Veeder to Harrison Loesch, Assistant Secretary who was in charge of Indian Affairs, Aug. 12, 1968.

109. *See* Act of July 15, 1958, Pub. L. No. 85-523, 72 Stat. 361.

110. United States v. 5677.94 Acres of Land, 162 F. Supp. 108 (D. Mont. 1958); Crow Indian Tribe of Indians of Montana v. United States, Civil No. 214 (D. Mont., filed Oct. 1, 1963).

111. United States v. 5677.94 Acres of Land, 162 F. Supp. at 108.

amount allowed in the legislation[112] authorizing a taking and compensation. In effect, then, the Crow were subjected at most only to a partial taking for specific and limited purposes. They were not subjected to a total divestiture of their property interests in their *Winters* rights in the Big Horn River which could justify allocation and sale of their waters by the Bureau of Reclamation. As the Supreme Court has stated: "The taking by condemnation of an interest less than a fee is familiar in the law of eminent domain."[113] This is certainly applicable in the Crow case.

CONCLUSION

Nowhere are the detrimental effects of piecemeal legislation relating to Indian rights more keenly felt than in the determination of water rights. Despite federal treaties and the existence of rights affirmed under *Winters*, the policy and practice of violation of their rights has continued to threaten the tribes of the Yellowstone River Basin. Pending litigation[114] by the northern Cheyenne and Crow tribes to protect their rights in the Tongue and Big Horn Rivers may clarify certain issues relating to these tribes.[115] However, the ultimate determination will probably turn on the application of federal policies formed in the face of the energy crises. Moreover, the historic reluctance of the Justice and Interior Departments to advocate Indian rights continues to render the protection of Indian reserved water rights difficult.

One issue is clear: It is detrimental to all concerned to persist in formulating grandiose schemes for developing coal-related industries in the region on the basis of highly misleading water supply projections that totally disregard the present and future demands on alleged firm water supplies.[116] Federal agencies often fail to present accurately the facts concerning the highly fluctuating water supplies and the needs of those already holding title of vested rights, either Indian or non-Indian. Mistakes in these estimates have disastrous consequences for local water users who are virtually without remedies once water has been committed by powerful political forces to uses which exceed anticipated supplies.

For a period of time a moratorium was imposed by the Secretary of the

---

112. Act of July 15, 1958, Pub. L. No. 85-523, 72 Stat. 361.

113. United States v. Cress, 243 U.S. 316, 328-29 (1916).

114. The Northern Cheyenne Tribe v. Tongue River Water Users Assoc., Civil No. 76-6 (D. Mont., filed Jan. 30, 1975); United States v. Tongue River Water Users Assoc., Civil No. 75-20 (D. Mont. filed Mar. 7, 1975); United States v. Bighorn Line Canal, Civil No. 75-34 (D. Mont., filed Apr. 17, 1975).

115. Of particular importance is the question whether the Indians are restricted to relief in the state of Montana or may also be granted relief in Wyoming, through whose territory their waters flow. *See* Willey v. Decker, 11 Wyo. 496, 73 P. 210 (1903).

116. *See* REPORT ON MONTANA-WYOMING AQUEDUCTS, *supra* note 1. *See also* U.S. DEP'T OF THE INTERIOR, WATER FOR ENERGY MANAGEMENT TEAM, REPORT ON WATER FOR ENERGY IN THE NORTHERN GREAT PLAINS AREA WITH EMPHASIS ON THE YELLOWSTONE RIVER BASIN 1-7 (1975).

Interior on sales of the water of the Big Horn River by the Bureau of Reclamation. Congress, too, has held comprehensive hearings on rights to the use of water in the entire Upper Missouri River Basin.[117] Appropriate legislation would, of course, go a long way toward resolving the complex factual, legal, and economic issues that have been raised by alternative energy programs affecting the Yellowstone River Basin. However, the suspension, early in 1976, of the moratorium on coal leasing increased the pressure to invade the rights of the Crow and Wind River Indians of the Big Horn as well as those of the Cheyenne on the Tongue River.[118] Even as comprehensive legislation is entertained and the Secretary of the Interior's promise to protect the interests of all western Indians is put to the test, the policies and principles established should not fail to conform to the concepts of water law reviewed here——concepts which are deeply rooted in the nation's history and Constitution.

---

117. Hearing set for June 26, 1975, reset for July 18, 1975. *See also* the discussion of these issues in the nomination proceedings of Interior Secretary Stanley K. Hathaway and particularly statements of Senator Metcalf in *Hearings on the Nomination of Stanley K. Hathaway to be Secretary of the Interior Before the Senate Comm. on Interior and Insular Affairs*, 94th Cong., 1st Sess. 82-93 (1975).

118. On the new regulations affecting the lease of federal lands for coal mining see 43 C.F.R. § 3040, *as amended*, § 3041, 49 Fed. Reg. 20252-273 (1976). *See also* N.Y. Times, May 12, 1976, at 68, col. 1. The Supreme Court also held that the Interior Department does not have to prepare an environmental impact statement on the regional effects on coal development in the northern Great Plains. Kleppe v. Sierra Club, 44 U.S.L.W. 5104 (U.S. June 28, 1976).

INDIAN WATER RIGHTS IN THEORY AND PRACTICE: NAVAJO EXPERIENCE IN THE COLORADO RIVER BASIN*

MONROE E. PRICE†

GARY D. WEATHERFORD††

Although Indian water rights are of critical economic importance, the nature and scope of these rights remain unclear. The Supreme Court has addressed itself to the issue infrequently, and most commentators have limited their discussions to an exegesis of the appellate arguments rather than engage in an analysis of the broader nature and context of these rights. Reservation water rights are of a very special nature: A right to water does not necessarily include a right to the capital investment necessary to realize the economic benefit of an entitlement, and limits on the uses of the water may be at odds with the original purposes of the reservation.[1] Because of recent and forthcoming federal legislation,[2] state unilateral action, and judicial decisions[3] on these questions, it is essential to understand how the Indians have

---

* Research for this article was supported by Grant No. NSF GL 34833 to the Legal-Institutional Subproject, and by Grant No. NSF 34832 to the Anthropology Subproject, of the Lake Powell Research Project from the Division of Environmental Systems and Resources of RANN (Research Applied to National Needs) in the National Science Foundation. Any opinions, findings, conclusions or recommendations expressed in this publication are those of the authors and do not necessarily reflect the views of the National Science Foundation. Invaluable research assistance was provided by John R. McCain, Political Science graduate student and Ph.D. candidate, University of Arizona, and Richard Conn, law student at the U.C.L.A. School of Law.

† Professor, School of Law, U.C.L.A.

†† Member, California Bar. Since this manuscript was submitted before Mr. Weatherford became Deputy Secretary for Resources, State of California, the views expressed herein are his own and do not necessarily represent those of his new employer.

1. For the argument that *Winters* doctrine rights may be applied to non-agricultural uses, see Leaphart, *Sale and Lease of Indian Water Rights*, 33 MONT. L. REV. 266, 275 (1972); Ranquist, *The Effect of Changes in Place and Nature of Use of Indian Rights to Water Reserved Under the "Winters Doctrine,"* 5 NAT. RES. L. 34, 37 (1971); Sondheim & Alexander, *Federal Indian Water Rights: A Retrogression to Quasi-Riparianism?*, 34 S. CAL. L. REV. 1 (1960); Veeder, *Winters Doctrine Rights—Keystone of National Program for Western Land and Water Conservation and Utilization*, 26 MONT. L. REV. 149, 170 (1965).

2. *See* recommendation for a "National Water Rights Procedure Act" and an Indian water rights act, in NATIONAL WATER COMM'N, WATER POLICIES FOR THE FUTURE 461-71, 477-83 (1973), detailing legislative proposals geared toward quantification of Indian water rights. *See also* S. 3298, 94th Cong., 1st Sess. (1976) (settlement of the water rights of the five Central Arizona Indian Tribes and providing for water projects which would permit those Indian groups to exercise their water rights).

3. Of particular importance is the decision in Colorado River Water Conservation Dist. v. United States, 96 S. Ct. 1236 (1976) which held that the McCarran Amendment, 43 U.S.C. § 666 (1970), permits the determination in state court of reserved water rights held by the United States on behalf of Indians.

had to bargain over their legal rights in the face of limited economic alternatives and the consequent difficulties that have been posed for implementation.

One of the most interesting contemporary opportunities to study the interplay between the definition and implementation of economic rights of an Indian reservation is provided by the experience of the Navajo tribe during the 1960s. The construction of Glen Canyon dam and Lake Powell has made possible major power projects requiring substantial use of water. To secure water for these uses, it was necessary to determine the extent to which the Navajo Reservation would share in the benefits of the river and its tributaries. The procurement of water rights to be used in the Navajo Generating Station at Page, Arizona became a vehicle for bargaining over the extent of Navajo entitlement to Colorado River water. In addition, the history of the Navajo Indian Irrigation Project provides an extraordinary opportunity to assess the difficulties involved in implementing a right once defined and bargained for in the context of a reservation dependent on federal largess for the financing of large-scale development.

Close scrutiny of these major incidents in the definition of economic rights on the Navajo reservation is important because of underlying assumptions about the status of Indian reservations and federal and tribal policy toward economic and cultural self-sufficiency. Since the nineteenth century, a basic principle of fundamental fairness in dealing with indigenous people in the United States has been the insulation of reservation resources from the constraints of the marketplace,[4] state taxation,[5] and state jurisdiction[6] at least until the Indian communities living on those lands are socially and culturally prepared fully to exploit those resources.[7] The growth of the guardian-ward ideal, buttressed by the concept of Indian tribal sovereignty, suggests that reservation lands were not subject to the laws of the states with respect to resource allocation. Yet at different times and places the principle of reservation insulation gave way to other forces, primarily the unyielding need

---

4. See Johnson v. McIntosh, 21 U.S. (8 Wheat.) 542 (1823).

5. See, e.g., The Kansas Indians, 72 U.S. (5 Wall.) 737 (1867), holding that, at least absent congressional consent, Kansas could not impose a property tax upon Indian lands. See also N. Margold's 1940 solicitor's opinion. Margold, Indians Not Taxed—Interpretation of Constitutional Provisions, 57 Interior Dec. 195 (1940).

6. Worcester v. Georgia, 31 U.S. (6 Pet.) 515 (1832).

7. In United States v. Clapox, 35 F. 575, 577 (9th Cir. 1888), Judge Deady based the reservation concept upon an educational function: "In fact, the reservation itself is in the nature of a school, and the Indians are gathered there . . . for the purpose of acquiring the habits, ideas, and aspirations which distinguish the civilized from the uncivilized man." The consequences of this view are explored in M. PRICE, LAW AND THE AMERICAN INDIAN 88-89 (1973). The rehabilitation strategy was reiterated in Winters v. United States, 207 U.S. 564, 576 (1908), where the Supreme Court explicitly recognized an early government policy aimed at changing the stereo-Indian lifestyle, of altering the "habits and wants of a nomadic and uncivilized people" in order to engender "a pastoral and civilized people."

of the settler community and their abundant descendants to utilize the reserved resources themselves. In the nineteenth century, this territorial imperative was reflected in the removal policy,[8] and later in the breaking up
of reservations through the Indian General Allotment Act[9] and transforma-
tion of the Indian Territory into modern states.[10] In the twentieth century,
the conflict between the reservation theory and the demand for resources has
sometimes been more subtle, and nowhere is this conflict more intense than
in the struggle for the waters of the Colorado River in the semiarid Southwest.

To situate the present conflict over Indian rights, it is important to understand the legislative and hydrological context of water distribution in the
Colorado River.[11] The first Colorado River Compact,[12] drafted in 1922, had
as its objective the apportionment of the Colorado River System[13] between
the hydrologically defined Upper and Lower Basins of the river.[14] This was
achieved when all of the basin states agreed that, of the estimated sixteen
million acre-feet average annual flow of the river,[15] the Upper and Lower
Basin each had the right to the beneficial consumptive use of 7.5 million
acre-feet, and the Lower Basin had the additional right to increase its beneficial consumptive use by one million acre-feet annually. The 1922 Compact
thus served to apportion the average flow of the river between the Upper
and Lower Basins, rather than among individual states. However, since not
all of the boundaries of basin states correspond with the hydrologically drawn
division between the Upper and Lower Basins, several states, including Arizona, have lands in both the Upper and Lower Basins. It is of great consequence for the present discussion, therefore, that almost all of Arizona's
lands within the Upper Basin are within the boundaries of the Navajo Reservation.

---

8. *See generally* G. FOREMAN, INDIAN REMOVAL (1932).

9. Indian General Allotment Act of 1887, ch. 119, 24 Stat. 288, *as amended*, 25 U.S.C. § 331
(1970). It has been estimated that during the interval spanning the passage of the Act and 1934,
when the allotment process was largely halted, tribal landholdings were reduced from approximately 138 million acres to about 48 million acres. *See* W. BROPHY & S. ABERLE, THE INDIAN,
AMERICA'S UNFINISHED BUSINESS 20 (1966).

10. *See, e.g.*, A. DEBO, THE RISE AND FALL OF THE CHOCTAW REPUBLIC 269 (2d ed. 1967).

11. A significant aid to that understanding is Meyers, *The Colorado River*, 19 STAN. L. REV. 1
(1966).

12. The Colorado River Compact, 70 CONG. REC. 324 (1928), consented to by Congress in
the Boulder Canyon Project Act, 43 U.S.C. § 617(1) (1970), was made effective by presidential
proclamation June 25, 1929, 46 Stat. 3000.

13. The Colorado River "system" is defined in article II(a) of the Compact as "that portion
of the Colorado River and its tributaries within the United States." Colorado River Compact,
art. II(a), 70 CONG. REC. 324 (1928).

14. The Upper Basin is comprised of lands from which water drains into the mainstream
above Lee Ferry, Arizona; the Lower Basin lands drain into the mainstream below this point.

15. This estimate, based on unusually high flows in the years immediately preceding 1922, is
approximately two million acre-feet per year higher than what is currently believed to be the
average annual flow. *See* Weatherford & Jacoby, *Impact of Energy Development on the Law of the
Colorado River*, 15 NAT. RES. J. 171, 183 table 1 (1975).

The second interstate compact affecting the law of the river is the Upper Colorado River Basin Compact of 1948.[16] This agreement elaborates on the 1922 Compact by apportioning the waters of the Upper Basin among the individual states involved.[17] States asserting rights under this apportionment scheme must have a beneficial use for a corresponding amount of water. Thus, the apportionment of the 1948 Compact in no case gives a state the right to divert water it cannot use, or to prevent another state from beneficially using such water.

The 1948 Compact thus appears to effect a final and comprehensive apportionment of Upper Basin waters. But the Upper Basin Compact also provides that "[n]othing in this Compact shall be construed as: (a) Affecting the obligations of the United States of America to Indian tribes."[18] The agreement, however, was only among the states; the affected reservations were not invited to the bargaining table. It was not determined how extensive the Indian rights were or against which state's apportionment they should be charged. Clearly the states acting alone could not agree to a diminution of Navajo rights. Navajo rights could, of course, be charged against the Arizona entitlement. But if the Navajos have a right in excess of Arizona's share, the effect would be to alter the apportionments of all other Upper Basin states. It is that legal possibility that came to be of significance in the 1960s.

In order to understand the nature and implications of competing claims to the waters of the Colorado River, it is particularly important to understand how the uncertainties of existing water law have forced tribes like the Navajo to bargain over their apparent rights in an attempt to achieve greater economic security. Indeed, a realistic assessment of the Indian's legal rights would be incomplete without an appreciation of why, under present circumstances, the implementation of bargained-for rights, though economically advantageous, may be achieved at the cost of weakening the political and cultural integrity of the tribe. It is in this complex interaction of social, economic, and political factors that an understanding of the legal concept of Indian water rights must necessarily be sought.

---

16. Act of April 6, 1949, ch. 48, 63 Stat. 31.

17. The Upper Colorado River Basin Compact, Act of April 6, 1949, ch. 48, art. III, § 2, 63 Stat. 31, grants Arizona 50,000 acre-feet per year of water. The balance was divided among the remaining states in the following proportions: Colorado 51.75 per cent, New Mexico 11.25 per cent, Utah 23.00 per cent, and Wyoming 14.00 per cent.

18. *Id.* art. XIX, 63 Stat. 42. Identical language can be found in its predecessor, Colorado River Compact, art VII, 70 CONG. REC. 324, 325 (1928). The clause might easily be construed as "a negative declaration to the effect that Indian rights are outside the reach of the interstate accord." Weatherford & Jacoby, *supra* note 15, at 179. However, the specificity of the state apportionments allocated by the Compact, as well as its directive that those apportionments are to be charged with Indian uses, suggest that that construction is by no means free from doubt. *See* R. Conn, Tribal Water Rights and the Navajo Generating Plant: An Analysis of Legal Issues 8-9, 1974 (unpublished manuscript on file with Professor Price).

I

THE *WINTERS* DOCTRINE REVISITED:
RIGHTS AND UNCERTAINTIES

Indian water rights are to the late twentieth century what Indian land rights were to the nineteenth, and many of the same utilitarian arguments applied to the scarcity of land have been applied to water in the last several decades.[19] The question often becomes not who owns the water but how can it best be used: for the reservations and their relatively few inhabitants or for the industrial metropolises of the Southwest.[20] Water rights are as critical for Indian well-being and development now as land rights were in the late nineteenth century.[21] But as with land, Congress has assumed enormous powers in the definition of Indian rights to water.[22] And the pressures and techniques to encourage Indian consent to the modification of Indian water rights are strikingly reminiscent of practices in the nineteenth century.

A.   The Issue of Quantum

A sharp contrast exists between the water law that has developed in the western states and on the Indian lands. Under the western doctrine of "prior

---

19.   The arguments are directed toward a common theme—the use of a limited and hence valuable resource—and reflect a common pattern. In assessing the validity of a 1908 agreement between the federal government and non-Indian landowners, which allocated 75 per cent of the flow of Ahtanum Creek to the latter and 25 per cent to the Yakima Indians, the Court of Appeals for the Ninth Circuit mirrored that pattern by briefly reviewing the history of federal dealings with the American Indian:

> That history largely supports the statement: "From the very beginnings of this nation, the chief issue around which federal Indian policy has revolved has been, not how to assimilate the Indian nations whose lands we usurped, but how best to transfer Indian lands and resources to non-Indians."

United States v. Ahtanum Irrigation Dist., 236 F.2d 321, 337 (9th Cir. 1956).

20.   The question is not a novel one. Underlying the legal contentions pressed by the non-Indian users in Winters v. United States, 207 U.S. 564 (1908), was the equitable claim that recognition of an implicitly reserved Indian right to water would ultimately destroy established Montana communities dependent upon the continued diversion of water from the Milk River. The tremendous amplification simply in the number of competing interests occasioned by the urban explosions that have occurred in the Southwest since the *Winters* decision adds to the difficulty of resolving the question of how a finite water resource can best be utilized.

> The urban-based "environmentalist" and "recreationist" demands clean water. The urban "voter" demands that limits be put on subsidies for agricultural development (while insisting upon low food prices). The urban "consumer" sustains a high-energy lifestyle which sends the electric utilities to the banks of the Colorado in search of powerplant sites. These often times inconsistent demands add up to an urban assault of major proportions on the rural reclamation ethic.

Weatherford & Jacoby, *supra* note 15, at 174.

21.   "Seize and take from the Indian people, by whatever means, their life-sustaining Winters doctrine rights to water and you take from them the basis for their continued existence as a separate and distinct people." Veeder, *Indian Water Rights in the Upper Missouri River Basin*, 48 N.D.L. REV. 617, 618 (1972). *See also* Young, *Interagency Conflicts of Interests: The Peril to Indian Water Rights*, 1972 LAW & SOCIAL ORDER 313.

22.   25 U.S.C. § 564 (1970).

appropriation," one may assert title to a specified quantity of water only as long as actual, beneficial use is made of that water.[23] Moreover, in times of shortage, a senior appropriator's right is satisfied in full before the junior appropriator obtains his share. It is a harsh, pragmatic, pioneer doctrine firmly rooted in the concept of present beneficial use.

By contrast, Indian water rights depend on future need rather than on present use. It was in *Winters v. United States*[24] that this right was first enunciated, and it is from this decision that many of the ambiguities of Indian water rights stem. In granting an injunction barring non-Indian users from interfering with the flow of the Milk River to the Fort Belknap Reservation, the Court held that, though the treaty establishing the reservation was silent as to water rights, the government's reservation of lands for the Indians implicitly carried with it a reservation of the water needed to make these lands "adequate and valuable" for their inhabitants. The Court further asserted that the rights of the Indians to such waters could not be diminished by application of state law.[25] However, the parties did not argue, and the Court did not decide, the precise standard for measuring the quantity of water reserved, and subsequent courts have not been able to agree on such a standard.[26]

The enormous implications of *Winters* and its potential for conflict between Indian and non-Indian users were highlighted when the issue was presented again in *Arizona v. California*.[27] Adopting the Master's finding that the tribes involved had a valid claim to about one million acre-feet annually[28] of the Lower Colorado River, the Court, reaffirming the reasoning in *Winters*, held that the United States "intended to deal fairly with the Indians by reserving for them the waters without which their lands would have been useless."[29] This reservation was necessary because economic competition for water, at that time, would have been ruinous.

Despite its support of *Winters*, *Arizona v. California* did not necessarily eliminate uncertainty concerning its meaning. First, there is the issue of quantum. Quantum (when coupled with priority) determines the strength of the Indian bargaining position with private or public agencies. The literature

---

23. Arizona v. California, 373 U.S. 546, 555 (1963); Tweedy v. Texas Co., 286 F. Supp. 383, 385 (D. Mont. 1968). *See generally* Veeder, *supra* note 1.

24. 207 U.S. 564.

25. "The power of the Government to reserve the waters and exempt them from appropriation under the state laws is not denied, and could not be." Winters v. United States, 207 U.S. at 577.

26. United States v. Ahtanum Irrigation Dist., 236 F.2d at 321; United States v. Walker River Irrigation Dist., 104 F.2d 334 (9th Cir. 1939); Conrad Investment Co. v. United States, 161 F. 829 (9th Cir. 1908).

27. 373 U.S. 546.

28. Actually the decree authorized one million acre-feet or that amount of water sufficient to irrigate the practicably irrigable acreage, whichever was less.

29. 373 U.S. at 600. *See also* M. PRICE, *supra* note 7, at 316-18, discussing *Arizona v. California* and quoting, *id.* at 317 from REPORT OF THE SPECIAL MASTER IN *Arizona v. California* 259 (1960).

abounds with the assertion that *Winters* implies the existence of automatically reserved water rights on Indian reservations and everywhere demands the same quantum test in determining how much water was reserved.[30] A close reading of the cases suggests that so clear and simple a definition of the *Winters* rights is not necessarily accurate. Under the *Winters* doctrine, "the basic question for determination was one of intent—whether the waters of the stream were intended to be reserved for the use of the Indians, or whether the lands only were reserved."[31] What is the exact holding of *Arizona v. California* with respect to quantum? The Supreme Court's definition of the Master's finding was that the water reserved "was intended to satisfy the future as well as the present needs of the Indian Reservations [and that] enough water was reserved to irrigate all the practicably irrigable acreage on the reservations.[32] In answer to Arizona's contention that the quantum standard should be fixed by the number of Indians, the court stated that "[h]ow many Indians there will be and what their future needs will be can only be guessed. We have concluded . . . that the only feasible and fair way by which reserved water for the reservations can be measured is irrigable acreage."[33] But the Court stopped short of making the irrigable acreage standard a universal and timeless test.[34]

The uncertainty of standard is also linked to the kind of decree a court will write as a result of its application. If the standard is one of potential irrigable acreage or future population, non-Indian water users will be unable to develop precise plans.[35] If the standard is calibrated on the basis of the

---

30. *See, e.g.*, Veeder, *supra* note 1.

31. United States v. Walker River Irrigation Dist., 104 F.2d at 336. Furthermore, the courts seem guided by the traditional principle that "treaties with the Indians and statutes disposing of property for that benefit have uniformly been given a liberal interpretation favorable to the Indian wards." 104 F.2d at 337. However, an intent must still be discovered, and all intents need not be the same. If intent, rather than a general rule of law, is the basis for *Winters*, each case must be looked at separately to determine the quantum standard. *Cf.* Cappaert v. United States, 44 U.S.L.W. 4756, 4759 (1976).

32. Arizona v. California, 373 U.S. at 600.

33. 373 U.S. at 601.

34. Indeed, the few words of the Court are themselves unsatisfactory. It is certainly true that the future Indian populations on the reservation "can only be guessed." But the number can be guessed with some range of accuracy, probably enough to use in fashioning a decree. As to the second part of the Court's modesty, its inability to define "what their future needs might be," the Court was merely begging the question. For as the cases and discussions of the Indian water right indicate, the critical issue involves the identification of those "future needs" that must be satisfied from the reserved rights.

35. A study by Sondheim and Alexander indicated that the amount of water reserved under an irrigable acreage test would often be many times the amount of water reserved under a test which was based on current usage and Indian population trends. Sondheim & Alexander, *supra* note 1, at 23. In one case, for example, the irrigable acreage on the Walker River Paiute Reservation was approximately ten thousand acres; the acreage actually cultivated was 2,100. United States v. Walker River Irrigation Dist., 104 F.2d 334. Almost five times as much water would be reserved under the *Arizona v. California* irrigable acreage standard. As Sondheim and Alexander put it, rather dramatically, "we are dealing with a problem where choice of a legal

amount of water needed by a stabilized population to continue cultivation of their lands,[36] no leeway will exist for increases in population. And if the order implementing a given standard is modifiable[37] or seeks to achieve finality,[38] it will partake of the same uncertainty or rigidity. It may be argued that the *Arizona* Court did not hold that the tribes had a perfected right to the flow measured by irrigable acreage, but rather that the Court was unable to determine a better method for ascertaining quantum.[39] Congress might authorize a hearing process in which a range of standards could be drawn on in formulating orders for different situations. But for the moment, the standard for measuring the quantum of reserved water remains unresolved.[40]

B. Purpose and Intent: The Federal Strategy

The measure of Indian water rights is closely linked to the federal purposes underlying the reservation of these rights. If the interest of the federal government is in fostering Indian agriculture, a very different entitlement will be involved than if the federal purpose is one of economic rehabilitation across a broad front. It remains unclear whether the quantum of water may vary with the definition of rehabilitation or changes in federal strategy. Although no answer has received judicial approval, a flexible approach is more consistent with national history. Reservations were established in part to aid the Indian community prepare for life in a white dominated society. The purpose of reservations might, then, vary somewhat from decade to decade.[41] If, under *Winters*, one must look to the original purpose to determine an intention to reserve waters, it may be argued that the federal government, in furtherance of its general rehabilitative purpose, must be prepared to shift water to municipal and industrial uses when such action is itself in the interests of the reservation. The *Winters* reserved rights would, then,

---

theory may well mean the difference between survival and dehydrated extinction for competing non-Indian irrigators." Sondheim & Alexander, *supra* at 24.

36. This was the standard applied in United States v. Walker River Irrigation Dist., 104 F.2d 334.

37. A flexible order was provided in Conrad Investment Co. v. United States, 161 F. 829 (9th Cir. 1908).

38. It is, however, important to distinguish finality from quantum. A court can take an approach which is liberal to the reservation in terms of the quantum of water available in the future, but which resolves the question finally. On the other hand, a court can award only modest in praesenti rights, leaving open the decree for modification on a showing of need by the reservation.

39. *Cf.* Burt, *Miranda and Title II: A Morganatic Marriage*, 1969 SUPREME COURT REV. 81, discussing Katzenbach v. Morgan, 384 U.S. 641 (1966); Pyramid Lake Paiute Tribe v. Morton, 354 F. Supp. 252 (D.D.C. 1973).

40. Not only the standard is at issue: there is also the question of time. Is the *Winters* right completely open-ended? Is it open-ended only until the time of quantification, whenever that occurs? Or does the time involved vary with each case?

41. *Cf.* United States v. Clapox, 35 F. 575, 577 (9th Cir. 1888).

constitute a class of uses any one of which could be important for the "improvement" of the Indians residing on the reservation.[42]

C. Alienation and Off-Reservation Use of Reserved Water Rights

Complicating the issue of the uses to which Indians may apply their water rights is the question of alienating these rights. No legislation specifically prohibits the alienation of Indian water rights. The Supreme Court, in *United States v. Powers*,[43] upheld the action of a lower court which had determined that non-Indian successors in interest to Indian allottees also hold the water rights implicitly conveyed to those allottees when the latter obtained titles to parcels of reservation land ceded by the tribe. However, the Supreme Court declined to define the precise nature or extent of the successors' rights in the water. A tribe may be able to lease or sell confirmed rights but it may not thereby be able to add to the quantity of water to which it is entitled.[44]

A similar question arises as to the location of use of reserved water rights. It is unlikely that under *Winters* a tribe could claim that it was going into the wholesale water leasing business as part of the "future needs of the reservation" and that all downstream users would thereafter have to lease water from the tribe. But even where a limitation has been set on quantum, it is unclear whether the exploitation of reservation water must be limited to the reservation itself. On the one hand, it may be argued that since tribes can use the proceeds from land leases for off-reservation investment so, too, it should be able to apply its water rights to various locations. On the other hand, if the purpose of the right is to make reservation lands livable, off-reservation uses could be held impermissible. Picking at the bones of *Winters* provides little guidance. Uncertainty about alienability and location of use renders it difficult for a tribe to assess the validity of a particular transaction and contributes to the hazards of the bargaining process.

D. Duration of Reservation Immunity

To say that there are reserved rights does not say how long those rights are reserved. One threat to these rights is the possibility that the Congress

---

42. If the shift in federal purpose resulted in an increased quantum of water for Indian use non-Indian users would, of course, raise the usual objection of uncertainty. Use does not, however, need to be linked solely to irrigable purposes. As in the Pyramid lake situation, one might look to the original purpose of maintaining the lake as a fishery to determine the quantum reserved, and then maintain that quantum even if the lake is later used for tourism and recreation.

43. 305 U.S. 527 (1939).

44. Tweedy v. Texas Co., 286 F. Supp. 383, 385 (D. Mont. 1968) explicitly suggests that possibility: "It seems clear . . . that need and use are prerequisite to any water rights on Indian reservations." The decision, however, has been severely criticized as being inconsistent with the established view of *Winters* doctrine rights as reserved rights distinct from appropriative rights. *See* Leaphart, *supra* note 1.

will terminate the reservation.[45] It could be argued that the purpose of the reservation was to give to the tribe a limited period of immunity from the rigors of the appropriation doctrine and state regulation. To be sure, under an approach which viewed such immunity as limited in time, it would be difficult for courts, unaided by Congress, to determine what the limit should be.[46] Yet we know that the trust of land is terminable and that Congress can ordinarily determine that an Indian resource can be subjected to state laws without effectuating a taking.[47] Congress could state that, as of a particular time, the community's entitlement to water would be subject to state regulation.[48] To avoid destruction of vested rights, the Congress would be obliged to state that existing, beneficially used rights, as quantified under *Winters* and *Arizona*, would maintain the vitality and priority held prior to the legislation and would be protected against taking by the fifth amendment.[49]

This approach is, however, wholly at war with the widely accepted view. It is more generally regarded that the *Winters* reservation was not only an immunity from state regulation, but the reservation of a fixed right by a collective group to a variable amount of water, the terms of the right being largely governed by the settlement.[50] Without clarification, however, the threat of subjecting reservations to state water laws will continue to affect the bargaining posture and planning capabilities of the Indian tribes.

1. *Technology*

Another uncertainty is whether changed technology is to be taken into account in defining the scope of the reserved right. When the Navajo Reservation was created, most Colorado River water was inaccessible because its

---

45. *See* the infamous H.R. Con. Res. 108, 83d Cong., 1st Sess. (1953).
46. *See* United States v. Cisna, 25 F. Cas. 422 (No. 14,795) (C.C. Ohio 1835); *cf.* United States v. Bailey, 24 F. Cas. 937 (No. 14,795) (C.C. Tenn. 1834).
47. *See* Johnson v. McIntosh, 21 U.S. (8 Wheat.) 542 (1823); *cf.* Goldberg, *Public Law 280: The Limits of State Jurisdiction Over Reservation Indians*, 22 U.C.L.A.L. REV. 535 (1975). Congressional action subjecting a tribe to state and local jurisdiction must, however, be interpreted strictly. Menominee Tribe v. United States, 391 U.S. 404 (1968); Santa Rosa Band of Indians v. King's County, Civil No. 74-1565 (9th Cir., filed Nov. 3, 1975). Since the Supreme Court has not determined that the federal government has authorized the states to impose zoning and other land use restrictions on Indian land there is no holding determining that a grant of regulatory jurisdiction to the state constitutes a compensable taking. *Cf.* Snohomish County v. Seattle Disposal Co., 389 U.S. 1016 (1967) (Douglas, J. dissenting from denial of certiorari).
48. Compare deferment of state taxation of lands conveyed to Alaska natives under the Alaska Native Claims Settlement Act, 43 U.S.C.A. § 1620(d) (1971).
49. Compare the concept of "recognized" and "unrecognized" rights to land in determining fifth amendment compensability. Northwestern Bands of Shoshone Indians v. United States, 324 U.S. 335, 355 (1945) (Jackson, J. concurring). *See also* 28 U.S.C. § 1360(b) (1970), which prohibits state courts assuming jurisdiction under 28 U.S.C. § 1360(a) (1970) from alienating, encumbering or taxing Indian property (specifically including water rights) that is held in trust, and forbids their regulating such property in a manner inconsistent with federal treaties.
50. *See* Veeder, *Indian Prior and Paramount Rights versus State Rights*, 51 N.D.L. REV. 107 (1974).

flow was deep in canyons. Enormous investment and the construction of Glen Canyon Dam now make the water more readily available.

Limiting technology seems a less principled way of defining the water right than looking to the purpose of the reservation. If the purpose of immunity from the doctrine of prior appropriation were to allow technology to catch up with the needs of reservation lands, a principle forcing inefficient uses of water resources would be intolerable. On the other hand, technology undoubtedly has a role to play in determining what is "practicably irrigable." It might be established that a tribe can employ whatever technology it chooses to extract and deliver water, but the quantum will be limited to what seemed practicably irrigable with reference to a technology at a fixed date. But what is practicable is a function both of technology and cost. It is hard to read into the *Winters* right a limit on the amount that the federal government can expend to assist in diversion projects and in the construction of works for beneficial uses. Similarly, the United States must be free to develop and apply its water technology to Indian reservations without judicial limitation on congressional appropriation.

A somewhat different issue is presented where private non-Indian users on the reservation apply vast resources and technology to the exploitation of the Indian right. One might argue that the *Winters* right was limited by the capacity of the tribe and the willingness of the federal government to provide the capital to effectuate the right. Circumscribing exploitation of the right by limiting the class of institutions that could participate would have been an effective way of placing a ceiling on the right. Such a rule would have a political safety valve for non-Indian competitors for water since they would have a significant, indeed dominant, say in the legislative process. By opening exploitation to private interests, control is lost over the extent to which "future needs" can burgeon.

A remote analogy can be found in state regulation of off-reservation hunting and fishing based on the mechanism used by the Indians in the exercise of their right. Many states have, for example, attempted to prohibit Indians from using set nets or gill nets at off-reservation sites. The *Puyallup* case dealt with the power of the state, in its pursuit of conservationist goals, to limit the use of set nets along the Columbia River.[51] Courts were asked to interpret the basic right of the Indians by determining whether a sharp advance in the means of exploiting the right could be prohibited or regulated. If subsistence was the basis of the right, then, it was thought, the state could ensure that techniques incompatible with subsistence fishing could be prohibited. On the other hand, in the most recent cases,[52] the courts seem to

---

51. Puyallup Tribe v. Department of Game, 391 U.S. 392 (1968); Department of Game v. Puyallup Tribe, 414 U.S. 44 (1973).

52. United States v. Washington, 384 F. Supp. 312 (W.D. Wash. 1974), *aff'd*, 520 F.2d 676

suggest that what was reserved was a quantum of fish—a fishery—and there is a positive duty on the part of the state to assure that the fishery is available. Technology is not so important as the quantum expectation.

II
PRINCIPLES IN CONTEXT

All of this is part and parcel of administering the "meaning" of *Winters* in the most technical sense. But there is a flaw in any doctrinal analysis that relies solely on an elaboration of legal principles. A principle has the potential to be effective only when asserted; and even then the assertion of a principle may be in vain. In the development of Indian resources the usefulness of a legal principle may be deeply affected by the availability of an appropriate forum,[53] adequate counsel,[54] and sufficient funds to sustain complex litigation. Sometimes a legal right may be used in a process of bargaining rather than principle vindication. Often, an Indian resource right is used by the tribal government, or the federal government as its representative, to obtain another sought-after goal for the tribe: In the treaty-making period, disputed claims to land were traded for seeming peace and certainty, while in the later nineteenth century so-called surplus lands were traded for additional money and individual allocations of land.[55] Today, a tribe may determine that it wishes a particular kind of economic or social development and that it is willing to exchange its uncertain water rights to further that particular goal.

Indeed, because tribes have traditionally not had the capital to exploit a resource by themselves, the exchange value of the resource has been a critical issue. The valuation of a resource for the purposes of exchange usually involves the allocation of risks among the parties to the exchange. There is the risk that the existence or costs of extracting a resource will prove too great, or that future government regulation may alter the value of the resource. In the case of the Indians' valuation of their water rights, there is the additional uncertainty of not knowing whether the outer logical boundaries of the *Winters* doctrine will really be possible of achievement. *Winters* is a cloud on the development of water in the arid regions of the Southwest. How much the states are willing to expend to see the cloud dispelled depends on how large and black that cloud is perceived to be.

Uncertainty may also exist in the social and political implications of asserting a resource right. Of considerable importance is the actual and per-

---

(9th Cir. 1975), *cert. denied*, 96 S. Ct. 877 (1976); Sohappy v. Smith, 302 F. Supp. 899 (D. Ore. 1969); Comment, *State Power and the Indian Treaty Right to Fish*, 59 CAL. L. REV. 485 (1971).

53. *See* note 3 *supra*.

54. *See* Price, *Lawyers on the Reservation: Some Implications for the Legal Profession*, 1969 LAW & SOCIAL ORDER 161.

55. *See* M. PRICE, *supra* note 7, at 441.

ceived viability of the tribal government that is asserting the *Winters* right. Because the national policy for decades was premised on the ultimate disappearance of tribal sovereignties and the assimilation of Indian people into the mainstream population, non-Indian competitors for water rights may have assumed that a policy of waiting was compatible with ultimate disappearance of the *Winters* cloud.[56] Indeed, the Indian's own scale of relative values may be influenced to a large extent by what the federal government has suggested is of greatest value to the development of the Indian society.

The Navajo experience in the 1960s provides an opportunity to examine the unfolding of the *Winters* right in this context. Throughout the decade, the pressure for power development and greater supplies of water for southwestern cities brought pressure for a resolution or definition of Navajo water rights. Extraordinary public expenditures were necessary before regional goals could be realized. Such expenditures were, however, inconsistent with the risk of uncertain sources of water. In particular, there were two occasions when the Navajo Tribe was obliged to determine whether it was interested in bargaining its *Winters* claim for other values. In 1962, Congress confirmed a tribal determination providing for federal financing of a massive irrigation project on the eastern portion of the reservation in exchange for a surrender of the Navajo priority to waters needed for the San Juan-Chama project. And again, in 1968, the tribe resolved to forebear from using Colorado River water on the western portion of the reservation in exchange for some monetary consideration and the promise of beneficial economic development, actions which made possible the construction of the Navajo Generating Station. In analyzing these two decisions, an effort will be made to appraise the efficacy of the *Winters* right by describing some aspects of the institutional context in which it was deployed.

A. The Navajo Generating Station

As indicated above, the Upper Colorado River Basin Compact of 1948 apportioned the consumptive use of 7.5 million acre-feet among Colorado, New Mexico, Utah, Wyoming, and Arizona. While the compact specifically declared that nothing within it affected the obligations of the United States to the Indian tribes,[57] it was generally assumed that the 50,000 acre-feet[58] allocated to Arizona would suffice to meet any Navajo claim. Although there was no question that the states, agreeing among themselves, could determine that Navajo uses in Upper Basin Arizona would be charged against Arizona's entitlement, it was far less certain that the states, even with congressional confirmation, could limit the Navajo entitlement itself.

---

56. See, for example, the discussion of the "New Policy" of 1917 in L. KELLY, THE NAVAJO INDIANS AND FEDERAL INDIAN POLICY 1900-1935, at 132 (1968).

57. Colorado River Compact, art. VII, 70 CONG. REC. 324, 325 (1928).

58. *Id.* art. III(a), at 325.

Vagueness on this issue had been imperative in 1948. There was no appetite to include the Navajos or other Upper Basin Indian tribes in the deliberations leading to the 1948 Compact. Nor was there a desire to confront and define the outer limits of the Navajo water right. *Winters* could be discounted as an obscure and perhaps obsolete piece of jurisprudence. Federal Indian policy in the post-war period was aimed at the reduction of "special rights" for Indian tribes.[59] The seeds of termination had already been planted. It would not have been absurd for the Upper Basin states to assume that the issue of potential Indian water claims would take care of itself.

By the mid-1960s, the virtues of postponement were no longer apparent. In 1964, the Salt River Project (SRP) applied for a permit to appropriate waters of the State of Arizona for the purpose of constructing a coal-fired electric generating station on the Navajo Reservation.[60] And in March 1965, the SRP applied for Lake Powell water from the Department of the Interior for the same purpose.[61] Most significantly, a consortium of electric utilities had been organized under the name "WEST," short for Western Energy Supply and Transmission. WEST would allow the several electric utilities to take advantage of economies of scale to provide the generation, transmission, and supply of electricity to their customers.[62]

To obtain the needed water, plant sites, and transmission rights of way, WEST would have to apply to the Department of the Interior. Inevitably, the terms upon which WEST was licensed to use these resources would be the subject of negotiation. Discussions between the Department of the Interior and WEST began in early 1965 on studies of power supply and related problems. With President Johnson's hope that a formula for joint public and private resource development in the Colorado Basin could be found, tentative agreement on a cooperative approach in the energy arena was initiated in early June 1965. Basically the agreement under discussion called for a gigantic pooling of the power resources of several large private and municipal power producers with those controlled by the Bureau of Reclamation. The private and municipal participants hoped to utilize existing giant steam-generating plants and proposed to produce firm, continuous power and to rely upon hydroelectric plants of the Bureau of Reclamation, present and future, to provide power during hours of peak consumption. Studies

59. *See* Watkins, *Termination of Federal Supervision: The Removal of Restrictions Over Indian Property and Person*, 311 ANNALS 47 (1957).

60. State of Arizona Application No. A-4753 (Dec. 19, 1964) (on file with the Arizona State Water Commission, Phoenix).

61. Letter from R.J. McMullin to Stewart L. Udall, March 22, 1965.

62. The participating members of WEST in the NGS were the Salt River Project (project manager), Los Angeles Department of Water and Power, Arizona Public Service Co., Nevada Power Co., Tucson Gas & Electric Co., and the U.S. Bureau of Reclamation. Indeed, as project manager, the prior actions of Salt River, described *supra*, were on behalf of the coalition.

on this as well as on cost and efficiency gains through future construction and integration of transmission lines were also initiated. Secretary Udall argued that without cooperative planning and coordination between the federal government and the public and private sectors of the utility industry, the probable result would be a less efficient and reliable power system.

By the spring of 1966, negotiations were under way between Secretary Udall and WEST to integrate WEST thermal power with the hydroelectric peaking power to be produced from the Hualapai and Marble Canyon dams. And by August 1966, a "preliminary letter agreement" had been entered into by the Secretary of the Interior and WEST laying down general guidelines for an arrangement that would be "mutual[ly] advantageous."[63]

By late 1966, interest in a Page power plant had considerably increased.[64] It had become clear that there would be no dams in the Grand Canyon to furnish pumping power for the Central Arizona Project. An alternative source of energy and a plan allowing for government participation in a private power plant, through prepayment of capital, was devised. Within a few months negotiations for a water service contract between the Salt River Project and the Bureau of Reclamation commenced.[65]

To build support and dampen potential conflict the SRP held a series of meetings with the Arizona Interstate Streams Commission, the Central Arizona Project Association, and the Arizona Power Authority.[66] Endorsement was sought for a plan to tap Arizona's share of the Upper Basin allocation for the cooling water needed at the plant.

On February 1, 1967, Secretary Udall unveiled the administration's new proposal for the Central Arizona Project (CAP).[67] This new arrangement

---

63. M. Udall, Language for Committee Report on H.R. 4671, Aug. 9, 1966 (unpublished manuscript on file with author). The Department of Interior informed the power companies involved in the Four Corners, Mohave, and Page power complexes that water service contracts, rights-of-way, permits and approvals could not be made unless they agreed upon arrangements to coordinate their fossil fuel generating resource with Department of Interior hydroelectric resources. *Hearings on Problems of Electrical Power Production in the Southwest Before the Senate Comm. on the Interior and Insular Affairs*, 92d Cong., 1st Sess. 1742 (1971). See also the exchange of letters between Stewart L. Udall and Jack Horton, President, Southern California Edison Company, in *id*. at 332-51.

64. *Hearings on Problems of Electrical Power Production in the Southwest*, *supra* note 63, at 1741.

65. *Id*. at 1741-42.

66. The meetings were to completely brief these organizations on the Page plant, the use of a part of the 50,000 acre-feet allocated to Arizona, and the benefits of the Page plant to Arizona citizens. In the case of the Interstate Streams Commission and the Central Arizona Project Association, the meetings were also devoted to requesting an endorsement of each for the consumptive use of part of Arizona's Upper Basin Allocation in the proposed Page plant. *Id*. at 1748.

67. U.S. DEP'T OF INTERIOR, SUMMARY REPORT: CENTRAL ARIZONA PROJECT WITH FEDERAL PRE-PAYMENT POWER ARRANGEMENT (1967). The CAP was revised in two significant areas. First, the CAP was to be an independent development without financial assistance from the Lower Colorado Basin Development Fund as proposed in legislation reported on during the Eighty-

provided that the federal government prepay a portion of the capital cost of a large thermal power plant and related transmission system which would be constructed near Page, Arizona, adjacent to Lake Powell, by a consortium of electric utility companies. Coal for the plant would be obtained from the Black Mesa fields on the Navajo Reservation.

By fall of 1968, Congress had passed a statute permitting federal pre-purchase of power from a thermal generating station.[68] It was clear from previous actions of WEST and its project manager, SRP, that the plant would be located at Page, utilizing water of the Upper Basin and coal from Black Mesa. All that was unsettled was the status of the water. Congress had commanded that the water used be charged against the 50,000 acre-foot Arizona entitlement.[69] But the unresolved question, which could result in disunity, was just how much water was available from the 50,000 acre-feet of Arizona's allocation for use by the power plant.

The total amount of water to be contracted could not be determined until definitive studies of present water usage in Arizona's Upper Basin were instituted and completed. An operating assumption, to avoid the possibility of conflict, was that unless all parties interested in the 50,000 acre-feet reached agreement,[70]

> there could be no multimillion dollar project using this water. The touch-stone of the effort to acquire the water supply was that negotiations with all entities having the basis for valid claim to Arizona's Upper Basin Allocation would take place and *that there be no effort to prosecute to final court conclusion the legal claim of any one or more of them.*

If the Navajos claimed water for their reservation in addition to the total water already in use and earmarked for the project, or if they claimed under the *Winters* doctrine that they were entitled to more than 50,000 acre-feet, the calculations of Upper Basin users would be sorely jeopardized. The Navajos had never agreed to a 50,000 acre limit on their water use for that portion of the reservation lying in Arizona and draining from the Upper Basin. The consent of the tribe to the construction of the Page plant (to be called the Navajo Generating Station, or NGS) was viewed as essential if the tribe's water rights were to be limited to 50,000 acre-feet and the needs of the NGS were to be charged against the reservation's thus limited settlement.

---

ninth Congress. Secondly, Marble Canyon was to be placed in an enlarged Grand Canyon National Park and final decision on the Hualapai Dam reserved for future congressional action. This meant there would be no dams on the Colorado River to provide power for the CAP. Instead, the Secretary of Interior would be authorized to make arrangements with non-federal interests to acquire the right to a portion of the capacity of the output of a large thermal power plant as necessary to serve project purposes.

68. Act of Sept. 30, 1968, Pub. L. No. 90-537, § 303, 82 Stat. 889, *as amended*, 43 U.S.C. § 1523 (1970).

69. *Id.*

70. *Hearings on Problems of Electrical Power Production in the Southwest, supra* note 63, at 1740 (emphasis added).

An agreement was eventually reached. Although it is somewhat ambiguous, and although there were conflicting interpretations after the fact, there were clearly those who believed that the final resolution consituted an effective recognition by the tribe that their entitlement to Upper Basin Colorado water in Arizona remained at 50,000 acre-feet. The resolution reads as follows.[71]

> 1. In consideration of the Secretary of the Interior executing a contract between the United States and Salt River Project Agricultural Improvement and Power District, operator of the coal-fuel power plant, committing the use of approximately 34,100 acre-feet of water per year for the power plant to be located on the Navajo Reservation near Page, Arizona, the Navajo Tribe of Indians agrees that they will not make demands upon the 50,000 acre-feet of water per year allocated to the State of Arizona, pursuant to the Colorado River Basin Compact, in excess of 50,000 acre-feet of water per year, of which 34,100 acre-feet of water per year shall be used by the coal fuel power plant to be located on the Navajo Reservation near Page, Arizona.

Explicit discussion of the *Winters* doctrine did not play a major part in the negotiations concerning the Navajo Generating Station and the ensuing resolution. Negotiations differ from litigation in the way the doctrine is used. In negotiations, the focus is on the quantity and form of consideration rather than on the fine points of legal argument. Yet legal rights are only barely beneath the surface, setting a background for the bargaining power of the parties. The written material prepared during the critical period, including the minutes of Tribal Council meetings, does not indicate any elaborate discussion of the potential claims that the Navajo Tribe might have had under the *Winters* doctrine in the Upper Basin. No effective challenge to the 50,000 acre-foot limitation was argued by the tribe. Instead, the emphasis was on the form of compensation that would be paid for a waiver of tribal claims to the water needed by the Salt River Project to operate the Navajo Generating Station.

The weak role that the *Winters* doctrine played in the deliberations can be explained in several ways. One possible explanation lies in the relation-

---

71. Navajo Tribal Council, Resolution No. CD-108-68, December 11, 1968 (Navajo Tribal Council minutes and resolutions are on file with the Office of the Clerk, Navajo Tribal Council, Window Rock, Arizona). The other significant parts of CD-108-68 for the *Winters* doctrine were:

RESOLVED: 3. It shall be understood that the Navajo Tribe's promise to limit its claim to 50,000 acre-feet of water per year shall only be for the term of the lifetime of the proposed power plant, or for 50 years, whichever shall occur first. . . .

WHEREAS: 6. Because the 34,100 acre feet of water per year must come from the 50,000 acre-feet of water allocated to the State of Arizona by the terms of the Upper Colorado River Basin Compact, the Salt River Project Agricultural Improvement and Power District must be assured that the Navajo Tribe will not assert, for the lifetime of the proposed coal-fuel power plant, or for the next 50 years, or whichever occurs first, claims for water in excess of 50,000 acre-feet per year. . . .

Id.

ship between the information gathered by the tribe and the ultimate tribal decision. Acting consistently with one's self interest is said to be "a function of choice and information."[72] It is thus assumed that the possibility of protecting one's interests declines where information and choice are unavailable or restricted. During the policy process, decision makers eventually develop a particular impression of the issue involved. Information is compiled and utilized on the basis of that impression. Likewise, their perception of the issue naturally makes them more receptive to what they want to hear. As a result, they are more favorably inclined towards data which support or justify actions they desire. All other information is extraneous and perhaps even induces conflict.

The overriding issue for the Navajo Tribe was the need for jobs and increased revenues. The tribal leaders perceived that a strong bargaining stance could jeopardize those economic goals, and the negotiations show that they were particularly receptive to information which was consistent with those goals. To the Indians, the main issue was not the threat to their water rights. Information in this regard was minimal and, when presented, it seemed to make no impression. Information of this type was overshadowed by the promise of near-term economic benefits from the NGS. Conflict could have resulted if information concerning *Winters* had received greater emphasis.

Of perhaps even greater importance were the sources from which the tribe drew its information. The Navajo Tribal Council gained its information primarily from the SRP, the Bureau of Reclamation, and the Upper Colorado River Commission—the entities that were negotiating with the tribe. Data on current water usage, irrigable acreage, future water use alternatives, and benefits to the tribe were primarily prepared by non-Navajo interests.[73] In-

---

72. H. Ingram, The Politics of Water Allocation 4, February 28, 1974 (unpublished paper presented before the American Association for the Advancement of Science, Committee on Arid Land, San Francisco).

73. By mid-1968 when the non-Navajo parties had already resolved that NGS use of water should be charged against the Navajos and that the Navajo claim should be limited to 50,000 acre-feet, it became imperative to assess the existing uses of water in the Upper Basin portion of the reservation. Accordingly, representatives of the Bureau of Reclamation, the Upper Colorado River Commission (UCRC), and the Resources Department of the Navajo Tribe undertook a water usage survey in the spring of 1968.

The survey estimated that there were 17,912 acre-feet of water in present use. However, the Arizona Interstate Streams Commission estimated that there were only 8,167 acre-feet in use. Unity, and the pressure of time, demanded that these differing estimates be immediately reconciled. A meeting was held on October 3, 1968 for just this purpose between the staffs of the Upper Colorado River Commission and the Arizona Interstate Streams Commission. It is not clear just how these differing estimates were reconciled but it should be noted that the average of the two estimates, about 18,040 acre-feet, was within ten acre-feet of the estimate of Navajo water usage in Arizona's part of the Upper Basin presented to the Navajos during the December negotiations. At that point, little effort was made to assess more carefully the scope of existing Navajo use. Despite the fact that the Solicitor had already ruled that *Winters* doctrine water could be put to nonagricultural use, there apparently was no effort to determine the Upper Basin potential of the Navajos for such a utilization of their water. The compromise

deed, the original resolution presented to the tribe was prepared by the Department of the Interior and the Bureau of Indian Affairs (BIA).

Potential, if not real, conflicts of interest inhered in this information gathering process. The BIA is but one agency of the Interior Department whose departmental policies often overwhelm competing or conflicting Indian interests.[74] The major BIA official at Window Rock was reported to have said that the only thing he could have done was resign if he did not follow the orders of the Secretary of the Interior to obtain a waiver of Navajo water rights.[75] One example involves the key perception of mutual benefits. The impression left by non-Navajo interests was that the coal mine and the power plant were intimately related. It is difficult to ascertain the exact amount of benefits accruing to the Navajo Tribe as a result of the negotiations. The most impressive total presented was a $3,045,000 annual contribution to the Navajo economy.[76] This certainly is large relative to the gross national product of the reservation, but a breakdown of that total is instructive: $1.6 million came from coal royalties, $1.4 million from wages, and only $45,000 from the plant site lease itself, about 1.5 per cent of the total benefits. From the $1.4 million in wages, only $200,000 would come from employment at Page, making a total of $245,000 per year. In this way, benefits from the mine were always included when arguing benefits from the Page project. It was true that the tribe could not benefit from the power plant without coal to burn, but coal royalties ultimately may not have been dependent on the existence of the Navajo Generating Station, although an opposite impression was left with the Tribal Council.[77]

Ideas of sovereignty and concepts of the trust responsibility are vital to understanding and evaluating the bargaining roles with respect to such major resource allocation decisions as the possible waiver of rights in the upper Colorado River Basin. There is the question whether the Bureau of Indian Affairs had the technical capacity to act in any trust role with respect to major resource decisions on the Navajo Reservation. A more modern percep-

---

struck by the Interstate Stream Commission and the Upper Colorado River Commission became the law of the case.

74. Chambers, *Discharge of the Federal Trust Responsibility to Enforce Legal Claims of Indian Tribes: Case Studies of Bureaucratic Conflict of Interest*, in STAFF OF SENATE COMM. ON THE JUDICIARY, 91ST CONG., 2D SESS., STUDY OF ADMINISTRATIVE CONFLICTS OF INTEREST IN THE PROTECTION OF INDIAN NATURAL RESOURCES (Comm. Print 1970).

75. Gallup Independent, May 31, 1969, at 1.

76. Navajo Tribal Council 344, December 9, 1968.

77. Graham Holmes, Superintendent at the Navajo Agency, said, "There's more coal here than they need at Bullhead City. So, if you're going to sell all this coal you've got to have both of these plans." *Id.* at 353. He also said, *id.* at 349, that "we don't find anything else you can do with the coal." A council member agreed, "we want the power plant located on the Navajo Reservation so our coal could be used." *Id.* at 354. It was also estimated that the wages paid, because of the multiplier effect, would mean an extra $8 to $10 million a year boost to the economy. No mention was made that this multiplier effect might be siphoned to non-Navajos in the border towns.

tion of the trust responsibility may be to have the federal government remain in the background, letting the reservation make its own decision with respect to the appropriate bargain.[78] Harmonizing the trust responsibility with rising expectations of sovereignty is difficult. But in the deliberations surrounding the resolution of Navajo water rights, the Department of the Interior played conflicting roles with respect to Colorado River water, roles that made it difficult objectively to advise the Navajo Tribe.

In terms of technical assistance to the tribe, little, if any, came from the Bureau of Indian Affairs itself.[79] As indicated, much of the data had been prepared and analyzed by the Bureau of Reclamation, an agency in the department with interests clearly adverse to those of the Navajo Tribe. The Bureau's consultations came primarily through the assistance of the solicitor's office and the participation of the superintendent's office of the BIA's Navajo Agency. Both sources of help were bound to propound the department's position. The BIA was not well equipped to evaluate alternatives. It has traditionally been viewed within the department as a weak and uninfluential branch. With few exceptions, economists, hydrologists, and other technicians would be found in the Bureau of Reclamation rather than the Bureau of Indian Affairs. Certainly, on this occasion, the BIA did not independently evaluate the needs of the tribe and make recommendations to it.

The conflict of interest between the Secretary of the Interior as trustee for the Navajo Tribe and as a public official responsible to a national and departmental constituency was apparent. First, the Department of Interior would obtain a portion of the capacity of the proposed plant as a result of the recent passage of the Colorado River Basin Project.[80] Indeed, the WEST proposal had its long range positive aspects for the future of Bureau of Reclamation projects in the region. For example, WEST was essentially a proposal to produce base load energy which could enhance the value of hydroelectric peaking power under circumstances of high demand and low supply. The existence of such large amounts of low cost base load energy could further enhance other projects proposed by the Bureau of Reclamation. The Bureau of Reclamation had close and beneficial working relationships with the consortium of power companies. The federal government was prepurchasing a sizable amount of power, contributing a sizable amount of the capital costs, and would undoubtedly help to facilitate negotiations for coal, water, and permission from the appropriate entities—the State of Arizona

---

78. *See* Chambers & Price, *Regulating Sovereignty: Secretarial Discretion and the Leasing of Indian Lands*, 26 STAN. L. REV. 1061 (1974).

79. Navajo Tribal Council 349, 353, 382, December 9-10, 1968. For example, the Bureau of Reclamation made the study of alternative uses for the water and concluded that the Page plant was the best.

80. Act of Sept. 30, 1968, Pub. L. No. 90-537, 82 Stat. 885.

and the Navajo Tribal Council.[81]

There is current debate over the proper role of the federal government in decisions involving the allocation of reservation resources.[82] The more traditional view is that the Secretary should have a veto power to determine that the decision made meets fair market value requirements and is consonant with the long term best interests of the tribe. The Secretary, under this view, cannot command that an action be taken over the opposition of the tribal government, and the views of the tribe should be given great weight before the Secretary forbids it from taking a particular action. A competing view is that the duty of the trustee is to insure that the tribal government is well informed and the consequences of alternate forms of action are well known. According to this view, the trustee's duty is to provide data and the basis for analysis but not to overrule the decision of the tribe itself.

Clearly, the federal government, in particular the Secretary of the Interior, played neither of these roles adequately in the NGS context. The deep and certain conflict of interest prevented the Secretary from performing the traditional trust role. The Bureau of Reclamation had too great a stake in the outcome. Nor did the Secretary perform the second role adequately, largely because of the lack of expertise and forcefulness of the Bureau of Indian Affairs. Here the United States was purporting to act as the trustee and the Navajo Tribe was relying on that representation. But nothing in the period leading up to the December 1968 resolution suggested that the role could be performed adequately by the department.

Another important factor in the negotiations involving the resolution of *Winters* rights was the relative economic strength of the parties and the consequent need to have an immediate settlement. In 1968, the Navajo Tribe was said to be severely underdeveloped: living, health, and educational standards were far below the national norm.[83] Unemployment was extraordinarily high. And oil royalties, upon which the tribe depended for many of its own services, were seriously depleted. As a political matter within the tribe, jobs were a matter of first priority. The value of immediate additional employment on the reservation had a political and social significance greater than more remote, but possibly more valuable, alternative uses of Colorado River water. The power plant construction would, furthermore, spur eco-

---

81. Not to be overlooked were the close ties, personal and/or business, that existed between certain members of WEST, members of the Department of the Interior and the CAP lobby. Two members of WEST that were to build the Page plant were the Salt River Project (SRP) and the Arizona Public Service Company (APS). Both these utilities were members of and contributed financial and personal support to the lobbying efforts of the Central Arizona Project Association. Arizona periodically sent a "task force" of persons with good Department of the Interior connections to testify at congressional hearings on the CAP.

82. Chambers & Price, *supra* note 78.

83. Aberle, *A Plan for Navajo Economic Development*, in 1 JOINT ECONOMIC COMM., 91ST CONG., 2D SESS., TOWARD ECONOMIC DEVELOPMENT FOR NATIVE AMERICAN COMMUNITIES 223 (1969).

nomic development in one of the most depressed areas of an already economically underdeveloped reservation.[84]

It would be difficult for a financially pressed tribal government, representing a constituency in need of economic benefits, to await the full blossom
of *Winters* rights. The reserved waters doctrine at the base of *Winters* assumes
that there will be a slow maturation of the tribe's purposes. At the heart of
Winters is the idea that the settler community should not be able to withdraw
and commit water that might be needed by the tribe at a future time as it
gains the machinery to exploit its resources. But the tribe itself may see the
need to cut short *Winters* delaying power. More limited economic development in the present has an appeal that postponed development may lack.
The tribe may well reason that the kind of federal financing necessary for
massive tribal growth and use of its resources will not be forthcoming, especially if the exploitation of resources by the tribe conflicts with the needs
of the dominant settler culture.[85]

It is possible to argue that the Navajo Tribe, having accepted the importance of a present settlement of *Winters* rights for economic development,
became a true member of a coalition of economic interests, albeit one that

---

84. At least 150 Navajos would be employed in site development and plant construction, followed by up to 20 Navajos employed in plant operation with an anual payroll of $200,000;
some 110 to 130 Navajos employed at coal mining with an annual payroll of $400,000; another
30-40 Navajos employed in supporting industries with an annual payroll of $300,000. The
34,100 acre-feet needed for the plant was portrayed as a "trade-off" for revenue, development,
and jobs. Also it was argued that the power plant was the only way the water was likely to be
used within the immediate future, if ever. The General Manager of SRP told the Tribal Council, "we believe that by combining water with Black Mesa coal we can produce an economic benefit which exceeds any other known use of those resources. . . . We need electricity which your
coal and water will produce to your benefit and ours." Navajo Tribal Council 366, December
10, 1968.
   One of the tribal attorneys was even more forceful:
      The question always posed to the Legal Department, is this a good deal when anything
      is brought up. Based upon the information that has been given us from the Resources
      Department of the Navajo Tribe, and looking at the legal problems to the best of our
      ability, I think that this is a good deal. The question that you might ask yourself is, if
      you don't agree with this deal, what are you going to do with the water? Can you think
      of anything that can be done with it that will bring $300,000,000.00 to the western Res-
      ervation and provide many, many jobs for the Navajos? Certainly, not agricultural use.
      And I don't know of any other company that is interested in coming to the western
      Reservation now or the next twenty or thirty years. The people of the western Reser-
      vation need jobs and they need the money.
Id. at 339.
   85. Because of the value of jobs, all the possible consequences of a decision to build a power
plant were not adequately identified or taken into account. The participants focused only on
the direct and immediate effects of the proposed power plant and ignored the possible long-
run consequences. Questions of whether the Reservation should be developed by capital intensive industry rather than by labor intensive industry and for what purposes were ignored.
What would happen when the life of the plant was over and the coal exhausted? A situation of
arrested development and stagnation was not recognized as a possibility. What could be the
adverse social effects of the plant on the surrounding population? What effect would it have
on tourism? The effect of the plant on the environment was not even mentioned.

perhaps did not exact sufficient tribute as a condition of entry. The tribe, like the other participants, would gain by becoming part of an alliance that could produce federal benefits available to all. A complex series of interrelated events would lead to enhanced economic development on the western reservation. Legislation and the waiver of possible water use rights were essential. To accomplish them, the participation of all members of the coalition was vital. Primarily, there was an emphasis on avoiding conflict. To confirm the mutual benefits it was necessary to minimize any focus on issues that would be divisive in the long term. Hewing to *Winters* doctrine rights would deviate from such predictable behavior. Insistence on the recognition of full *Winters* rights would have constrained the participation of the Navajo Tribe in the coalition.[86]

B. The Navajo Indian Irrigation Project

It is not sufficient to determine the manner in which the Navajos, or a similarly situated Indian tribe, participates in the bargaining process. For it may well be the case that participation is apparent rather than real, that the ultimate distribution of resources will be a function of power in the society rather than a function of participation in the process of decision-making or the manipulation of a legal right. In the study of the Navajo Generating Station, an attempt was made to look at the pattern of participation. From that perspective, it was possible to view the tribe as a ratifier rather than a bargainer. In the case of the Navajo Indian Irrigation Project, the trappings of actual participation were more in evidence. Indeed, in the case of NIIP (as the project is known), enough time has passed so that problems of imple-

---

86. The likelihood that this would have been the outcome was dramatically illustrated a few months after passage of the 1968 resolution. DNA, an OEO legal services program, established several years before, published a written statement and a brief concerning the *Winters* implications of the 1968 transaction. As opposed to the tribe, DNA as an institution was not nurtured in a tradition of mutual accommodation. Unlike all previous presentations, DNA reviewed the status of the tribe's water rights under the *Winters* doctrine with special attention to the implications of *Arizona v. California*. The stress was on the continuing undefined right and the need for time for the tribe to evaluate the right in terms of the benefits from the construction of the plant at Page. The reaction of all the parties, including the tribe, was to exclude the offending parties from the decision making process. In this instance, the DNA was depicted as "interfering" and "causing a helluva turmoil among a lot of innocent people." Two strategies were employed by the anti-DNA group to dampen conflict: (1) to deny flatly that the *Winters* doctrine was involved in any way in Resolution CD-108-68 and the pending resolution and (2) to restrict severely the implications or interpretations of the *Winters* doctrine.

Note the following statements by a member of the Navajo Tribal Council:

[T]he federally supported agency, DNA, are now interfering with the Navajo Tribe's governing body and officials. . . . But here we are, the Navajo Tribal Council, representing our Navajo Tribe and trying to do what is right and trying to make use of our water rights by getting some revenue, get money from it and make use of it. Why should the DNA representatives try to interfere with what we are trying to do for the Navajo Tribe and trying to utilize our water rights in order to get revenue.

Navajo Tribal Council 198, June 3, 1969.

mentation of the bargain can be discerned. Like the Navajo Generating Station episode, the history of the Navajo Indian Irrigation Project provides data for assessing the meaning of the *Winters* rights.

1. *The Bargaining Process*

The initial boundaries of the Navajo Reservation were created by treaty in 1868 on land encompassing a stretch of the San Juan River, a tributary of the Colorado. When the utility of the water in the Colorado River system was being parceled out between the states in the 1922 and 1948 compact negotiations, however, the Navajos were not invited to sit at the bargaining table. It was assumed that their rights were protected by federal representatives and by the disclaimer clauses in the compacts. Non-Indians avoided consultation with the tribe partly because they viewed tribal sovereignty as mythological and tribal entities as existing more for purposes of education and internal tribal stability than for purposes of resource management and relationship with other governments. Indeed a formal tribal government did not exist on the reservation until shortly after the 1922 Compact. Moreover, at the time of the Upper Basin compact negotiations, the clear trend of federal Indian policy was toward the destruction of tribal political entities and the ultimate amalgamation of Indian communities into the states in which they were situated. The states involved had also set to work through their new Upper Colorado River Commission to put together a package of public works projects—collectively known as the Colorado River Storage Project (CRS)—which would provide benefits for each state.

Unlike the experience with the Navajo Generating Station, Navajo interest in the allocation of public works projects and their impact on Colorado River entitlements was expressed early in the deliberations. In 1948, the Navajo Tribal Council (NTC), aware of the emerging competition, requested the prompt development of irrigation projects to use San Juan River water and urged Congress not to approve any other uses of San Juan River water without the full protection of Navajo water rights.[87] By the end of 1950, the joint efforts of the Bureau of Indian Affairs and the Bureau of Reclamation produced an interim planning report favoring construction of a storage facility and an irrigation project for the Navajos.[88] New Mexico objected to the planning report, claiming that the only way the "legitimate needs" of New Mexico could be fulfilled would be for the report to include competing non-Indian projects for "concurrent authorization," including a San Juan-Chama project which would divert headwaters of the San Juan system across

---

87. Navajo Tribal Council, Resolution, December 8, 1948.
88. U.S. DEP'T OF THE INTERIOR, REGIONAL DIRECTOR'S REPORT OF DECEMBER 1950 ON COLORADO RIVER STORAGE PROJECT AND PARTICIPATING PROJECTS, UPPER COLORADO RIVER BASIN, in H.R. DOC. No. 364, 83d Cong., 2d Sess. 59-87 (1954).

the divide into the Rio Grande River system which serves Albuquerque.[89]

In the spring of 1951, after federal and state representatives had spent time exploring possible formulas for accommodating projects on both sides of the divide, the Navajo Tribal Council requested an "active voice in the negotiations and in the selection of project sites."[90] NTC representatives and consultants began to participate directly in planning meetings and conferences.[91]

Soon it became clear that the states wanted the acreage and water figures fixed for the Navajo project. The Navajo Tribal Council was told that approval by the states of the irrigation project would depend on its size.[92] The impression was conveyed that the conflict within New Mexico was delaying the Upper Colorado River Storage Project proposal. The Tribal Council chairman displayed an acute awareness of the political necessity of compromise: "If we are going to use all the water of the River . . . we will never have a project."[93] Another councilman mused, "We will never see the water again if it goes over the mountain."[94] The council was being cautiously prepared for the likelihood of compromise both by its own attorney and a BIA attorney.[95]

Early in 1952, the Navajo Tribal Council met and resolved that it wanted an irrigation project with a net area of 122,000 acres and a preferential right to divert and use 610,000 acre-feet of water annually to supply such a project. The council also asserted that it had "a prior and preferential right to all of the waters of the San Juan River and its tributaries for use on the Navajo Tribal lands."[96]

---

89. Letter from John Bliss, State Engineer of New Mexico to Oscar Chapman, Secretary of the Interior, June 12, 1951, in *id.* at 307. It was assumed at this time that New Mexico's 11.25 entitlement under the 1949 Compact represented about 838,000 acre-feet of water and that, after deducting reservoir losses and depletions for authorized or existing irrigation projects, approximately 600,000 acre-feet was available for future development. U.S. Dep't of the Interior, *Report of the Technical Comm. on Use of Waters of San Juan River in New Mexico*, in STATE ENGINEER OF NEW MEXICO, A REVIEW OF THE SAN JUAN RIVER PROBLEM IN NEW MEXICO 20 app. IV, item 1 (1953). New Mexico was purporting to assert its control over these unappropriated waters as trustee on behalf of the public.

90. *Id.* at 21. *See generally* Lawson, *The Navajo Indian Irrigation Project: Muddied Past, Clouded Future*, 9 THE INDIAN HISTORIAN 19 (1976).

91. Within a few months the Navajo Tribal Council consultant was speaking in terms of a 118,000 acre, gravity-flow irrigation project for the Navajos and was confirming the water supply projections of federal and state staff people which indicated that the expected water shortages from all of the proposed New Mexico projects would be tolerable for such an irrigation project. *See* H. PERSON, REPORT ON POTENTIAL IRRIGATION DEVELOPMENT ON NAVAJO INDIAN RESERVATION IN SAN JUAN RIVER BASIN 5 (1951); Statement of H.T. Person, Navajo Tribal Council, Minutes of Meeting, August 22, 1951.

92. Statement made by J.R. Riter, Navajo Tribal Council, *supra* note 9, at 59.

93. *Id.* at 56.

94. Statement by Sam Gorman, *id.* at 54.

95. Statements by Norman Littell and H.T. Person, *id.* at 62-63.

96. Navajo Tribal Council, Resolution No. CJ-4-52, January 18, 1952. The land reserved for the Navajos by the Treaty of 1868 encompasses a significant stretch of the San Juan River.

Navajo participation was not only early but constituted an effective determinant of the structure of the arrangement among the competing political interests. Rather than object totally to a Navajo storage and irrigation project, New Mexico sought to have the Navajo project linked to a controversial San Juan-Chama diversion project through concurrent authorization. Other Upper Basin states indicated that their support of a Navajo project would be forthcoming if, in the process, Navajo claims to the tributaries would be limited and defined. Furthermore, it became clear that bargaining for support would not only involve the quantity of the Navajo right, but also its allocation in time of shortage. Indeed, in 1952 and 1953 negotiations almost ceased because of the sharing of shortage issue. All the Upper Basin states had an interest in a resolution of the conflict, and the Navajo Tribe perceived that it shared this interest.

The stalemate over the San Juan River projects was to continue, however, and was memorialized in the 1956 enactment of the Colorado River Storage Project Act. The Navajo Indian Irrigation Project and the San Juan-Chama Project were listed as "priority planning" projects in the Act,[97] but were not authorized. Planning reports on these projects had been prepared in 1955 but departmental approval had been withheld pending resolution of the conflicting water use claims concerning the San Juan. For the remainder of 1956 and most of 1957, the competition between the east slope and west slope in New Mexico continued as each side reviewed its negotiating position and claims. In early 1957, Navajo tribal leadership began to support a proposal for a smaller irrigation project on higher quality crop land, a plan that would necessarily free a greater quantity of water for industrial use.

In late 1957, an important series of meetings was held, involving representatives of the Navajo Tribal Council, the New Mexico Interstate Stream Commission, and the BIA, relating to a draft bill for the simultaneous authorization of the Navajo Indian Irrigation Project (NIIP) and the San Juan-Chama Project (SJCP). The New Mexico Interstate Stream Commission approved the draft bill in mid-October[98] and the Navajo Tribal Council adopted a resolution approving that bill on December 12, 1957.[99] The draft bill provided for a sharing of shortages by NIIP and SJCP proportionate to their respective diversion requirements, and thereby called for a compromise of the 1868 water right priority date enjoyed by the Navajos. Several reasons for the compromise were presented to the Navajo Tribal Council by the tribal attorney, the consulting engineer, the BIA land operations engineer, and the State Engineer of New Mexico.

The tribal attorney explained that in time of water shortage under west-

---

97. Act of April 11, 1956, ch. 203, 70 Stat. 105, *as amended*, 43 U.S.C. § 620 (1970).
98. New Mexico Interstate Stream Comm'n, Resolution of October 17, 1957.
99. Navajo Tribal Council, Resolution No. CD-86-57, December 12, 1957.

ern water law, a prior right carries with it the right to use the water to the exclusion of others, if need be. He stated that under the *Winters* doctrine, the priority date is the date the reservation is established. He then told the Navajo Tribal Council that there were several reasons why he was commending the sharing-of-shortages provision of the draft bill to them:[100]

> [T]he first one is if the irrigation had first priority and got a full supply of water, even in years of shortage, the people who come in later, meaning the industrial users, would not get any water at all some years. What would happen? You would not get any industrial users. If they could not depend on the water supply, they would not come in. You would not get industrial development. Industrial development I think, and I believe you agree with me, is just as important to the Navajo people as irrigation, maybe more so, so if the Navajo Tribe were to insist on first priority on irrigation projects, it would be killing off all the industrial jobs that the Navajos would otherwise get. It would be killing off the Utah Construction Project that we have all worked so hard for. The next reason is if we did not have this Section in the Bill, we would never get through Congress. If this were not in the Bill, the only project that would be feasible would be irrigation projects. The Trans-Mountain and industrial development would not be feasible. They are reimbursable projects. They help to pay for Government work in New Mexico. If this were left just as this, it would just be a grant to the Navajo Tribe and the people from New Mexico would not support it and the Congressional delegates would not support it and we would not get anything.

The consulting engineer applied flow records for the 1927-1954 period to two alternatives: one that subordinated industrial and municipal uses to NIIP and SJCP and another that equated all those uses. He concluded that the shortages NIIP would have experienced over that period if it had no superior priority would have been sporadic and tolerable.[101]

The Navajo Tribal Council approved the draft bill containing the provision whereby all but preexistent users would share shortages proportionately.[102] The Navajos were willing to sacrifice the priority of their water right for such anticipated benefits as industrial development and a heavily subsidized irrigation project. Thus, by 1958, a "horse trade" had been made.

In mid-June 1962,[103] Congress finally authorized construction of the

---

100. Navajo Tribal Council, Minutes of Meeting 68-69, December 11, 1957.
101. *Id*. at 75-76.
102. Navajo Tribal Council, *supra* note 99.
103. Between 1958 and 1962 Navajo and non-Indian interest groups from New Mexico had jointly appeared before congressional committees and lobbied for authorization of the New Mexico projects. Various authorization bills had received favorable treatment in the Senate but were repeatedly tied up in the House Committee on Interior and Insular Affairs, largely due to the opposition of California and Colorado representatives. California interests opposed the projects, as they had the overall Colorado River Storage Project, on the grounds that it was financially unsound. Representative Wayne Aspinall of Colorado, who was pushing for reclamation projects within Colorado on the Animus and La Plata, which are tributaries of the San Juan River, was concerned that the New Mexico projects might compete for the same water supply as those Colorado projects. During the legislative deliberations on the NIIP project, Aspinall made a record several times for the limitation of Navajo water claims. *E.g.*, *Hearings*

NIIP and San Juan-Chama projects.[104] After almost a century of promises and a decade of active promotion, a largescale Navajo irrigation project was approved—but was far from built.

The 1962 Act authorizing the Navajo Irrigation Project seemed to culminate the Navajo bargaining effort. An unquantified *Winters* right, with all its uncertainties, had been converted to the promise of water works that could be of use to the Navajo people. Something was surrendered in terms of the Navajo's ultimate claim—compromise of a priority which probably would have made shortage-sharing unnecessary—in exchange for a promise of substantial federal funds to develop a portion of the Navajo economy that was desperately in need of nourishment. Bargaining seemed effective. The Navajos had seemingly employed the *Winters* right as a weapon, foreclosing transbasin diversion of water from the Colorado River system until a substantial benefit had been conferred on the Navajo people. By working through a national political forum, the Navajos could gain non-regional support for their position. And when it appeared that there was independent support for the Navajo project, the other regional participants in the coalition embraced it as enhancing the political strength of their collective approach to Congress.

The Navajo Indian Irrigation Project also represents a diligent effort by the Bureau of Indian Affairs and the tribe itself toward more active participation in the allocation of water resources and the federal largess. The period prior to 1962 was filled with study and analysis of alternate positions on the shape of such an irrigation project. And yet, more than a decade later, there are serious doubts about the basic premises of the project and the likelihood of ultimate success. The project was portrayed to Congress as one that would foster small farm agriculture on the eastern portion of the Navajo

---

on H.R. 2352, H.R. 2494, & S. 72 Before the Subcomm. On Irrigation and Reclamation of the House Comm. On Interior and Insular Affairs, 86th Cong., 2d Sess. 70 (1960); Hearings on H.R. 2552, H.R. 6541, & S. 107 Before the Subcomm. on Irrigation and Reclamation of the House Comm. on Interior and Insular Affairs, 87th Cong., 1st Sess. 22, 30-31, 33, 56-57 (1961).

104. Act of June 13, 1962, Pub. L. No. 87-483, 76 Stat. 96, *as amended*, 43 U.S.C. §§ 615, 620 (1970); Act of Sept. 25, 1970, Pub. L. No. 91-416, 84 Stat. 867 (codified in 43 U.S.C. § 615 (1970)). The Act of 1962, among other things, authorized a maximum of $135 million for the Secretary of the Interior to "construct, operate, and maintain the Navajo Indian irrigation project for the principal purpose of furnishing irrigation water" to about 110,630 acres, at an average annual diversion of 508,000 acre-feet. Liability for repayment of construction costs is to be "within the capability of the land to repay," and is to be charged as liens against the land, conditionally payable only if and when the land passes out of Indian status. Section 2 incorporated section 4(d) of the Act of April 11, 1956, ch. 203, 70 Stat. 107, which in turn subjects Indian lands to the Act of July 1, 1932, ch. 369, 47 Stat. 564. The Secretary of the Interior is directed to declare a trust over certain federally owned land to the east of the reservation for inclusion in the project, upon payment by the Navajos of the full appraised value. The Act also authorizes the acquisition of other land suitable for the project and permits it to be held in trust status as well. The Secretary is authorized to include municipal and industrial capacity in the NIIP system. Water use is not to occur without approved contracts and the contracts must make provision for the sharing of shortages. Before entering into contracts the Secretary must take into account the diversion requirements of NIIP and SJCP.

reservation. In many ways, the Project had at its heart a sense of the Navajo people and the future development of the land that may have been erroneous. In terms of cost to the nation of the implementation of the project, and in terms of per family benefits to the Navajo people, the Navajo Indian Irrigation Project has been open to increased critical analysis. In addition, the national implementation of the bargain is itself questionable. Federal support for the project has been slow and uneven while federal support for its exchange-counterpart, the San Juan-Chama Project, has moved steadily ahead to completion. Both of these aspects—the cultural premises of the bargain and its implementation by Congress—must be examined to understand the career of the *Winters* right.

2. *The Agricultural Premise*

One hypothesis of Jorgensen[105] and others is that the reservation is a satellite of the metropolis, that its resources will be diverted primarily for the use of the dominant culture and the benefit of more powerful interests within that culture. The underlying planning and hope of the Navajo Indian Irrigation Project clearly sought a different objective. *Winters* rights were to be utilized essentially to achieve a goal harmonious with the *Winters* case itself. In a classic *Winters* sense, arid land would be irrigated and Navajo families would prosper thereby. Limited Navajo irrigation development had existed in the vicinity of Shiprock since 1900 and various schemes for large-scale projects had been entertained for fifty years. But only with the pressure of trans-basin diversion and the need for a resolution of the Navajo claim was the possibility of farming development a real one. The water resource was finally to be turned inward, finally to assist in achieving the kind of self-contained community foreseen in the nineteenth century. The Navajos, with the assistance of the massive infusion of regulated water, would be enabled to make the culturally significant switch from a quasi-nomadic existence to a pastoral community. The virtue of the project, in terms of its theoretical basis, was that a natural resource that was appurtenant to the reservation would be converted to enriching the lives of the Navajos with minimum diversion to the external, settler society.

Between 1950, when the concept of the Navajo Indian Irrigation Project was formalized, and 1975, the ideas that were at the heart of the project seemed to dissolve. The Navajo Tribe has come to see the economic future of the reservation more in terms of industrial development than agriculture. And the tribe's perception of the appropriate utilization of the *Winters* right has altered accordingly. Moreover, there has been an increasing sense that the agricultural ideal of the nineteenth century is ill-suited to the current Navajo family. As the massive project is studied and restudied, corporate

105. J. JORGENSEN, THE SUN DANCE RELIGION, POWER FOR THE POWERLESS (1972).

agriculture more and more replaces the family farm as the preferred mode of use of the irrigated lands. Both of these tendencies yield results that are closer to the Jorgensen hypothesis, for the move toward industrialization and corporate farming implicates non-Navajo interests far more substantially in the Navajo economy.

In 1966, Secretary Udall asked the Bureau of Reclamation to reevaluate completely the irrigation project. The reevaluation was being prompted, in part, by "exciting new opportunities for industrial development."[106]

> These include particularly the opportunity to use the coal resource of the Navajo Indian for steam generation of electric power and to develop related industries, including petro chemicals. Accordingly, we are not at all sure that it will be serving the Navajos well to dedicate all of their available water for agricultural purposes and by so doing foreclose possibilities for industrial and recreational development which would seem to offer more possibilities to advance the economic opportunities of the Tribe. I would like to emphasize that studies we will make are intended solely to assist the Tribe in making the best use of its water. Our studies are not intended in any way to affect the Tribe's entitlement to the water or the construction of those facilities that would be necessary for delivery.

The resulting Task Force for Reevaluation of NIIP met in the spring of 1966, after being instructed by the Commissioner of Reclamation to abide by the 508,000 acre-feet diversion and 254,000 acre-feet depletion figures in the reevaluation study, but to consider alternate sizes of 110,000, 77,000 or 62,000 acres for NIIP.[107] A smaller NIIP could provide residual water, among other things, for thermal power and petro-chemical development. The Navajos generally were hostile to the idea of reevaluation in 1966. Reportedly, they had first heard about the reevaluation in the newspapers.[108] They were upset by an expression of personal opinion by the State Engineer of New Mexico to the effect that New Mexico wanted to put its water entitlement to economic use without unnecessary delay, and that if NIIP was not going to use its authorized amount, the "residual water" ought to be "returned to the pool at Navajo Reservoir, available for contract and allocated where those needs first arise whether they are on or off the reservation."[109] The Navajos rejected an opportunity to designate a representative to serve on the reevaluation task force. While the subsequent report of the task force recommended that a full-sized NIIP project be continued, it included two significant caveats. First, it recognized that the future might hold other opportunities for resource development besides agriculture and

106. Letter from Stewart Udall to Clinton P. Anderson, February 16, 1966.
107. Letter from Floyd Dominy, Commissioner of Reclamation to Regional Director, Amarillo, Texas, March 29, 1977, in Navajo Tribal Council, Task Force for Reevaluation of Navajo Indian Irrigation, Minutes of Meeting, April 8, 1966.
108. *Id.* at 12-13.
109. *Id.* at 11.

that such development would require water. Second, the reevaluation accentuated a change in thinking relating to the developments of family farms in the project. Congressional committees previously had been told that approximately 1,200 family farms would be established, a plan that would be compatible with a standard BIA policy holding that the "development and extension of irrigation projects on Indian reservations are primarily for the benefit of resident reservation Indian families."[110] The 1966 reevaluation study emphasized the necessity of recognizing that sociocultural differences between Indian and non-Indian farmers demanded "fresh thinking and perception" in the planning of NIIP farm development.[111] The plans should be so compatible with the indigenous culture as to "avoid past pitfalls and failures in Indian irrigated farming," many of which were catalogued by the study. Farm development should proceed on the basis of creating large land blocks of 2,000 or 3,000 acres, within which assignments of varying sizes would be made to individual Navajo farms. Unassigned acreage could be "operated by a managed farm enterprise employing either Navajo laborers or the farmers and family members in the block." The major goal, however, ought to remain the "family farm."[112] This goal was to become more and more remote in the ensuing months and years. Less than a month after Secretary Udall approved the reevaluation study, the Commissioner of Indian Affairs disclosed further doubts as to whether irrigated agriculture, as non-Indians knew it, was culturally suitable for the Navajos.[113] NIIP thereafter emerged as an agri-business development.[114]

---

110. Statement of Phileo Nash, B.I.A. Commissioner, in *Hearings on H.R. 5279 Before a Subcomm. of the Senate Comm. on Appropriations*, 88th Cong., 1st Sess. 107 (1963).

111. U.S. DEP'T OF THE INTERIOR, BUREAU OF RECLAMATION, REEVALUATION REPORT NAVAJO INDIAN IRRIGATION PROJECT, NEW MEXICO, X-1 app. (1966).

112. *Id*. at X-16, 18.

113. Memorandum from Robert Bennett, B.I.A. Commissioner to Graham Holmes, Area Director, January 13, 1967.

114. In 1970 the Navajo Tribal Council created a tribal enterprise called Navajo Agricultural Products Industry (NAPI) to manage agricultural development on the Reservation, particularly within NIIP. This tribal enterprise approach had been used before with the Forest Products Industry and the Navajo Tribal Utility Authority. NAPI has a management board composed of Navajos and non-Indians with farming and reclamation experience. The board has been overseeing pilot projects and development plans for NIIP.

The Agricultural Experiment Station of the New Mexico State University has conducted agricultural studies related to NIIP. One 1972 study concluded that, due to a lack of experienced Navajo farmers, the tribal enterprise approach was preferable initially to 320-acre individual farms. The study estimated that investment capital of $56.5 million would be needed to develop the project on a tribal enterprise scale with a good mix of field, seed and vegetable crops, and livestock. It was predicted that federal assistance, over and above private financing, would be needed. No net expendable income could be expected until the fourth year (about $2 million), thereafter it would rise to about $7.5 million by the twelfth year. NEW MEXICO STATE UNIVERSITY, AGRICULTURAL EXPERIMENT STATION, ALTERNATIVE FORM ORGANIZATIONAL STRUCTURES FOR THE NAVAJO INDIAN IRRIGATION PROJECT 183, 188-95 (1972). This large-scale, agri-business farm unit approach to NIIP can be criticized for its apparent failure to take into account elements of the indigenous native culture and for its inability to provide incentives for individual

3. *Implementing the Bargain*

The second major issue in *Winters* implementation relates to the process of federal financing of the works necessary for the Navajo project. In terms of understanding techniques for the resolution of *Winters* uncertainties, it is critical to appreciate the complexities that arise after a bargain is struck, the right is quantified, or there is congressional authorization for the project. Authorization is but the first step in the long journey to the completion of a federal water resource project.[115] The real commitment of Congress comes when it backs up the authorization with the appropriation of money. To determine the implications of a bargain, one must look at the appropriation process as critically as at the original authorization. The Navajo Indian Irrigation Project, it will be recalled, was a bargained-for exchange for the San Juan-Chama diversion project. Both were concurrently authorized in the 1962 legislation, one to serve the Navajos and the other to supplement the water supply of the settler culture of New Mexico. The pattern of appropriations is instructive. In the case of NIIP, Congress met the 1962 authorization of $135 million with appropriations of only $1.8, $4.7, and $6.5 million for fiscal 1964, 1965, and 1966, respectively.[116] San Juan-Chama, authorized for $85.8 million by comparison, received approximately $1 million more than this amount over the same three-year period.[117] By the late 1960s, the splendor of the reclamation ethic had been tarnished and the Bureau of the Budget was ordering slowdowns on public works projects. An estimated two to three year delay in the water delivery schedule for NIIP resulted.[118] NIIP was 16 per cent completed in 1969, whereas the San Juan-Chama Project was 57 per cent completed and on schedule;[119] and the figures

---

Navajos. Concerns are being expressed that Navajo income and employment will not be adequately maximized.

115. *See generally* N. ELY, AUTHORIZATION OF FEDERAL WATER PROJECTS (National Water Comm'n Legal Study No. 12, 1971).

116. *See* Statement of David F. Cargo, Governor of the State of New Mexico, in *Hearings on H.R. 17619 Before a Subcomm. of the Senate Comm. on Appropriations*, 91st Cong., 2d Sess. 4054 (1970).

117. $1.6 million for Fiscal 1964; $5.9 million for Fiscal 1965; and $7.7 million for Fiscal 1966. *See Hearings on Public Works Appropriations for 1967 of the House Comm. on Appropriations*, 89th Cong., 2d Sess. 410 (1966); *Hearings on Public Works Appropriations for 1966 Before a Subcomm. of the House Comm. on Appropriations*, 89th Cong., 1st Sess. 409 (1965); *Hearings on Public Works Appropriations for 1965 Before a Subcomm. of the House Comm. on Appropriations*, 88th Cong., 2d Sess. 422 (1964).

118. Exchange between Senator Carl Hayden and Robert Bennett, B.I.A. Commissioner, in *Hearings on H.R. 9029 Before a Subcomm. of the Senate Comm. on Appropriations*, 90th Cong., 1st Sess. 784 (1967).

119. Statement of Robert Bennett, B.I.A. Commissioner, in *Hearings on H.R. 12781 Before a Subcomm. of the Senate Comm. on Appropriations*, 91st Cong., 1st Sess. 166 (1969); *see* U.S. DEP'T OF THE INTERIOR, BUREAU OF RECLAMATION, PROJECT DATA SHEET, UCRBF—SAN JUAN CHAMA PARTICIPATING PROJECT, COLORADO-NEW MEXICO (1969), in *Hearings on H.R. 14159 Before a Subcomm. of the Senate Comm. on Appropriations*, 91st Cong., 1st Sess. 2973 (1969).

for 1970 were about 17 per cent and 65 per cent, respectively.[120] Strong pleas
to Congress on behalf of NIIP by members of the New Mexico delegation,
the Governor, the State Engineer, and federal officials led to enactment of a
1970 law increasing the authorization ceiling for NIIP to $206 million (1970
prices).[121] However, appropriations remain well below that ceiling. As of
1975 a total of $86 million had been appropriated for NIIP.[122]

Water has been scheduled for delivery on the first block of 10,000 acres
in 1976. In March of 1975 the State of New Mexico, prompted by an unquantified water right claim of the Jicarilla Apaches, filed a lawsuit in state
court to adjudicate water rights in the New Mexico stretch of the San Juan
River system,[123] putting at issue Navajo water rights in the San Juan. It is
unclear to what extent the litigation will cause delays in funding or water
delivery for NIIP. One recent analysis suggests that over-contracting of supplies now poses the possibility of water shortages within the New Mexico
portion of the San Juan system and could reduce deliveries to NIIP.[124]

Certainly, numerous reasons can be cited for the differential treatment
of the two projects and the delay in appropriations for the Navajo Indian

---

120. Statement of Charles Corke, in *Hearings on H.R. 17619 Before a Subcomm. of the Senate
Comm. on Appropriations*, 91st Cong., 2d Sess. 2021 (1970).

121. 43 U.S.C. § 615oo (1970).

122. The following NIIP appropriation figures were supplied by Harold Boyd, Assistant
Project Manager for NIIP Construction, Bureau of Reclamation, Farmington, New Mexico,
April 21, 1975.

Year	Actual Appropriations
1963	$ 300,000
1964	1,800,000
1965	4,700,000
1966	6,500,000
1967	6,498,000
1968	5,300,000
1969	3,548,000
1970	5,300,000
1971	3,800,000
1972	8,900,000
1973	10,500,000
1974	14,000,000
1975	15,200,000
	$86,346,000

123. State of New Mexico, *ex rel*. State Engineer v. United States, Civil No. 75-184 (D.N.M.,
filed March 13, 1975).

124. *See* R. Hughes, Gasification and the NIIP: A Study of Upper Basin Water Availability
in New Mexico, 9 (undated and unpublished paper on file with the DNA).

Considering the diversion requirement of 370,000 a[cre] f[eet]/yr, for the NIIP as presently conceived, the absence of any competent studies indicating return flow, the fact
that the NIIP water contract will probably be the last San Juan water contract to come
before Congress, and the stiff statutory prohibitions against operating the project so
as to put New Mexico over its Article III Compact allocation, it is difficult to reach
any other conclusion but that every new diversion of San Juan water in New Mexico—
including particularly the water ear-marked for the gasification projects—will ultimately result in a severe reduction in the size of the NIIP.

Irrigation Project. Among those reasons were changed technology in the projected irrigation system, yielding some dispute about the nature of the diversion right for NIIP,[125] and some lingering uncertainty about the basic purpose and cost-effectiveness[126] of the project itself. But an alternative explanation, consistent with the course of events, lies in the reduced power of the Navajo Tribe after its bargaining advantage had been relinquished. The uncertainties of the *Winters* right could be employed to hold hostage a trans-basin diversion. But once the *Winters* right was compromised and the San Juan-Chama diversion project was authorized, the weight of the Navajo stance diminished. The appropriation process, the ultimate test of strength in Congress, was one in which the mythology of the family farm and the utility of the NIIP as a mechanism for clearing other projects was far more closely scrutinized. Perhaps only as the project more closely approximates the Jorgensen model—only as the reservation land becomes more significantly a source for non-Navajo development—will NIIP progress toward completion.

CONCLUSION

Rights can be weapons, but their potency rests on a number of factors. Although elaboration of the legal issues inherent in the *Winters* doctrine is essential to an understanding of its implications, the extent to which tribes can deploy its potential rests heavily on congressional support, judicial constancy, changing conceptions of reservation purposes and goals, developmental alternatives, and the costs to all parties of striking a bargain. No less important is the role of intergovernmental bodies entrusted with the power of fashioning resource allocation decisions. The fact that the Navajo were not represented in the formulation of the Colorado River Compacts or were not before the interstate stream commissions, and the fact that consortia of power companies have close links to state governments but not to the tribes

---

125. Originally planned as a gravity-flow system, NIIP was expected to result in a net depletion of 254,000 acre-feet in a return flow of an equal amount. Sprinkler irrigation now is planned which will reduce the diversion from 508,000 acre-feet to 370,000 acre-feet, causing a net depletion of 230,000 acre-feet and returning 140,000 acre-feet to the San Juan. The issue accentuated by this change was whether the Navajo entitlement is 508,000 acre-feet, irrespective of the amount of net depletion, or 254,000 acre-feet, in net depletion. Late in 1974, the Deputy Solicitor of the Department of the Interior ruled that the tribe is entitled to the smaller net-depletion amount. Navajo Indian Irrigation Project—Water Entitlement of Navajo Tribe, memorandum from David E. Lingren, Deputy Solicitor to John C. Whittaker, Under Secretary of the Interior, December 6, 1974.

126. For example, Senator Bible of Nevada offered the suspicion in 1970 that NIIP was a "totally marginal project." *Hearings on H.R. 17619, supra* note 116, at 2022. Congressman Hosmer of California had argued in 1955 that if the $200,000 expected to be spent in bringing water to each Navajo family farm in NIIP were invested instead at a five per cent yield, the income would double that produced by farming. *Hearings on H.R. 270, H.R. 2836, H.R. 3383, H.R. 3384, & H.R. 4488 Before the Subcomm. on Irrigation and Reclamation of the House Comm. on Interior and Insular Affairs,* 84th Cong., 1st Sess. 234 (1955).

involved, have a deep effect on the way *Winters* rights are subject to bargain and negotiation. Similar importance attaches to the fact that the Bureau of Indian Affairs, as operating trustee, has been unable to supply the expertise necessary to counter the Bureau of Reclamation's assessments of technical alternatives. Often non-Indians simply postpone the resolution of Indian rights, hoping that they will disappear or that courts will not interfere with a developed pattern of resource reliance. Even if a compromise is reached, failure to obtain congressional appropriations may undermine the bargain.

The stark truth of the matter is that, beginning at the turn of the century, the offices and powers of national government were marshalled to plan, construct, and finance non-Indian agricultural development in the West, and nothing comparable was done for the Native American. Conveniently, this disparity could be rationalized, in part, by the assumption, grounded in the *Winters* doctrine, that early-priority Indian water rights were unaffected by non-Indian development and could successfully be exercised at any point in time, without regard to intervening non-Indian development. As the resource demands of urban areas increase, and reservations are mined or industrialized to meet these demands,[127] the uncertainties of the *Winters* doctrine provide a context in which legal rights become the subject of complex negotiation whose purpose and outcome vary in accordance with a broad range of social, economic, and political factors.

---

127. The study, L. ROBBINS, THE IMPACT OF POWER DEVELOPMENTS ON THE NAVAJO NATION (Lake Powell Res. Project Bull. No. 7, 1975) indicates that energy-related industrialization on the Reservation is not significantly improving the economic condition of the Navajo people as a whole.

THE ALASKA NATIVE CLAIMS SETTLEMENT ACT: A FLAWED VICTORY

ARTHUR LAZARUS, JR.*
W. RICHARD WEST, JR.†

For the eighty thousand natives of Alaska (Indians, Eskimos and Aleuts), passage of the Alaska Native Claims Settlement Act of 1971 (ANCSA)[1] constituted a triumph over long-time governmental inertia. With increasing urgency,[2] the natives had pressed their claims of aboriginal title to virtually all the 375 million acres of land within the state. While Congress proved nominally willing to preserve such claims,[3] almost a century had elapsed without action to confirm or extinguish them.[4] By 1969-1970, however, the rapidly escalating rate of economic development in Alaska, combined initially with pressure from a more sympathetic administration,[5] impelled a reluctant state

---

* Member, Fried, Frank, Harris, Shriver & Kampelman, Washington, D.C. Mr. Lazarus represents Doyon, Ltd., one of the twelve Alaska Native Regional Corporations, and has served as a legal consultant to both the Alaska Federation of Natives and the Alaska Native Foundation.

† Associate Attorney, Fried, Frank, Harris, Shriver & Kampelman, Washington, D.C. Mr. West is a member of the Southern Cheyenne and Arapaho Tribes of Oklahoma.

1. Act of December 18, 1971, Pub. L. No. 92-203, 85 Stat. 688 (codified at 43 U.S.C. § 1601 (Supp. IV, 1974)). The Alaska Native Claims Settlement Act of 1971 will be referred to hereinafter as the "Claims Act" or "ANCSA." Throughout, reference and quotation will be to the original sections of the Claims Act as embodied in 85 Stat. 688 while citation will be to the present codification of the Claims Act in 43 U.S.C. § 1601.

2. Absent federal recognition of their aboriginal rights, the natives faced a constant danger that the United States could (and might) dispose of the lands they claimed without incurring even the obligation to pay just compensation. Tee-Hit-Ton Indians v. United States, 348 U.S. 272 (1955).

3. See Act of July 7, 1958, Pub. L. No. 85-508, 72 Stat. 339; Act of June 6, 1900, ch. 786, 31 Stat. 321; Act of May 14, 1898, ch. 299, 30 Stat. 409; Act of March 3, 1891, ch. 543, 26 Stat. 989; Act of May 17, 1884, ch. 53, § 8, 23 Stat. 24; Lazarus, *Native Land Claims in Alaska*, 7 AM. INDIAN 39 (1958).

4. The Indian Claims Commission Act, which was enacted in 1946, has served as the principal legislative vehicle for settling the claims of Indians against the United States. See 25 U.S.C. § 70 (1970). This legislation, however, has not been utilized by Alaska Natives for the reasons noted by the House of Representatives in its report on the House version of the Claims Act:

> The Indian Claims Commission has not been available to the Natives in Alaska, in a practical sense, because the great bulk of the aboriginal titles claimed by the Natives have not been taken or extinguished by the United States. The United States has simply not acted.

H.R. REP. No. 523, 92d Cong., 1st Sess. 4 (1971).

5. In response to native requests, supported by such Indian-interest organizations as the Association on American Indian Affairs, Inc., Secretary of the Interior Stewart L. Udall in late 1966 imposed an informal and unannounced moratorium upon the patenting of lands selected by the state pursuant to section 6 of the Alaska Statehood Act. Act of July 7, 1958, Pub. L. No. 85-508, 72 Stat. 339. Before leaving office, Secretary Udall issued Public Land Order No. 4582, 34 Fed. Reg. 1025 (1969), formally withdrawing all unreserved public lands in Alaska from disposition

and, subsequently, private industry to join the natives in seeking a comprehensive legislative determination of their land rights.[6] The Claims Act soon followed.

The victory for the native cause achieved through ANCSA was overwhelming, both comparatively and absolutely. In June 1967, Secretary of the Interior Stewart L. Udall recommended to Congress a legislative settlement which included the grant of trust title in up to fifty thousand acres for each native village (a maximum of about ten million acres) and authorization for the Alaska Attorney General to sue for the value of any remaining native lands at 1867 prices.[7] By July 1969, Secretary of the Interior Walter J. Hickel had raised the administration's suggested price for the extinguishment of native claims to $500 million and ownership of up to ten million acres.[8] Under the Claims Act, the natives in fact will receive fee title to over forty million acres of land, payments from the United States Treasury of $462.5 million over an eleven year period, and a royalty of two per cent up to a ceiling of $500 million on mineral development in Alaska.[9] This settlement provides far more money and leaves far more land in native ownership than any previous treaty, agreement, or statute for the extinguishment of aboriginal title in our nation's history.

In addition to funds and resources, however, the Claims Act presents the natives of Alaska with a unique challenge. Rejecting traditional federal-Indian relationships, Congress directed that the settlement be administered through corporations organized under state law, and defined the precise manner in which native funds and income from native property were to be allocated.[10] Within this statutory framework, though, the natives retain relatively unfettered control over their assets, and are free from Bureau of Indian Affairs supervision.[11] ANCSA thus reflects a new departure in government dealings

---

pending a determination of native rights, and during the course of his confirmation hearings Secretary-designate Walter J. Hickel, former Governor of Alaska, agreed to honor the Udall "land freeze" for two years.

6. *See generally* M. BERRY, THE ALASKA PIPELINE: THE POLITICS OF OIL AND NATIVE LAND CLAIMS (1975). The switch in the state's position from opposition to native land claims legislation and the subsequent change in industry attitudes from indifference to active support stemmed in substantial part from native successes in the courts. Specifically, in Alaska v. Udall, 420 F.2d 938 (9th Cir. 1969), the Court of Appeals for the Ninth Circuit, in rejecting a state attack upon the validity of the land freeze, ruled that lands claimed by the natives could not be deemed, as a matter of law, "vacant, unappropriated, and unreserved" and thus subject to selection under the Statehood Act. In Native Village of Allakaket v. Hickel, Civil No. 706-70 (D.D.C., filed Oct. 18, 1972), the District Court for the District of Columbia enjoined construction of the Alaska pipeline across native lands.

7. U.S. Dep't of Interior, News Release (June 16, 1967) (on file with authors).

8. *See generally* Senate Interior Comm. Amendment No. 112, in *Hearings on S. 1830 Before the Comm. on Interior and Insular Affairs*, 91st Cong., 1st Sess., pt. 2, at 197-98 (1969).

9. *See* 43 U.S.C. §§ 1605(a), 1608, 1611, 1612 (Supp. IV, 1974).

10. *Id.* §§ 1606(d), 1607(a).

11. The settlement is to be effected "without establishing any permanent racially defined institutions, rights, privilges, or obligations, without creating a reservation system or lengthy ward-

with Indians—a policy which places on the natives alone the crucial task of translating the immediate benefits of the settlement into permanent, socially and economically productive enterprises.

Unfortunately, the language of the Claims Act frequently is ambiguous, and serious difficulties already have arisen in its implementation. The object of this article is to identify those major legal problems which have surfaced to date, to suggest possible answers to some of the crucial issues, and to discuss whether the provisions of ANCSA offer the natives a reasonable chance of meeting the law's challenge.

I

THE PRINCIPAL PROVISIONS OF THE CLAIMS ACT

The Claims Act not only effected a comprehensive legislative settlement of all aboriginal land titles and claims,[12] it also enabled Alaska to resume land selections under the Statehood Act,[13] and removed a major legal obstacle to construction of the Alaska pipeline and a potential cloud upon the titles of all non-natives claiming rights to land in the state under federal law. What the natives received, or were required to do in return, is summarized below.

A.   The Native Corporations

Pursuant to section 7(a) of the Claims Act, the Secretary of the Interior divided the State of Alaska into twelve geographic regions composed, as far as practicable, of natives having a common heritage and sharing common interests. In order to qualify for benefits under ANCSA, the natives of a particular region first had to organize a Regional Corporation under the "busi-

---

ship or trusteeship, and without adding to the categories of property and institutions enjoying special tax privileges . . . ." *Id.* § 1601(b).

12. *Id.* § 1603. The legal and factual background of the settlement is set forth in S. REP. No. 405, 92d Cong., 1st Sess. 71-83, 88-89 (1971). *See also* H.R. REP. No. 523, 92d Cong., 1st Sess. 3-6 (1971); H.R. REP. No. 746, 92d Cong., 1st Sess. 34 (1971).

Courts, however, have noted certain exceptions to the proposition that the Claims Act settled all Alaska Native claims based upon aboriginal title. In Edwardsen v. Morton, 369 F. Supp. 1359 (D.D.C. 1973), the Arctic Slope Native Association sued the Secretary of the Interior to recover damages caused by the United States' allegedly unlawful transfer of native lands to the State of Alaska, and for its purportedly illegal authorization of certain third-party trespasses on the natives' lands. The defendant moved for summary judgment on the ground that such claims had been extinguished by section 4 of the Claims Act. *See* 43 U.S.C. § 1603 (Supp. IV, 1974). The district court rejected the government's defense, and held that ANCSA had not effected an extinguishment of native claims based on defendant's "pre-Settlement Act trespasses." Edwardsen v. Morton, *supra* at 1379.

Legislation was introduced in the Ninety-fourth Congress which was directed towards overruling the *Edwardsen* case by amending section 4 of ANCSA to include the trespass claim alleged by the Arctic Slope Native Association. *See* S. 1824, 94th Cong., 1st Sess. § 15(b) (1975). The proposed legislation, however, was not included in the Claims Act amendments ultimately enacted by Congress. *See* Act of January 2, 1976, Pub. L. No. 94-204, 89 Stat. 1145.

13. *See* notes 5, 6 *supra*.

ness for profit" laws of the State of Alaska.[14] Section 7(g) of the Claims Act provides that each "Regional Corporation shall be authorized to issue such number of shares of common stock, divided into such classes of shares as may be specified in the articles of incorporation to reflect the provisions of this Act, as may be needed to issue one hundred shares of stock to each Native enrolled in the region . . . ."[15] Until December 18, 1991, stock in the Regional Corporations is subject to a restriction upon alienation and carries voting rights only if the holder is a native.

Within each region, eligible native villages must also organize under state corporation laws before receiving benefits under the Act.[16] These Village Corporations are neither stockholders in nor subsidiaries of the Regional Corporations,[17] but the Claims Act nonetheless requires the Regional Corporations to supervise the redistribution to Village Corporations of monies received from the Alaska Native Fund and from timber and mineral resources,[18] to withhold money until acceptable plans have been approved by the Regional Corporation for the use of distributable funds,[19] and to review and approve the articles of incorporation, including proposed amendments and annual budgets of the Village Corporations for a period of five years.[20]

---

14. 43 U.S.C. §§ 1606(d), 1607(a) (Supp. IV, 1974). Section 7(c) of ANCSA, 43 U.S.C. § 1606(c), provides that, "[i]f a majority of all eligible Natives eighteen years of age or older who are not permanent residents of Alaska elect . . . to be enrolled in a thirteenth region . . . the Secretary shall establish such a region for the benefit of the Natives who elected to be enrolled therein, and they may establish a Regional Corporation . . . ." The Secretary ruled that a majority of the adult natives who are nonresidents of Alaska did not elect to form a thirteenth region, but his determination has been overturned by a federal district court, and a thirteenth Regional Corporation was organized on January 1, 1976. Alaska Native Ass'n of Oregon v. Morton, Civil No. 2133-73; Alaska Fed'n of Natives Int'l v. Morton, Civil No. 2141-73 (D.D.C., filed Dec. 30, 1974). Moreover, the district court's decision was confirmed by the Act of January 2, 1976, Pub. L. No. 94-204, § 8, 89 Stat. 1145, 1149.

15. 43 U.S.C. § 1606(g) (Supp. IV, 1974).

16. *Id.* § 1607(a). At the present time all of the more than two hundred native villages in Alaska certified by the Secretary of the Interior as eligible for benefits under the Act have organized as business corporations pursuant to Alaska law.

17. All of the stockholders of a Village Corporation also are stockholders of the Regional Corporation for their region, but only some of the stockholders of the Regional Corporation will be stockholders of any particular Village Corporation. Under the Claims Act, the Village Corporations do not own stock of the Regional Corporation, and the Regional Corporation does not own stock of the Village Corporations.

18. 43 U.S.C. § 1606(j) (Supp. IV, 1974). *See* text at notes 7-8, 10-11 *supra.*

19. A Regional Corporation may withhold money otherwise distributable to a Village Corporation

until the village has submitted a plan for the use of the money that is satisfactory to the Regional Corporation . . . [and] may require a village plan to provide for joint ventures with other villages, and for joint financing of projects undertaken by the Regional Corporation that will benefit the region generally.

43 U.S.C. § 1606(l) (Supp. IV, 1974).

20. *Id.* § 1607(b). This vesting of authority in one set of private corporations over the business, assets, and affairs of a second independent set of private corporations appears unprecedented in the annals of American legal history.

B. The Alaska Native Fund

Section 6 of the Claims Act establishes in the United States Treasury an Alaska Native Fund[21] into which money from two major sources is to be deposited. The Fund is to receive federal appropriations in the total amount of $462,500,000 over an eleven year period beginning with the fiscal year 1972, the year during which the Act became effective. In addition, a share in the amount of two per cent of specified federal and state mineral revenues is to be paid into the Fund, without regard to any time limitations, until such payments reach $500 million.[22]

Section 6(c) of the Claims Act provides that, after completion of a native roll by the Secretary, all money in the Fund "shall be distributed at the end of each three months of the fiscal year among the Regional Corporations organized pursuant to section 7 on the basis of the relative numbers of Natives enrolled in each region."[23] Pursuant to section 7(j) of ANCSA, however, during the first five years following enactment, not less than 10 per cent of all money received by the Regional Corporations from the Fund must be distributed among their stockholders and, in addition, not less than 45 per cent of such money during the first five year period and 50 per cent thereafter is to be distributed by the Regional Corporations to Village Corporations and to the class of regional stockholders who are not residents of native villages which have organized Village Corporations.[24] Thus, ANCSA specifically mandates that initially at least 55 per cent, and subsequently at least 50 per cent, of all money distributed from the Fund to Regional Corporations shall be redistributed to their stockholders, to non-residents of villages, and to Village Corporations.

C. Land Entitlement Under the Claims Act

Pursuant to section 11(a) of the Act, the Secretary of the Interior has withdrawn over one hundred million acres of "public lands"[25] in Alaska "from

---

21. *Id.* § 1605. [Hereinafter the Alaska Native Fund will be referred to as "Fund."]

22. *Id.* § 1608.

23. *Id.* § 1605(c). The final roll was certified by the Secretary of the Interior on December 18, 1973, and the balance of the money then held in the Fund was distributed to the Regional Corporations immediately thereafter. Previously, the corporations had received small advances from the Fund pursuant to special congressional authorization in order to conduct necessary business activities. *See* Second Supplemental Appropriations Act of May 27, 1972, Pub. L. No. 92-306, 86 Stat. 163, 167; Interior Dep't Appropriations Act for the Fiscal Year Ending June 30, 1973, Pub. L. No. 92-369, 86 Stat. 508, 510. The roll was ordered reopened by the Act of January 2, 1976, *supra* note 14, to accommodate those natives who missed the filing deadline.

24. 43 U.S.C. § 1606(j) (Supp. IV, 1974).

25. "Public lands" are defined in section 3(e) of ANCSA as
all Federal lands and interests therein in Alaska except: (1) the smallest practicable tract, as determined by the Secretary, enclosing land actually used in connection with the administration of any Federal installation, and (2) land selections of the State of Alaska

all forms of appropriation under the public land laws, including the mining and mineral leasing laws, and from selection under the Alaska Statehood Act . . . ."[26] Village Corporations had the collective right, before December 18, 1974, to select up to twenty-two million acres from the lands so withdrawn, with the exact land entitlement of each village being dependent upon its population.[27] The difference between the acreage actually selected by Village Corporations and the authorized twenty-two million acres is to be allocated by the Secretary among eleven Regional Corporations (excluding southeastern Alaska) on the basis of the number of natives enrolled in each region, and then is to be reallocated by the Regional Corporations to the villages "on an equitable basis after considering historic use, subsistence needs, and population."[28] The Village Corporations will receive a fee simple "patent to the surface estate in the lands selected,"[29] while the Secretary of the Interior is directed to "issue to the Regional Corporation for the region in which the lands are located a patent to the subsurface estate in such lands . . . ."[30] The Act also provided that Regional Corporations could obtain title to an additional sixteen million acres of land selected prior to December 18, 1975 from withdrawn public lands.[31]

---

which have been patented or tentatively approved under section 6(g) of the Alaska Statehood Act, as amended . . . or identified for selection by the State prior to January 17, 1969.
Id. § 1602(e).

26. *Id.* § 1610(a).

27. *Id.* §§ 1611(a), 1615(a). In villages outside southeast Alaska, the Village Corporations are entitled to select a minimum of three townships (69,120 acres) for a population between twenty-five and ninety-nine and a maximum of seven townships (161,280 acres) for a population over 600. *Id.* § 1613(a). All villages in southeastern Alaska are limited to land selections of one township (23,040 acres), regardless of population. *Id.* § 1613(b).

28. *Id.* § 1611(b).

29. *Id.* §§ 1613(a), 1613(b).

30. *Id.* § 1613(f).

31. *Id.* § 1611(c). Sealaska Corporation, organized by the natives of southeastern Alaska, and the thirteenth Regional Corporation, which will be organized under section 7(c) of the Claims Act, *see* note 14 *supra*, are not entitled to make these section 12(c) selections. In addition, since eligibility for section 12(c) selections is determined on a land-loss formula, only six Regional Corporations actually so qualify.

In exercising rights under section 12(c), lands withdrawn pursuant to subsection 11(a)(1) must be selected before lands withdrawn pursuant to subsection 11(a)(3) may be selected, provided that "within the lands withdrawn by subsection 11(a)(1) the Regional Corporation may select only even numbered townships in even numbered ranges, and only odd numbered townships in odd numbered ranges." 43 U.S.C. § 1611(c) (Supp. IV, 1974). The purpose of this provision was to prevent native corporations in combination from controlling large, solid blocks of land.

Section 14(c) provides that "[i]mmediately after selection by a Regional Corporation, the Secretary shall convey to the Corporation title to the surface and/or the subsurface estates, as is appropriate, in the lands selected." *Id.* § 1613(e). As a practical matter, the Bureau of Land Management will not be able to complete the required survey of native land selections for decades, so the Secretary will have difficulty in issuing a patent promptly. In recognition of this fact, the land selection regulations provide for issuance of interim conveyances. 43 C.F.R. § 2650.0-5(h) (1974).

Although Regional Corporations will receive full title to their own land selections and a fee simple patent to the subsurface estate under lands selected by native villages, groups, and individuals, ANCSA further provides that these corporations will not enjoy the entire benefit of this property. Section 7(i) of the Claims Act requires that each Regional Corporation divide among all twelve Regional Corporations on an annual basis 70 per cent of the revenues derived from the timber resources and subsurface estate patented to it.[32] Moreover, as in the case of the Fund, section 7(j) provides that, during the five years following enactment, not less than 10 per cent of all funds received by a Regional Corporation under section 7(i) must be distributed among its stockholders and, in addition, not less than 45 per cent of such revenues during the first five year period, and 50 per cent thereafter, shall be distributed by the Regional Corporation to Village Corporations established in its region, and to the class of its stockholders who are not residents of native villages having organized Village Corporations.[33] Thus, ANCSA vests substantial real property interests in the Regional Corporation, but further dictates that each Regional Corporation must share its revenues from timber and subsurface resources with other Regional Corporations, Village Corporations, and certain stockholders.

II

A SURVEY OF ISSUES WHICH HAVE ARISEN
IN THE IMPLEMENTATION OF THE CLAIMS ACT

Implementation of the Alaska Native claims settlement scheme has already produced a significant number of troublesome questions concerning the scope and meaning of its provisions. A new statute—especially one as complicated and unique as the Claims Act—is under the best of circumstances bound to produce problems of interpretation, but in the case of ANCSA this problem has been complicated by the frequent ambiguity of its language and the relative dearth of revealing legislative history. Moreover, as the following discussion will show, the executive agencies to which issues arising under ANCSA have been presented are not responding with the cooperative spirit and sympathetic understanding to which the natives are entitled.

The Regional Corporations also possess a land entitlement under section 14(h) of ANCSA which is not to exceed two million acres, including the subsurface estate beneath lands patented to native groups and individuals. 43 U.S.C. § 1613(h) (Supp. IV, 1974).

32. 43 U.S.C. § 1606(i) (Supp. IV, 1974).

33. *Id.* § 1606(j).

A. Threshold Questions—Village Eligibility and the Boundaries of Regional Corporations

Although the Act listed 205 native villages as presumptively eligible for land selections and monetary benefits,[34] the Secretary of the Interior was empowered to add other villages to the list[35] and, more importantly, declare ineligible any village with less than twenty-five native residents or one possessing a modern, urban character the majority of whose residents are non-native.[36]

The federal regulations implementing these provisions were written, as the natives had requested, with an eye towards favoring village eligibility.[37] Thus, building upon the previously issued enrollment regulations which equated "residence" with domicile,[38] a key paragraph of the village eligibility regulations provided that, for purposes of finding twenty-five or more native residents in a village, a "Native properly enrolled to the village shall be deemed a resident of the village."[39] Although the regulations required that a village possess "an identifiable physical location," that location need be evidenced only by "occupancy consistent with the Natives' own cultural patterns and life style" and through use by as few as thirteen natives during 1970.[40] Finally, the

---

34. *Id.* §§ 1610(b)(1), 1615(a).

35. *Id.* § 1610(b)(3).

36. *Id.* § 1610(b)(2). Native villages determined to be ineligible by the Secretary are still entitled, pursuant to section 14(h) of ANCSA, to receive some lands as native groups. *See id.* § 1613(h).

37. The area of village eligibility served as the specific occasion for one of the more curious interpretations of the Claims Act offered by the Office of the Solicitor of the Department of the Interior. The Solicitor was asked to determine whether the Secretary of the Interior possessed authority after June 18, 1974 to determine the eligibility of native villages for benefits under ANCSA. Sections 11(b)(2) and 11(b)(3) provide that the Secretary shall make determinations concerning village eligibility within two and a half years following the enactment of ANCSA.

Proponents of the position that the Secretary continued to have authority to decide eligibility questions after June 18, 1974 relied on the established principle of Indian law that federal statutes affecting the rights and affairs of Indians must be liberally construed in their favor. Squire v. Capoeman, 351 U.S. 1, 2 (1956); Carpenter v. Shaw, 280 U.S. 363, 366-67 (1930); Choate v. Trapp, 224 U.S. 665, 675 (1912). In order to escape this rule, the Solicitor gratuitously observed that the Claims Act is not Indian legislation. Interior Dep't Sol. Op. M-36876, 81 Interior Dec. 316 (1974). The Solicitor subsequently "revised" his opinion on village eligibility and eliminated (but did not officially withdraw) his gratuitous observation. Interior Dep't Sol. Op. M-36877 (Jan. 7, 1975), 82 Interior Dec. 15. Shortly thereafter, however, the Solicitor again construed the Claims Act adversely to native property interests, as if ANCSA were a public land law and not legislation for the benefit of Indians. *See* Interior Dep't Sol. Op. M-36880 (July 8, 1975), 82 Interior Dec. 325.

38. 25 C.F.R. § 43h.1(k) (1975).

39. 43 C.F.R. § 2651.2(b)(1) (1975).

40. *Id.* § 2651.2(b)(2). In order to preserve the eligibility of villages destroyed or abandoned because of the 1964 Alaska earthquake and tidal wave, the regulations further provided that "no village which is known as a traditional village shall be disqualified if it meets the other criteria specified in this subsection by reason of having been temporarily unoccupied in 1970 because of an act of God or government authority occurring within the preceding 10 years." *Id.* § 2651.2(b)(2).

standards for determining that a village is urban and modern in character were set too high to cover any native village.[41]

The Alaska Native Claims Appeal Board, which is empowered to pass on questions of village eligibility, adopted the position that it had jurisdiction to reconsider the residence of persons placed on the final roll approved by the Secretary of the Interior.[42] As a consequence, two listed villages (Pauloff Harbor and Uyak) and eight unlisted villages challenged in court board decisions denying their eligibility.[43] The significance of the village eligibility cases, however, lies not in the substantive issues involved, but in the fact that the natives' early exposure to administration of ANCSA led to rulings by a federal agency which actually granted less than the law and the regulations seemed to promise.

Similar difficulties have arisen in the determination of boundary disputes between the Regional Corporations. When the Secretary, in December 1972, directed that any dispute should be settled under the arbitration provisions of the Act[44] "within 90 days from the receipt of this letter,"[45] several Regional Corporations which were dissatisfied with the borders he had proposed sought judicial relief compelling other Regional Corporations to submit boundary questions to arbitration boards.[46] In almost all instances the Regional Corporation seeking an order for arbitration prevailed. Again, the significance of the boundary dispute cases lies not in the substantive issues involved,[47] but in the fact that the unity of purpose achieved by the natives prior to passage of the Claims Act broke down so quickly after its enactment.

---

41. *Id.* § 2651.2(b)(3).

42. *See, e.g., In re* Village of Afognak (1974) (appeal before the Alaska Native Claims Appeal Board). Under the regulations, the Director of the Juneau Area Office, Bureau of Indian Affairs, made the initial determination concerning eligibility, 43 C.F.R. § 2651.2(a)(4) (1975), but his decision was subject to appeal to the Alaska Native Claims Appeal Board. The decision of this ad hoc board was submitted to the Secretary for his personal approval. *Id.* § 2651.2(a)(5).

43. In a memorandum and order handed down on November 14, 1975, a federal district court upheld the eligibility of all the native villages. Koniag, Inc. v. Kleppe, 405 F. Supp. 1360 (D.D.C. 1975).

44. 43 U.S.C. § 1606(a) (Supp. IV, 1974).

45. Letter from Rogers C.B. Morton, Secretary of the Interior to John Borbridge. Dec. 11, 1972. In subsequent litigation concerning the arbitration of boundary disputes, the authority of the Secretary of the Interior to establish administratively the ninety-day deadline was challenged successfully. *See* Central Council of the Tlingit & Haida Indians v. Chugach Native Ass'n, 502 F.2d 1323, 1325 (9th Cir. 1974).

46. *See, e.g.,* Central Council of the Tlingit & Haida Indians v. Chugach Native Ass'n, 502 F.2d at 1325; Ahtna, Inc. v. Doyon Ltd., Civil No. A-198-72 (D. Alas., filed Jan. 18, 1973). The agreement entered into by Sealaska Corporation and the Chugach Native Association as a result of the *Tlingit and Haida Indians* litigation has been confirmed by the Act of January 2, 1976, Pub. L. No. 94-204, § 11, 89 Stat. 1145, 1150.

47. The location of a Regional Corporation's border obviously influences the number of natives who will be considered as "enrolled" in the region for purposes of distributing land and monetary benefits under ANCSA. *See, e.g.,* 43 U.S.C. §§ 1605(c), 1606(i) (Supp. IV, 1974).

B. Corporate and Tax Issues Relating to the Native Corporations
and to the Monetary Benefits Distributed Under the Claims Act

In administering and distributing the substantial monetary benefits conferred on native corporations by the Claims Act, the Regional Corporations have had to determine not only what the general tax consequences of ANCSA are, but also how such consequences should be allocated between the Regional and Village Corporations. Furthermore, provisions in the Act authorizing the native corporations to distribute stock to their shareholders have raised obvious questions about the applicability of federal securities laws.

1. *Tax Consequences Attaching to the Distribution of Revenues and Moneys Under the Claims Act*

Among the more important tax questions which have arisen under the provisions of ANCSA[48] are the following: (1) whether money earned from the Alaska Native Fund prior to distribution to the Regional Corporations is subject to federal income taxes upon receipt by the Regional Corporations and/or upon redistribution to Village Corporations and individual natives under section 7(j) of the Claims Act; (2) whether distributions which must be made by Regional Corporations to the Village Corporations under sections 7(i) and 7(j) of ANCSA should be taxed to the Regional or the Village Corporations; and (3) whether income on mandatory distributions earned prior to distribution is taxable to the Regional Corporation or the Village Corporation.

a. Interest or other earnings on Fund money before distribution

In accordance with section 6(a) of the Claims Act,[49] Congress appropriated $12,500,000 during fiscal year 1972, $50 million during fiscal year 1973, and $70 million during fiscal year 1974 for deposit in the Alaska Native Fund.[50] A small portion of this money was advanced to the Regional Corporations[51] while the balance earned interest either as a deposit in the United States Treasury or a qualified bank until distribution to the Regional Corporations on December 19, 1973.[52] The Claims Act, its legislative history, and relevant

---

48. One such issue already has been eliminated by the Act of January 2, 1976, which effected a number of corrective amendments to the Claims Act. *See* Act of January 2, 1976, Pub. L. No. 94-204, § 13, 89 Stat. 1145, 1154. The 1976 Act amended section 21 of ANCSA to provide explicitly that until January 1, 1992, the stock of any native corporation, including the right to receive dividends from such stock, shall not be included in the gross estate of a decedent under sections 2031 and 2033 of the Internal Revenue Code. *See generally* H.R. REP. No. 729, 94th Cong., 1st Sess. 33 (1975).

49. 43 U.S.C. § 1605(a) (Supp. IV, 1974).

50. *See* Act of Oct. 4, 1973, Pub. L. No. 93-120, 87 Stat. 429, 431; Act of Aug. 10, 1972, Pub. L. No. 92-369, 86 Stat. 508, 510; Act of May 27, 1972, Pub. L. No. 92-306, 86 Stat. 163, 167

51. *See id.*

52. Under date of December 28, 1973, the Comptroller General ruled that, upon certification of the final native roll by the Secretary on December 18, 1973, Fund money lost its status as

authorities all support the conclusion that the "interest" portion of Fund distributions to the Regional Corporations is not subject to federal income tax
upon receipt or upon distribution.[53] Section 21(a) of the Claims Act provides
a tax exemption for "revenues" originating from the Fund, with no distinction drawn between principal and interest.[54] Section 6(c) of the Act directs
that, after completion of the native roll by the Secretary, "all money in the
Fund," with an exception not here material, "shall be distributed . . . among
the Regional Corporations," and such "money," which necessarily includes
both principal and accumulated interest, is the only revenue originating from
the Fund to which the statutory tax exemption possibly could relate. Only the
income earned from the investment of this revenue is subject to taxation.
Thus the statutory pattern, which is repeated in provisions affecting taxation
of native land, is to immunize native property from taxation until its receipt,
and thereafter to permit taxation of the income from these assets "to the same
extent as such revenues or proceeds are taxable when received by a non-
native individual or corporation."[55] Indeed, since the Village and Regional
Corporations are treated as Indian tribes for purposes of the interest earned
on the deposit of their funds,[56] and since Indian tribes are not entities subject

---

"tribal funds" and no longer would qualify for interest-bearing deposit pursuant to 25 U.S.C. §§
161a, 162a (1970). In passing the Act of January 2, 1976, Congress effectively overruled the
Comptroller General. *See* Act of Jan. 2, 1976, Pub. L. No. 94-204, § 5, 89 Stat. 1145, 1147. For
purposes of sections 161a and 162a, the Alaska Native Fund now shall be considered Indian trust
moneys until the date on which distributions are made from the Fund under section 6(c) of the
Claims Act.

 53. Nonetheless, the question has been pending before the Internal Revenue Service since
May 1974. IRS's unreasonable delay in responding to the request for tax rulings typifies the
natives' frustration with federal agencies in trying to make ANCSA work.

 54. 43 U.S.C. § 1620(a) (Supp. IV, 1974). In substance, the Alaska Native Fund is indistinguishable from any of the numerous judgment funds deposited in the Treasury to the credit of
Indian groups. Distributions of principal and interest from these funds have also been declared
to be tax exempt. Act of Oct. 19, 1973, Pub. L. No. 93-134, 87 Stat. 466, 468 (codified at 25
U.S.C. § 1407 (Supp. IV, 1974)).

 55. 43 U.S.C. § 1620(d) (Supp. IV, 1974). The legislative history of ANCSA lends additional
support to the conclusion that interest earned upon Fund money prior to distribution to the
Regional Corporations is not subject to federal income taxes upon such distribution. Whereas the
Act does not expressly provide for the payment of interest on money actually appropriated and
deposited in the Treasury, section 6(a)(2) does call for the payment of four per cent interest
upon money authorized to be appropriated which in fact is not appropriated within six months
after the fiscal year during which the money was payable. In explaining the former omission,
Senator Bible, the Floor Manager of the Conference Report, declared in response to a question
from Alaskan Senator Gravel:

  [I]t is the committee's intention that the Secretary of the Treasury shall use his existing
  statutory authority to invest and manage the Alaska Native Fund pending enrollment
  and to credit any interest so earned to that fund. When the enrollment is completed, *the*
  total balance, including accrued interest will be paid to regional corporations in accordance with
  the bill.

117 Cong. Rec. 46967 (1971) (statement of Senator Alan Bible) (emphasis added).

 56. Letter from Elmer B. Staats, Comptroller General of the United States to Rogers C.B.
Morton, Secretary of the Interior 6, October 31, 1972.

to income tax statutes,[57] it follows that the interest or other income earned upon Fund money during the period before distribution to the Regional Corporations should not be subject to federal income tax upon receipt by the Regional Corporations or, following partial redistribution pursuant to section 7(j) of ANCSA, upon receipt by stockholders, Village Corporations, and non-village residents.[58]

b. Distributions mandated by the Claims Act

Section 7(i) of ANCSA requires the distribution to all twelve Regional Corporations of 70 per cent of the revenues which a Regional Corporation receives from the disposition of its timber resources and subsurface estate.[59] Furthermore, Regional Corporations are directed by section 7(j) to distribute to their stockholders, to Village Corporations in their region, and to certain nonvillage residents a portion of the funds and revenues which the Regional Corporations receive under sections 6(c) and 7(i).[60] These statutory provisions establish the basic pattern for the allocation of Fund money, resource revenues, and certain other income under ANCSA. The intent of Congress plainly was to accord all natives a meaningful stake in the land claims settlement, either directly or through a two-tier structure of Regional and Village Corporations which they were to own.

The question that arises—and upon which neither the Internal Revenue Service nor the courts have yet ruled—is whether income which the Regional Corporations must distribute to Village Corporations and individual natives under the Claims Act is taxable to the Regional Corporations or the ultimate distributees, or possibly both. The language of the Claims Act is clear in that Regional Corporations do not take funds, revenues, or other income which the law mandates be shared or redistributed[61] as beneficial owners or even under a claim of right, but instead are mere conduits, the instruments chosen by Congress to receive and pass along funds which the federal government would have practical difficulties in itself disbursing. The courts have, moreover, repeatedly held that taxes may not be charged against one who has no right to retain the income earned.[62] Therefore, the Regional Corporations

---

57. Rev. Rul. 284, 1967-2 Cum. Bull. 55, 58.

58. Revenue Ruling 67-284, of course, further states that "[t]ribal income not otherwise exempt from Federal income tax is includible in the gross income of the Indian tribal member when distributed or constructively received by him." The potential application of this rule to the interest portion of the 10 per cent distribution from the Fund money to individual natives, however, is precluded by section 21(a) of ANCSA.

59. 43 U.S.C. § 1606(i) (Supp. IV, 1974).

60. Id. § 1606(j).

61. See Healy v. Commissioner, 345 U.S. 278 (1953).

62. See, e.g., Commissioner v. Brown, 54 F.2d 563 (1st Cir. 1931), cert. denied, Burnet v. Brown, 286 U.S. 556 (1932); Seven-up Co., 14 T.C. 965 (1950), acquiesced in, 1950-2 Cum. Bull. 4. See also Ford Dealers Advertising Fund, Inc., 55 T.C. 761 (1971), aff'd, 456 F.2d 255 (5th

should not be subject to federal income tax with respect to any revenues which must be distributed to other Regional Corporations pursuant to section 7(i) of the Act, or with respect to any funds, revenues, or other income which must be distributed under section 7(j) to their stockholders, to Village Corporations, and to the class of their stockholders who are not village residents.[63]

c. Earnings upon mandated distributions

ANCSA is silent as to when or how frequently the Regional Corporations are required to distribute funds in accordance with section 7(j), and is equally unrevealing concerning the powers or responsibilities of the Regional Corporations to invest withheld funds. However, after receipt of a Fund distribution,[64] or a resource revenue sharing payment pursuant to section 7(i),[65] the Regional Corporations as a practical matter will need thirty to sixty days to up-date their books and process checks effecting a redistribution of the money to Village Corporations and individual native stockholders. At least three sets of circumstances also exist under which the Regional Corporations may be well advised temporarily to withhold redistribution of some or all of such receipts for an even longer period:

(1) The Village Corporations and individual natives may be entitled to a distribution of resource revenues and Fund money at approximately the same time, so that two distributions could be combined if one were briefly delayed.

Cir. 1972); Broadcast Measurement Bureau, Inc., 16 T.C. 988 (1951), *acquiesced in*, 1951-2 Cum. Bull. 2.

63. Section 7(m) of the Act provides that, "[w]hen funds are distributed among Village Corporations in a region, an amount . . . shall be distributed as dividends to the class of stockholders who are not residents of those villages," and a question thus may arise as to whether at least the money so paid out as "dividends," including, in particular, the distributable portion of "all other net income" under section 7(j), should be included in the gross income of the Regional Corporations. In this regard, Congress appears to have used the term "dividends" in section 7(m) in its primary sense as "an individual share of something distributed among a number of recipients," Webster's Third New International Dictionary 633 (1966); Black's Law Dictionary 565 (4th ed. 1968), and not as the word is specially defined under section 316 of the Internal Revenue Code. *See* Int. Rev. Code of 1954, § 316.

First, the language of the Act makes clear that village nonresidents receive payments under section 7(m) not because they are stockholders of a Regional Corporation, but rather because they are not stockholders of a Village Corporation. Second, section 7(j) directs the Regional Corporations to distribute 45 to 50 per cent of certain revenues to Village Corporations and non-village residents regardless of whether the Regional Corporations, in the light of all their activities, have "earnings and profits"; under section 316 of the Code, on the other hand, a dividend by definition must be derived from "earnings and profits." Finally, section 21(a) of ANCSA clothes Fund income with a tax exemption upon receipt by an "individual Native through dividend distributions," a clear congressional use of the word "dividend" in a context where the meaning that this term possesses under section 316 of the Code could not possibly have been intended.

64. Under section 6(c) of ANCSA, distributions from the Fund are made on a quarterly basis. *See* 43 U.S.C. § 1605(c) (Supp. IV, 1974).

65. Resource revenues under section 7(i) will be distributed twice a year, at the end of the calendar year in some cases and at the end of a June 30 fiscal year for all other Regional Corporations. *See id.* § 1606(i).

(2) A Fund distribution or resource revenue payment may be so small as to make immediate redistribution economically undesirable, especially to individual natives. This situation is likely with respect to three out of every four Fund distributions during early years, when no appropriated money will have been deposited and, as is now the case, the contributions from the two per cent royalty under section 9 of ANCSA remain relatively low.[66]

(3) Under section 7(1) of the Act, a Regional Corporation is empowered to withhold section 7(j) distributions to a Village Corporation "until the village has submitted a plan for use of the money that is satisfactory to the Regional Corporation."

The Regional Corporations originally placed 55 per cent of the December 19, 1973 Fund distribution, and will continue to place 55 to 50 per cent, as the case may be, of future Fund money and resource revenue payments, in interest-bearing deposits or short-term investments pending redistribution of the money to the Village Corporations and individual native stockholders. Since section 21(a) of the Act provides that the tax exemption accorded revenues originating from the Alaska Native Fund "shall not apply to income from the investment of such revenues," and since ANCSA contains no special tax exemption for resource revenues, the question arises as to whether income earned upon the distributable portion of these funds is attributable for tax purposes to the Regional Corporations.

Case law and a published ruling of the Internal Revenue Service both stand for the proposition that interest or other earnings upon money which the Regional Corporations must distribute to Village Corporations and individual natives in accordance with section 7(j) of the Act is not income of the Regional Corporations. In *Rupe Investment Corporation v. Commissioner*,[67] the court held that an investment banker possessing stock as a conduit between a buyer and seller was not entitled to claim a dividends-received credit, the overriding principle being that such income will be attributed to the beneficial owner of the underlying asset. Furthermore, in Revenue Ruling 69-96,[68] the Service determined that annual dividends received (and used to reduce future premiums) on a group credit life insurance policy, which was administered by a farm production credit association for the benefit of its member-borrowers, were not income to the association since it was acting solely as an agent in handling the dividends.[69] Similarly, interest or other income earned during

---

66. Under section 7(j), Regional Corporations are required to distribute to natives 10 per cent of royalties received under section 9 of the Act. The distribution of March 31, 1974, for example, amounted to 71 cents per native.

67. 266 F.2d 624 (5th Cir. 1959).

68. 1969-1 Cum. Bull. 31.

69. In Revenue Ruling 69-96, the Service emphasized that the association's books must "clearly establish that it is acting as a mere trustee or conduit" with respect to dividend payments. Rev. Rul. 96, 1969-1 Cum. Bull. 32. The books and records of the Regional Corporations clearly establish their position as conduits of the statutorily mandated distributions.

the period after receipt and before redistribution on that portion of Fund money and resource revenues received by the Regional Corporations which must be redistributed under section 7(j) of ANCSA to their stockholders, the class of their stockholders who are not village residents, and Village Corporations should not be taxable to the Regional Corporations.

2. *The Applicability of Federal Securities Laws*

The Claims Act requires the issuance of shares of stock by Regional Corporations and business-for-profit Village Corporations to natives residing within the native corporations' respective geographical areas. The authority of the Regional and Village Corporations to issue stock raised obvious questions about the applicability to such actions of the key federal securities statutes —namely, the Securities Act of 1933,[70] the Securities Exchange Act of 1934,[71] and the Investment Company Act of 1940.[72]

Only the Investment Company Act of 1940 ever became a matter of active concern for the native corporations.[73] In 1974 the Securities and Exchange Commission promulgated a temporary rule which, in granting the corporations a partial exemption from the requirements of the Act, made a number of its provisions applicable.[74] Furthermore, in late 1975 the Commission issued notice of a proposed permanent rule which would have reduced drastically the

---

70. 15 U.S.C. § 77a (1970).

71. *Id.* § 78a.

72. *Id.* § 80a-51.

73. On its face the 1933 Act does not apply to the native corporations. Only securities which are offered or sold for "value"—*i.e.*, those for which consideration has been given in exchange —are subject to the provisions of the Act. *See* 15 U.S.C. § 77b(3) (1970). Since section 7 of ANCSA appears to state that all eligible natives are entitled to receive one hundred shares of stock, and the Claims Act contains no intimation that the Regional Corporation must, or even may, be paid value for the securities issued, the 1933 Act is inapplicable. And since none of the Village Corporations in fact received value for stock issued, they are not subject to the requirements of the Act.

The legal relevance of the Securities and Exchange Act of 1934 remained an academic issue because of the Securities and Exchange Commission's notion that the native corporations were investment companies. The registration requirements of the Investment Act of 1940, rather than those of the 1934 Act, were said to be applicable to such companies.

74. 17 C.F.R. § 270.6c-2 (1975) (Rule 6c-2(T)). Specifically, the temporary rule provided the following:

> Any corporation organized pursuant to the [Claims Act] shall be temporarily exempt from all provisions of the Act except Sections 8(a), 9, 17, 36, and 37 subject to the following conditions: Any company claiming exemptions pursuant to this rule shall file annually with the Commission copies of the reports required by section 7(o) of the Settlement Act and shall maintain and keep current the accounts, books, and other documents relating to its business which constitute the record forming the basis for such information and of the auditor's certification thereto.

scope of the exemption contained in the temporary rule.[75]

The growing controversy over the applicability of the Investment Company Act of 1940, however, was mooted by Congress' enactment in early 1976 of Public Law 94-204.[76] The legislation amended the Claims Act to provide that any "corporation organized pursuant to [ANCSA] shall be exempt from the provisions of the Investment Company Act of 1940 . . . the Securities Act of 1933 . . . and the Securities Exchange Act of 1934 . . . as amended, through December 31, 1991."[77]

C. Distributions of Land and Monetary Benefits

In view of the great stakes involved, the most numerous and by far the most controversial issues which have arisen in the implementation of ANCSA concern the proper allocation of land and money. Thus, major debates have developed over the final regulations issued by the Secretary relating to land selections by native corporations, departmental guidelines for the retention of public use easements upon the lands selected, and the provisions of the Claims Act governing the distribution of Fund monies and section 7(i) resource revenues.

1. Issues Relating to Land Selections and the Use of Native Lands

Section 11(a) of the Claims Act[78] provides for the withdrawal from the public lands of twenty-five townships around each native village[79] pending selection by native corporations of the lands to which they are entitled. Subsection 11(a)(3) further provides that if the Secretary of the Interior determines that the lands withdrawn pursuant to subsections 11(a)(1) and (2) are "insufficient," he "shall withdraw three times the deficiency from the nearest unreserved, vacant and unappropriated public lands," and, in making any

---

75. Investment Company Act Release No. 8902 (Aug. 22, 1975) (proposed rule 6c-2); see 39 Fed. Reg. 8936 (1975).

76. Act of Jan. 2, 1976, Pub. L. No. 94-204, 89 Stat. 1145.

77. Act of Jan. 2, 1976, Pub. L. No. 94-204, § 3, 89 Stat. 1147. The amendment does require, however, that

any . . . corporation which, but for this section, would be subject to the provisions of the Securities Act of 1934 shall transmit to its stockholders each year a report containing substantially all the information required to be included in an annual report to stockholders by a corporation which is subject to the provisions of such Act.

In a somewhat belated recognition of the broad exemption created by Public Law 94-204, the Securities and Exchange Commission rescinded its proposed rule 6c-2 on February 6, 1976. See Investment Company Act Release No. 9148 (Feb. 6, 1976); 41 Fed. Reg. 8342 (1976).

78. 43 U.S.C. § 1610(a) (Supp. IV, 1974).

79. Only nine townships were withdrawn around the ten villages of southeastern Alaska. See id. § 1615(a).

such deficiency withdrawal, he shall, "insofar as possible, withdraw public lands of a character similar to those on which the village is located . . . ."[80] Section 17(d)(2) of ANCSA,[81] on the other hand, also directs the Secretary to withdraw up to eighty million acres of unreserved lands in Alaska for possible inclusion in the National Park, Forest, Wildlife Refuge, and Wild and Scenic Rivers Systems.

In setting aside lands under the Claims Act, the Secretary engaged in a balancing act, and not all of the original deficiency withdrawals for the benefit of natives ended up either close to the related village or similar in character to the village lands. Most of the Regional Corporations, after subsequent negotiations, managed to convince the Secretary to promulgate amended withdrawals which were reasonably satisfactory.[82] With respect to his land selection regulations and easement guidelines, though, the Secretary has proved more obdurate.

a.   Federal regulations implementing land selection procedures
     established under section 12 of the Claims Act

Section 12(a)(1) of ANCSA provides that in the so-called "first round" village land selections, "the Village Corporation for each Native village . . . shall select . . . all of the township or townships in which any part of the village is located, plus an area which will make the total selection equal to the acreage to which the village is entitled under section 14."[83] Section 12(a)(2) further provides that "[s]elections made under . . . subsection (a) shall be contiguous and in reasonably compact tracts, except as separated by bodies of water or by lands which are unavailable for selection, and shall be in whole sections and, wherever feasible, in units of not less than 1,280 acres."[84] Section 12(b) of the Claims Act, dealing with the second round village selections, on the other hand, merely recites that each "Village Corporation shall select the acreage allocated to it from the lands withdrawn by subsection 11(a)."[85]

On May 10, 1973, the Secretary of the Interior issued regulations[86] purporting to implement sections 12(a) and 12(b) of ANCSA. Despite a number of similarities between the Interior Department land selection regulations and the corresponding provisions in ANCSA, the regulations implementing sections 12(a) and (b) differ from the statute in several important respects. First,

---

80.   *Id.* § 1610(a)(3).

81.   *Id.* § 1616(d)(2).

82.   The major exception was Cook Inlet Region, Inc. which was unable to conclude satisfactory negotiations with the Secretary. *See* Cook Inlet Region, Inc. v. Morton, Civil No. A-40-73 (D. Alas., filed Feb. 20, 1975). Cook Inlet's situation, however, apparently was resolved in recent legislation. *See* Act of January 2, 1976, Pub. L. No. 94-204, § 12, 89 Stat. 1145, 1150.

83.   43 U.S.C. § 1611(a)(1) (Supp. IV, 1974).

84.   *Id.* § 1611(a)(2).

85.   *Id.* § 1611(b).

86.   43 C.F.R. § 2650.0-1 (1975).

sections 2651.4(b) and (c) of the regulations impose on all village land selections certain restrictions to which only section 12(a) selections are subject under the precise language of ANCSA. Section 2651.4(b), for example, requires that selections under sections 12(a) and (b) satisfy "compactness" and "contiguity" criteria, whereas section 12(a)(2) of the Claims Act makes these criteria applicable only to the first round village land selections.

Second, the "compactness" requirement in the regulations is far more expansive than its statutory antecedent in the Claims Act. Section 2651.4(b) of the regulations provides expressly that "the total *area* selected shall be reasonably compact . . . ."[87] By contrast, section 12(a)(2) of ANCSA requires only that selections "made . . . shall be . . . in reasonably *compact tracts* . . . ."[88] In other words, the Claims Act provides that land selections under section 12(a) must be composed of a number of compact tracts, but a Village Corporation is not compelled to choose lands in a manner which makes the total area selected compact.

Finally, the Secretary's regulations add various restrictions to the land selection process which appear nowhere in section 12 of the Claims Act. Thus, section 2651.4(b) provides that a Village Corporation's land selection shall not be considered "compact" if it excludes (1) "other lands available for selection within its exterior boundaries," or (2) "lands which are similar in character to the village site or lands ordinarily used by the village inhabitants . . . ."[89] Similarly, section 2652.3(c) of the regulations contains a direction, unmentioned in ANCSA, that "[w]henever a regional selection is made in any township, the regional corporation shall select all available lands in that township [*i.e.*, up to 23,040 acres]."[90]

The differences between the land selection limitations imposed by the Claims Act and the restrictions imposed by the regulations are not mere technical distinctions, but have rather drastic practical implications for the Regional and Village Corporations. Quite obviously, these corporations need flexibility in selecting lands under ANCSA for resource and subsistence purposes, while the deviations of the regulations from the Claims Act are aimed at reducing that flexibility. As a consequence, several Regional and Village Corporations filed suits challenging portions of the land selection regulations.[91] Significantly, while he did not amend the regulations, the Secretary settled this litigation by entering into stipulations which, through waiv-

---

87. *Id.* § 2651.4(b) (emphasis added).
88. 43 U.S.C. § 1611(a)(2) (Supp. IV, 1974) (emphasis added).
89. 43 C.F.R. § 2651.4(b) (1975).
90. *Id.* § 2652.3(c). This regulation and others relating to the Secretary's guidelines for land selections by native corporations have been challenged on the ground that they are not authorized by ANCSA. *See* Chugach Natives, Inc. v. Kleppe, Civil No. 75-2113 (D.D.C., filed Dec. 18, 1975).
91. Arctic Slope Regional Corp. v. Morton, Civil No. 73-1563 (D.D.C., filed Feb. 26, 1974); Doyon, Ltd. v. Morton, Civil No. 74-1463 (D.D.C., filed Oct. 4, 1974).

ers, accorded the native corporations all the latitude in making land selections which they had initially sought and which the Claims Act seemed to provide.

b. The reservation of federal easements on lands selected by native corporations

Out of the twenty-two substantive sections in ANCSA, twenty-one deal directly with the settlement of native claims and one—section 17—adopted at the insistence of conservation organizations, deals more broadly with land use planning in Alaska. Buried in the land use section is a provision authorizing the Secretary of the Interior to reserve public easements upon lands patented to Regional and Village Corporations.[92] Under date of July 8, 1975, the Solicitor for the Department of the Interior issued an opinion which expresses the view that the Secretary possesses a broad power to reserve public easements on native lands pursuant to section 17(b) of the Claims Act, and, more particularly, that the Secretary's authority under subsection 17(b)(3) to determine which public easements are necessary is not limited to selecting among the easements identified by the Land Use Planning Commission (LUPC) under subsection 17(b)(1).[93] In addition, based upon his self-generated premise of broad secretarial power, the Solicitor further concluded that reserved easements upon native lands are not restricted to the types of easements described in subsection 17(b)(1) of the Claims Act.

The Solicitor is plainly wrong as a matter of law and of policy. In short, subsection 17(b)(3) must be read in context, with that context being the totality of ANCSA under which the United States, in exchange for the extinguishment of aboriginal claims to virtually all of Alaska, guaranteed the natives clear title to some forty million acres of land. Congress would have been guilty of a breach of faith if, as the Solicitor suggests, the Secretary were authorized—under a subordinate provision in a section of ANCSA largely unrelated to the claims settlement—to override the dominant purpose of the statute and carve out from the native lands (without payment of compensation) an unlimited number of easements for an unrestricted number of public uses.[94]

---

92. 43 U.S.C. § 1616(b) (Supp. IV, 1974).

93. Interior Dept't Sol. Op. M-36880 (July 8, 1975), 82 Interior Dec. 325. On February 24, 1975, the Department of the Interior had circulated for comment proposed guidelines for implementing section 17(b) of ANCSA which presupposed a broad authority in the Secretary to reserve easements. LUPC and the natives challenged the validity of this assumption, and the later Solicitor's opinion was issued in an obvious attempt to shore up the Secretary's position.

94. According to the Solicitor, "[s]ince Section 17(b)(3) is not the sole source of authority for the Secretary to reserve easements, the scope of that authority must be discussed in the context of his total authority." Interior Dep't Sol. Op. M-36880, at 1 (July 8, 1975), 82 Interior Dec. 325. Section 26 of the Claims Act provides, on the other hand, that "[t]o the extent that there is a conflict between any provisions of this Act and any other Federal laws applicable to Alaska, the provisions of this Act shall govern." 43 U.S.C. § 1601 (Supp. IV, 1974). Thus, to the extent that the Secretary has other statutory powers—r.g., 43 U.S.C. §§ 932, 945 (1970)—to create easements

As the prime basis for his position, the Solicitor points out that, while the House version of the Claims Act[95] did not contain a land use section, section 24(d)(3) of the Senate bill[96] did provide, in part, that "[p]rior to granting any patent under this Act the Secretary shall consult with the Planning Commission and *shall reserve such public easements as the Planning Commission has identified and recommends.*"[97] In conference, the language requiring the Secretary to reserve easements recommended by LUPC "was vigorously opposed by the House members of the Conference Committee and by the Executive Branch,"[98] and eventually this language was dropped out of the Claims Act. From this fact, the Solicitor finds a congressional intent that the Secretary's authority be "broadened to look beyond the Planning Commission and to make individual determinations on questions concerning easements."[99]

The Solicitor has misread ANCSA's legislative history. In eliminating the mandatory aspect of easement reservations, Congress did not intend to *broaden* the authority of the Secretary, but rather to *lessen* the authority of the Planning Commission. In other words, instead of being required to reserve all easements identified by LUPC, the Secretary was authorized under subsection 17(b)(3) of the Claims Act to pick and choose among the easements so identified in order to reserve only those he determines are necessary. Nothing in ANCSA or in its legislative history supports the Solicitor's proposition that the Conference Committee suddenly vested in the Secretary a broad authority to reserve easements on native lands which he would not have possessed under any previous version of the legislation.[100]

Once the Secretary's authority to reserve easements is placed in correct perspective, LUPC's power to identify such public easements assumes its proper significance. Specifically, subsection 17(b)(1) of the Claims Act provides that the easements identified by the Commission must be either: (1) "across lands selected by Village Corporations and the Regional Corporations," or (2) "at periodic points along the courses of major waterways . . . ."[101] This

---

on lands in Alaska which are inconsistent with his powers under ANCSA, such statutes do not add to his authority to reserve easements on native lands, but rather are inapplicable.

95. H.R. 10367, 92d Cong., 1st Sess. (1971).

96. S. 35, 92d Cong., 1st Sess. § 24(d)(3) (1971).

97. Interior Dep't Sol. Op. M-36880, at 2-3 (July 8, 1975), 82 Interior Dec. 325 (emphasis added).

98. *Id.* at 4.

99. *Id.* at 5.

100. Subsection 17(b)(2) required LUPC, in identifying public easements, to "consult with appropriate State and Federal agencies," review "proposed transportation plaus," and "receive and review statements and recommendations from interested organizations and individuals on the need for and proposed location of public easements . . . ." 43 U.S.C. § 1616(b)(2) (Supp. IV, 1974). According to the Solicitor's interpretation of the statute, this congressionally directed activity is largely meaningless.

101. 43 U.S.C. § 1616(b)(1) (Supp. IV, 1974).

statutory language shows on its face that LUPC actually has little flexibility in selecting the scope and location of the public easements which it will recommend to the Secretary.

Thus, contrary to the Solicitor's assertion,[102] the Claims Act does not authorize the Commission or the Secretary to reserve "site" easements on lands to be patented to native corporations. Rather, it authorized easements *across* native land selections[103] for such public purposes as "transportation, utilities," and access to adjoining state and federal lands "for recreation, hunting . . . and such other public uses as the Planning Commission determines to be important."[104] Any other construction of the Claims Act would violate the intent of Congress in ANCSA to convey lands to profit-making native corporations for their own use and development.

Whether the Secretary, notwithstanding the Solicitor's views, ultimately will recognize the statutory limitations upon his authority to reserve easements across native lands remains to be seen.[105] If not, section 17(b) of ANCSA, like so many other provisions of the Claims Act, will be headed for resolution in

102. Interior Dep't Sol. Op. M-36880, at 7 (July 8, 1975), 82 Interior Dec. 325. Citing a number of state cases involving special circumstances, the Solicitor argues that "across" can mean "over" or "on." *Id.* The Solicitor then argues on the basis of a reference to "recreation sites" and "camp sites" in the Conference Report that the Secretary has authority "to reserve site easements for [all] public uses . . . ." *Id.* Finally, the Solicitor argues that "public use" can extend to any matter of "public health, recreation and enjoyment," *id.* at 6, the logical extension of this thesis being that the Secretary can reserve an "easement" on native lands for a hospital or public building. The short answer to this bootstrap argument is that no evidence exists that Congress intended so to define the Secretary's easement authority, and the plain language of the Claims Act appears to the contrary.

103. This conclusion is supported by the Joint Statement of the Conference Committee on ANCSA, which recites in part:
   Subsection 17(b) of the conference report is substantially the same as Section 24(d) of the Senate amendment. This subsection provides for the advance reservation of easements and camping and recreation sites *necessary for public access across lands granted to Village and Regional Corporations.*
H.R. REP. No. 746, 92d Cong., 1st Sess. 44 (1971) (emphasis added).

104. 43 U.S.C. § 1616(b)(1) (Supp. IV, 1974). Similarly, with respect to access through water transportation, subsection 17(b)(1) makes clear that LUPC should identify, and the Secretary may reserve, easements only at "periodic points" and only along "major waterways." Thus, contrary to the apparently prevailing view in the Department of the Interior, the Secretary does not have authority to reserve "continuous shorelines easements," even though he may feel such easements desirable for public travel. Draft memorandum from Royston C. Hughes, Chairman of the Alaska Task Force to Jack O. Horton, Assistant Secretary for Land and Water Resources 6-7, Feb. 24, 1975. Furthermore, since a non-navigable body of water by definition does not constitute a waterway, the Secretary's power can be exercised only in relation to the most important rivers and lakes of Alaska.

105. Thus far, the Secretary, unfortunately, appears to be following the questionable legal advice being provided by his solicitor. On February 12, 1976, the Secretary promulgated an order relating to guidelines for local easements which, while departing from the Solicitor's recommendations in some particulars, essentially reflects the approach he suggested. 41 Fed. Reg. 6295 (1976). On May 4, 1976, the Alaska Federation of Natives and six Regional Corporations filed suit seeking a declaratory judgment that the Secretary's easement guidelines are in excess of his authority under law. Calista Corp. v. Kleppe, Civil No. 76-0771 (D.D.C., May 4, 1976).

the courts. Unfortunately, while any such litigation is pending, the issuance of patents to the native corporations will be delayed and their use and development of the land correspondingly deferred.

2. Problems Relating to the Distribution of Funds

A number of significant and controversial legal issues have arisen in connection with the distribution of funds under provisions of the Claims Act to the Regional and Village Corporations. First, at least one Regional Corporation has contended that it is not obligated to share with other corporations section 7(i) resource revenues which are derived from lands not yet patented to the resource-owning corporation.[106] Second, the Secretary of the Interior's decision to exclude, for purposes of computing the amount of distributions from the Alaska Native Fund to each Regional Corporation, natives residing in "reservation" villages already has resulted in litigation. Finally, although not yet an acute legal question, provisions in section 7(j) of ANCSA relating to the distribution of funds by Regional Corporations to Village Corporations and other designated distributees are likely to cause future controversy.

a. Distributions of section 7(i) resource revenues

Section 7(i) of ANCSA provides for the division of 70 per cent of all timber and mineral revenues on an annual basis among twelve regional corporations.[107] Potentially, resource revenues will be a major source of income for all the Regional Corporations and the proper construction of section 7(i), therefore, is a question of utmost concern.

1. The obligation of Regional Corporations to share benefits received from the disposition of section 7(i) resources prior to patenting of the land

The contention that a Regional Corporation is under no obligation to share with other Regional Corporations benefits received from the disposition of section 7(i) resources prior to patenting of the land seems a tenuous proposition at best. To permit a resource-rich Regional Corporation to dispose of substantial rights in its subsurface resources before the land has been selected—an event over which only the resource-owning Regional Corporation

---

106. At least nine of the Regional Corporations entered into agreements covering the exploration and development of oil, gas, and other minerals underlying lands in their regions—even though the lands involved in the agreements had not yet been patented to the respective corporations. The legal question posed in this part of the article was clarified in Aleut Corp. v. Arctic Slope Regional Corp., Civil No. 75-53 (D. Alas., filed July 9, 1976), and Doyon, Ltd. v. NANA Regional Corp., Civil No. 74-1531 (D.D.C., filed May 5, 1976), which held that section 7(i) revenues were not exempt from the sharing requirement merely because no formal patent had been issued on the land containing the resources.

107. 43 U.S.C. § 1606(i) (Supp. IV, 1974).

would have control—and then retain the consideration paid because the land has not yet been patented, would frustrate the overriding congressional purpose of assuring all natives a fair share of the wealth.

Other provisions in the Claims Act indicate that Congress limited distributable resources to "timber resources and [the] subsurface estate patented to it"[108] only because Congress did not anticipate that Regional Corporations would have the ability to derive revenues from withdrawn land prior to patenting. By explicitly affirming, in section 22(i),[109] the Secretary of the Interior's power to administer land withdrawn for native selection "prior to conveyance," Congress established that the Regional Corporations could not effectively dispose of legal interests in such property. In short, in agreements disposing of section 7(i) resources, Regional Corporations have not sold rights in withdrawn land, which section 22(i) of ANCSA gives the Secretary exclusive authority to do, but rather have negotiated a present sale of future interests, the subsurface resources in lands which will be "patented to it."[110] Furthermore, nothing in the land selection regulations issued by the Secretary to implement the Claims Act lends any support to the argument that a Regional Corporation can dispose of property rights in withdrawn lands apart from the resources ultimately to be "patented to it."[111]

---

108. *Id.* § 1606(i). A reasonable construction of the phrase is that it probably was intended by Congress to identify what lands were subject to the distribution requirements of section 7(i) rather than *when* such requirements became applicable. In other words, only lands patented to the native corporation under ANCSA would be affected by section 7(i). Those lands acquired in some other fashion—such as by purchase—would not be.

109. *Id.* § 1621(i).

110. Section 10(d) of H.R. 10367, the House bill from which section 22(i) of ANCSA was drawn, provided "for the continuation of present management" of withdrawn land "until the land is either patented or returned to its use prior to withdrawal." H.R. REP. No. 523, 92d Cong., 1st Sess. 27 (1971). The Conference Committee rejected the provisions of section 16(b) in the Senate bill, S. 35, which would have sharply limited the powers of the Secretary in administering withdrawn lands in order to enhance native rights. S. REP. No. 405, 92d Cong., 2d Sess. 36, 145-46 (1971).

The principle that a Regional Corporation possesses no legally recognizable interest in withdrawn lands which can be transferred independently of its rights in patented lands is confirmed in the Secretary of the Interior's land selection regulations. *See* 43 C.F.R. § 2650 (1975). Section 2650.1(a)(2)(i) of Title 43 of the Code of Federal Regulations, for example, which deals with the "interim administration" of lands withdrawn in aid of native land selections, specifically provides that, prior to conveyance under the Claims Act, the Secretary need only obtain and consider "the views of the concerned regions or villages" before making contracts or issuing leases with respect to the land. In a similar vein, sections 2650.4-2 and 2650.4-3 declare, respectively, that upon issuance of a patent to a Regional Corporation, "the grantee thereunder shall succeed and become entitled to any and all interests . . . of the United States as lessor" but prior leases "shall continue to be administered . . . by the United States after the conveyance has been issued, unless the responsible agency waives administration." 43 C.F.R. §§ 2650.4-2, 2650.4-3 (1975).

111. The validity of this conclusion can best be illustrated by referring to one of the agreements which is at issue in Doyon, Ltd. v. NANA Regional Corp., Civil No. 74-1531 (D.D.C., filed May 5, 1976). Under an agreement entered into with NANA, Standard Oil Company of California will have exclusive rights of prospecting and exploration in those "lands and/or subsurface estates within the NANA Region, subject to selection by NANA, the Village Corporations, Native Groups

2. *The manner in which an accounting for section 7(i)*
   resources should be rendered

Before a Regional Corporation can share section 7(i) resource revenues
with other Regional Corporations, accounting guidelines governing such distributions will have to be established. Following established legal authority the
word "revenues," which is left undefined in section 7(i), should be construed
broadly to include all compensation for the disposition of rights and interests
in subsurface resources, regardless of whether such consideration assumes the
form of cash payments, goods, services or benefits, which would not have
been received but for the section 7(i) transaction.[112]

Moreover the Claims Act and its legislative history[113] offer rather compel-

---

and individual Natives . . . pursuant to the Alaska Native Claims Settlement Act." Exploratory
Option Agreement Between NANA Regional Corporation, Inc. and Standard Oil Company of
California 1, January 17, 1973 (unpublished document on file with authors). Standard obviously
will derive benefits under its agreement with NANA solely from those lands and subsurface
estates which actually are patented to NANA. Indeed, patenting or interim conveyance of the
land to NANA is a condition precedent to the lease by Standard. Exploratory Option Agreement,
supra at 5-6. This language in the contract leads rather ineluctably to the conclusion that the
consideration paid by companies such as Standard to Regional Corporations wishing to dispose of
their mineral resources is attributable directly to patented land and is encompassed within section
7(i) of ANCSA.

112. Numerous legal authorities have interpreted the term "revenues" to include a wide variety of benefits. Moreover, courts have stated on repeated occasions that revenues include income.
See Donald v. Metropolitan Life Ins. Co., 200 S.C. 7, 15, 20 S.E.2d 395, 398-99 (1942); Trefry v.
Putnam, 227 Mass. 522, 529, 116 N.E. 904, 908 (1917). The term "income" has been interpreted
to encompass not only money or cash payments, but also services which have value to the recip-
ient. *See generally* J. MERTENS, LAW OF FEDERAL INCOME TAXATION § 6.05, at 28 (1974). Viewed in
realistic economic terms, revenues received in the form of cash benefits are indistinguishable
from benefits received in the form of rights or services. Both types of benefit constitute good
consideration, and, assuming all parties to the transaction are fully knowledgeable about market
prices, the amount of any cash payments promised for the acquisition of interests in land will
fluctuate in direct relationship to the value of any required payments in kind.

Moreover, the broad construction of the term "revenues" which is described above has been
adopted by courts which have been called upon to interpret the word within the context of
ANCSA. In Aleut Corp. v. Arctic Slope Regional Corp., Civil No. 75-53 (D. Alas., filed July 9,
1976), and Doyon, Ltd. v. NANA Regional Corp., Civil No. 74-1531 (D.D.C., filed May 5, 1976),
the court confirmed the proposition that the term "revenues" in section 7(i) should be construed
in a liberal manner to include all forms of consideration which would not have been received but
for the section 7(i) transaction.

113. Section 9(j)(1) of the Senate version of the Claims Act speaks in terms of "net proceeds,"
rather than "gross revenues." S. 35, 92d Cong., 1st Sess. § 9(j)(1) (1971). *See also* S. REP. No. 405,
92d Cong., 1st Sess. 120, 125 (1971). Nor is a contrary interpretation of "all revenues" required
by the legislative history of the original House version of section 7(i) of the Claims Act. Section
6(g) of H.R. 10367 contained the following provisions:

   All revenues received by each corporation from the subsurface estate patented pursuant
   to this Act shall be divided by the corporation among all twelve regional corporations
   organized pursuant to this section according to the number of Natives enrolled in each
   region pursuant to section 5.

H.R. 10367, 92d Cong., 1st Sess. § 6(g) (1971) (emphasis added). The House Committee on
Interior and Insular Affairs explained that this provision was included in the bill to guarantee
that all natives would "benefit equally from any minerals discovered within a particular region."
H.R. REP. No. 523, 92d Cong., 1st Sess. 6 (1971). Leaving aside the question of whether ANCSA

ling evidence that when Congress referred to the distribution of "all revenues" from timber and subsurface resources it meant net, rather than gross, revenues. If the term were defined as gross revenues, the Claims Act would reduce significantly the incentive of any Regional Corporation to develop "the timber resources and subsurface estate patented to it."[114] No statutory provision exists for the sharing of expenses among Regional Corporations, and all development costs, therefore, would be charged against the resource-owning Regional Corporation's retained 30 per cent—perhaps even to the extent of exceeding it. Furthermore, since the productive use of a natural resource necessarily entails some expenses on the part of the owner—if no more than the cost of negotiating and administering a lease—the conclusion that "all revenues" means "gross revenues" would violate the 70-30 split between the twelve Regional Corporations and the resource-owning Regional Corporation which Congress established.[115]

A determination must also be made for accounting purposes of what constitutes allowable deductions to arrive at net proceeds. Allowable deductions should encompass all reasonable charges which are legitimately incurred by the resource-owning Regional Corporation to obtain or retain section 7(i) revenues. As a matter of fairness, such costs properly could include: (a) all business expenses (as that term is defined in the Internal Revenue Code) incurred in the development or production of a section 7(i) resource; (b) all direct administrative costs related to the production of section 7(i) revenues, plus a reasonable allocation of other overhead; and (c) a fair share of pre-development costs, including amortization of land selection costs relating to timber and the subsurface estate which have not otherwise been classed as business expenses.

In addition, a Regional Corporation should not be permitted to use a depletion deduction or income taxes as offsets against its section 7(i) revenues. The deduction of a depletion allowance and income taxes would represent in the first instance the insertion into the section 7(i) distributions formula of tax concepts which are unrelated to actual receipts. Furthermore, the disallowance of such deductions guarantees that the distribution of section 7(i) revenues will not be affected by the resource-owning corporation's tax situation,

---

actually achieved this objective, the Committee could not possibly have intended that "all revenues" mean "gross revenues," since such a construction would result in obviously disproportionate distributions, with the patentee Regional Corporation's absorbing all expenses, while the other Regional Corporations reap benefits without cost.

114.   43 U.S.C. § 1606(i) (Supp. IV, 1974).

115.   In Doyon, Ltd. v. NANA Regional Corp., Civil No. 74-1531 (D.D.C., filed May 5, 1976), the court held in substance that the phrase "all revenues" in section 7(i) connoted a "net" rather than "gross" concept. The theory of net revenues adopted by the court, however, is quite restrictive, and would not permit the deduction of overhead or direct administrative costs related to the production of section 7(i) income, or a share of land selection costs attributable to timber and the subsurface estate.

and the 70-30 split of resource revenues mandated by Congress, therefore, will be carried out in terms of real dollars.

Revenues attributable to timber and subsurface resources, and thus subject to section 7(i) distributions, should, moreover, be calculated on the basis of the value of the resource in place. Any other formula would have to reflect gains or losses from business operations, and such an approach involves more than resource revenue sharing.

In the case of passive development, such as the sale of standing timber or a standard oil and gas lease, a rebuttable presumption should exist that the contract price or royalty payment constitutes the fair market value of the resource in place. Where active development by the Regional Corporation occurs, such as production through a subsidiary or joint venture or the receipt of non-cash consideration, a determination of the revenue attributable exclusively to the resource will become more difficult, and appropriate accounting procedures may have to be worked out on a case-by-case basis. Finally, in the event a Regional Corporation sells property outright, and the property sold is a subsurface interest or land having a highest and best use for timber operations, a rebuttable presumption should exist that the sales price represents the fair market value of these resources. The opposite rebuttable presumption should apply if the land is without trees or has no known mineral values.

A Regional Corporation's accounting for section 7(i) revenues also will be determined in part by the nature of the duty a resource-owning corporation owes to other Regional Corporations in its disposition of section 7(i) resources. The relationships among the native corporations created under the Claims Act are unique and, in terms of legal responsibilities, largely unclarified, but the resource-owning Regional Corporation certainly appears to owe no greater duty to the other Regional Corporations than it does to its own stockholders. Such a standard is further justified by the fact that it conflicts with no provision of the Claims Act, the basic rules that govern such a relationship are well-defined and easily applied, and there is no inconvenience in maintaining the same standard for intercorporate relations as for manager-stockholder relations.

Assuming a resource-owning Regional Corporation's duties to other Regional Corporations are the same as those which a corporation owes to its stockholders, then the native corporation distributing section 7(i) revenues is not required to obtain the consent of, or to advise, other Regional Corporations before it enters into agreements disposing of section 7(i) resources. Courts consistently have adhered to the general rule that "the board of directors, and not the stockholders, controls the conduct of the corporation's business, and necessarily controls the corporation's property with reference to all matters within and incidental to such business."[116] This legal rubric often has

---

116. Hanrahan v. Anderson, 108 Mont. 218, 231, 90 P.2d 494, 499 (1939); *accord*, Fontaine v.

been applied for the specific purpose of rejecting stockholders' claims that corporate property had been disposed of without their consent,[117] and the distributee Regional Corporations can advance no justification for claiming superior rights.[118]

Finally, section 7(i) of the Claims Act provides explicitly that distributions are to be made on an "annual" basis.[119] At the end of any given year, the amounts which a resource-owning Regional Corporation must pay over to all twelve Regional Corporations are determinable, and the failure of the resource-owning corporation to make payments promptly means that it is retaining the use of funds belonging to others. Thus, in the absence of agreement to the contrary among the Regional Corporations, the resource-owning corporation could logically be found liable to pay interest upon distributable funds from the end of its fiscal year to the date of distribution.

As a practical matter, however, the accountants for the Regional Corporations will not be able to calculate section 7(i) revenues for some time after the close of the fiscal year, and, in recognition of this fact, the resource-owning corporation probably should not be required to pay interest on distributable amounts unless it fails to distribute such funds to the other Regional Corporations within a reasonable period—thirty days, for example—after the end of the fiscal year in which the section 7(i) revenues are or were received.

b.   The exclusion of natives residing in "reservation" villages for purposes of making distributions to regional corporations from the Alaska Native Fund

In addition to issues relating to the distribution of section 7(i) resource revenues, a serious question also has arisen concerning the exclusion, for purposes of making distributions to Regional Corporations from the Alaska Native Fund, of those natives who resided in villages which elected "to acquire title to the surface and subsurface estate in any reserve set aside for the[ir]

Brown County Motors Co., 251 Wis. 433, 437-38, 29 N.W.2d 744, 747 (1947). *See also* ALASKA STAT. § 10.05.174 (1968).

117.   *See, e.g.,* McCloskey v. New Orleans Brewing Co., 128 La. 197, 203-04, 54 So. 738, 740 (1911).

118.   The Claims Act appears to contain no provisions which would indicate that resource-owning Regional Corporations are required to adhere to a more rigorous standard—such as that which normally is imposed on trustees. Congress made clear in section 2(b) of the Claims Act that the settlement of aboriginal claims "should be accomplished rapidly . . . without creating a reservation system or lengthy wardship or trusteeship . . . ." 43 U.S.C. § 1601(b) (Supp. IV, 1974). No provision elsewhere in ANCSA indicates that Congress intended the Regional Corporations to possess in relation to each other a status which was denied the Secretary of the Interior. Furthermore, section 7(i) places no obligation upon a resource-owning Regional Corporation "prudently" to develop the "timber resources and subsurface estate patented to it," and such language is employed to define the duty of a statutory trustee. *See generally* United States Nat'l Bank & Trust Co. v. Sullivan, 69 F.2d 412, 415 (7th Cir. 1934).

119.   43 U.S.C. § 1606(i) (Supp. IV, 1974).

use,"[120] rather than participate in the regular land selection procedures of the Act. In determining a Regional Corporation's share of Section 6(c) monies, the Secretary has excluded the native residents of such villages on the ground that when Congress employed the phrase "natives enrolled in each region"[121] to describe eligibility, it actually meant "stockholders in each Regional Corporation." Furthermore, he argued, any other action would result in an "unjustified disparity of benefits among the stockholders of the various regional corporations which cannot be rationally supported."[122]

The exclusion of reservation villagers is questionable on several grounds.[123] The status of reservation villager and "enrolled Native" are not mutually exclusive categories. The term "Native" is defined in section 3(b) of ANCSA in part as follows:[124]

> "Native" means a citizen of the United States who is a person of one-fourth degree or more Alaska Indian (including Tsimshian Indians not enrolled in the Metlaktla [sic] Indian Community) Eskimo, or Aleut blood, or combination thereof . . . . Any decision of the Secretary regarding eligibility for enrollment shall be final . . . .

The definition of "Native" in the Claims Act, therefore, does not exclude natives residing in reservation villages, and, indeed, makes no reference, explicit or implicit, to the necessity for eliminating such natives from the pop-

---

120. *Id.* § 1618(b).

121. After completion of the roll prepared pursuant to section 5, all money in the Fund . . . shall be distributed at the end of each three months of the fiscal year among the Regional Corporations organized pursuant to section 7 on the basis of the relative numbers of Natives enrolled in each region. *Id.* § 1606(i).

122. Letter from Kent Frizzell, Solicitor of the Department of the Interior to Arthur Lazarus, Jr. 2, Sept. 25, 1974. The specific Regional Corporations which have been prejudiced by the Secretary's determination are Doyon, Limited and Bering Straits Native Corporation. Specifically, if the Secretary had included natives residing in reservation villages for purposes of calculating these corporations' shares of Fund distributions, Doyon would have been paid approximately $735,000 more and Bering Straits would have been paid about $3,170,000 more by the end of September 1975. (No further distributions have been made since that date.) Furthermore, on the basis of the Secretary's September 17, 1974 population figures, failure to count residents of the section 19(b) villages among the numbers of natives enrolled in each of these regions for purposes of section 6(c) ultimately will cost Doyon over $2,900,000 and Bering Straits almost $12,500,000 in total distributions out of the Fund.

123. In 1974 Doyon, Limited and Bering Straits Native Corporation, the two Regional Corporations prejudiced by the Secretary's decision, brought suit to challenge its legality. *See* Doyon, Ltd. v. Morton, Civil No. 74-1463 (D.D.C., filed Oct. 4, 1974). On May 13, 1975, the action, which originally was filed in the District Court for the District of Columbia, was transferred to the District of Alaska. *See* Doyon, Ltd. v. Hathaway, Civil No. 75-89 (D. Alas., transferred May 13, 1975). On July 9, 1976, the District Court for the District of Alaska, in an opinion based largely on the same reasoning which is discussed below, held that the Secretary of the Interior had acted illegally in excluding, for purposes of making distributions from the Fund, natives enrolled in section 19(b) villages.

124. 43 U.S.C. § 1602(b) (Supp. IV, 1974). An identical definition of the word "Native" appears in the regulations which have been issued to implement section 3 of the Claims Act. 25 C.F.R. § 43h-1(g) (1975).

ulation count under section 6(c).[125] Indeed, the fact that, in another provision[126] dealing with the revocation of existing reservations, Congress expressly declared members of the Metlakatla Indian Community to be ineligible for benefits, but made no similar declaration with respect to the native residents of reservation villages, indicates that Congress intended that the native residents of villages which elected to acquire title to their reserves pursuant to section 19(b) would remain classified as "Natives" under the provisions of the Claims Act.

Reservation villagers are also clearly "enrolled" natives for purposes of the Act. The Secretary has promulgated a roll of Alaska Natives which shows the natives residing in reservation villages as being enrolled in their respective regions,[127] and such natives, therefore, quite literally are "Natives enrolled" in these regions within the meaning of section 6(c).[128]

The plain meaning of the words in section 6(c) therefore dictate that Fund distributions be made on the basis of all "Natives enrolled in each region," including the residents of reservation villages. Even assuming the language of section 6(c) were ambiguous, a close analysis of ANCSA renders somewhat dubious the Secretary's assertion that Congress intended to say "stockholders in each Regional Corporation" when it actually said "Natives enrolled in each region." It is clear from an analysis of other provisions in the Act that, when Congress wanted to use the word "stockholder," it had no difficulty in doing so.[129] The absence of the term from section 6(c) leads to the conclusion that Congress intended what it said—namely, that monies from the Fund should be distributed on the basis of the relative numbers of natives enrolled in the respective regions.

---

125. Nor for that matter does section 3(b) purport to exclude native residents of section 19(b) villages from the definition of "Native" for any other purpose. Section 19(b) stipulates that, in the event a village elects to acquire title to its reserve, "the enrolled residents of the Village Corporation shall not be eligible to receive Regional Corporation stock." Section 19(b) does not provide that residents of reservation villages no longer shall be considered "Natives," and such individuals remain subject to all other provisions of ANCSA relating to natives and Native Corporations. *See*, *e.g.*, 43 U.S.C. §§ 1607(c), 1617, 1620(d) (Supp. IV, 1974).

126. 43 U.S.C. § 1618(a) (Supp. IV, 1974).

127. Every native is enrolled in a region. *Id.* § 1604(b). If the native residents of the reservation villages were not listed on the Secretary's roll, they would not have been eligible to form a Village Corporation under section 8 of ANCSA or to conduct an election under section 19(b). *Id.* §§ 1607, 1618(b).

128. Under the Claims Act, a "decision of the Secretary regarding eligibility for enrollment shall be final." *Id.* §§ 1602(b), 1604(a).

129. Thus, section 7(j) directs the Regional Corporations for five years to distribute not less than 10 per cent of the benefits derived by them under sections 6(c) and 7(i) "among the *stockholders* of the twelve Regional Corporations." 43 U.S.C. § 1606(j) (Supp. IV, 1974) (emphasis added). Furthermore, section 7(k) provides that funds distributed by Regional Corporations among Village Corporations shall be divided on the basis of the relative numbers of stockholders. *Id.* § 1606(k). Finally, section 7(m) establishes a formula for determining the manner in which certain funds will be distributed among those Regional Corporation stockholders who are not residents of a village. *Id.* § 1606(m).

Finally, consideration must be given to the Secretary of the Interior's assertion that, if taken literally, the language of section 6(c) would result in an "unjustified disparity of benefits among the stockholders of the various regional corporations." To state the Secretary's conclusion conversely, the Claims Act purportedly requires close to mathematical equality in the distribution of benefits among the various Regional Corporations.

An objective reading of ANCSA reveals a number of instances in which Congress, for a variety of reasons, did not provide that the stockholders of all Regional Corporations were to share the benefits of the claims settlement equally. First, the thirteenth Regional Corporation is not eligible to share in resource revenues pursuant to section 7(i) and is not permitted to make land selections under section 12.[130] Furthermore, section 7(j) of the Act establishes a minimum percentage for payments by the thirteenth Regional Corporation to its stockholders out of Fund distributions which differs from the minimum statutory requirement for other Regional Corporations.[131]

Second, Sealaska, the Regional Corporation for southeastern Alaska, is not eligible for land selections under section 12 of ANCSA.[132] Moreover, the native villages in southeastern Alaska, regardless of size, are limited to ownership of only one township, and thus, on a per shareholder basis, Sealaska's subsurface entitlement is markedly lower than the entitlement of the other eleven Regional Corporations, whose villages may select from three to seven townships, depending upon their size.[133] Congress also allowed Sealaska's stockholders to retain, without debit against distributions from the Alaska Native Fund,[134] the judgment of $7,546,053.80 for the loss of aboriginal lands entered by the Court of Claims in *Tlingit and Haida Indians v. United States*,[135] and appropriated by Congress in 1968.[136]

Third, section 12(c) of the Claims Act contains a complex land-loss formula which will result in an unequal distribution of land among the Regional Corporations.[137] In general, Congress directed that sixteen million acres of land would be allocated among some, but not all eleven, eligible Regional Corporations on the basis of the relative amounts of land to which claims were being relinquished by the natives within each region, regardless of the size of each region's native population. In fact, only six Regional Corporations qualify for section 12(c) land selections. Thus, the fair market values of stock in the various Regional Corporations, calculated on the basis of total assets

---

130. *Id.* §§ 1606(i), 1611.
131. *Id.* § 1606(j).
132. *Id.* § 1611.
133. *Id.* §§ 1613, 1615.
134. *Id.* § 1615(c).
135. 389 F.2d 778 (Ct. Cl. 1968).
136. Act of July 9, 1968, Pub. L. No. 90-392, 82 Stat. 307.
137. 43 U.S.C. § 1611(c) (Supp. IV, 1974).

—land as well as funds—will and were intended to differ materially.

Finally, as previously pointed out, section 7(i) of ANCSA provides that each Regional Corporation may keep 30 per cent of the revenues received from its timber resources and subsurface estate, and that 70 per cent of such revenues shall be divided annually among all twelve Regional Corporations.[138] This feature of the Act clearly creates a bonus for the stockholders of resource-rich Regional Corporations, like the Arctic Slope Native Corporation, which, on a per shareholder basis, will receive a far larger portion of resource revenues than the other Regional Corporations.

In summary, a number of observations can be offered with respect to the Secretary of the Interior's decision to eliminate natives residing in reservation villages from his calculations for purposes of determining the appropriate shares of the Regional Corporations in Fund distributions. First, such natives unquestionably are natives enrolled in their respective regions and, based upon the plain language of the Claims Act, their exclusion by the Secretary seems erroneous. Secondly, though Congress may have been motivated by the concept that all natives would receive a fair share of benefits distributed under ANCSA, the law as written does not in fact achieve anything approaching mathematical equality in the allocation of benefits. Finally, section 6(c) is yet another portion of the Claims Act which, instead of facilitating smooth administration of the settlement, has tended to cause conflict among the Regional Corporations and the dissipation of their money and energy in thankless litigation.

c. The distribution of funds under section 7(j) of the Claims Act

Perhaps the most crucial legal problem presented by ANCSA for future years is the construction of section 7(j). This section of the Claims Act provides:[139]

> (j) During the five years following the enactment of this Act, not less than 10% of all corporate funds received by each of the twelve Regional Corporations under section 6 (Alaska Native Fund), and under subsection (i) (revenues from the timber resources and subsurface estate patented to it pursuant to this Act), and all other net income, shall be distributed among the stockholders of the twelve Regional Corporations. Not less than 45% of funds from such sources during the first five-year period, and 50% thereafter, shall be distributed among the Village Corporations in the region and the class of stockholders who are not residents of those villages, as provided in subsection to it [sic].

The specific issue posed by section 7(j) is whether the Regional Corporations must distribute 45 per cent of their "other net income" during the first five year period following enactment of ANCSA and 50 per cent thereafter

---

138. *Id.* § 1606(i).
139. *Id.* § 1606(j).

among the Village Corporations and the class of stockholders who are not village residents. This question does not involve simply the division of money betweeen Regional and Village Corporations. The answer to the question in all likelihood will determine whether the Regional Corporations can survive as profit-making institutions, since any corporation which must give away 50 per cent of its "net income" and at the same time pay taxes upon 100 per cent of its income will operate at a perpetual deficit.[140] The issue turns on whether the phrase "from such sources," which appears in the second sentence of the section, includes as one of its antecedents the term "all other net income," which appears in the first sentence of the section, or refers only to funds received as resource revenues or from the Alaska Native Fund.

Read and considered carefully, section 7(j) on its face appears more susceptible to the interpretation that the phrase "from such sources" was not intended to encompass the net earnings of Regional Corporations. The antecedents for the phrase, which are found in the first sentence, are "funds received . . . under section 6 (Alaska Native Fund) and under subsection (i) (revenues from timber resources and subsurface estate patented to it pursuant to this act) . . . ."[141] The term "all other net income," which also appears in the first sentence, is not used subordinately to "funds," but instead is a separate category of money subject to distribution only under the 10 per cent formula.

The legislative history of section 7(j) also lends support to the proposition that Congress did not intend the Regional Corporations to distribute 45 to 50 per cent of their earnings and profits from business investments to Village Corporations and village nonresidents. In the Conference Report on the bill which became ANCSA, the Committee commented with respect to section 7(j):[142]

> Each Regional Corporation must distribute among the Village Corporations in the region not less than 50 percent of its share of the $962,500,000 grant, and 50 percent of all revenues received from the subsurface estate. *This provision does not apply to revenues received by the Regional Corporations from their investment in business activities.*

---

140. Applying the federal corporate income tax rate (including surtax) of 48 per cent, 26 U.S.C. § 11 (1970), and the Alaska corporate income tax rate (including surtax) of 9.4 per cent, CCH State Tax Handbook [¶ 220] 10 (1975), each Regional Corporation will pay out over one-half its net income in taxes.

If "net income," as used in section 7(j) of ANCSA, were defined to mean "net income after taxes," or if any distributions mandated by section 7(j) were deemed a deduction from income before calculation of taxes, then the Regional Corporations, of course, would not be legally obligated to pay out over 100 per cent of their income. The corporations, however, still would not have sufficient income—apart from retained section 7(i) revenues—to pay reasonable dividends to their stockholders or to use as working capital in new ventures.

141. 43 U.S.C. § 1606(j) (Supp. IV, 1974).

142. H.R. Rep. No. 746, 92d Cong., 1st Sess. 36 (1971) (emphasis added).

Finally, no legitimate reason exists for requiring Regional Corporations to pay out 50 per cent of their net income to Village Corporations and village nonresidents. Congress intended all natives and native corporations to share in the monetary settlement effected by ANCSA, so the allocation of Fund distributions provided in section 7(j) appears entirely appropriate. Similarly, title to all subsurface resources is vested in the Regional Corporations pursuant to the Claims Act, so the sharing of section 7(i) revenues also seems logical. The Village Corporations, however, are under no obligation to split their net income from business activities with the Regional Corporations, and no economic justification can be found in the Claims Act for saying the Regional Corporations must share comparable income with the Village Corporations.[143]

CONCLUSION

This article has described and analyzed the major issues which have arisen to date in the operation of the Alaska Native Claims Settlement Act of 1971. Briefly summarized, the enactment of ANCSA marked the successful conclusion of the Alaska Natives' long quest for a settlement of their aboriginal land claims, but passage of the Claims Act also has signaled the beginning of a period during which natives will face a host of new and difficult legal problems in implementing the complex, unique, and often ambiguous settlement scheme created by Congress. Moreover, in their efforts to make ANCSA work, the natives are encountering with increasing frequency not only a lack of support from the concerned federal agencies, but also divisions within their own ranks. In a very real sense, therefore, the complete and final settlement intended by Congress, and for which the natives have strived, still lies many years in the future.

A study of the Claims Act should not conclude without mention of the most serious practical problem inherent in its provisions. Assuming a native population of approximately 80,000, the typical Village Corporation having

---

143. The third sentence in section 7(j), which provides that, "[i]n the case of the thirteenth Regional Corporation, if organized, not less than 50% of all corporate funds received under section 6 shall be distributed to the stockholders" also gives support for the conclusion that the phrase "from such sources" does not include the net income of Regional Corporations. 43 U.S.C. § 1606(j) (Supp. IV, 1974). This provision for the thirteenth Regional Corporation is the counterpart of the provision for the other twelve Regional Corporations contained in the second sentence. In other words, the thirteenth Regional Corporation is not entitled to share in section 7(i) resource revenues, but is entitled to distributions from the Fund. Other than taking into account this difference between the thirteenth and the other twelve Regional Corporations, the third sentence of section 7(j) imposes substantially the same distribution requirement upon the former as the second sentence imposes upon the latter. Nonetheless, without mention of income, the third sentence requires only the distribution of 50 per cent of Fund moneys received by the thirteenth Regional Corporation, and if Congress intended to require the twelve Regional Corporations to distribute income under the second sentence of section 7(j), the Claims Act would have required the thirteenth Regional Corporation to do the same under the third sentence.

150 shareholders is entitled to receive in distributions from the Alaska Native Fund about $433,000 in appropriated funds over an eleven year period (an average of less than $40 thousand annually) and an additional $468,750 from the two per cent royalty (section 9) over an indefinite period, or a total of about $900 thousand. In the Alaskan economy, particularly as inflated by the current pipeline construction boom, this income flow is hardly sufficient to pay full-time corporate staff, much less provide the cash needed for business investments or community improvement. This capital shortage obviously can be made up only if the natives' subsurface resources begin at an early date to produce substantial revenues. For the ordinary village resident, therefore, the legal nuances of ANCSA are largely irrelevant, and it is the land for which they fought so fiercely which ultimately will determine whether ANCSA represents a dream or a delusion.

A DYNAMIC VIEW OF TRIBAL JURISDICTION TO TAX NON-INDIANS*

CAROLE E. GOLDBERG†

Domestic dependent nations are permitted an existence in the United States so long as they are weak.[1]

Just as Indian land was the object of white settlers in the nineteenth century, so Indian minerals are the object of white-dominated urban centers hungry for additional sources of energy in the twentieth century. If Indian tribes are to benefit from contemporary circumstances, however, it will probably be necessary to alter the political and economic system associated with the allocation of these resources. In order to achieve this goal, tribes may choose, among other means, to bargain for a percentage of the profits derived from access to their resources. Greater benefits, however, may result from the exercise by Indian tribes of the power to tax non-Indian developments on reservation lands.[2]

The imposition of taxes on non-Indians poses a set of legal issues that cannot be considered in a political and institutional vacuum. Despite the long-standing legal characterization of Indian tribes as "semi-sovereign"

---

* This article was supported by the National Science Foundation, RANN Division, Research Grant Number NSF 61-294-22 to the Lake Powell Research Project.

† Professor of Law, University of California, Los Angeles School of Law.

1. M. SHEPARDSON, NAVAJO WAYS IN GOVERNMENT 113 (American Anthropological Ass'n Memoir 96, 1963).

2. Traditionally, Indian tribes have settled for fixed royalties in exchange for mineral leases. Taxation can be a more lucrative future alternative to royalties than joint venture investment because it can supplement long term royalty agreements that have failed to keep pace with current market prices. For example, coal is now worth three to four times as much as when leases for extraction of much of Navajo coal were signed, "but the Navajos still receive 15¢ to 25¢ a ton . . . whereas Montana receives a royalty of 40¢ or more for coal taken from state lands and the Crow Indians receive a sliding scale with a 40¢-a-ton minimum." Reno, *High, Dry and Penniless*, 220 THE NATION 359, 361 (1975). Furthermore, the gains possible from taxation of massive new industrial developments are staggering. The New Mexico Revenue Commission has estimated that contemplated coal gasification plants on the eastern end of the Navajo Reservation would bring in the following sums at current prices and tax rates: $20 million per plant from a tax on contractors for the value of the completed project; $51 million from a sales tax on coal sold to power the gasification plants (assuming seven such plants operating for twenty-five years); over $3 million per year from severance and natural resource excise taxes; $12.5 million from a property tax on production; plus additional sums from income taxation of non-Navajos. *Gasification Plants Face Sales Tax*, Farmington (N.M.) Daily Times, Feb. 17, 1975, at 8, cols. 1-5. If tribal taxation could preempt state taxation, all these revenues could go far towards meeting the goals of the Navajo Tribe's recently adopted Ten-Year Plan. NAVAJO NATION, THE NAVAJO TEN-YEAR PLAN (1972). According to the plan, $3.8 billion is needed over the next ten years if Navajos are to enjoy a standard of living at the national average. *See also* OFFICE OF PROGRAM DEVELOPMENT, NAVAJO TRIBE, THE NAVAJO NATION: OVERALL ECONOMIC DEVELOPMENT PROGRAM (1974).

entities,[3] tribes have been reluctant to assert as broad a range of jurisdictional powers as those exercised by the states.[4] They have recognized that a legal victory may lead to a political defeat, that gains in one area may result in the unwelcome imposition of new restraints or requirements in another. Therefore, to understand the implications of the legal doctrine of Indian taxing power it is essential to take a dynamic view of the relation between legal constructs on the one hand, and on the other, the political-institutional context of their development. Using the large, energy-rich Navajo Nation as a case study, this article will explore the legal, political, and institutional limitations on the exercise by Indian tribes of the power to tax non-Indians.

I

THE ORIGIN AND FUNCTIONS OF NAVAJO TRIBAL GOVERNMENT

The ability to extend the range of Indian tribal powers depends, in large part, on the political structure that has developed as the result of various federal, state, and tribal relationships. The current division of Navajo tribal government into executive, legislative, and judicial branches[5] was set by and intended to further the aims of the federal government. Prior to contact with whites the Navajo possessed no centralized government or overall leader, disputes being resolved with the aid of non-hereditary clan leaders and respected mediators.[6] Following the military defeat of the Navajo and the imposition of the resettlement provisions of the Treaty of 1868, the tribe was

---

3. Worcester v. Georgia, 31 U.S. (6 Pet.) 515 (1832).

4. To the extent that modern Indian governments have punished, taxed, zoned, or otherwise regulated activities on their reservations, they have generally done so only if those activities were undertaken by Indians of their own tribe or another. *See, e.g.,* TASK FORCE ON INDIAN-STATE GOVERNMENT RELATIONS, STAFF REPORT ON TAXATION, STATE OF SOUTH DAKOTA D1-10 (1973), describing tax collection agreements between the state and the Pine Ridge Tribe, whereby the state agreed to collect and return a four per cent sales tax which the tribe had levied on Indian purchases on the reservation. The state collects a four per cent tax on non-Indian purchases on the reservation.

5. The legislative branch consists of a Tribal Council whose members are elected by Navajos from designated districts within the reservation. Secretary of the Interior, *Rules for the Tribal Council,* in R. YOUNG, NAVAJO YEARBOOK 407 (1961); 2 N.T.C. (Navajo Tribal Code) § 101 (1972). There are standing committees, 2 N.T.C. §§ 361-802 (1972), and an Advisory Council that exercises the Council's powers when it is not in session. 2 N.T.C. §§ 341-49 (1972). The executive branch consists of a tribal Chairman, Vice-Chairman, and numerous administrative departments, the Chairman and Vice-Chairman being elected by vote of all enrolled members of the tribe. *Rules for the Tribal Council,* in R. YOUNG, *supra* at 408; 2 N.T.C. §§ 4, 281-89 (1972). The judicial branch has several trial courts and an appellate court in which cases are heard de novo. Judges are appointed by the Chairman with the approval of the Council. 7 N.T.C. §§ 101, 131-73 (1969). For a description of the Navajo judiciary, *see* Davis, *Court Reform in the Navajo Nation,* 43 J. AM. JUD. SOC'Y 53 (1959); JUDICIAL BRANCH, NAVAJO NATION, ANNUAL REPORT (1973). Navajo institutions are among the most complex of Indian tribes. Compare, for example, the tribal governments described in detail in AMERICAN INDIAN LAWYER TRAINING PROGRAM, INDIAN TRIBES AS GOVERNMENTS (1975).

6. A. WILLIAMS, NAVAJO POLITICAL PROCESS 6-7, 24 (1970); M. SHEPARDSON, *supra* note 1, at 3.

subject to varying federal policies. In the 1920s the federal government sponsored the creation of an elected tribal government. The purpose of this program was to establish "indirect rule" of the tribe, to legitimize federal decisions concerning the allocation of reservation resources, and to further the assimilation of the Navajo into the dominant society.[7] The current Navajo Tribal Council still functions under by-laws issued by the Secretary of the Interior in 1938.[8] There is no tribal constitution authorizing the Council, since the Navajos declined to accept the provisions of the Indian Reorganization Act of 1934 which would have required such a constitution,[9] the Secretary of the Interior refused to approve an independently drafted Navajo constitution,[10] and the constitution authorized by the Navajo-Hopi Rehabilitation Act[11] was never promulgated. The Secretary of the Interior attempts to exercise considerable control over the Council as it is presently constituted, approving or disapproving resolutions and budget items, and even calling for the Council to convene.[12] It is debatable whether all such powers are authorized by law.[13]

Tribal courts, known as Courts of Indian Offenses, also were originally established by the Secretary of the Interior to hear civil and criminal cases against reservation Indians. The Indian judges for these courts were appointed by the Commissioner of Indian Affairs and paid for with federal funds until 1950, when the Tribal Council resolved that they be elected by the Navajo people.[14] Finally, in 1959 the Council provided for abolition of the Navajo Courts of Indian Offenses and establishment of the current Navajo judicial system which is an instrumentality of the tribe free from control of the Department of the Interior.[15]

While these contemporary governing institutions of the Navajo Tribe are a federal imposition on traditional Navajo forms of government, they are not fully equivalent to their federal, state, and local counterparts. The Navajo Tribe has few lawyers involved in any branch of government, and its legislature and court system have modest professional staffs.[16] Statutory law is

---

7. A. WILLIAMS, *supra* note 6, at 18-26.

8. See *Rules for the Tribal Council*, in R. YOUNG, *supra* note 5.

9. R. YOUNG, *supra* note 5, at 377; *see* 25 U.S.C. § 476 (1970).

10. R. YOUNG, *supra* note 5, at 379-82.

11. 25 U.S.C. § 636 (1970).

12. A. WILLIAMS, *supra* note 6, at 26.

13. See text accompanying notes 45-52 *infra*.

14. See Davis, *supra* note 5.

15. Navajo Tribal Council, Resolution No. C0-69-58, October 16, 1958 (codified in scattered sections of 7, 8 N.T.C.).

16. The Tribal Council is assisted by personnel of the Navajo Tribal Legal Office, consisting of two or three state-licensed lawyers. 2 N.T.C. §§ 951-53, 953(10) (1972). Although there is no express provision in the Navajo Tribal Code for law clerks for Navajo judges, the judges may by rule of court provide for the creation of such positions. 7 N.T.C. § 254 (1969). Currently there

codified in desultory and haphazard fashion. While the tribe is expanding its administrative bureaucracy, it lacks a full complement of specialists possessing the expertise necessary to cope with the growing number of complex decisions related to environmental degradation, cultural change, resource utilization, and planned development.[17] Bureaucracy exists more on flow charts than in organizational behavior.

Tribal taxation of non-Indians disturbs this federally created political structure in several respects. First, and most obviously, it involves the Indians in assertions of power over non-traditional, non-Indian activity. Second, it can provide the resources necessary to fund a thoroughly professional tribal bureaucracy, capable of maximizing tribal advantages from outsiders' development. Third, it can enable the tribe to become self-sufficient and self-sustaining, reducing the arguments in favor of making the reservation subject to state jurisdiction and terminating trust status. With taxing power over non-Indians, the tribe acquires the potential for equivalence with state governments. Accordingly, it is important to appreciate the new conception of tribal government inherent in the exercise of tribal taxing power over non-Indians, and the political and institutional alterations that may follow from that conception. The possibility of such alterations may lead the courts to redefine the sources of and limitations on tribal taxing power, and Congress to exercise its prerogative to redistribute power over reservation activities. This dynamic is central to the actual development of the legal doctrine of Indian taxing power.

II

SOURCES OF NAVAJO TAXING POWER

Early decisions of the United States Supreme Court proclaimed that Indian tribes possessed all sovereign powers over domestic matters within their territorial boundaries unless the United States decreed to the contrary.[18] This sovereign power has even been declared free of restrictions emanating from the Bill of Rights.[19] Since taxing power over all activities conducted on a sovereign's territory is an ordinary incident of sovereignty, under Supreme Court precedent the Navajo Tribe ought to possess this power unless Congress has withdrawn it.[20] In fact, Congress has not attempted to do so. The

---

are law school graduates working for the court of appeals. Professionals who can provide probation and parole services are sorely needed. ANNUAL REPORT, *supra* note 5, at 17.

17. *See* Cortner, *Development, Environment, Indians, and the Southwest Power Controversy*, 4 ALTERNATIVES 14, 19 (1974).

18. Worcester v. Georgia, 31 U.S. (6 Pet.) 515 (1832); *Ex Parte* Crow Dog, 109 U.S. 556 (1883).

19. *E.g.*, Native Am. Church v. Navajo Tribal Council, 272 F.2d 131 (10th Cir. 1959); Barta v. Oglala Sioux Tribe, 259 F.2d 553 (8th Cir. 1958).

20. Iron Crow v. Oglala Sioux Tribe, 231 F.2d 89, 99 (8th Cir. 1956).

1868 Treaty with the Navajos confirms their power to banish undesirable non-Indians from the reservation.[21] And the Indian Reorganization Act of 1934, although not accepted by the Navajos, manifests Congress's intent that tribal governments possess taxing powers.[22] The Solicitor of the Department of the Interior, however, has not been willing to extend the broad judicial pronouncements about sovereignty to the ultimate conclusion of recognizing tribal power to impose criminal sanctions on non-Indians for offenses committed on the reservation.[23] Nevertheless, this limited view of tribal sovereignty need not jeopardize tribal taxing power over non-Indians.[24]

In fact the historic definition of Indian sovereign powers is itself a function of the federal government's conception of what tribal governments would want and ought to regulate. As Indian-white contacts expanded, the scope of tribal sovereignty contracted, and the justification for the retention of certain powers was based largely on a recognition of Indian cultural distinctiveness, their geographic isolation, and the perils of precipitous assimilation.[25] If tribes

---

21. Treaty With the Navajo Indians, art. II, 15 Stat. 667, 668 (1869); see Dodge v. Nakai, 298 F. Supp. 26 (D. Ariz. 1969).

22. 25 U.S.C. § 476 (1970); see Barta v. Oglala Sioux Tribe, 259 F.2d 553.

23. 77 Interior Dec. 113 (1970). The use of authority in this opinion is thoroughly criticized in Baldassin & McDermott, *Jurisdiction Over Non-Indians: An Opinion of the "Opinion,"* 1 AM. INDIAN L. REV. 13 (1973). The Solicitor's position, based on a few early lower federal court decisions, has been that Indian tribes are limited to the sanction of banishing non-Indians from the reservation. The implication is that Indian tribes have such distinctive values that it would not be proper to subject a non-Indian to their ordinary modes of punishments, notwithstanding this is ordinarily the risk any alien takes upon entering a foreign country. However, the analogy between whites working on an Indian reservation and Americans working abroad, although appealing, is not fully warranted. Americans do not expect to be able to share the values of local decision-makers when they are abroad. A white on a reservation, however, may have different expectations because he or she is still in his or her own home country.

Despite the broad judicial pronouncements about sovereignty, the Solicitor's opinion implies that Indian tribes are more like private clubs or businesses, capable of imposing sanctions only on those who acquiesce. Contrary to this theory, however, the code adopted by the Department of Interior for Courts of Indian Offenses authorizes criminal jurisdiction over Indians who are not members of the tribe in whose court they are tried. 25 C.F.R. § 11.2 (1975). At the same time, it excludes even non-Indians who have consented to jurisdiction, although civil jurisdiction is allowed over non-Indians in such cases. 25 C.F.R. § 11.22 (1975). This characterization of Indian tribes was rejected by the Supreme Court quite recently in United States v. Mazurie, 419 U.S. 544 (1975). Recently several tribes have attempted to acquire criminal jurisdiction over non-Indians by posting notices at the boundaries of the reservation that entry will constitute consent to criminal jurisdiction. See discussion in Vollmann, *Criminal Jurisdiction in Indian Country: Tribal Sovereignty and Defendants' Rights in Conflict,* 22 U. KAN. L. REV. 387, 394 (1974); 4 NAT'L AMERICAN INDIAN COURT JUDGES ASS'N, JUSTICE AND THE AMERICAN INDIAN, EXAMINATION OF THE BASIS OF TRIBAL LAW AND ORDER AUTHORITY 50-56 (1974).

24. The tribe could simply banish any non-Indian who had failed to pay his taxes (lease provisions to the contrary notwithstanding). Indeed, court decisions of the 1950s confirm this point. Barta v. Oglala Sioux Tribe, 259 F.2d 553; Iron Crow v. Oglala Sioux Tribe, 231 F.2d 89. *See also* 55 Interior Dec. 14, 45 (1934), in which the Associate Solicitor affirmed the power of the tribe to tax nonmembers who accept privileges of trade and residence. This power was written into the Oglala Sioux Constitution and approved by the Secretary of the Interior. M. PRICE, LAW AND THE AMERICAN INDIAN 717 (1973).

25. *Ex Parte* Crow Dog, 109 U.S. 556 (1883).

now attempt to expand their powers to include taxation of non-Indians, the courts may alter their own construction of tribal sovereignty, limiting its scope to enrolled members of the tribe or its implementation to conformity with the Federal Constitution.

Recent decisions by the Department of the Interior and the United States Supreme Court indicate that a redefinition of tribal sovereignty to limit it to Indians in general, or to tribal members in particular, is unlikely. The solicitor has withdrawn his official opinion denying the existence of tribal criminal jurisdiction over non-Indians,[26] and has failed to disapprove several tribal ordinances imposing criminal jurisdiction over non-Indians on a theory of implied consent.[27] Furthermore, the Bureau of Indian Affairs's (BIA) policy of contracting with Indian tribes to provide services formerly administered by BIA personnel suggests that strengthening of administrative apparatus on reservations is an important goal.[28]

Most important, in January 1975, the Supreme Court delivered its opinion in *United States v. Mazurie*,[29] which reaffirmed the existence of wide tribal authority over non-Indians. The case did not deal with that issue squarely, since the question was whether the federal government could delegate law-making power over non-Indians to the tribes, not whether the tribes themselves could make these laws. Nevertheless, the Supreme Court asserted that the delegation of authority was easier to sustain because the delegate tribe possessed "a certain degree of independent authority over matters that affect the internal and social relations of tribal life,"[30] in this case the distribution and use of intoxicants on the reservation. The Court seemed anxious to avoid a direct statement that tribes could impose such regulations absent federal delegation, but it is difficult to develop a credible theory that would support the federal delegation but not the independent authority.

Of course, the Supreme Court still could define narrowly the class of activities by non-Indians on the reservation that affect the tribe's internal and social relations. For example, confusion and discussion abound in case law and commentary over whether a crime committed by one non-Indian against another non-Indian ought to be classified as such.[31] Conceivably taxation of

---

26. Memorandum from Kent Frizell, Solicitor, Dep't of the Interior, to Regional and Field Solicitors, Bureau of Indian Affairs, Jan. 25, 1974, in 1 INDIAN L. REP. no. 2, at 51 (1974).

27. Vollmann, *supra* note 23, at 394.

28. T. TAYLOR, THE STATES AND THEIR INDIAN CITIZENS 142-43, 160-67 (1972). This practice was approved of and facilitated by Congress in the Indian Self-Determination and Education Assistance Act of 1974, Pub. L. No. 93-638, §§ 102-10, 88 Stat. 2203.

29. 419 U.S. 544.

30. 419 U.S. at 557.

31. For a criticism of the case law holding crimes by non-Indians against non-Indians to be outside federal or tribal jurisdiction see Canby, *Civil Jurisdiction and the Indian Reservation*, 1973 UTAH L. REV. 206, 208-10; Taylor, *Development of Tripartite Jurisdiction in Indian Country*, 2 SOLICITOR'S REV. 1, 70-71 (1973); Vollmann, *supra* note 23, at 395. Recent lower court authority

non-Indians solely for the purposes of raising revenue might be viewed as a matter unrelated to regulation of internal tribal affairs, even though revenues might be used to redistribute income or to finance needed social services or cultural events. The trend does not seem to be in that direction, however. Rather, it seems to favor reaffirmation of Indian tribes as "unique aggregations possessing attributes of sovereignty over both their members *and their territory.*"[32]

Ironically, it is delay by Indian tribes in asserting these powers that ultimately may jeopardize their claim to sovereignty, especially to sovereignty that preempts the states. Most Indian tribes, including the Navajos, have not often attempted to assert and thereby test their sovereign powers with respect to non-Indians. For example, the general provisions for civil and criminal jurisdiction in Navajo tribal courts specify that the defendant must be an Indian.[33] A resolution to expand this jurisdiction to non-Indian defendants has been introduced in the Tribal Council, but has not even come to a vote.[34] Quite recently, however, in response to supportive precedent in the courts[35] and a supportive opinion by the Solicitor of the Department of Interior,[36] the tribe has asserted jurisdiction over non-Indians who violate tribal laws regulating hunting and fishing.[37] Similar resolutions, confined to a narrow range of non-Indian activities, have also passed the Council in recent years,[38] though

---

suggests that the commentators are having some impact. *See* Oliphant v. Schlie, Civil No. 511-73C2 (W.D. Wash., filed Apr. 5, 1974) (appeal pending) (upholding tribal jurisdiction over non-Indian charged with resisting arrest by tribal police officer and assaulting the officer); Ortiz-Barraza v. United States, 512 F.2d 1176 (9th Cir. 1975) (upholding the power of tribal police to stop and search non-Indians suspected of violating state or federal law, for purposes of excluding them under applicable tribal law).

32. United States v. Mazurie, 419 U.S. at 557 (emphasis added).

33. 7 N.T.C. § 133(a), (b) (1969).

34. Navajo Tribal Council, Proposed Resolution, *amending* Navajo Tribal Council, Resolution No. CJA 5-59, Jan. 9, 1959 (codified in 7 N.T.C.) (To Include Civil and Criminal Jurisdiction Over Non-Indians) (on file with the author). From the tribe's point of view, it was probably too large an initial step into the realm of jurisdiction over non-Indians. It might have produced a test case involving very little tribal interest. An attempt by the Tribal Council to institute a system of hunting and fishing licenses applicable to non-Indians and enforced by tribal courts was thwarted in the late 1960s, when counsel for the tribe contended with misplaced conviction that the tribe possessed no enforcement power. Navajo Tribal Council, Minutes of Meeting 129-40, February 3, 1969. The Resolution as eventually adopted required that non-Indians found in violation of tribal hunting and fishing laws be delivered to federal authorities. 23 N.T.C. § 109 (1969).

35. *E.g.*, Quechan Tribe of Indians v. Rowe, 350 F. Supp. 106 (S.D. Cal. 1972); *see* Comment, *Indian Regulation of Non-Indian Hunting and Fishing*, 1974 WIS. L. REV. 499. *See also* Oliphant v. Schlie, Civil No. 511-73C2 (W.D. Wash., filed Apr. 5, 1974).

36. *See* Memorandum, *supra* note 26.

37. Navajo Tribal Council, Resolution Nos. CAU-46-73, CJN-38-75, June 18, 1975. Significantly, the tribe also has authorized the training and hiring of special tribal law enforcement officers who will be concerned only with arresting people pursuant to these laws. Navajo Tribal Council, Resolution No. CJN-38-75, June 18, 1975 (Exhibit "D": Plan of Operation for the Establishment of a "Wildlife Enforcement Section" Within the Fish and Wildlife Department).

38. One resolution that grants tribal jurisdiction over forcible entry and detainer actions against any "person," has been upheld by the Navajo Court of Appeals as applied to a non-Indian corporation. Navajo Tribe v. Orlando Helicopter Airways, Inc., Civil No. 1-12 (Navajo Ct.

not necessarily as part of a deliberate plan gradually to extend jurisdiction over non-Indians.[39] More directly, in January 1974, the Tribal Council authorized the establishment of a Navajo Tax Commission that would report back to the Council on the prospects of taxing non-Indians.[40] Indicative of the tribe's restraint on this issue is the fact that the Commission was not appointed until April 1976. Meanwhile, the State of New Mexico has moved closer to taxing the same non-Indian assets and income the tribe may want to tap.[41]

Three factors account for the tribe's reluctance to pursue the substantial revenues to be gained from taxing non-Indians. First, many Council members have feared that new taxes will have to be imposed on Navajos as well as non-Navajos.[42] Second, the Council has sensed that the costs of designing and enforcing a tax structure will, at least initially, be too great a burden.[43] And finally, there has been concern that the structure of the tribe will be adversely affected when, as part of expanding its jurisdiction, the tribe may have to provide services to non-Indians, share special rights (e.g., voting, jury duty) with non-Navajos, and create a more Anglicized political structure. It is reasonable for tribal leaders to expect that after courts have reaffirmed, and the tribe has asserted, new and far-reaching sovereign powers, courts, the Department of Interior, and Congress will initiate fresh discussions of the limits on how tribal authority may be exercised.

III
SOURCES OF POSSIBLE RESTRICTIONS ON TRIBAL TAXING POWER

A. Federal Power to Approve or Disapprove Tribal Council Decisions

The courts have been willing to recognize broad tribal power over Indians in part because they recognize as a restraining factor the requirement that the

---

App., filed Jan. 12, 1972); see Note, Indian Tribal Courts—Jurisdiction—Navajo Court Jurisdiction Over Non-Indian Defendants, 18 ST. LOUIS U.L.J. 461 (1974). Another authorizes the recently established Navajo Environmental Protection Commission to seek imposition of fines on non-Indian as well as Indian polluters. Navajo Tribal Council, Resolution No. CAU 72-72, Aug. 10, 1972.

39. Navajo Tribal Council, Minutes of Meeting, Nov. 21, 1969, concerning Navajo Tribal Council, Resolution No. CN-100-69, November 21, 1969 and Navajo Tribal Council, Resolution No. CAU-72-72, August 10, 1972.

40. Navajo Tribal Council, Resolution No. CJA-6-74, January 16, 1974. The tribe had before it a study prepared by Professor Gerald Boyle of the Department of Economics, University of New Mexico, concerning appropriate sources of tax revenue on the reservation. G. BOYLE, REVENUE ALTERNATIVES FOR THE NAVAJO NATION (University of New Mexico Working Papers in Economics 1973).

41. See Farmington (N.M.) Daily Times, supra note 2.

42. Navajo Tribal Council, Minutes of Meeting 41-64, January 16, 1974. This fear was fed by a consultant's report on Navajo taxation which recommended imposition of a payroll tax. See G. BOYLE, supra note 40, at 13-15.

43. The tribe does not even have an adequate means of auditing and enforcing royalty and lease obligations of lessees. G. BOYLE, supra note 40, at 17-19.

Secretary of the Interior must approve all tribal ordinances.[44] Because of its unusual origin, the Navajo Tribal Council enjoys more independence from the Secretary of the Interior than do most tribal governments. Had the Navajos adopted a constitution under the Indian Reorganization Act of 1934, it probably would have followed the BIA's model provisions, including a requirement that all tribal resolutions be approved by the Secretary before becoming effective.[45] Since the Navajos refused not only that invitation to establish a constitution, but also the more personal one embodied in the 1954 Navajo-Hopi Rehabilitation Act,[46] the Council continues to act under some sketchy rules promulgated by the Secretary of the Interior in 1938—rules intended to be only temporary. Thus, although the Navajo Tribal Council operates as if the Navajo people had formally vested it with their sovereign power, it is technically the creation of secretarial rules. These rules do not, however, define or limit what the Council may do. Neither do they require secretarial approval of all tribal resolutions. They simply provide for elections and terms of office for members of the Tribal Council, the Chairman, and the Vice-Chairman.[47] While Congress could limit the Council's powers and require secretarial approval, it has not done so.[48]

The Navajo Tribal Code nevertheless contains statements that tribal law and order regulations must be approved by the Secretary before becoming effective.[49] While tax laws do not fall into this category, it has been the general practice for many years for the tribe to submit resolutions to the Secretary for his signature. A signal that this practice may be terminated is the holding of the Court of Appeals for the Navajo Tribe in the case of *Navajo Tribe of Indians v. Holyan*. The court concluded that even where the tribe has expressly provided for secretarial approval, the submission is unnecessary and the Secretary's action "a meaningless formality."[50] According to the court, Congress and the Secretary have not ordered the submission, and the tribe cannot voluntarily relinquish its sovereignty. In spite of this decision, submission of resolutions to the Secretary continues.

---

44. Thus, the Court in United States v. Mazurie, 419 U.S. 544, 558 n.12 (1975) noted with favor that the Secretary must approve any tribal ordinance limiting sale of liquor on the reservation before violation of the ordinance becomes a federal offense. *See* text accompanying notes 29-30 *supra*.

45. *See* M. PRICE, *supra* note 24, at 717-19.

46. 25 U.S.C. § 636 (1970).

47. *See Rules for the Tribal Council*, in R. YOUNG, *supra* note 5.

48. It is debatable whether, in the absence of specific congressional direction, the secretary could require such approval under the general delegation of authority in 25 U.S.C. § 2 (1970). Although there is little judicial guidance to its limits, this section has been interpreted narrowly in recent years. *E.g.*, Organized Village of Kake v. Egan, 369 U.S. 60, 63 (1962); Norvell v. Sangre de Cristo Dev. Co., 372 F. Supp. 348, 354-55 (D.N.M. 1974), *rev'd on other grounds*, 519 F.2d 370 (10th Cir. 1975).

49. 7 N.T.C. § 1(e) (1969); 17 N.T.C. § 1 (1969).

50. Navajo Tribe of Indians v. Hoylan, Civil No. 8-22 (Navajo Ct. App., filed Aug. 22, 1973).

Although there seems to be no direct secretarial barrier to Navajo imposition of taxes on non-Indian development, the absence of such a barrier will not necessarily enhance the sovereign powers of the tribe. The existence of a potential federal check, as in the *Mazurie* case[51] and as is true for most Indian tribes, may make courts more relaxed about recognizing tribal power to tax non-Indians, or more inclined to find a taxing ordinance within the permissible limits of the Indian Civil Rights Act. On the other hand, the Secretary *can* exercise some indirect control over Navajo legislation. Under section seven of the Navajo-Hopi Rehabilitation Act, tribal power to appropriate "funds" is subject to secretarial approval.[52] Whether expenditures of tax revenues collected by the tribe are subject to this limitation is uncertain. The reference may only be to rentals, royalties, and federal appropriations. But assuming *any* tribal funds may be spent only after secretarial approval, some indirect federal supervision of tribal policies does exist, although perhaps not enough to convince courts that tribal jurisdiction over non-Indians will reflect dominant values and political preferences.

B. The Indian Civil Rights Act

Another well-spring of federal power to regulate Indian tribes, that may shape the use of tribal taxing power, is the Indian Civil Rights Act.[53] Enacted in 1968, this statute was designed to restrain the actions of tribal councils with respect to Indians and non-Indians[54] by requiring conformity with the dominant values expressed in the Bill of Rights.[55] The Act does not render all ten constitutional amendments applicable to the tribes; nor is it clear that the language in the Act making certain amendments applicable to tribal governments means the same in a tribal context as it does elsewhere.[56]

These limits on tribal powers are relevant to an examination of the dynamics of Navajo taxing power over non-Indians in two very different ways. First, they dictate how the tribe must structure and administer the taxes

---

51. *See* note 44 *supra*.

52. 25 U.S.C. § 637 (1970).

53. *Id.* §§ 1301-41.

54. Although early commentators on the Act doubted its applicability to non-Indians, judicial decisions have found it applicable. *Compare* Note, *The Indian Bill of Rights and the Constitutional Status of Tribal Governments*, 82 HARV. L. REV. 1343, 1364 (1969), *with* Dodge v. Nakai, 298 F. Supp. 17, 26 (D. Ariz. 1968) *and* Oliphant v. Schlie, Civil No. 511-73C2 (W.D. Wash., filed Apr. 5, 1974).

55. This requirement was influenced by the fact that the earlier court decisions had suggested that Indian tribes were not subject to the Bill of Rights at all. The legislative history of the Act is described from competing points of view in Ziontz, *In Defense of Tribal Sovereignty: An Analysis of Judicial Error in Construction of the Indian Civil Rights Act*, 20 S.D.L. REV. 1 (1975) and de Raismes, *The Indian Civil Rights Act of 1968 and the Pursuit of Responsible Tribal Self-Government*, 20 S.D.L. REV. 59 (1975). *See* cases cited at note 19 *supra*.

56. Comment, *The Indian Bill of Rights and the Constitutional Status of Tribal Governments*, 82 HARV. L. REV. 1343 (1969).

it decides to impose. They may, for example, prevent the Navajo Tribe from taxing only non-Indians or non-Navajos.[57] Second, and more seriously, these limits open the possibility that tribal sovereignty will be subject to greater restraints in areas other than taxation should the tribe attempt to impose a tax on non-Indians, even if that tax is itself acceptable under the Act.

The major structural restriction on Navajo taxing power is the equal protection clause inserted in the Indian Civil Rights Act. Supreme Court interpretations of the equal protection provisions of the fifth and fourteenth amendments specify that ordinarily a law which treats groups of people differently must be rationally related to the achievement of some legitimate statutory purpose.[58] However, where the law distinguishes between people with respect to their ability to exercise some constitutional right,[59] or classifies people on the basis of an individual characteristic, such as race, that is beyond individual control and has historically been the basis for invidious treatment,[60] the law must be *necessary* to achieve a compelling state interest. Very few laws have survived this latter requirement.[61]

Under these standards, a law taxing non-Indians or non-Navajos might survive, even though it smacks of discrimination against a racial or alien group. The Supreme Court has indicated that it will rarely second-guess legislative determinations about who should bear tax burdens, no matter which group receives the heavier burden.[62] Moreover, distinctions involving Indians have not always been subjected to the rigorous scrutiny imposed on other racial distinctions. In the Supreme Court's 1974 decision in *Morton v. Mancari*,[63] a federal statute giving preference to members of federally recognized Indian tribes in BIA hiring and promotions was upheld because the Court found that the classification was not racial but "political." The Court emphasized that people who are racially Indian but not members of federally recognized tribes

---

57. The Navajos currently grant preferences to tribal members in determining rentals for lease of tribal lands. Navajo Advisory Committee, Resolution No. ACJ-48-56, 1956, described in K. GILBREATH, RED CAPITALISM 39 (1973). Concern about the likely imposition of taxes on Navajos along with non-Navajos is partly responsible for lack of speed in implementing the Navajo Tax Commission. *See* text accompanying note 42 *supra*.

58. This principle is articulated in Reed v. Reed, 404 U.S. 71 (1971).

59. *E.g.*, Dunn v. Blumstein, 405 U.S. 330 (1972).

60. *E.g.*, Loving v. Virginia, 388 U.S. 1 (1967) (race); Graham v. Richardson, 403 U.S. 365 (1971) (alienage).

61. One notable exception is the law that produced the internment of Japanese-Americans in detention camps during World War II. Korematsu v. United States, 323 U.S. 214 (1944).

62. Thus in Kahn v. Shevin, 416 U.S. 351 (1974), Mr. Justice Douglas joined the Court in upholding the distribution of tax burdens on the basis of sex, even though he joined the plurality opinion in an earlier case viewing sex discrimination with the same suspicion as race discrimination. Frontiero v. Richardson, 411 U.S. 677 (1973) (opinion of Mr. Justice Brennan). Since allocation of tax burdens is perceived to be within the peculiar competence of local governing bodies, the Supreme Court is inclined to find a discriminatory tax law adequate to withstand any level of scrutiny.

63. 417 U.S. 535 (1974).

would not qualify. Thus, the requirement of a "compelling state interest," applicable to racially discriminatory laws, will not necessarily apply whenever a distinction is drawn between Indians and non-Indians.

A tax imposed solely on non-Navajos would have a strong chance of surviving the less stringent rational relation test. Indeed, the demonstration of a reasonable relationship between such discrimination and a legitimate statutory purpose often has been found, as in *Morton*, where the goal of furthering Indian self-government sufficed. Federal (as opposed to tribal) discrimination in favor of Indians will almost always satisfy this requirement because of the federal government's trust and guardianship responsibilities with respect to Indians and the special constitutional provisions giving Congress authority over Indian affairs. A tax imposed by the Navajo tribe only on non-Navajos cannot be justified as easily. A justification based simply on the desire to favor one "political group" (Navajos) over others (non-Navajos) would be circular as well as suspect, given that the group imposing the tax was the exempt group. A rationale based on the fact that tribal members own the tribal resources might be plausible, however, since the tax would be on outsiders for the privilege of operating on the tribal territory. A more convincing argument would rest on the need to overcome the hardships and disadvantages long suffered by the Indians. This kind of justification sufficed to support a sex discriminatory tax,[64] although it has never been applied by the Supreme Court to racial discrimination as such.[65]

Even if a tax on non-Navajos would not be acceptable on constitutional equal protection grounds, it is conceivable that the equal protection clause of the Indian Civil Rights Act imposes different requirements. A substantial body of legal literature[66] argues that constitutional doctrine should be modified in interpreting identical provisions in the Indian Civil Rights Act, to take into account the distinctive culture and institutions of reservation tribes. Thus, for example, while tribes frequently make distinctions on the basis of blood quantum in distributing benefits among tribal members,[67] distinctions which might well fall under the fifth and fourteenth amendments as racial classifications,[68] these same distinctions might be upheld under the Indian Civil Rights Act as necessary to preserve tribal integrity, to maintain long-

---

64. Kahn v. Shevin, 416 U.S. 351 (1974).

65. The issue was avoided in DeFunis v. Odegaard, 82 Wash. 2d 11, 507 P.2d 1169 (1973), *vacated as moot*, 416 U.S. 312 (1974).

66. *See* articles cited in de Raismes, *supra* note 55, at 59 n.2.

67. *See, e.g.*, the Crow Creek Tribe's requirement that certain Tribal Council candidates be at least one-half blood, upheld in Daly v. United States, 483 F.2d 700, 705 (8th Cir. 1973).

68. There are some early Supreme Court decisions upholding federal distinctions among enrolled tribal members on the basis of blood quantum. *E.g.*, United States v. Waller, 243 U.S. 452 (1917). None, however, squarely faced the equal protection issue. For a discussion of these cases see Vieira, *Racial Imbalance, Black Separatism, and Permissible Classification by Race*, 67 MICH. L. REV. 1553, 1577-81 (1969).

standing tribal traditions, or to recognize tribal ownership.[69] Some commentators would allow this deference only in situations where the tribal action reflects long-standing tradition essential to tribal culture,[70] forgetting that although many modern tribal institutions have structures similar to those in white society they operate in uniquely Indian ways.

Under either standard of review, however, a tax only on non-Navajos would be little easier to justify under the Indian Civil Rights Act than under the fifth or fourteenth amendment. Separate treatment of outsiders for purposes of matters such as voting, jury service, issuance of grazing permits, and perhaps even freedom of speech, may be justifiable to maintain tribal identity and distinctiveness. The problem is that special taxation of outsiders has no connection with these values, except perhaps as a means of regulating entry by outsiders, or protecting the income and property of Indians whose traditional pursuits do not leave them with sufficient funds to pay taxes. Yet these possible connections are not viable if the tribe is simultaneously pursuing a policy of encouraging non-Indian enterprises on the reservation,[71] or if the tax exemption for Navajos applies to non-Indian style entrepreneurs as well as sheep herders.

Assuming the Navajos are willing to tax their own people and outsiders alike (relying, for example, on steep graduation beyond a certain low income, or taxes on major industry only), the Indian Civil Rights Act may introduce a very different kind of restraint on the tribe. On the one hand, the potential in the Act for imposition of dominant values on tribal actions may enhance the likelihood that taxing power and other jurisdiction over non-Navajos will be upheld in the courts.[72] On the other hand, the quid pro quo for this expanded jurisdiction over non-Indians might well be an increasing inclination on the part of the courts to force Indian governments into the mold of state

---

69. Other distinctions between "constitutional" requirements on and off reservations might be justified by the need for informality on reservations where bureaucratic institutions have not developed and government operates as an extended family. Ziontz, *supra* note 55, at 47-78. Imagine, for example, the impact on reservations of a holding that criminal cases with potential jail sentences must be heard by attorney judges. Such a requirement exists as a matter of due process in California. Gordon v. Justice Court for Yuba Judicial Dist., 12 Cal. 3d 323, 525 P.2d 72, 115 Cal. Rptr. 632 (1974).

70. de Raismes, *supra* note 55, at 82-85.

71. NAVAJO NATION, *supra* note 2, at 73-80.

72. Ziontz, *supra* note 55, at 56-57 and de Raismes, *supra* note 55, at 81-82, agree on this point. The Supreme Court's approving reference to the Indian Civil Rights Act in United States v. Mazurie, 419 U.S. at 558 n.12, which upheld tribal jurisdiction over non-Indians, reinforces this opinion. Although claims have been made that application of tribal rules to non-Indians violates due process because resident non-Indians cannot participate in formulating the rules, these claims have generally not led to invalidation of the rules themselves. *See* Memo, *Jurisdiction of Indian Tribes to Prohibit Aerial Crop Spraying Within the Confines of a Reservation*, 78 Interior Dec. 229 (1971), advising that Fort Hall Business Council Resolution No. 56-70, prohibiting all aerial spraying, does not violate due process served under 25 U.S.C. § 1302(8) (1970) as to non-Indian lessees who had no opportunity to present their view on the measure prior to its enactment. A similar claim was rejected in United States v. Mazurie, 419 U.S. 544, 558 n.12 (1975).

and local entities by interpreting the Indian Civil Rights Act provisions to mean the same thing as their Bill of Rights counterparts. For example, tribal rules limiting voting in tribal elections to enrolled members of the tribe might be invalidated on a theory analogous to the one used to strike down long residency requirements for voting in state elections,[73] given the fact that there is no way to become part of the tribal body politic except by birth.[74] Or tribal rules limiting service on juries or in tribal offices to Indians might be struck down on a theory analogous to those used in recent cases challenging exclusion of aliens from juries or civil service employment.[75]

This result should not be surprising if it is true that tribal power will be viewed expansively by the courts only so long as it is exercised within the bounds intended by the federal architects of tribal governments. As soon as tribal government appears to acquire the independence and permanence that significant exercise of taxing power brings, as soon as its institutions develop and Anglicize to the point where effective exercise of such jurisdiction is possible, and as soon as the tribe clearly indicates that its sovereign concern is everything that affects its territory (not simply its people), the courts may balk at deference to tribal definitions of expedient legislation that differ from dominant societal values, and courts may require participation by non-Indians in the legislative (*e.g.*, taxing) process.

The Indian Civil Rights Act may have been enacted in contemplation of expanded tribal jurisdiction over non-Indians. Simultaneously Congress was encouraging long-term leasing of reservation lands to non-Indians,[76] yet making it impossible for states to acquire jurisdiction over reservation Indians without consent of the affected Indians.[77] The Civil Rights Act was the only remaining protection against imposition of alien cultural or political values on non-Indians. Thus tribal sovereignty may receive a freer rein the longer tribes choose to retain their self-contained, distinctive way of life. The Supreme Court's very different responses to non-normative policies of the expansionist Mormons on the one hand,[78] and the isolated Amish on the other,[79] illustrate

---

73. *See, e.g.*, Dunn v. Blumstein, 405 U.S. 330 (1972).

74. 1 N.T.C. § 102 (1969).

75. *See* Sugarman v. Dougall, 413 U.S. 634 (1973) (state civil service); Mow Sun Wong v. Hampton, 500 F.2d 1031 (9th Cir. 1974) (federal civil service); Travers, *The Constitutional Status of State and Federal Governmental Discrimination Against Resident Aliens*, 16 HARV. INT'L L.J. 113 (1975). Even a Navajo might demand non-Indians on his jury under current definitions of the right to a representative jury. Peters v. Kiff, 407 U.S. 493 (1972).

76. 25 U.S.C. § 415(a) (1970). Ninety-nine-year leases of Navajo land were first authorized in 1960. Pub. L. No. 86-505, 74 Stat. 199 (1960).

77. 25 U.S.C. §§ 1321-26 (1970).

78. *See* Reynolds v. United States, 98 U.S. 145 (1878), upholding anti-polygamy laws in the face of challenge under the Free Exercise Clause; M. SHEPARDSON, *supra* note 1, at 113, where she notes "[t]he futile efforts of the Mormons to establish an independent State of Deseret . . . ."

79. *See* Wisconsin v. Yoder, 406 U.S. 205 (1972), striking down state compulsory school laws as applied to the Amish, whose religion. forbade formal education.

this point. It is unlikely that the Navajos will be permitted to retain their sovereign distinctiveness while selecting out portions of the reservation for lucrative development by non-Indians. Since the cases suggest that tribal powers over non-Indians are not about to be denied altogether,[80] the important question is how far the courts will go in fitting tribal governments to non-Indian models. The Indian Civil Rights Act is a powerful tool for accomplishing that purpose; and fears related to possible invocation of the Act may induce the tribe to negotiate with industry and competing sovereigns over revenues rather than assume the risks attendant with bold exercise of power.

C.   Secretarial Power to Approve or Disapprove Leases

As trustee for tribally held and allotted Indian lands, the Secretary of the Interior or his delegate must approve every lease of that property.[81] When the lease is for a very long term, Congress has required that prior to approval the Secretary shall first satisfy himself that adequate consideration has been given to "the availability of police and fire protection and other services [and] the availability of judicial forums for all criminal and civil causes of action arising on leased lands . . . ."[82]

These secretarial powers can affect the exercise of Navajo taxing powers in several ways. Indirectly, the Secretary could refuse to approve leases generally or hinder the process of lease approval if he disfavored some tribal tax. More directly, the Secretary could refuse to approve a particular lease unless it contained a provision in which the tribe surrendered its power to tax. Several major industrial leases entered into by the tribe over the last fifteen years, including the lease for the Four Corners Power Plant and the Navajo Generating Station, contain just such waivers, although not necessarily at secretarial insistence.[83] For example, the Four Corners lease prohibits taxation of property located on leased lands, leasehold rights granted in the lease, ownership, construction, and operation of facilities, generation or transmission of power, sale or disposal of power, company income, or sale or delivery of fuel to the company until 2005, when the tribe is then permitted to levy only a property tax, and at a rate one-half that of New Mexico or Arizona. Here is recognition of the tribe as property-owner, entitled to rents and royalties, but not as sovereign, entitled to taxes.[84]

Whether such lease provisions are enforceable against the tribe is unclear.

---

80. *See* text accompanying notes 26-32 *supra*.

81. 25 U.S.C. § 415 (1970). For a thorough description of the leasing process see Chambers & Price, *Regulating Sovereignty: Secretarial Discretion and the Leasing of Indian Lands*, 26 STAN. L. REV. 1061 (1974).

82. 25 U.S.C. § 415(a) (1970).

83. *See* G. BOYLE, *supra* note 40, at 7-8.

84. This view of the tribe may be fostered by its counsel, who have always been private law firms rather than an "in-house" staff of government lawyers.

If a hypothetical state that had agreed to forego assessing certain taxes later imposed those very taxes, the taxpayer would have a constitutional defense or claim based on the section of the Federal Constitution prohibiting any state from impairing the obligations of contracts.[85] The Supreme Court has held, over powerful dissent, that a sovereign state is capable of contracting away its taxing powers.[86] By contrast, a sovereign is incapable of contracting away its police power or its power of eminent domain.[87] In deference to the sovereign, however, courts have gone out of their way to construe narrowly any exercise of the power to contract away taxing authority, to construe broadly any state constitutional restriction on contracting away taxing authority, and to characterize tax exemptions as legislative measures rather than contracts.[88]

This body of law is not easily related to the situation of the Navajo Tribe. The constitutional prohibition on impairment of the obligations of contracts has not been applied to Indian tribes under the Indian Civil Rights Act. It is uncertain, however, whether that means that a tribal tax imposed subsequent to an agreement not to tax would be treated simply as a potential deprivation of property without due process or would be subjected to more searching constitutional examination. A recent decision by the Navajo Court of Appeals[89] makes it clear that Navajo sovereign immunity[90] will not save the tribe from suit if such claims are made under the Civil Rights Act. Should they be brought, the tribe might nevertheless invoke other precedents construing narrowly any arguable exercise of the power to contract away taxing authority. Following these precedents, the courts might decline to find any authorization for the Tribal Council to enter into such agreements, and invalidate the waivers. The tribe may be wary of suggesting such an approach, however, because it calls into question many principles the tribe would not want threatened—such as the Tribal Council's personification of all sovereignty possessed by the Navajo people, notwithstanding the lack of any constitution. Nevertheless, the tribe might argue that while the Council may have broad regulatory authority in the absence of a constitution, it wants the authority in the absence of a constitution to cede further sovereign powers in a contract. In one way or another, then, the tribe may be able to elude its agreement not to tax existing major industry on the reservation.

---

85. U.S. Const. art I, § 10.
86. Dartmouth College v. Woodward, 17 U.S. (4 Wheat.) 518 (1819); New Jersey v. Wilson, 11 U.S. (7 Cranch) 164 (1812).
87. Annot., 173 A.L.R. 15, 31 (1948).
88. *Id.* Thus, it might be possible to argue that the Tribal Council does not have sufficient authorization from the secretary to contract away tribal taxing power.
89. Halderman Dennison v. Tucson Gas & Electric Co., Civil No. 12-74 (Navajo Ct. App., filed Dec. 23, 1974).
90. *See, e.g.,* Thebo v. Choctaw Tribe, 66 F. 372 (8th Cir. 1895); cases cited in Ziontz, *supra* note 55, at 32 n.124 (immunity in federal court). This immunity can be lifted by Congress. Hamilton v. Nakai, 453 F.2d 152 (9th Cir. 1971).

Even if the validity and enforceability of agreements not to tax are doubtful, secretarial insistence on including such provisions in leases might fail to comport with the Secretary's trust responsibility.[91] In the case of long-term leases, however, the Secretary might justify such action on the basis of Congress's direction that he insure there has been adequate consideration of the availability of public services and judicial forums prior to approving such leases. Restrictions on tribal taxing power might be deemed appropriate to avoid possible tribal preemption of state taxing power under circumstances where the state is being relied on to provide the services and forums. The surrender of tribal taxing power would have to be carefully tied to this rationale, however, if the Secretary ever attempted to invoke it. For example, the tribe would have to be permitted to tax if it ever became willing and able to provide necessary services and court facilities.

In both indirect and direct ways, then, the Secretary may be able to restrain tribal taxing power through exercise of control over leasing tribal lands. As in the case of other federal controls, the existence of this potential for secretarial control may make the courts more comfortable about the prospect of recognizing tribal jurisdiction over non-Indians. But the price of this acceptability is the possibility of a secretarial veto whenever tribal sovereignty is exercised in ways that threaten non-Indian interests.

D.   Inhibitions Emanating from State Taxing Power

As state and tribal governments compete for tax revenues arising from reservation activities by non-Indians, judicial doctrines and legislation that have protected tribes from state incursion may weaken. Not only do state officials fear that tribes may obtain advantages the states wish for themselves, or that tribal decisions will affect people who do not participate in their formulation, but they are also concerned that the states will be burdened by the demands for protection and education of non-Indians on the reservation without being allowed the necessary compensating revenues.[92] State power to tax non-Indians on the reservations may preclude tribal taxation because of an explicit congressional grant of exclusive state power, because state taxation preempts tribal taxation even in the absence of congressional action, or because, as a practical matter, tribes are placed in an unfavorable bargaining

---

91. See Chambers & Price, *supra* note 81; Chambers, *Judicial Enforcement of the Federal Trust Responsibility to Indians*, 27 STAN. L. REV. 1213, 1232-34 (1975). The secretary might take the position that a waiver of taxing power would increase the return measured in terms of rentals and royalties. *But see* Price & Weatherford, *Indian Water Rights in Theory and Practice: Navajo Experience in the Colorado River Basin*, 40 LAW & CONTEMP. PROB. no. 1, at 97 (1976).

92. This concern with state responsibility for services in the absence of state entitlement to revenues already exists with respect to Indians, as courts have held Indians entitled to participate in state governmental benefits despite their immunities from state taxes. *See* Goldberg, *Public Law 280: The Limits of State Jurisdiction Over Reservation Indians*, 22 U.C.L.A.L. REV. 533 (1975).

position when they try to impose taxes on non-Indian lessees in addition to those already levied by the state.

1. *Congressional Authorization for Exclusive State Taxing Power*

As part of its plenary control over Indian affairs,[93] Congress has the power to confer exclusive jurisdiction on the states to tax Indians as well as non-Indians on reservations. Congress has never acted, however, to confer such jurisdiction on the states as a general matter.[94] The closest Congress has come to conferring broad jurisdiction on the states is the enactment in 1953 of Public Law 280,[95] which required six states[96] and authorized the remainder to assert jurisdiction over reservation Indians. The Act was amended in 1968 to provide that no jurisdiction could be asserted by states merely *authorized* to assume it unless the affected Indians first consented in a referendum.[97] In addition, the 1968 amendments permitted states that had been compelled to assume jurisdiction under Public Law 280 to return (retrocede) such power to the federal government.[98]

The statute preserved the tax-exempt trust status of Indians lands,[99] although one circuit court of appeals has read the exemptions as permitting taxation of non-Indian leasehold interests in trust property.[100] In addition, the Supreme Court held recently that the statute does not authorize any kind of state taxation of reservation Indians.[101] Because Public Law 280 is addressed to state jurisdiction over Indians, this holding does not mean that states possessing jurisdiction under Public Law 280 may not tax non-Indians if they could have done so had the statute never been enacted. However, the decision does make it clear that Public Law 280 was not a broad or exclusive

---

93. *Id.* at 535, 563-67.

94. While one might construe Congress's directive to the Secretary to consider jurisdictional problems before approving long-term leases as a delegation of this authority, the Secretary has never promulgated comprehensive regulations. The only relevant regulations concern application of state zoning laws to leased lands. 25 C.F.R. § 1.4 (1974). They were adopted prior to the legislation incorporating this directive. 25 U.S.C. § 415(a) (1970). For a suggestion that such regulations be promulgated see Note, *Need for a Federal Policy in Indian Economic Development*, 2 N.M.L. Rev. 71, 79-80 (1972).

95. Act of Aug. 15, 1953, ch. 505, 67 Stat. 588-90 (now codified, *as amended*, in scattered sections of 18 and 28 U.S.C.). For an analysis of the Act, *see* Goldberg, *supra* note 92.

96. Alaska, California, Minnesota, Nebraska, Oregon, and Wisconsin, with the exception of certain named reservations, fell into this category.

97. 25 U.S.C. §§ 1321-26 (1970).

98. *Id.* § 1323. For a discussion of retrocession see Goldberg, *supra* note 92, at 558-92. Public Law 280 jurisdiction has been assumed in whole or in part by Florida, Idaho, Iowa, Montana, Nevada, North Dakota, South Dakota, and Washington. *Id.* at 567-69 and accompanying notes.

99. The Act also preserved treaty and statutory rights with respect to hunting, fishing, and land use even after states had acquired this jurisdiction. 28 U.S.C. § 1360(b) (1970); 18 U.S.C. § 1162(b) (1970).

100. Agua Caliente Band of Mission Indians v. County of Riverside, 442 F.2d 1184 (9th Cir. 1971), *cert. denied*, 405 U.S. 933 (1972).

101. Bryan v. Itasca County, 96 S. Ct. 2102 (1976).

grant of state taxing power over Indians and non-Indians on reservations.

Federal law does appear to authorize state taxation of mineral extraction on Indian trust lands.[102] However, this limited provision does not render state taxing power exclusive.

2. State Preemption of Tribal Taxing Power Over Non-Indians Absent Congressional Authorization

More interesting is the scope of state taxing power when the state possesses no Public Law 280 jurisdiction.[103] This is the case on the Navajo reservation: Arizona, New Mexico, and Utah—the states containing the Navajo Reservation—did not assume jurisdiction prior to 1968 (although Utah did so afterwards),[104] and the Navajos have never voted in favor of such jurisdiction.[105]

In the absence of congressional allocation of exclusive jurisdiction to the states, the states nevertheless have argued that their exercise of regulatory power over non-Indians on reservations can preempt any tribal powers. One potential judicial response to increased assertiveness of tribes like the Navajo may be to strengthen the doctrinal underpinning of the states' argument. The source of this argument involves Supreme Court cases denying federal (and by implication, tribal) jurisdiction over crimes committed by one non-Indian against another on the reservation in favor of exclusive state jurisdiction.[106]

It is unlikely that the law will evolve in this direction, however. The logic of the original cases upholding exclusive state jurisdiction is under increasing attack, as commentators point out that activities by non-Indians may legitimately concern the tribe.[107] These observations are correct even if the tribal government is still functioning merely as a transitional agent of assimilation and indirect rule. Laws prohibiting interference with activities of tribal police,[108] traditional Indian ceremonies or burial grounds,[109] or tribal deci-

---

102.   25 U.S.C. § 398 (1970); see British-American Oil Producing Co. v. Board of Equalization, 299 U.S. 159 (1936). For an interpretation of this statute that would deny state taxing power over lessees engaged in mineral production while permitting state taxation of the royalties Indian tribes receive from such production see Comment, *The Case for Exclusive Tribal Power to Tax Mineral Lessees of Indian Lands*, 124 U. PA. L. REV. 491, 515-20 (1975).

103.   The number of states lacking Public Law 280 jurisdiction may well increase if legislation is passed permitting tribes to effect retrocessions. See S. 1328, 94th Cong., 1st Sess. (1975).

104.   Arizona has improperly asserted Public Law 280 jurisdiction over air and water pollution, but the assumption has never been challenged. ARIZ. REV. STAT. ANN. §§ 36-1801, 1865 (1974). For a critique of Arizona's effort see Goldberg, *supra* note 92, at 554-57. Utah's assumption is found in UTAH CODE ANN. §§ 63-36-9 -21 (Spec. Supp. 1975).

105.   Under the Act, the Navajos in Arizona, New Mexico, or Utah could accept the Act for their territory independently of the rest.

106.   *E.g.*, Draper v. United States, 164 U.S. 240 (1896).

107.   See note 31 *supra*.

108.   See Oliphant v. Schlie, Civil No. 511-73C2 (W.D. Wash., filed Apr. 5, 1974).

109.   See 1 NATIONAL AMERICAN INDIAN COURT JUDGES ASS'N, *The Impact of Public Law 280*

sions to limit the sale of liquor on the reservation[110] would fall within such appropriate federal and tribal regulation. Accordingly, there is no reason to assume that state efforts to control non-Indians in these respects ought to be exclusive, especially so long as one sovereign is not requiring parties to do what the other prohibits.[111] Indeed, as will be discussed below, it is not even reasonable that state jurisdiction in such areas ought to prevail when it conflicts or overlaps with exercise of tribal sovereignty. Thus a general rule rendering state jurisdiction preemptive with respect to non-Indians will be more and more difficult to justify.

The Supreme Court's decision in *Mazurie*[112] confirms this impression. There the State of Wyoming already had laws providing for licensing of the sale and distribution of liquor. Non-Indians who had complied with those laws were prosecuted under federal law for selling liquor on the reservation in violation of different tribal regulations respecting the same subject. Without referring to the cases supporting exclusive state jurisdiction over crimes by and against non-Indians, the Court announced that tribal jurisdiction over non-Indians persisted despite state legislation on the same subject, at least in the case of "matters that affect the internal and social relations of tribal life."[113] Thus, if tribal jurisdiction to tax non-Indians exists in the absence of state efforts to tax, that jurisdiction can probably survive the exercise of any concurrent state taxing power.

Whether such "double taxation"[114] would discourage location of development on Indian reservations is a separate problem. Certain activities, such as mineral extraction, are not mobile, although resources on Indian reservations compete with resources located elsewhere. However, the most lucrative tax sources—industrial works and employees—could be located either on or off reservations.

Upon the Administration of Justice on Indian Reservations, in JUSTICE AND THE AMERICAN INDIAN (1973).

110. *See* United States v. Mazurie, 419 U.S. 544 (1975).

111. Such situations rarely occur. The likelihood of their occurring is discussed in the debate over dividing the Ninth Circuit Court of Appeals into two circuits, each containing part of California. Problems would ensue if the two circuits in California imposed conflicting requirements. Comm'n on Revision of the Federal Court Appellate System, *The Geographical Boundaries of the Several Judicial Circuits: Recommendations for Change*, 62 F.R.D. 223, 238-39 (1974).

112. United States v. Mazurie, 419 U.S. 544.

113. *Id.* at 557.

114. This would not be the constitutionally forbidden form of double taxation which involves multiple actions by a single sovereign. Generally speaking, it is permissible for more than one sovereign to tax property or activities, if the property or activities fall within more than one jurisdiction. Apportionment is required, however, if, for example, property is used in two different states. *See, e.g., In re* McLean Trucking Co., 281 N.C. 375, 189 S.E.2d 194 (1972). None of this precedent concerns a hypothetical situation in which territory falls within two states' boundaries, the only situation that would approximate an Indian reservation.

3. Can Tribal Taxation Preempt State Taxation?

Tribal fears of multiple taxation would vanish if a tribal tax could render any state tax on the same activity or property illegal. Existing Supreme Court doctrine provides support for such an argument in the absence of congressionally authorized state taxation.[115] The Court has held that states have no jurisdiction over reservation activities or property where that jurisdiction would interfere with "the right of reservation Indians to make their own laws and be ruled by them"[116] or would "affect the internal and social relations of tribal life."[117] State regulation of non-Indians has not generally been regarded as an interference with tribal government or society.[118] Thus in *Norvell v. Sangre de Cristo Development Company*,[119] the District Court of New Mexico upheld the state's power to impose a leasehold and gross receipts tax on a non-Indian company leasing Indian lands for the creation of a recreation home subdivision adjacent to a large city. While recognizing that the taxes would adversely affect the commercial value of the Indian land, the court held that such taxes did not "do violence to the governmental powers of the pueblo."[120] The Indians might have argued that higher rentals were part of an overall development plan that would be undermined by state taxation.[121] But since the tribe had no plans to provide any services to the development and the burden for their provision would have fallen entirely on the state and local governments, it is understandable that the court failed to perceive any threat to the Pueblo's sovereignty from the imposition of state taxation.

A very different application of the doctrine enunciated in *Norvell* may, therefore, be expected when the tribe has an ongoing interest in non-Indian activity or property on the reservation: for example, when the tribe is already taxing the same matters, has a major financial interest in the venture,[122] is

---

115. For an example of such a tax, *see* note 102 *supra* and accompanying text.

116. Williams v. Lee, 358 U.S. 217, 220 (1959).

117. United States v. Mazurie, 419 U.S. at 557.

118. Cases involving state taxation of non-Indians include Confederated Salish & Kootenai Tribes v. Moe, 392 F. Supp. 1297 (D. Mont. 1975), *aff'd*, 96 S. Ct. 1634, 1645 (1976); Oklahoma Tax Comm'n v. Texas Co., 336 U.S. 342 (1949); Thomas v. Gay, 169 U.S. 264 (1898); Utah & Northern Ry. v. Fisher, 116 U.S. 28 (1885); Kahn v. Arizona State Tax Comm'n, 16 Ariz. App. 17, 490 P.2d 846 (1971).

119. 372 F. Supp. 348 (D.N.M. 1974), *rev'd on other grounds*, 519 F.2d 370 (10th Cir. 1975).

120. 372 F. Supp. at 358.

121. Such a showing might have brought the case closer to the cirumstances of White Mountain Apache Indian Tribe v. Shelley, 107 Ariz. 4, 480 P.2d 654 (1971), in which the Arizona Supreme Court extended tribal sovereign immunity from suit to a profit-making entity authorized under the tribal charter as a means of furthering the tribe's economic development plans. Absent that kind of showing, the Pueblo in *Norvell* appeared to be acting more as a landowner than as a sovereign whose powers were under attack.

122. The tribe might, for example, lease to a corporation incorporated under tribal law, with itself or some tribal enterprise as a minor but not insignificant shareholder. The tribal shares might be in exchange for a lower lease price or a contribution of minerals to the project under-

providing services and governmental support, or the venture is integrally connected with tribal economic development. Of course, it is not easy to predict how much tribal involvement is enough to preclude state jurisdiction. It may be that the mere existence of a tribal tax will suffice, on the theory that an infringement of tribal sovereignty always exists where state and tribe attempt to derive revenue from the same source. But where the purpose of a state taxing scheme is seen as the regulation of various activities, the provision of a higher level of public services, or the redistribution of income, tribes will probably have to be doing more than simply collecting tax revenues in order to preempt state jurisdiction.

An example of a situation that would present a compelling case for tribal preemption of state taxing power is a proposed "new town" for the Navajo Reservation to house Navajo and other employees of contemplated coal gasification plants in the eastern reservation. The plans as presented in a consultant's report[123] suggest joint participation by the Navajo Nation and gasification companies in creating a non-profit development corporation to lease the land for the town, prepare the physical and social plan, obtain long-term financing for construction, promote retail and service uses in the new town, and so on. When the property has been developed and transferred to individuals for residential, business, and industrial use, a local governmental body accountable to the Navajo Tribal Council would set policy and provide public services other than education. The ultimate goals would be enhancement of reservation life through creation of a uniquely Navajo urban environment and the increase in tribal capacity to benefit economically from extraction of its precious resources.[124] Given the connection between revenue raising and tribal plans for management of non-Indians' activities on the reservation, a court might be inclined to prohibit state intervention in tribal fiscal plans as an infringement on tribal sovereignty. What makes the case particularly appealing is the tribal provision of most public services.

Doctrinally, the preemptive impact of tribal taxes would seem to depend on what the tribe does in addition to taxing. Practically, it may also depend on how long the tribe waits to institute a taxing scheme. Since state taxes on non-Indians are probably permissible in the absence of a tribal taxing scheme, it may be more difficult for courts to disrupt state expectations or to invali-

---

taken on leased land. A state tax on the corporation itself (as opposed to a tax on dividends paid the non-Indian shareholders) then would be a direct and impermissible burden on the tribe, even if a fraction of the corporate tax was assessed corresponding to the fraction of non-Indian shareholders. *Cf.* Makah Indian Tribe v. Callam County, 73 Wash. 2d 677, 440 P.2d 442 (1968) (community property of Indian wife and non-Indian husband wholly exempt from state personal property tax).

123. DEVELOPMENT RESEARCH ASSOCIATES, HOUSING AND COMMUNITY SERVICES FOR COAL GASIFICATION COMPLEXES PROPOSED ON THE NAVAJO RESERVATION (1974).

124. *Id.* at 11-2, 11-3.

date a tax that has been permissible for years.[125] Accordingly, the tribe ought to resolve doubts about its taxing power in favor of attempting to invoke it, since delay in doing so may destroy its preemptive force. At the same time, it must avoid premature assumptions that cannot be accompanied by sufficient additional tribal involvement.

Finally, the prospects for tribal taxation preempting state taxation should be evaluated in light of the dynamic of tribal sovereignty suggested in this article. It is quite possible that even under the propitious circumstances of the "new town" discussed above, tribal taxing power will not be found preemptive, because the courts are reluctant to acknowledge Indian tribes as such powerful and independent governing entities. The permanence and self-sustaining nature of such a "new town" government would not be consonant with the prevailing assumptions about tribal government.

As reservation peoples and development blend in with surrounding non-Indian communities, the Navajo Tribe will be pressured either to take on characteristics and responsibilities of non-Indian governments, or to surrender powers to the states—if not by state taxation, then by termination.[126] While the former alternative may preserve tribal taxing power, it is uncertain that even the relatively wealthy and advanced Navajos are capable of assuming the responsibility; even if they are capable, they may do so at the expense of tribal exclusivity and cultural distinctiveness. To avoid such negative consequences, as well as costly litigation, it may be necessary for the tribe to seek a congressionally sanctioned compromise or to negotiate directly with the states for sharing of revenues and responsibilities.[127]

---

125. By analogy, because the Supreme Court has been unwilling to review lower court decisions ruling against challenges to state assumptions of jurisdiction under Public Law 280, courts have begun upholding state jurisdiction in order to avoid defeating expectations of those who have relied on it. Tonasket v. State, 84 Wash. 2d 164, 525 P.2d 744, 753 (1974).

Interestingly, for the case of the Navajos, Arizona and New Mexico are moving quickly to impose leasehold taxes as substitutes for a property tax. See Reno, supra note 2, at 362. New Mexico already imposes personal property, severance, and sales taxes on the Four Corners power plant complex, located on Indian land. These taxes have never been challenged in court. See Farmington (N.M.) Daily Times, supra note 2.

126. See Agua Caliente Band v. County of Riverside, 442 F.2d 1184 (1971) (upholding leasehold tax in a Public Law 280 state); see note 98 supra. T. TAYLOR, supra note 28, at 153 n.17 states that

[t]he non-Indian population might not support continued trust status for a wealthy Indian group over an extended period of time. However, various State governments are experimenting with a possessory interest tax which, if held legal by the courts, may erode the tax protection provided by trust and therefore take the pressure off eliminating trust status, as such, even for a wealthy Indian group.

127. Preliminary steps in the direction of negotiation are evident in AMERICAN INDIAN LAW CENTER, TAXATION AND SOVEREIGNTY (1975), written for the New Mexico Commission on Indian Affairs.

CONCLUSION

Tribal taxing power over non-Indians seems to have a firm basis in current judicial doctrine, as does state taxing power. Furthermore, there are few direct federal restraints on the exercise of this tribal power, and little likelihood that state taxation will preempt it. Indeed, under certain circumstances the tribes may preempt the state with their taxes. The legal framework is dynamic, however, and may change as tribes such as the Navajo depart from their original weak governmental form. Federal restraints may be increased through the mechanism of the Indian Civil Rights Act, especially in the direction of homogenizing tribal governments with state and local counterparts. Freedom from state taxation may be available only if the tribes take on functions traditionally performed by the state.

Significantly, both of these developments propel a strong tribe like the Navajo in the direction of becoming a state itself, a subordinate entity within a state, or a commonwealth such as Puerto Rico. To the extent that the courts perceive these consequences with fear or concern, the judicial tendency may be to deny tribal taxing power over non-Indians altogether. The result will depend largely on what tribes such as the Navajo do wth respect to conceiving and implementing their power to tax. The ultimate lesson, however, is that jurisdictional doctrine cannot be understood apart from the historical, political, and institutional framework within which it is applied. Jurisdictional rules may be framed in terms of sovereignty, but they evolve as prevailing assumptions about the functions of power change and as the consequences of the exercise of that power change as well.

TOWARD A MORE COHERENT POLICY FOR FUNDING INDIAN EDUCATION

DANIEL M. ROSENFELT*

In 1969 the Special Senate Subcommittee on Indian Education published the results of its extensive study, concluding that "our Nation's policies and programs for educating American Indians are a national tragedy."[1] The Nixon administration,[2] independent scholars,[3] and public interest groups[4] reached similar conclusions not only as to the deplorable state of Indian education, but also with respect to the most important new policy needed to bring improvement: increased Indian participation in and control of Indian education programs.[5]

In six short years, dramatic changes have taken place both in Washington and in Indian communities throughout the nation. The Indian Education Act of 1972 (IEA)[6] established broad new programs of federal financial assistance to Indian children enrolled in public schools and created a new bureau within the United States Office of Education to administer the Act.[7] In 1975 the Bureau of Indian Affairs drastically revised the regulations governing its Johnson-O'Malley program (JOM).[8] Earlier in that year Congress passed a wide-ranging Indian Self-Determination[9] and Education Assistance Act[10] which

---

* Associate Professor of Law, Gonzaga University School of Law; formerly Senior Staff Attorney, Center for Law and Education, Harvard University; Staff Attorney, California Indian Legal Services, Native American Rights Fund Division.

1. SPECIAL SUBCOMM. ON INDIAN EDUCATION, COMM. ON LABOR AND PUBLIC WELFARE, INDIAN EDUCATION: A NATIONAL TRAGEDY—A NATIONAL CHALLENGE, S. REP. NO. 501, 91st Cong., 1st Sess. XIV (1969).

2. MESSAGE FROM THE PRESIDENT OF THE UNITED STATES, RECOMMENDATIONS FOR INDIAN POLICY, H.R. Doc. No. 363, 91st Cong., 2d Sess. 6 (1970).

3. E.g., 5 R. HAVIGHURST, THE NATIONAL STUDY OF AMERICAN INDIAN EDUCATION: THE EDUCATION OF INDIAN CHILDREN AND YOUTH 27 (1970).

4. E.g., NAACP LEGAL DEFENSE AND EDUC. FUND, AN EVEN CHANCE 59-64 (1971) [hereinafter cited as AN EVEN CHANCE].

5. See generally Rosenfelt, Indian Schools and Community Control, 25 STAN. L. REV. 489 (1973).

6. 20 U.S.C. §§ 241aa, 887c, 1211a (Supp. III, 1974).

7. Id. § 441.

8. 40 Fed. Reg. 51303 (Nov. 4, 1975).

9. Pub. L. No. 93-638, 88 Stat. 2203 (Jan. 4, 1975). Title I of the Indian Self-Determination and Education Assistance Act establishes no new major programs, but it directs the Secretary of Interior, upon the request of any Indian tribe, to enter into a contract with tribally sponsored organizations to conduct or administer all or a portion of any Indian program now conducted by the Department of Interior. Id. § 102(a). A similar provision applies to the Indian Health Service programs administered by the Department of Health, Education and Welfare. Id. § 103(a). Since education is the largest program administered by the Department of Interior's Bureau of Indian Affairs, the effect of this Act is to pave the way for eventual Indian control of the existing federal school system.

10. Title II of P.L. 638 is known as the Indian Education Assistance Act and consists of two

modified programs administered by the Bureau of Indian Affairs and the United States Office of Education. Indian parents in communities throughout the nation now participate in education program formation to a greater degree than before,[11] and some Indian organizations operate and administer their own programs.[12]

These recent innovations, however, have emerged less as the product of carefully planned reform than as a result of partisan politics,[13] organizational[14] and personal[15] rivalries, and differing philosphies and priorities at every decision-making level from the presidency, through Congress and the federal agencies, to the Indian tribes[16] and communities.[17] The inevitable re-

---

parts. Part A amends the Johnson-O'Malley Act, 25 U.S.C. §§ 452-55 (1970), and is discussed in the text accompanying notes 149-61 *infra*. Part B authorizes a new program of school construction and is discussed in the text accompanying notes 64-66 *infra*.

11. *See, e.g.*, Testimony of Morris Thompson, Comm'r of Indian Affairs, in *Hearings on Dep't of the Interior and Related Agencies Appropriations for 1975 Before a Subcomm. of the House Comm. on Appropriations*, 93d Cong., 2d Sess., pt. 1, at 158 (1974) [hereinafter cited as *FY 1975 House Appropriations Hearings*].

12. *Cf.* Testimony of Morris Thompson, Comm'r of Indian Affairs, in *Hearings on Dep't of the Interior and Related Agencies Appropriations Fiscal Year 1975 Before the Senate Comm. on Appropriations*, 93d Cong., 2d Sess., pt. 3, at 1315-18 (1974).

13. The Nixon Administration, for example, consistently opposed the Indian Education Act of 1972 whose most prominent sponsor was Senator Edward M. Kennedy. *Cf.* D. RATHER & G. GATES, THE PALACE GUARD 197-202 (1975). In fairness, that administration opposed other education programs on philosophical grounds.

14. The two federal agencies concerned with Indian Education, the Bureau of Indian Affairs and the United States Office of Education, have failed to coordinate their activities and have given each other only minimal cooperation despite continuous urging by Indian people and concerned congressmen.

15. In the United States Senate, for example, the Interior and Insular Affairs Committee, which has jurisdiction over the Department of Interior, is chaired by Senator Henry Jackson. The Committee on Education and Labor with responsibility for the Office of Education has Senators Kennedy and Mondale among its senior members. In framing Indian education legislation, a great deal of energy was expended by each committee staff in trying to outmaneuver the competing committee.

16. Indian tribal governments have generally opposed the extension of federal benefits to urban Indians. Their concern has been that a large increase in the number of eligible "Indian beneficiaries" of a program will result not in increased appropriations, but in reduced sums going to the reservations. A secondary source of antagonism towards urban Indians derives from the notion that many persons now claiming benefits as "Indians" turned their backs on the reservations when the going was tough. Many of these urban dwellers are said to have tried to deny their Indian heritage. Further, urban Indians are viewed by some tribal leaders as too militant and disrespectful of custom and tradition.

17. Within the larger Indian tribes, it is common to find differences on major issues between the elected tribal government and local community representatives. To some extent this is a result of the different constituencies represented. In some tribes, there is a burgeoning women's movement apparent in the local communities which views with some distaste the male dominated tribal council. Most often, however, tribal council members concerned with economic development and natural resources place lower priority on educational matters than do local community representatives.

The tribal-local conflict may surface when the question of parent participation or veto power in an education program is sought to be lodged in some Indian group. For example, section 202 of the Indian Self-Determination and Education Assistance Act adds a new section 5 to the Johnson-O'Malley Act providing for the establishment of a locally elected parent committee to

sult is some duplication, some waste, and some inconsistency in federal programs for Indian education. A key factor in the formulation of a coherent approach to Indian education is the design of funding legislation. In addition to the direct impact of funding on the delivery of educational services, disputes concerning discrimination and jurisdiction often are exacerbated by confusion over funding.

In recognition of this condition, Congress required the Secretary of the Interior to submit a comprehensive analysis of the interrelationship between five major federal programs designed to assist Indian children in public schools.[18] The Secretary's study, completed in October 1975,[19] should stimulate extended discussions among persons concerned with Indian education. In addition, the congressionally created American Indian Policy Review Commission will, as part of its final report, address itself to the problems of Indian education policy.[20] This article is one attempt to examine selected Indian educational policy issues from the perspective of funding and to offer suggestions for making federal aid programs more effective.

About 80 per cent of the 350,000 American Indian school children attend public schools.[21] At least half of these children attend schools funded in large measure by local property taxes. However, the remaining half attend schools in "reservation" districts containing blocks of Indian land held in trust by the United States and exempt from real property taxation.[22] Accordingly, in reservation districts the federal government provides Impact Aid funds in lieu of local property taxes and special assistance for school construction.

"Supplemental" or "categorical" programs supply additional sums for the special educational needs of selected groups of students. Funded at almost two billion dollars,[23] the largest of these national programs, Title I of the Elemen-

---

approve or disapprove the proposed JOM program. 88 Stat. 2213 (Jan. 4, 1975). At the same time, section 102(a) directs the Secretary of Interior to enter into a contract to administer the JOM program upon request of the tribe. 88 Stat. 2206 (Jan. 4, 1975). Approval for such a tribal request is not required from the locally elected parent committee. Already, for instance, the Portland area office has received a request to contract from the Colville Confederated Tribes followed by expressions of opposition from local JOM parent committees.

18. Indian Self-Determination and Education Assistance Act, § 203, 88 Stat. 2214 (Jan. 4, 1975).

19. The report, entitled "Study of Title II of P.L. 93-938," was actually prepared by contract with the National Indian Education Association.

20. Pub. L. No. 93-580, 88 Stat. 1910 (Jan. 2, 1975).

21. Statistics on Indians and Indian education are notoriously inaccurate, partially because there is no commonly accepted definition of the term "Indian." The general figures used in this article are extrapolations from inconsistent data published by the Bureau of Indian Affairs and the United States Office of Education.

22. See, e.g., Squire v. Capoeman, 351 U.S. 1, 9 (1956) (recognizing the tax-exempt status of tribal and restricted Indian lands). See generally Israel & Smithson, Indian Taxation, Tribal Sovereignty and Economic Development, 49 N. Dak. L. Rev. 267 (1973).

23. House Comm. on Educ. and Labor, Elementary and Secondary Education Amendments of 1974, H. R. Rep. No. 805, 93d Cong., 2d Sess. 14 (1974).

tary and Secondary Education Act of 1965,[24] is limited to persons who are "educationally deprived," and thus includes both reservation and non-reservation Indian children among the participants. Exclusive benefits are provided Indian children by the Indian Education Act of 1972 (IEA)[25] and the Johnson-O'Malley Act of 1934 (JOM).[26] The IEA, funded at forty-two million dollars in fiscal year 1975,[27] provides for entitlement grants to public school districts enrolling Indian children for supplemental programs, certain discretionary grants, and adult education funds. The main thrust of the broadscale Johnson-O'Malley program in recent years has been to provide supplemental programs to meet the special educational needs of Indian children in public schools.[28] In fiscal year 1975 JOM was funded at twenty-eight million dollars.[29] All of the federal programs are available to reservation school districts but only Title I and the IEA serve non-reservation Indians.

In evaluating each of these programs it is necessary to pose several important questions: (1) how do these programs operate in practice; (2) to what extent do they result in duplication of benefits or inefficiency in administration; and (3) what legislative or administrative changes, if any, would render them more effective.

I

BASIC SUPPORT

Districts enrolling Indian children, like most of the nation's school districts, are experiencing difficulty in generating sufficient funds for the operation and maintenance of the basic school program. Some contributing factors such as inflation and increased taxpayer militance are nationwide phenomena. In addition, most of the Indian districts are in rural portions of states that have fewer resources to expend on education than the national average.[30] Finally, federal agencies have begun to enforce more rigorously regulations

---

24. 20 U.S.C. § 241 (1970). The Title I program was extended by Congress for an additional five years by the Education Amendments of 1974, Pub. L. No. 93-380, 88 Stat. 484 (Aug. 21, 1974).

25. 20 U.S.C. §§ 24laa, 887c, 1211a (Supp. III, 1974).

26. 25 U.S.C. §§ 452-55 (1970).

27. *Hearings on Dep't of the Interior and Related Agencies Appropriations for 1976 Before a Subcomm. of the House Comm. on Appropriations*, 94th Cong., 1st Sess., pt. 3, at 327 (1975) [hereinafter cited as *FY 1976 House Appropriations Hearings*].

28. *See* Testimony of Morris Thompson, Comm'r of Indian Affairs, in *FY 1976 House Appropriations Hearings* 61. In fiscal 1975, 75 per cent of JOM monies were spent for supplemental programs. *Id.*

29. *FY 1976 House Appropriations Hearings* 56.

30. In 1973 the following states with significant Indian populations spent less than the nationwide median of $810 for the education of each pupil: Arizona ($771), Idaho ($629), Maine ($739), Nevada ($799), New Mexico ($732), North Carolina ($668), North Dakota ($719), Oklahoma ($660), and South Dakota ($760). U.S. OFFICE OF EDUCATION, THE INDIAN EDUCATION ACT OF 1972: REPORT OF PROGRESS FOR THE FIRST YEAR OF THE PROGRAM Table 2 (1974).

which prohibit the use of federal supplemental funds for basic support.[31] This federal action so acutely affects predominantly Indian districts that the problem has been brought to the attention of Congress.[32]

Legally, the states, rather than the federal government, have the duty to provide education services for Indian children. The Supreme Court has ruled emphatically that the opportunity for public education, "where the state has undertaken to provide it, is a right which must be made available to *all* on equal terms."[33] Indian children, as citizens of the state in which they reside, are entitled to a free public education to the same extent as other citizens.[34] It has long been held by both state[35] and federal[36] courts that the provision of Indian schools by the Bureau of Indian Affairs does not justify the exclusion of Indian children from public schools. Nor do the Indian treaties impose on the federal government a generalized responsibility for the education of Indian children.[37]

Many persons from states with large Indian populations, incorrectly believing that the federal government is responsible for the education of Indians,[38]

---

31. Widespread misuse of federal funds in Indian school districts was documented in AN EVEN CHANCE 2-4. Subsequently, a federal court *held* that Title I and Johnson-O'Malley funds could not be used for basic support. Natonabah v. Board of Educ., 355 F. Supp. 716 (D.N.M. 1973). These events, accompanied by heightened community awareness, received attention from the United States Office of Education and the Bureau of Indian Affairs. In the case of BIA, the JOM regulations were revised and tightened. *See* discussion in text accompanying notes 107-57 *infra*.

32. Indian Self-Determination and Education Assistance Act, § 203(2)(A), 88 Stat. 2214 (Jan. 4, 1975).

33. Brown v. Board of Educ., 347 U.S. 483, 493 (1954) (emphasis added); Rosenfelt, *supra* note 5, at 502-06; *cf.* Letter from John Kyl, Assistant Secretary of the Interior to Henry M. Jackson, Chairman, Committee on Interior and Insular Affairs, Aug. 3, 1973, in *Hearings on S. 1017 Before the Subcomm. on Indian Affairs of the Senate Comm. on Interior and Insular Affairs*, 93d Cong., 1st Sess. 85-86 (1973). Assistant Secretary Kyl's letter appears to make the following points: (1) Legal responsibility for the education of Indian children rests with the states; (2) the acutal responsibility is exercised by both entities (state and federal) "in certain complicated ways"; (3) because it is "difficult" to educate Indian children, the federal government has a "moral" responsibility to help the states.

34. Some Indians did not become citizens until the Citizenship Act of 1924, ch. 233, 43 Stat. 253 (codified in 8 U.S.C. § 1401(a)(2) (1970)). Others had become citizens through treaty or the General Allotment Act of 1887. Responsibility for the education of non-citizen Indians rested with the federal government. The shift in responsibility from the federal government to the states is discussed in Rosenfelt, *supra* note 5, at 492-506. The lingering questions concerning responsibility for Indian education are traceable in part to this historical background.

35. Grant v. Michaels, 94 Mont. 452, 23 P.2d 266 (1933); Piper v. Big Pine School Dist., 193 Cal. 664, 226 P. 926 (1924); Crawford v. District School Bd., 68 Ore. 388, 137 P.217 (1913).

36. United States v. Dewey County, 14 F.2d 784 (8th Cir. 1926), *aff'd sub nom.* Dewey County v. United States, 26 F.2d 434 (8th Cir. 1928), *cert. denied*, 278 U.S. 649 (1928).

37. *See* Rosenfelt, *supra* note 5, at 492-93, 503. The provision of education may, however, be required as part of the broad federal trust responsibility to the Indians. *See* Chambers, *Judicial Enforcement of the Federal Trust Responsibility to Indians*, 27 STAN. L. REV. 1213, 1243-46 (1975).

38. *E.g.*, Senator Paul Fannin is perhaps the most influential person who espouses this view. In *Hearings on S. 1017*, *supra* note 33, at 160-61, he stated that, "It is my opinion that the Federal Government has full responsibility for financing the education of those Indian children whose parents reside on reservation land." Senator Fannin's position, set forth more fully in SENATE COMM. ON INTERIOR AND INSULAR AFFAIRS, INDIAN SELF-DETERMINATION AND EDUCATION AS-

resent the expenditure of local funds for the education of Indians and often defeat school bond levies which would benefit Indian students.[39] Furthermore, both state and federal education officials, responsive to the popular confusion of this issue, countenance disparities in educational programs provided to Indians by state and local government which exceed most of the overt discrimination formerly practiced against blacks in the deep South.[40] It is important, therefore, to indicate how federal assistance more than compensates for the burden placed on local districts and how the structure of federal programs bears on the overall problem of basic support.

A.   Public Law 81-874[41]

Indian children generate P.L. 874 money for public school districts because their parents live and work on property held in trust by the federal

---

SISTANCE ACT, S. REP. No. 762, 93d Cong., 2d Sess. 30 (1974), is to the effect that where the tax-exempt status of Indian lands makes it impossible for a *local* school district to generate enough monies to operate an adequate educational program, the federal government is obliged to supply necessary funds.

39.   *See, e.g.*, Testimony of Myron Jones in Indian Education Act of 1971, in *Hearings on H.R. 8937 & S. 2482 Before the General Subcomm. on Education of the House Comm. on Education and Labor*, 92d Cong., 2d Sess. 163-64 (1972).

40.   The most striking evidence of the toleration of blatant disparities related to race occurs in the failure to provide adequate school facilities to house Indian students. In the State of Alaska, for example, 135 predominantly Native villages lacked *any* secondary school facilities as of October 5, 1972, while all but ten predominantly white settlements had such facilities. A portion of the litigation initiated by Alaska Natives to rectify this disparity is reported in Hootch v. Alaska State Operated School System, 536 P.2d 793 (Alas. 1975). In the Gallup-McKinley school district in New Mexico, a federal district court concluded that the local school district had allocated school construction monies in a manner which denied "a fair share (indeed, any real share at all) to those schools with overwhelmingly Indian enrollments." Natonabah v. Board of Educ., 355 F. Supp. at 723. The southern portion of Utah's San Juan school district includes the Navajo Indian Reservation where more than 50 per cent of the district's pupils reside. The district's two secondary schools are located many miles to the north in the towns of Monticello and Blanding. Most Indian children who wish to attend secondary school must be bused distances over one hundred miles each day. After Navajo parents brought suit, the district agreed to construct additional schools on the reservation. Sinajini v. Board of Educ., Civil No. 74-346 (D. Utah, consent decree Aug. 15, 1975), in 2 INDIAN L. REP. no.12, at 9 (1975).

In each of these three instances, Indian parents were forced to retain attorneys in attempting to rectify practices which were clearly discriminatory. Not until federal, state, and local education officials were confronted with the facts in litigation were meaningful efforts toward corrective actions undertaken.

Nor are the disparities in the examples given above limited to building facilities. In Alaska during FY 1972, the state legislature appropriated 37 per cent less state money for the educational program in the district with the largest Native enrollment than the state-wide average. In the Gallup-McKinley district, the federal court found disparities in the allocation of equipment, instruction expenditures, operational expenditures, and misuse and misallocation of JOM and Title I funds, all to the detriment of Indian students. In the San Juan school district in Utah, an out of court settlement of the litigation required the district to institute the kind and type of bilingual program now mandated by civil rights statutes. *See, e.g.*, 20 U.S.C.A. § 1703(c) (Supp. 1976).

41.   Act of Sept. 30, 1950, Pub. L. No. 81-874, 64 Stat. 1100, *as amended*, 20 U.S.C. §§ 236-41-1 (1970). This law, the Federally Impacted Areas Act, together with the School Facilities Construction Act, 20 U.S.C. §§ 631-47 (1970), are commonly referred to as "Impact Aid" laws. *See generally* U.S. DEP'T OF HEALTH, EDUCATION AND WELFARE, ADMINISTRATION OF PUBLIC

government. Although the original impetus for the Impact Aid program resulted from the defense activities of the federal government, the federal trust and tax-exempt status of Indian lands warranted inclusion of Indians in the program.[42] While Indians attract a mere five per cent of the annual P.L. 874 appropriation of $600 million,[43] the $31,137,000 allocated to school districts encompassing Indian reservations constitutes the most important single source of revenue for many of those districts. These monies are unrestricted, and they sometimes amount to as much as 40 to 60 per cent of the total operational budget of a reservation school district.[44] The Indian-controlled Rocky

---

LAWS 81-874 & 81-815, TWENTY-THIRD ANNUAL REPORT OF THE COMM'R OF EDUCATION (1975).

P.L. 874 is designed to assure that a federal connection, such as living on tax-exempt Indian land, will not cause any financial burden to local school districts. Payments are computed by multiplying the number of children whose parents live on Indian land by the amount which "comparable" school districts spend per pupil from local sources. Additional funds are provided where parents work but do not live on Indian land. In the event that the sum received by the district is not enough to provide a level of education equivalent to that maintained in comparable districts or if there are unusual geographical features in a district which affect the cost of education, the Commissioner of Education is authorized to make necessary adjustments.

42. Rosenfelt, *supra* note 5, at 497-99; *see* AN EVEN CHANCE 1-10.

43. *Cf. Hearings on Dep't of Labor and Health, Education and Welfare Appropriations for 1976, Before a Subcomm. of the House Comm. on Appropriations*, 94th Cong., 1st Sess., pt. 5, at 269 (1975); *FY 1976 House Appropriations Hearings* 342.

44. A representative sample of predominantly Indian districts as reported in TWENTY-THIRD ANNUAL REPORT OF THE COMM'R OF EDUCATION, *supra* note 41, Table 1, at 28 shows the following:

State & District	Net Payment Estimated 1972-73*	Current Expenditures†	Per cent**
Arizona	14,527,743	299,846,649	4.8
Window Rock	904,852	2,527,421	36
Chinle C.S.D. No. 24	1,205,710	2,886,103	42
Peach Springs S.D. No. 8	46,036	97,305	47
Kayenta E.S.D. No. 27	305,142	1,037,343	34
Minnesota	3,505,450	427,133,123	0.8
Red Lake I.S.D. No. 38	449,143	1,087,039	41
Montana	6,019,439	93,529,336	6.4
Browning E.S.D.	655,856	1,461,806	45
Elem S.D. No. 87	172,573	379,212	46
New Mexico	14,667,549	182,185,419	8
Gallup-McKinley	2,995,331	11,500,000	26
I.S.D. No. 22	1,602,780	5,100,000	31
Cuba	251,120	786,100	32
North Dakota	4,784,078	57,636,379	8
New Town	100,461	172,734	58
South Dakota	5,732,911	62,356,889	9
Shannon I.S.D. No. 1	709,324	1,198,000	59
Todd County I.S.D.	667,760	1,313,300	51

* Includes revenue from three sections of P.L. 874, §§ 2, 3, 4, *as amended*, 20 U.S.C. §§ 237-39 (1970).

† Total operational expenditures

** Calculated by author

Boys School Board of Montana did not exaggerate when it explained to a congressional committee:[45]

> P.L. 874 funds are the life blood of Reservation schools. To date, P.L. 874 has been a remarkably stable source of funding. Funding has been stable because impact aid, going to school districts in 375 Congressional Districts, has a powerful constituency and strong political appeal. The funding of the Reservation schools is relatively secure because—and probably only because—each Congressman and Senator, in voting the interests of his own constituents, at the same time, perhaps unwittingly, votes the interests of the Reservations.

There is good reason to continue funding P.L. 874 for children living on Indian reservations. Although reservation Indians pay no real property taxes, their status as citizens entitles them to educational services. Without P.L. 874 the education of Indian children would place a financial burden on local school districts. Because the location of Indian reservations within one state rather than another may be viewed as fortuitous, it seems appropriate that taxpayers from all the states should contribute to the expenses of educating reservation Indians. In this sense Indian reservations are analogous to other federal installations.

Although P.L. 874 does not directly compensate state government for their contributions to Indian education and although Indians living on trust land pay no state income tax on earnings from Indian land, it does *not* follow that the states suffer a financial burden requiring additional federal relief as a consequence of Indian education. Indian people, tribal governments, and reservation economic enterprises generate considerable taxable wealth to the states. Mining, tourism, manufacturing, governmental services, conventions and the like all result in substantial taxable income to state government. This Indian contribution to the state's economy is rarely acknowledged when state officials complain about the indisputably high cost of rural (Indian) education. If all factors were considered, no state government could demonstrate a net loss of tax revenue due to the unique status of Indian reservation land.[46]

---

45. Education Amendments of 1971, *Hearings on S. 659 Before the Subcomm. on Education of the Senate Comm. on Labor and Public Welfare*, 92d Cong., 1st Sess., pt. 4, at 1784 (1971).

46. Two recent judicial opinions contain data which are instructive. In Prince v. Board of Educ. ____ N.M. ____, 543 P.2d 1176 (1975), non-Indian taxpayers unsuccessfully challenged the right of Indians residing on tax-exempt land to vote in school board and school bond elections, and to have proceeds from school bonds used to construct schools on the reservation. The Supreme Court of New Mexico found that almost 97 per cent of the taxable wealth of the district was located on the Navajo reservations on land leased from the tribe by corporations. Although the land itself is not taxable, the corporate buildings and property are assessed as taxable personal property. In Confederated Salish & Kootenai Tribes v. Moe, 392 F. Supp. 1297 (D. Mont. 1975), *aff'd*, 96 S. Ct. 1634, 1645 (1976), a three-judge federal court held the imposition of a state cigarette tax on reservation smoke shops invalid. In response to the argument that Indians who receive the benefits of state citizenship must accept the tax burdens as well, the court examined data on the economic contributions made to the state and counties by the tribes and the federal government. It found that "(a) the amount contributed by the Federal Government is substantial; (b) the funds expended by both the Federal Government and Tribes contribute to the economic

B. Equitable Distribution of Funds

Disparities exist within, as well as between, schools and school districts
.ducating Indian children. Within districts with racially identifiable schools,
.ısparities will often be found in the services provided and expenditures allotted. Sometimes a hint of these disparities can be gleaned from the Title I
comparability report,[47] but more often a rather thorough audit is required to
ferret out the necessary data. The most conspicuous disparity, however, cannot be hidden: the quality of school facilities serving Indian children will almost invariably compare unfavorably with facilities serving non-Indians. Even
when the predominantly Indian schools are new, they tend to be overcrowded and lack adequate supporting facilities such as cafeterias, gym-
nasiums, restrooms, and vocational education shops.[48]

The time has come to confront directly this clear discrimination against
Indian children. For many years, the federal government has expended ever-
increasing sums of money to assist the education of Indians and in so doing it
has unwittingly subsidized racial discrimination.[49] The easiest way to eliminate
this discrimination is to direct the United States Office of Education's Office
of Civil Rights to conduct a compliance review of each district and each state

---

well being of the Reservation, and (c) non-Indians benefit from at least part of the expenditures."
392 F. Supp. at 1314-15. The court was not, however, able to determine if the state or local governments suffered any net tax loss.

47. In order to receive Title I funds, the local education agency must submit a report which
includes data prescribed by 45 C.F.R. § 116.26 (1975) which demonstrates that state and local
funds allocated to Title I schools are comparable to funds allocated to non-Title I schools. The
purpose of this requirement is to assure that Title I funds can be used to meet the special
educational needs of educationally deprived children and are not used to "supplant" (take the
place of) state and local funds.

48. See note 40 supra. Natonabah v. Board of Educ., 355 F. Supp. 716 involved a school district consisting of thirteen schools which were predominantly Indian and twelve schools predominantly non-Indian. The evidence showed that 24.9 per cent of the Indian students attended
classes in portable or makeshift classrooms compared to 11.7 per cent of non-Indians attending
school under similar circumstances. There was an 18 per cent disparity in the value of the buildings which Indians attended compared to those attended by non-Indians. These disparities
were held to constitute racial discrimination.

The discussion here focuses on disparities in the allocation of resources. Other types of racial
discrimination beyond the scope of this article but regularly found in Indian public school districts include: failure to provide a bilingual/bicultural curriculum, see Lau v. Nichols, 414 U.S. 563
(1974); misclassification of Indians as educationally mentally retarded, see, Kirp, Schools as Sorters:
The Constitutional and Policy Implications of Student Classification, 121 U. PA. L. REV. 705 (1973); and
uneven application of suspension and expulsion sanctions, see Hawkins v. Coleman, 376 F. Supp.
1330 (N.D. Tex. 1974); Yudof, Suspension and Expulsion of Black Students from the Public Schools:
Academic Captial Punishment and the Constitution, 39 LAW & CONTEMP. PROB. no. 2, at 374 (1975).

49. Where the state and/or the local school district fails to provide Indians with sufficient
educational services or facilities to meet minimum standards, federal aid programs such as
Johnson-O'Malley and Public Law 81-815 have been used to make up some of the difference.
These federal subsidies reward those districts which provide least assistance to Indians. In practice, little effort is made to separate those states and districts which are unable to provide necessary educational services from those which are unwilling to do so. In each of the many instances
where the amount of state or local resources provided for Indians is less than that provided to
others, racial discrimination exists. Cf. Natonabah v. Board of Educ., 355 F. Supp. 716.

enrolling Indian students which receives P.L. 874 funds on their account. Where violations are found the district or state should be required to prepare a plan designed to eliminate the discrimination within a time frame acceptable to both the Office of Education and the Indian tribe whose members are affected. In the event agreement cannot be reached, P.L. 874 funds should be withheld and the Department of Justice should be instructed to institute suit against the state and district in question to compel the reallocation of state monies to compensate for the withheld federal monies.

C.   Interdistrict Disparities

Interdistrict funding disparities are no less critical. Districts enrolling reservation Indian children have long been faced with a chronic inadequacy of monies to support basic school programs.[50] All too often the Indian children have been blamed for an inequity caused by state systems of school finance which make revenue a function of the taxable wealth of the local school district. More than a dozen states have overhauled school finance laws based on property taxes in order to achieve greater equity between school districts.[51] The President's Commission on School Finance recommended a federal incentive grant program to induce the states to assume responsibility for the full funding of equitable state education programs.[52] The cost of eliminating the disparities, estimated by the Commission at four to five billion dollars, may explain why thus far no action has been taken.

Although Indian education may not be a sufficiently broad issue to warrant the imposition of new finance schemes in all states, there is a more limited approach which may well be feasible for districts educating reservation Indian children. These districts receive P.L. 874 monies. Until the 1974-1975 school year, states which provide "equalization"[53] monies to local districts were not permitted to consider federal impact aid monies in calculating entitlements of the districts for equalization funds.[54] In 1974, however, in order to

---

50. Testimony of Herbert Jacobson, Planning Officer, Office for Indian Education, in FY 1976 House Appropriations Hearings 307-08; cf. Additional Views of Senator Paul Fannin, in S. REP. No. 762, supra note 38, at 30. A thorough study comparing the amount of monies available for basic support to public school districts educating Indians with statewide or national averages has not been published.

51. See 2 EDUCATION COMM'N OF THE STATES, MAJOR CHANGES IN SCHOOL FINANCE: STATEHOUSE SCORECARD (Res. Brief No. 2, 1974).

52. PRESIDENT'S COMM'N ON SCHOOL FINANCE, SCHOOLS, PEOPLE, & MONEY, THE NEED FOR EDUCATIONAL REFORM, FINAL REPORT 36-37 (1972).

53. Equalization monies are those provided by a state to local school districts in order to make each district equally able to support some level of education expenditure predetermined by the state. The amount of equalization monies allocated to local districts is inversely proportional to the taxable wealth of the district. Almost all states provide some form of equalization assistance.

54. 20 U.S.C. § 240d (1970); Carlsbad Union School Dist. v. Rafferty, 300 F. Supp. 434 (S.D. Cal. 1969); Hergenreter v. Hayden, 295 F. Supp. 251 (D. Kan. 1968); Douglas Independent School Dist. No. 3 v. Jorgenson, 293 F. Supp. 849 (D.S.D. 1968); Shepheard v. Godwin, 280 F.

encourage the states to distribute more equalization funds, Congress amended P.L. 874 to permit funds under that Act to be taken into account in computing entitlements for state equalization funds.[55]

Congress should further amend the statutes to provide that in districts where more than ten per cent of the enrollment consists of Indian children living on tax-exempt land, P.L. 874 payments may be considered for state equalization purposes only if funds available for basic support from state and local sources equal one hundred dollars or more per pupil above the state average.[56] Such a standard would *not* require states to fund Indian districts at one hundred dollars above the state average; rather, it would prohibit states from considering P.L. 874 monies for state equalization purposes unless the requisite standard was met. It bears some emphasis that until the 1976 fiscal year, states could not consider P.L. 874 revenue at all in their allocation of equalization funds. The effect of this proposal would be modest, but it would increase the flow of basic support funds to those districts most in need.[57]

In order to assure sufficient operating funds for public schools on or near Indian reservations, federal policy should, therefore, be based on three elements: (1) P.L. 874 monies should continue to be appropriated so that the tax-exempt status of Indian land does not constitute a financial burden to local school districts; (2) racial discrimination against Indian students by public school districts should be identified, acknowledged, and rooted out; and (3) the federal government should exercise the leverage afforded by P.L. 874 to require states to allocate a fair share of education monies to local school districts which educate Indian children. In this manner schools and school districts educating Indian children can receive a more equitable allocation of funds for general operating expenses without increased federal expenditures. Federal monies can then be concentrated in those areas where the states and local school districts must have federal financial assistance to provide an exemplary education for Indian children.

II
School Construction Programs

The most immediate financial problem in Indian education today is the shortage of school construction funds.[58] In 1953, when the government

---

Supp. 869 (E.D. Va. 1968); *see* Note, *The Dilemma of Federal Impact Area School Aid*, 55 Minn. L. Rev. 33 (1970).

55. 20 U.S.C. § 240(d)(2) (1970).

56. More precisely, separate computations should be required for elementary and secondary school expenditures.

57. By increasing support for both Indian and non-Indian students, a contribution might also be made to the reduction of friction between the races in districts encompassing Indian reservations.

58. Construction Assistance for Indians under P.L. 815 amounted to $5,528,000 in 1973, $11,200,000 in 1974, and $10,500,000 in 1975. *FY 1976 House Appropriations Hearings* 327. As of

sought to transfer Indian students to public schools as part of the policy of "termination" of the special status of Indians, Congress amended the School Facilities Construction Act (Public Law 81-815) to provide construction funds for public schools attended by Indians.[59] There are two ways school districts can qualify for P.L. 815 funds. If one-third of the student population or region served is Indian, districts can receive construction funds if they show that they are making an effort to raise money through tax programs or other financial means and have insufficient funds to provide facilities to their students. If these conditions are met, funds may be used for any school in the district, even those that serve no Indian students. Alternatively, districts with as little as a 10 per cent Indian enrollment or land base may qualify under the statute without a showing of additional financial effort or insufficiency of funds. Districts qualifying under this provision, however, may only apply funds received to those schools in the district actually serving Indian students or reservation areas.[60] Ironically, the first provision, section 14(a), is not objectionable even though it is possible that none of the federal monies will be spent on schools for Indians. To qualify for 14(a) funds a district must have allocated all its construction funds on an equitable basis and utilized available local resources including bonding authority to serve all students. If such a district still finds itself unable to raise sufficient construction monies because of the tax-exempt status of Indian land, then the federal government should provide additional assistance.

By contrast, districts receive section 14(b) funds without any showing of reasonable diligence to utilize other resources and without any showing of financial need. Section 14(b) seems to imply that a local district is free to discriminate against Indians by allocating state and local construction monies for facilities serving non-reservation students and awaiting federal funds for the construction of schools serving the reservations. All too often this is precisely what occurs.[61]

The principle of equal educational opportunity is too important to be further ignored. Congress should require all qualifying districts to demon-

---

June 20, 1974 the backlog of eligible but unfunded applications for construction under P.L. 815 for districts serving Indian children amounted to $39,607,624. *Hearings on Dep't of Labor and Health, Education and Welfare Appropriations for 1976, supra* note 43, at 262. This represents a small portion of the total construction need which in the most comprehensive survey was estimated to be in excess of $163,000,000. *See generally* F. McKinley, Public School Survey of Construction Aid Needs Related to the Education of Reservation Indian Children (1972). This study examined the construction needs of 162 school districts in 21 states which enroll reservation Indian children.

59. 20 U.S.C. § 631-47 (1970). By the Act of August 8, 1953, ch. 400, § 1, 67 Stat. 526, Congress expressly provided for assistance to districts whose ability to finance needed construction was impaired on account of the immunity from taxation of Indian lands. These provisions now appear at 20 U.S.C. § 644 (1970).

60. 20 U.S.C. §§ 644(a), 644(b) (1970). *See also* 45 C.F.R. § 114.16 (1975).

61. *See, e.g.,* Natonabah v. Board of Educ., 355 F. Supp. at 721-22.

strate that funds have been distributed equitably and that available local resources, including bonding authority, are inadequate for the needs of all students in the district because of the tax-exempt status of Indian land. In the case of the many districts guilty of past discrimination against Indians, federal grants should be converted to loans, with funds being repaid from state and local revenues. Furthermore, local districts that refuse to provide adequate facilities for the education of Indians should, if necessary, be compelled by the courts to make necessary expenditures.[62]

Beginning in 1970, Congress took action designed to provide increased federal construction funds for reservation Indian school districts. It amended P.L. 815 to place Indian schools in the highest priority category together with military bases and natural disasters.[63] The new Indian Education Assistance Act of 1975 provides an additional federal source for school construction monies.[64] Since 75 per cent of these funds must be allocated on the basis of priorities established under section 14 of P.L. 815, it is apparent that in this instance Congress deliberately intended to duplicate an existing federal program to provide a mechanism for increasing appropriations. The remaining 25 per cent of the funds under the new act may be spent to assist tribes in constructing facilities for schools they control, but this latter provision is limited to "previously private" schools.[65] The statute should be amended to allow a wider range of eligibility[66] and to enable the Bureau of Indian Affairs to make grants to public school districts that are effectively excluded by the rigid guidelines and priorities of P.L. 815.[67]

---

62. *See* Griffin v. County School Bd., 377 U.S. 218 (1964); Sinajini v. Board of Educ., in 2 INDIAN L. REP. no. 12, at 9 (1975).

63. 20 U.S.C. § 644(c) (1970).

64. Pub. L. No. 93-638, § 204(b), 88 Stat. 2215 (Jan. 4, 1975).

65. *Id.* § 208 provides in part: "The Secretary is authorized and directed to provide funds, pursuant to this Act . . . to any tribe or tribal organization which controls and manages any previously private school." *Id.* § 204(c) provides: "The Secretary may expend not more than 25 per centum of such funds . . . on any school eligible to receive funds under section 208 of this Act." The limitation to "previously private" schools appears to have been deliberately imposed by the House which eliminated broader language contained in the Senate-passed bill. *Compare* S. REP. No. 762, *supra* note 38, at 15 *with* H. REP. No. 1600, 93d Cong., 2d Sess. 18 (1974). The Department of Interior opposed provisions in the Senate bill which would have permitted the Secretary of Interior to have broad authority to assist public school districts serving Indian children on the ground that such authority would duplicate the program administered under Pub. L. No. 81-815, 64 Stat. 967 (1950). Letter from John Kyl to James A. Haley, May 17, 1974, in H. REP. No. 1600, *supra* at 36.

66. Former BIA schools now operated by tribal organizations are not eligible for funds under this regulation. *See* 40 Fed. Reg. 51283 (Nov. 4, 1975).

67. For example, there are several public school districts, notably in Alaska, which educate large numbers of Indians and have urgent construction needs but do not qualify under existing priorities. The priority system for approval of P.L. 815 projects is based on the percentage of children living on tax-exempt land in the district and the percentage of children who are unhoused (*i.e.*, without minimum school facilities) in the district. *See* 45 C.F.R. §§ 114.4, 114.5 (1970). The State of Alaska—with a large native population, high construction costs, and an almost total lack of secondary school facilities in predominantly native towns and villages—received

III
Supplemental Programs

The Indian Education Act, Title I, and Johnson-O'Malley are the three programs which fund projects designed to meet the special educational needs of Indian children. There is some overlap in the objectives of these programs, but at present funding levels it is by no means clear that the overlap results in duplication of benefits or waste. The purpose of this section is to examine each program as it operates today, to assess the extent of overlap and duplication, and to suggest corrective actions which Congress and federal agencies might take to increase the efficacy and equity of educational services to Indian children.

This discussion proceeds on two assumptions. The first—thoroughly documented elsewhere—is that Indian children do have special educational needs which require compensatory programs.[68] Indian boys and girls enter school on a par with children from other racial backgrounds, but with each advancing year Indian children as a group perform less well and by the time they reach secondary school age they drop out at an alarming rate. The purpose of the supplemental programs discussed below is to provide relevant programs geared to the needs of Indian children in the hope that this failure in the education system can be stemmed. The second assumption is that there is a great need for restraint by Congress in revising Indian education programs. Major needs in Indian education have been identified, legislation has been enacted, and projects throughout the nation are only now beginning to address the priorities set by Indian people. There is no indication that any of the existing supplemental programs for public schools is basically defective.

It is important to note that Indian people, for the first time, actively participated in the formulation and modification of the proposals which ultimately became the Indian Education Act of 1972, the 1974 Johnson-O'Malley regulations, and the Indian Self-Determination and Education Assistance Act. The programs which are in place today result from the incalculable investment of time and energy over a period of five years by Indian people in most of the major tribes and communities, and to a surprising extent these programs represent a consensus of collective Indian opinion. Radical changes by

---

a mere .9 per cent of the total section 14 funds appropriated from 1954 through 1973. It is not clear whether this is because (1) the state failed to apply, (2) Alaska Natives are not considered "federally connected," or (3) the availability of schools in the cities of Anchorage and Fairbanks and BIA facilities in Oklahoma and Oregon did not qualify native children as "unhoused." It is probable that construction needs for Alaska Natives exceed 50 per cent of the total needs of all other states at this time. *See* Hootch v. Alaska State Operated Schools, 536 P.2d 793 (Alas. 1975), discussed in note 40 *supra*. In contrast with Alaska, the State of Arizona received 34 per cent of all section 14 funds, Twenty-third Annual Report of the Comm'r of Education, *supra* note 41, at 130.

68. *See, e.g.*, authorities cited in notes 1 through 4 *supra*.

Congress in the public school supplemental programs—at this early date
—might be viewed as a breach of faith by Indian people. This discussion,
then, is an attempt to identify aspects of existing programs which, if modified,
might facilitate the more direct achievement of present goals and priorities.

A. The Indian Education Act of 1972

The Indian Education Act of 1972[69] (IEA) is the most comprehensive federal program designed to meet the special educational needs of Indian children. With present funding levels at forty-two million dollars, IEA programs
reach approximately 1,500 school districts in thirty-eight states and serve
more than 250,000 Indian children enrolled in public schools.[70] The statute
defines "Indian" broadly, and contains no restrictions with respect to blood
quantum or place of residence.[71] The IEA is, therefore, the only Indian education program which serves the special educational needs of urban as well as
reservation Indian children.

The Act establishes three broad programs. Part A[72] provides categorical
grants to local education agencies based on the number of Indian children
enrolled and the average per pupil expenditure in the state. Funds must be
spent to meet the special educational needs of Indian children for programs
such as those providing bicultural and/or bilingual classes, culturally relevant
curriculum materials, guidance, and counseling.[73]

---

69. 20 U.S.C. §§ 241aa, 887c, 1211a (Supp. III, 1974).

70. *FY 1976 House Appropriations Hearings* 283-290.

71. 20 U.S.C. § 1221h (Supp. III, 1974) provides:

For the purposes of this title, the term "Indian" means any individual who (1) is a
member of a tribe, band, or other organized group of Indians, including those tribes,
bands, or groups terminated since 1940 and those recognized now or in the future by
the State in which they reside, or who is a descendant, in the first or second degree, of
any such member, or (2) is considered by the Secretary of the Interior to be an Indian
for any purpose, or (3) Is an Eskimo or Aleut or other Alaska Native, or (4) is determined to be an Indian under regluations promulgated by the Commissioner, after consultation with the National Advisory Council on Indian Education, which regulations
shall further define the term "Indian."

Present regulations merely repeat the statutory definition. 45 C.F.R. § 187.2 (1975).

72. 20 U.S.C. § 241aa (Supp. III, 1974).

73. Although Part A is an "entitlement program," applications are not approved unless the
local education agency complies with the statutory requirements for parent, community, and Indian involvement. Applicants for Part A funds must demonstrate that the proposed project has
been developed:

(i) in open consultation with parents of Indian children, teachers, and, where applicable, secondary school students, including public hearings at which such persons have had
a full opportunity to understand the program for which assistance is being sought and to
offer recommendations thereon, and

(ii) with the *participation and approval* of a committee composed of, and selected by,
parents of children participating in the program for which assistance is sought, teachers,
and where applicable, secondary school students of which at least half the members shall
be such parents.

20 U.S.C. § 241dd(b)(B) (Supp. III, 1974) (emphasis added). In addition, the applications must
set forth specific plans for operation, administration, and evaluation. 20 U.S.C. § 241dd(a) (Supp.

It has been argued that federal funds should not be disbursed on a formula basis regardless of need but should be used to develop programs which can then be adopted and funded by local education agencies.[74] However, it is important to remember that Part A serves Indian children who are not reached by any other Indian oriented education program. There are approximately 162 school districts in this country, located on or near Indian reservations, which educate a significant number of Indian students.[75] But approximately half of the 3,200 additional public school districts which are eligible[76] to receive Part A funds have taken advantage of this program to identify the Indian children in their communities and to develop special programs for them.[77] If Part A entitlements were not funded, it seems highly unlikely that districts with a small percentage of Indian students would perceive the special needs of that minority as warranting attention when competing requests from larger groups cannot be met. The entitlement aspect of Part A must, therefore, be continued if assistance is to reach non-reservation Indian students.

There are, however, two problems associated with Part A funding. First, the statute makes the level of funding dependent upon each state's average per pupil expenditure.[78] The purpose of the provision is to take account of the variation in cost of delivery of educational services. Unfortunately, the variation among the states, ranging from a low in Arkansas of $578 to a high in New York of $1549,[79] appears to reflect factors, such as the relative affluence of the states, which are unrelated to the actual cost of educational services. The Part A allocation formula should, therefore, be adjusted to pro-

---

III, 1974). In fiscal years 1973 and 1974, almost 25 per cent of the applications submitted were denied by the Office of Indian Education for failure to comply with these requirements. U.S. OFFICE OF EDUCATION, *supra* note 30, at 13; *FY 1976 House Appropriations Hearings* 287. It appears, therefore, that there is a serious effort by the administrators of this program to prevent the misuse of funds so widespread in earlier education programs. *See, e.g.,* AN EVEN CHANCE.

74. U.S. Commissioner of Education, John Ottina, advocated this position in the 1975 Appropriations Hearings but failed to persuade the Congressional Appropriations Committee. *See FY 1975 House Appropriations Hearings* 402-04.

75. *Cf.* synopsis of National Indian Training Research Center survey of construction needs of public school districts enrolling reservation Indian children in *id.* at 179.

76. Local education agencies are eligible for grants under Part A if they have ten Indian students or the Indian enrollment constitutes 50 per cent of the total enrollment. Every local education agency, however, which serves a single Indian child located in the states of Alaska, California, and Oklahoma or located on or near an Indian reservation is eligible. 20 U.S.C. § 241bb(a)(2)(B) (Supp. III, 1974). In practice, districts with negligible Indian enrollments do not apply for funds.

77. Statement of U.S. Office of Education, Office of Indian Education, in *FY 1976 House Appropriations Hearings* 287.

78. *See* 20 U.S.C. § 241bb (Supp. III, 1974). By contrast, Title I allocations used the state average per pupil expenditures as a basis for computation only when the state average is higher than the national average. 20 U.S.C. § 241c (1970). Congress further refined the method of computation in 1974 by providing that the state average per pupil expenditure would be used so long as it was not less than 80 per cent nor more than 120 per cent of the national average. Education Amendments of 1974, § 103(a)(2), Pub. L. No. 93-380, 88 Stat. 484 (Aug. 21, 1974).

79. U.S. OFFICE OF EDUCATION, *supra* note 30 Table 2, at 9.

mote increased equity between the states. In 1974, Congress modified the Title I formula for precisely this reason, and now the state average per pupil expenditure is utilized only if it is not less than 80 per cent nor more than 120 per cent of the national average.[80] In the case of Part A there is an additional consideration, not present in Title I: many of the eligible districts depend for a substantial part of their basic support on P.L. 874 which itself is distributed on the basis of per pupil expenditures of "comparable" districts within the state. The P.L. 874 formula works to the disadvantage of children from poor states and regions. The Part A allocation formula can be used to ameliorate the present disparities in resource allocation by substituting for the state average per pupil expenditure the national average figure.[81]

In addition to modifying the allocation formula, the present level of Part A funding must also be increased in order to operate meaningful education programs. In 1973, for example, the City of Cleveland, Ohio, received only $24,305 to develop and operate a program for its 349 Indian students.[82] In each of the last three years the number of eligible districts and the number of funded applications have risen at a faster rate than appropriations.[83] The combination of increased Part A appropriations and the reallocation of Title I funds, suggested below, would raise the IEA program to a size where it could have a meaningful impact.

Part B of the IEA[84] authorizes discretionary grants to improve educational opportunities for Indian children. The statutory language is broad enough to cover almost any proposal relating to Indian education, and funded projects thus far emphasize teacher training, "alternative" schools for dropouts, curriculum development, and early childhood guidance and counseling.[85] Unlike Part A, eligible applicants under Part B include Indian tribes and organizations, BIA schools, institutions of higher education, and state and local education agencies. Applications submitted by Indian organizations receive priority under Part B except for training projects, and in that instance, projects which involve the training of Indians receive priority.

Since Part B is the only program which enables the concentration of substantial funds on a limited number of projects, there is no apparent overlap or duplication with other programs. In order for Part B to discharge its

---

80. *See* note 95 *infra. See also* H.R. REP. No. 805, *supra* note 24, at 13-14.

81. For the state of Alaska, which has a large native enrollment and which presently spends almost twice as much per pupil as the national average, special provisions would be required. Within that state, costs in isolated Eskimo villages are dramatically higher than in cities such as Ketchikan or Sitka. New York is the only other state which would be substantially and adversely affected by the proposed new formula.

82. *FY 1975 House Appropriations Hearings* 423.

83. *FY 1976 House Appropriations Hearings* 287.

84. 20 U.S.C. § 887c (Supp. III, 1974).

85. *See* HEW News Release 3-12 (Aug. 12, 1974), listing Part B grant recipients and grant purposes.

unique function, however, the program administration must be systematically scrutinized to insure that (1) resources are sufficiently concentrated on the few most meritorious projects, (2) unproductive and unsuccessful projects are not refunded, and (3) each project provides an appropriately detailed evaluation of its effectiveness in achieving its purposes.[86]

Finally, Part C of the Indian Education Act authorizes grants to Indian tribes and organizations and to state and local agencies for programs of adult education.[87] The most striking feature of Part C is its low level of funding: three million dollars in fiscal years 1974 and 1975.[88] As recently as 1969, the Senate's Special Subcommittee on Indian Education reported that forty thousand Navajo Indians, nearly a third of the entire tribe, are functionally illiterate in English and the average educational level of all Indians under federal supervision is five school years.[89] Although adult education is widely acknowledged to be of prime importance, it has received comparatively little attention and inadequate funding.[90] It would seem appropriate for an organization such as the National Advisory Council on Indian Education to conduct a review and an analysis to determine whether adult education is receiving the appropriate priority among Indian education programs.

B. Title I

A cornerstone of President Lyndon Johnson's War on Poverty, Title I of the Elementary and Secondary Education Act of 1965,[91] was the first and most significant federal aid program to recognize that economically and edu-

---

86. There is no reason to believe that Part B has been administered other than in the most exemplary manner. The concerns enumerated here arise from observations of tendencies exhibited by administrators of other federal programs. *See, e.g.*, Testimony of Myron Jones, in *Hearings on H.R. 8937 & S. 2482, supra* note 39, at 167.

87. 20 U.S.C. § 1211a (Supp. III, 1974).

88. *FY 1976 House Appropriations Hearings* 296.

89. S. REP. No. 501, *supra* note 1, at XII.

90. *See, e.g.*, SPECIAL EDUCATION SUBCOMM., NATIONAL COUNCIL ON INDIAN OPPORTUNITY, THE FIRST REPORT TO THE PRESIDENT OF THE U.S., BETWEEN TWO MILESTONES 87-90 (1972). There are two other federal programs, both funded through the states, which provide some assistance to Indian adults. The Adult Education Act of 1966 is designed to serve under-educated adults, primarily those with less than an eighth grade education. 20 U.S.C. § 1201 (1970). The House Committee on Education and Labor recently reported evidence that for every dollar invested in these adult education programs, there has been a return to the government of more than eleven dollars in tax revenue resulting from increased earnings of students. H.R. REP. No. 805, *supra* note 24, at 66. Since the level of funding is based on population, states with large Indian populations such as Alaska, Arizona, Montana, New Mexico, North Dakota, and South Dakota each received less than $500,000 per year in fiscal 1974. *Id.* at 47-48. Nationally, the Office of Education estimates that approximately $1,000,000 under this act was spent on adult Indians. *FY 1976 House Appropriations Hearings* 347. The states receive larger grants through Part B of the Vocational Education Act, 20 U.S.C. § 1241 (1970). The Office of Education estimates that approximately four million dollars per year is spent to provide some vocational training to Indians of all ages. *FY 1976 House Appropriations Hearings* 346.

91. 20 U.S.C. §§ 236-44a (1970).

cationally deprived children may need compensatory educational programs in order to perform well in school.[92] Although its overall success is unclear, Title I has performed one important function well: it provides substantial federal financial assistance to the public school districts with the greatest need.[93] The overwhelming majority of this nation's public school districts received Title I funds amounting to a total of some $1.8 billion in fiscal year 1975.[94] Funds are dispersed by the United States Office of Education to the states which, in turn, approve, fund, and monitor projects proposed by local school districts for educationally disadvantaged children. The amount of Title I funds allocated to each local district is based on the number of its students from low income families and the state's average per pupil expenditure.[95]

Within a given school district, however, the "concentration" and "targeting" requirements of Title I operate to exclude many low income or disadvantaged children from Title I benefits. In order to insure that most of the children who receive Title I services are in fact poor, local school officials must select as target schools for Title I services those which have concentrations of children from low income families equal to or greater than the percentage of such children in the district as a whole.[96] Children in non-target schools, in most instances, may not participate in the Title I program.[97] In 1970, only two-thirds of public school Indians attended Title I target schools.[98] Within each target school, moreover, the Title I programs must be concentrated "on those children who are most in need of special assistance."[99] School administrators, therefore, are required to exclude some children in order to concentrate on the few most in need.

The kind and type of Title I program offered may not reflect the educational judgment of a school administrator so much as it reflects the wishes of the Parent Advisory Council (PAC).[100] While the PAC is advisory in the sense

92. *Cf.* 20 U.S.C. § 241a (1970); S. Rep. No. 146, 89th Cong., 1st Sess. 1 (1965).

93. H. Rep. No. 805, *supra* note 24, at 4-7.

94. *Id.* at 4.

95. 20 U.S.C. § 241c (1970). In general terms, each school district's entitlement is computed by multiplying the total number of children from low income families (as defined by the Act) by 40 per cent of the state average per pupil expenditure provided the state average is not less than 80 per cent nor more than 120 per cent of the national average.

96. 45 C.F.R. § 116.17d (1975); U.S. Dep't of Health, Education, and Welfare, Office of Education, ESEA Title I (Program Guide No. 44, Guideline 1.1, 1969).

97. *Cf.* 45 C.F.R. § 116.17a (1975), which authorizes an exception for educationally deprived children residing outside the project area "if such a participation will not dilute the effectiveness of the project with respect to children residing in the project area." In practice, the exception is rarely invoked.

98. Bureau of Social Science Research, Inc., Federal Funding of Indian Education: A Bureaucratic Enigma 53 (1973).

99. U.S. Dep't of Health, Education and Welfare, Office of Education, ESEA Title I (Program Guide No. 44, Guideline 4.2,4.7, 1969); *cf.* 45 C.F.R. § 116.17(c) (1975). Within the target schools, program participants are identified in terms of their educational needs and are not limited to children from poor families.

100. The Education Amendments of 1974, § 131, Pub. L. No. 93-380, 88 Stat. 479 (Aug. 21,

that it has no power to veto a decision of the school district, in some communities it plays a key role in setting priorities for the Title I program. In districts where Indians constitute the majority of Title I participants, the Title I PAC is likely to be composed largely of Indian parents and the priorities of the Title I program may correspond to the special educational needs of Indian students.[101] Conversely, in many rural and almost all urban school districts, Indians constitute a small portion of the Title I students, and often the programs are designed to meet the needs of Chicano, black, or other children.

For all of these reasons, large numbers of eligible Indian children do not participate in Title I programs.[102] When the Office of Education lists the many "Indian" education programs which it funds, it now acknowledges in a footnote that in the case of Title I "the dollars drawn to that district as a result of the presence of Indians do not necessarily benefit those Indians."[103] Title I, then, is an example of inconsistency in federal programs with respect to Indian education. Although reservation Indian students generally benefit from Title I to a greater extent than urban students, there are many instances in which reservation children participate to a limited extent.

The advent of Part A of the IEA, a program similar to Title I and also administered by the United States Office of Education, may provide a mechanism through which the diversion of Title I benefits from Indian students could be curtailed. Quite simply, a portion of the Title I "Indian allocation" to each public school district could be transferred to the IEA Part A program and administered as part of it.[104] A 50 per cent reallocation of each district's Title I "Indian" monies to Part A would produce a more equitable

---

1974), now require each local education agency to establish a district wide Title I parent advisory council (PAC) *and* a PAC for each Title I target school. Title I parents must constitute a majority of PAC members, and the members must be chosen by parents in each school attendance area. The function of the PAC is to advise the local education agency in the planning, implementation, and evaluation of the Title I program. This amendment to Title I strengthens the present regulation which in 1972 made PACs mandatory. 45 C.F.R. § 116.17(c) (1975).

In the early years of Title I, the parent advisory council was optional and in most districts existed, if at all, in name only. *See* AN EVEN CHANCE 51-54. More recently, many school administrators have begun to accept the notion that parents should play a role in education policy, and parents themselves have become more determined to be heard.

101. In Indian communities perhaps more than others, the legitimacy and necessity of parent advisory councils is accepted. Under both Part A of the IEA and JOM, Indian parent committees analogous to the Title I PAC are more than advisory; they now have full veto power over the proposed program. 45 C.F.R. § 186.17(f) (1975); § 273.16(a)(2), 40 Fed. Reg. 51306 (1975).

102. Smith and Walker, in their study of federal funding of Indian education, cite unpublished U.S. Office of Education data showing that nationwide only 34 per cent of Indian students participate in Title I, *supra* note 9. *See also* AN EVEN CHANCE 39-40.

103. *E.g., FY 1976 House Appropriations Hearings* 330. Impact Aid is another program in this same category.

104. While there is presently no specifically designated Title I "Indian allocation" per se, local education agencies determine the number of low income students and the racial composition of Title I eligible children. Using these data, the "Indian allocation" of Title I monies can be readily determined.

distribution of benefits with only a change in bookkeeping entries, and both programs would continue substantially as before. In this manner a greater percentage of funds received by the district because of the presence of Indian students would actually be spent for their benefit. The designation of Title I "target schools"[105] should also be modified to reflect the reallocation of funds.[106] This would allow some districts serving non-Indian disadvantaged children to offer Title I programs at previously ineligible schools.

In a handful of predominantly (more than 90 per cent) Indian school districts, the proposed reallocation of Title I monies to Part A would effectively eliminate the Title I program. But because Indian children in each of these districts constitute more than 90 per cent of the students, the purpose of the Title I program (to provide compensatory education to educationally deprived children) and of the Part A program (to meet the special educational needs of Indian students) should in actuality be almost identical.

Neither the Indian Education Act nor its regulations contain language expressly excluding non-Indians from the Part A program. It would seem possible, therefore, to achieve a consolidation of the programs without creating administrative, ethical, educational, or legal nightmares. A "90 per cent Rule" could be adopted specifically for the 90 per cent Indian districts so that non-Indians would not be excluded from the program on the basis of race. Thus, if a remedial reading program were offered, students would participate based on educational need. Of course, if the district ran a bilingual program in Yupik Eskimo, a non-Indian child might be excluded because he lacked the special educational need that the program was designed to meet. The 90 per cent rule should result in increased administrative efficiency without diluting the "Indian" nature of the Part A program.

C. The Johnson-O'Malley Act

In 1934 Congress passed the Johnson-O'Malley Act (JOM),[107] which contains broad authority for the Secretary of Interior to contract with states and

---

105. Title I target schools are those which have concentrations of children from low income families equal to or greater than the percentage of such children in the district as a whole. If, for example, 40 per cent of the children in the district are from low income families, then each school with a student body consisting of more than 39 per cent low income children will be a "target school."

106. This is necessary in order to prevent undue concentration of benefits to Indian students at Title I target schools at the expense of non-Indian students. To take an extreme and oversimplified example, assume a district consisting of two schools of equal size, A and B. School A has a 100 per cent Indian enrollment and 90 per cent low income children. School B has no Indian enrollment, but 60 per cent of its students are from low income families. School A is a Title I target school, School B is not. Under the proposal, School A will receive 66 per cent of all Title I funds through the reallocation to Part A, and if the "targeting" criteria are unmodified it will also receive the remainder of the funds directly through Title I. If, however, only 50 per cent of the Indian students were counted for targeting purposes, then School B would be designated as a target school and would receive Title I funds. But if School B had only 10 per cent low income children, then quite properly School A would continue to receive all the Title I funds.

107. 25 U.S.C. §§ 452-54 (1970).

other entities for the education of Indian children. In order to encourage states to accept responsibility for Indian education, the Bureau of Indian Affairs, in the 1950s, promulgated a regulation which committed JOM funds "to accommodate unmet financial needs of school districts related to the presence of large blocks of non-taxable Indian-owned property in the district."[108] Although the funds supplied under JOM and P.L. 874 were initially regarded as mutually exclusive,[109] Congress amended the Impact Aid law in 1958 so that school districts could qualify for funds under both programs.[110] The BIA then amended its regulations to provide that "[w]hen school districts educating Indian children are eligible for Federal aid under Public Law 874 . . . supplemental aid under [JOM] . . . will be limited to meeting educational problems under extraordinary or exceptional circumstances."[111] It seems apparent, then, that Congress intended P.L. 874 funds to provide general revenue "in lieu of taxes," while JOM monies were to be devoted to special programs for Indians. Only in extraordinary or exceptional circumstances might JOM monies be used for basic support.[112]

The BIA, however, failed to promulgate any standards or criteria by which the existence of extraordinary or exceptional circumstances could be ascertained. In practice the BIA often failed to administer the JOM program in any meaningful way, relying instead on the respective state departments of education.[113] The states, however, frequently took the position that they were entitled to use JOM monies for any purpose not prohibited by the BIA. As a result, the following practices became common:

------

108. This provision was in force until 1974. The position that the BIA acted contrary to the intent of Congress in so limiting the JOM program is set forth in the Senate Subcommittee's Report on Indian Education, S. REP. No. 501, *supra* note 1, at 38-39. *See also* Sclar, *Participation by Off-Reservation Indians in Programs of the Bureau of Indian Affairs and the Indian Health Service*, 33 MONT. L. REV. 191, 210-11 (1972).

109. Act of Sept. 30, 1950, Pub. L. No. 81-874, § 2, 64 Stat. 1101; *see* Rosenfelt, *supra* note 5.

110. Act of Aug. 12, 1958, Pub. L. No. 85-620, § 201(b), 72 Stat. 559; *see* discussion in Rosenfelt, *supra* note 5.

111. 25 C.F.R. § 33.4(c), *as amended*, 40 Fed. Reg. 51282 (Nov. 4, 1975).

112. Section 201(b) of P.L. 620 amended P.L. 874 to permit school districts to receive both JOM and P.L. 874 monies. The House Committee report sets out the intention of this amendment:

> H.R. 11378 makes a significant change in the treatment of school districts educating Indian children, by enabling them to accept payments under Public Law 874 without forfeiting the right to obtain payments under the Johnson-O'Malley Act for special services and for meeting educational problems under extraordinary or exceptional circumstances . . . H.R. 11378, in amending Public Law 874 in this connection, prevents any duplicate payments for the same services.

H.R. REP. No. 1532, 85th Cong., 2d Sess. 3 (1958). Section 33.4(c) was promulgated contemporaneously and should have been read against this background. *See* Natonabah v. Board of Educ., 355 F. Supp. at 725-26.

113. Prior to 1970, all JOM contracts were with state departments of education rather than with Indian tribes or organizations. The contracts consisted of approximately four pages with few provisions, other than verbatim repetitions of applicable federal regulations, limiting the use of funds.

1) School districts used JOM monies as general aid, *i.e.*, supplementing general operating funds and therefore ignoring special Indian education needs;

2) Indians had little voice in how JOM monies were spent;

3) JOM fund recipients were not held accountable and no evaluations were made to determine whether the money was being properly used;

4) the BIA failed to use its contracting authority with incorporated tribes and non-profit groups;

5) funds were allocated only to districts with large tax-exempt Indian reservations and allotments, while off-reservation districts with Indian children having special educational needs were ignored; and

6) the allocation of funds between and within states varied widely and followed no coherent or decipherable pattern.[114]

Indeed, until 1972, the BIA did not even require that JOM funds be kept separate from the general operating revenues of local school districts.

In the late 1960s and early 1970s pressure mounted from Indian interest groups[115] and congressional committees for the reform of the JOM regulations. In response, the BIA tightened the accounting procedures of the program and increased parent participation,[116] but the promulgation of new regulations was stalled by old guard resistance within the BIA, pressures from some state departments of education, and divisions within the Indian community.[117] Impetus for change was added when the District Court for

---

114. *See* Rosenfelt, *New Regulations for Federal Indian Funds,* 10 INEQUALITY IN ED. 22 (1971); Testimony of Myron Jones and Sefferino Tenorio, in *Hearings on H.R. 8937 & S. 2482, supra* note 39, at 137-75.

115. These organizations included the Native American Rights Fund, the Harvard Center for Law and Education, Americans for Indian Opportunity, the NAACP Legal Defense and Education Fund, Inc., and the Institute for the Development of Indian Law. The single most effective group, however, was the National Indian Leadership Training (new Indian Education Training) of Albuquerque, New Mexico, headed by Myron Jones.

116. Although the BIA has long been regarded by many as one of the most inept bureaucracies in the government, *e.g.,* OUR BROTHER'S KEEPER (E. Cahn ed. 1969), it nevertheless retains widespread support among Indian tribal people. To a considerable extent this support reflects approval of the BIA practices of consulting with and listening to representatives of Indian communities. When both S. REP. NO. 501, *supra* note 1, at 44 and AN EVEN CHANCE 51 criticized the BIA for failing to insure parent participation in the JOM program, the BIA set out to address that shortcoming and did so in relatively short order. *See* testimony of Morris Thompson, in *Hearings on the Dep't of the Interior and Related Agencies Appropriations Fiscal Year 1975, supra* note 12, at 1312.

117. Fierce bureaucratic infighting occurred within the BIA between two factions. One group embraced most of the findings of the Senate Subcommittee and *An Even Chance* and eagerly sought reform of the JOM program. A second group appeared to act defensively concerning past BIA practices and seemed responsive to the positions of states and local school districts which argued forcefully for a continuation of JOM as basic support. Between 1972 and 1974, the BIA was almost institutionally incapable of reaching a decision on an issue such as this because (1) the position of Commissioner was vacant, (2) the administrative measures to implement Indian preference personnel policies within the bureau had caused divisiveness between white and Indian BIA employees which overshadowed most other issues, and (3) the national Indian community had not yet reached a position of unanimity regarding JOM. The principal issue which divided

New Mexico ruled that the use of JOM monies for basic support by the Gallup-McKinley school district was illegal,[118] and a consent decree in New Mexico bound the BIA to issue new regulations for use in that state.[119] Finally, in 1974, a group of thirty-eight Indian organizations presented an alternative set of regulations[120] to those that had been developed by the Department of Interior.[121] For perhaps the first time ever, a large number of diverse Indian organizations, working together to produce what they called the "Red Regs," virtually dictated to the Bureau of Indian Affairs a solution to a complex issue. Key members of Congress joined in support[122] and the regulations, promulgated on August 21, 1974, contain the substance of the Red Regs.[123]

D. New Regulations

The 1974 JOM regulations made several basic changes in the program. Eligibility for benefits is no longer tied to residence on tax-exempt federal land;[124] funds may be spent only for Indians and need not be spent in

---

the Indian community was whether off-reservation or urban Indians would be eligible for JOM funds.

118. Natonabah v. Board of Educ., 355 F. Supp. 716, 725-29 (D.N.M. 1973).

119. Denetclarence v. Board of Educ. of Independent School Dist. No. 22, Civil No. 8872 (D.N.M., filed Feb. 14, 1974), incorporating Agreement of Parties dated Dec. 14, 1973).

120. Participants included major national organizations such as the National Congress of American Indians, the National Indian Education Association, and the Coalition of Indian Controlled School Boards, as well as such important regional organizations as the Alaska Federation of Natives, the All-Indian Pueblo Council of New Mexico, and the Small Tribes of Western Washington. Attorneys from the Native American Rights Fund coordinated the effort.

121. 25 C.F.R. § 33 (1975), *as amended*, 40 Fed. Reg. 51282 (Nov. 4, 1975). The proposed regulations omitted many of the reforms upon which there had already developed a broad consensus, including parent participation.

122. *E.g.*, Senator James Abourezk, Chairman of the Committee on Interior and Insular Affairs' Subcommittee on Indian Affairs, Congressman Lloyd Meeds, Chairman of the House Committee on Interior and Insular Affairs' Subcommittee on Indian Affairs, and Congressman Sidney Yates, Chairman of the House Appropriations Subcommittee on the Department of Interior and Insular Affairs. In a dramatic meeting held on August 16, 1974 in a large conference room in the Senate Office Building, BIA officials, Indians, and congressmen addressed the issue of why the BIA had not adopted the "Red Regs." Assembled were representatives from most of the thirty-eight organizations that had drafted the "Red Regs" as well as a large number of Indians from other organizations and tribes, some of the most influential members of Congress concerned with Indian Affairs, the Associate Solicitor for Indian Affairs of the Department of Interior, the Commissioner of Indian Affairs, and a group of BIA education officials. Spokespersons for the Indian groups included LaDonna Harris of Americans for Indian Opportunity, Kirke Kickingbird of the Institute for the Development of Indian Law, and Charles Wilkinson of the Native American Rights Fund. The show of unity had its desired effect.

123. 25 C.F.R. § 33 (1975). These regulations have been modified and renumbered because of the enactment of the Indian Self-Determination and Education Assistance Act which amends the Johnson-O'Malley Act as discussed in text accompanying notes 158-70 *infra*. With few exceptions, the substance of the 1974 Regulations is not significantly affected. *See* 40 Fed. Reg. 51303 (Nov. 4, 1975).

124. Sections 273.11, 273.12, 273.13, 40 Fed. Reg. 51303 (Nov. 4, 1975) contain no reference to tax-exempt land.

schools;[125] a system for equitable distribution of funds between and within states is established;[126] the use of JOM for basic support is sharply circumscribed though not prohibited;[127] parent participation provisions give Indian parents full veto power over proposed programs;[128] and a system of fiscal accountability is established.[129] Despite these major improvements, some issues still require further attention.

E.   Eligibility for Benefits

The new regulations obscure rather than resolve the sensitive issue of whether urban Indians may participate in JOM programs. Program beneficiaries are defined as: "Indian students . . . recognized by the Secretary as being eligible for Bureau services."[130] Although there may have been no intention to make substantial changes in the scope of JOM, the language chosen definitely includes many—though not all—urban Indians.

Despite many formal statements to the effect that the BIA has no responsibility for providing services to urban Indians,[131] some services are in fact provided to Indians who reside in urban areas. Urban Indians, for example, are eligible to receive BIA scholarships to colleges,[132] they may receive health services at Indian Health Services hospitals,[133] and if they are beneficial owners of trust property they receive BIA property management services.[134] These people, therefore, are indisputably "eligible for Bureau services."

While education programs are essential to meet the needs of urban Indians, the Bureau of Indian Affairs with its agencies located on the reservations is not particularly well equipped to administer those programs. With adequate funding, Part A of the IEA can meet the needs of urban Indians. Since urban Indians in the past have been excluded from JOM, moreover, no widespread community expectations would be defeated by limiting the pro-

---

125.   §§ 273.12, 273.37, 40 Fed. Reg. 51303 (Nov. 4, 1975). *But see* text accompanying notes 162-70 *infra*.

126.   § 273.13, 40 Fed. Reg. 51303 (Nov. 4, 1975). *But see* text accompanying notes 144-46 *infra*.

127.   §§ 273.33-.34, 40 Fed. Reg. 51303 (Nov. 4, 1975).

128.   *Id.* §§ 273.16-.17.

129.   *Id.* §§ 273.47, 273.48, 273.50.

130.   *Id.* § 273.12.

131.   *E.g.*, MESSAGE FROM THE PRESIDENT OF THE UNITED STATES, H.R. DOC. No. 363, *supra* note 2, at 9. ("The Bureau of Indian Affairs is organized to serve the 462,000 reservation Indians. The BIA's responsibility does not extend to Indians who have left the reservation, but this point is not always clearly understood.") Testimony of Morris Thompson, in *FY 1976 House Appropriations Hearings* 45.

132.   25 C.F.R. § 32.1 (1975) expressly authorized loans and grants to non-reservation Indians.

133.   Although these facilities are located on the reservations, services are provided to any Indian who presents himself at an I.H.S. clinic or hospital regardless of where he lives. Sclar, *supra* note 108, at 201.

134.   The services provided in connection with real property include maintenance of records, leasing, and probate. Trust funds are managed to increase their earnings. *See id.* at 199 and authorities cited therein.

gram. Accordingly, Congress should act to confine the JOM program to reservation areas.[135]

F. Basic Support

The new regulations which sharply circumscribe the use of JOM monies for basic support appear to acknowledge, at long last, that such payments effectively subsidize discrimination by the states against Indian school districts.[136] Districts now receiving JOM basic support payments will be phased out over a three year period.[137] Under these circumstances, one would expect the regulations to contain no continuing authorization for basic support payments, but that is not the case.[138] The cutting off of basic support funds to local districts will cause hardship until the states revise their programs of assistance to take up the slack. It remains to be seen whether the

---

135. An Act of Congress appears necessary to limit those eligible for JOM participation to certain geographic areas. See authorities cited in note 108 *supra*. Following the suggestion made by the Supreme Court of the United States in construing other legislation that the BIA may limit services based on "rationally made priorities," Morton v. Ruiz, 415 U.S. 199, 230 (1974), the BIA inserted a priority provision for contracts "which would serve Indian students on or near reservations." The BIA would be hard pressed to defend its present funding practices which award JOM monies to groups in urban areas such as Albuquerque, New Mexico and Rapid City, South Dakota but deny funds to groups in Seattle and Phoenix. The new regulations also embody an effort to define the term "reservation" to include non-reservation persons in Alaska and Oklahoma with the effect that off-reservation Indians in such places as Minnesota and Wisconsin are excluded. § 273.2(o), 40 Fed. Reg. 51303 (Nov. 4, 1975).

136. To receive basic support funds, a school district must establish that:
  (i) It cannot meet the applicable minimum State standards or requirements without such funds.
  (ii) It has made a reasonable tax effort with a mill levy at least equal to the State average in support of educational programs.
  (iii) It has fully utilized all other sources of financial aid, including all forms of State aid and Pub. L. 874 payments. The State aid contribution per pupil must be at least equal to the State average.
  (iv) There is at least 70 percent eligible Indian enrollment within the school district.
  (v) It shall clearly identify the educational needs of the students intended to benefit from the contract.
  (vi) It has made a good faith effort in computing State and local contributions without regard to contract funds pursuant to this part.
  (vii) It shall not budget or project a deficit by using contract funds pursuant to this Part.
§ 273.13(b)(1), 40 Fed. Reg. 51303 (Nov. 4, 1975). In addition, upon receipt of an application for operational support, either the Area Director or the Commissioner must make a "federal written determination and findings supporting the need for such funds." §§ 273.24(e), 273.27(c), 40 Fed. Reg. 51303 (Nov. 4, 1975).

137. § 273.31(a), 40 Fed. Reg. 51303 (Nov. 4, 1975).

138. It appears that tribally operated schools may qualify for JOM basic support funds provided only that the funds are used to meet "established State educational standards or Statewide requirements." §§ 273.33, 273.13(b)(2), 40 Fed. Reg. 51303 (Nov. 4, 1975). While BIA operational funding of tribal alternative schools is clearly desirable, it is not at all clear that these funds should be taken off the top of the JOM supplemental program. Further, this use of JOM for basic support was not discussed with Indian communities and organizations, and understandably the BIA's insertion of this provision has stimulated objections. *See* 40 Fed. Reg. 51286 (Nov. 4, 1975).

BIA is capable of enforcing this significant change in the JOM program.[139]

G. Equitable Apportionment of Funds

In the past the BIA claimed that funds were distributed to the different states on the basis of need.[140] In fact, the method of distribution was arbitrarily based in large measure on the previous year's allocation.[141] Thus, in 1973, Nebraska was allocated $944 for each eligible JOM pupil while South Dakota received $318, Washington received $179, and Idaho received $279.[142] Similarly, within individual states the allocation between school districts varied widely.[143]

The 1974 regulations require apportionment of JOM supplemental funds among states based on the number of eligible students. This figure is then adjusted by taking into account the actual cost of delivering educational services in the state, which, like Part A of the IEA, is determined by reference to the state average per pupil expenditure.[144] Although allocations based on the state average per pupil expenditures represent a vast improvement over past practices, the method of allocation can and should be further refined in order to ameliorate the disparities in educational resources among the states.

Within each state the JOM regulations require that funds be distributed among the contractors so that each will receive approximately the same amount for each eligible Indian student.[145] Again, the regulations have opted

---

139. The BIA has "waived" some of the new requirements such as the 70 per cent Indian enrollment in a district so that otherwise ineligible districts may continue to receive JOM basic support funds. Public schools on the Navajo Reservation face severe financial problems. *See* NAVAJO DIVISION OF EDUCATION, SURVIVAL OF THE PUBLIC SCHOOLS (1975). However, this is due to Arizona's discriminatory finance scheme which yields unreasonably low levels of state aid to these schools. Arizona may threaten to close some of these reservation schools if the BIA does not exercise its discretion to release additional basic support funds. Similar problems exist in South Dakota.

140. *See* former 25 C.F.R. § 33.4(b) (1975). It will be noted that the regulation refers to the need of the school district rather than the need of the Indian students.

141. *E.g.*, Independent School Dist. No. 22 in New Mexico has regularly received a generous allocation of JOM funds despite the fact that in two recent years it generated a cash surplus of operating funds in excess of one million dollars. This information was developed in the course of preparing the case of Denetclarence v. Independent School Dist. No. 22, Civil No. 8872 (D.N.M., filed Feb. 14, 1974). *See also* testimony of Buck Benham, Assistant Area Director of Education, Bureau of Indian Affairs; Sam Mackey, Education Specialist, Bureau of Indian Affairs; and James McLarry, Acting Director of Indian Education, New Mexico State Dep't of Education, in *Hearings on H.R. 8937 & S. 2482, supra* note 39, at 120-21.

142. These figures are derived from U.S. DEP'T OF INTERIOR, FISCAL YEAR 1973 STATISTICS CONCERNING INDIAN EDUCATION 39, Table 16 (1974) and BIA data showing Johnson-O'Malley funding by states in *Hearings on Dep't of the Interior and Related Agencies Appropriations Fiscal Year 1975, supra* note 12, at 1324-25.

143. *E.g.*, AN EVEN CHANCE 13.

144. § 273.31, 40 Fed. Reg. 51303 (Nov. 4, 1975). The regulation requires only that allowance be made for the actual cost of delivering services in each state, but in practice the BIA has used state average per pupil expenditures to make the adjustments.

145. §§ 273.31(b), 273.31(3), 40 Fed. Reg. 51303 (Nov. 4, 1975).

for equity and stability. One consequence is that the funds will not necessarily be allocated to those most in need, but since there is no satisfactory way to make a meaningful determination of educational need and since the commissioner retains discretion to make exceptions to per capita allocations where a community can demonstrate special needs, the regulation appears as satisfactory as can be expected. In addition, several of the programs administered by the Office of Education are discretionary, and relative need is presumably considered in these allocations.[146]

H. JOM Today

In hearings considering the 1975 appropriations request for JOM, Senator Alan Bible, Chairman of the Senate Appropriations Subcommittee, made the following statement: "Johnson-O'Malley has been a bugaboo for years around here. I do not know if anybody has been particularly satisfied. We get a lot of complaints on it."[147] Clearly Senator Bible's dissatisfaction with the JOM program was well founded. Many of the past problems have been sufficiently eliminated or ameliorated by the new regulations (which had not been promulgated when Senator Bible spoke) to warrant continuation of the program.

The strongest argument for the abolition of JOM is the possibility of duplication with IEA, Part A, which—like JOM—provides monies on a per capita basis for educational programs to meet the special educational needs of Indian children. While there is an undeniable overlap in permissible expenditures under the two programs, the relevant inquiry would seem to be whether or not the overlap results in the duplication of benefits to Indian children. Given the present low level of appropriations, the likelihood of duplication of benefits appears remote. In fiscal year 1975, for example, Congress appropriated only $23 million for Part A which resulted in an average distribution of only $85 per pupil,[148] and JOM yielded an average of $203 per pupil.[149] In most of the reservation school districts which now operate both programs, the level of basic support is far below the national average[150] so that there is a broad area to be covered by compensatory programs.

In the future, however, Part A funding should be substantially increased

---

146. In addition to IEA, Part B, the U.S. Office of Education administers discretionary programs for bilingual education, 20 U.S.C. § 880(b) (1970); dropout prevention (ESEA Title VIII); and school libraries (ESEA Title II).

147. *Hearings on Dep't of the Interior and Related Agencies Appropriations Fiscal Year 1975, supra* note 12, at 1319.

148. *FY 1976 House Appropriations Hearings* 287. This sum does not include a ten per cent set aside for Indian controlled schools located on or near reservations which are not local educational agencies. 20 U.S.C. § 241bb(b) (Supp. III, 1974).

149. This figure was derived by dividing the 1975 appropriation of $28,352,000 by 105,000 eligible Indian students. *FY 1976 House Appropriations Hearings* 26-27, 56. In 1975, 25 per cent of the JOM appropriation went for basic support.

150. *See, e.g.,* testimony of Herbert Jacobson, Planning Officer, Office for Indian Education, in *FY 1976 House Appropriations Hearings* 307-08.

in order to insure that off-reservation children will receive a fair share of relevant educational services. As Part A funding begins to approach its full authorization of approximately $387 million,[151] Congress could appropriately decrease its support of JOM. At present, however, the availability of monies from both JOM and Part A makes it possible for reservation Indian communities to establish priorities such as early childhood projects, curriculum development, and remedial reading and to allocate the available funds in an orderly manner.

Given the substantial improvements made by the 1974 regulations, there are several compelling reasons why the JOM supplemental program should be continued for reservation Indian children. First and foremost, Indian communities have in recent years been more actively involved in JOM than with any other education program. JOM parent committees exist on almost every federal reservation in the nation, and Indian parents have invested incalculable time and energy in attempting to devise sound programs for their communities. Should Congress terminate the JOM program, many Indian people would feel a deep sense of betrayal to their hopes and aspirations. Indeed, the active involvement of Indian parents in the education of their children contributes to the greater potential success of the entire program. The assistance given to facilitate their involvement should, therefore, be continued.

Secondly, the JOM program is far more flexible than any of the other federal education assistance programs—a situation uniquely desirable for the varied circumstances facing Indian reservation communities and educational institutions. JOM funds may be used in school or in the community, for parental costs related to education, for travel, or for summer programs. Moreover, JOM contractors may be an Indian corporation, a school district, or a state. In contrast, recipients of grants under Title I and IEA, Part A, must be local educational agencies (*i.e.* public school districts) and as a result the educational programs funded by those acts are likely to be tied to a traditional "school." Yet the geographical dispersion of rural reservation Indian children may make it more desirable to hold an educational program at some other location.

Thirdly, reservation school districts, taken as a whole, have fewer resources of all types—financial, cultural, educational—than do non-reservation school districts taken as a whole. Most reservation students live in comparatively isolated communities. The cost of a trip to the state capital or to a large art museum is likely to be greater for a reservation student than for an urban student. In short, the spectrum of needs which can be addressed by compensatory education are demonstrably greater for most reservation students than for most urban students. The perpetuation of the JOM program provides a useful vehicle to accommodate these needs.

---

151. *FY 1976 House Appropriations Hearings* 287.

I. Duplication of Administration

Where both JOM and the IEA, Part A programs operate in school districts, there is presently some duplication of administrative expenses which can be avoided. For example, both programs require committees of Indian parents to review, develop, and approve proposed projects. These parent committees can be combined, as was apparent to Congress when, in section 202 of the Indian Education Assistance Act, it provided, "in the discretion of the affected tribal governing body or bodies,"[152] for the utilization of one board for both purposes. In view of the differing requirements for composition of the parent committees under the two programs[153] and the possibility of different views concerning the best means to meet the educational needs of Indian students, ·it is conceivable that in some instances the two committees should not be combined. The tribal governing body is usually sufficiently informed to make the appropriate determination.[154]

Where the JOM contract administrator is an Indian corporation, expenses of administration will be incurred which might be saved if all contracts were required to be run through the state and public school district. As a policy matter, however, Congress has decided to encourage Indian administration of Indian programs even if it will result in some additional administrative expense. The experience gained by the Indian corporation in program management may itself be viewed as educational and the fact of Indian control may promote increased Indian participation in the funded programs. Finally, it will be noted that the JOM program administered by the BIA prevents the centralization of all federal education programs in the United States Office of Education. In the past, this separation has resulted in lack of coordination between the two agenices.[155] Part of the duplication can be reduced by coor-

---

152. Pub. L. No. 93-638, § 202(5)(b), 88 Stat. 2212 (Jan. 4, 1975).

153. *Compare* 20 U.S.C. § 241dd(b)(2)(B) (Supp. III, 1974) and 45 C.F.R. § 186.15-16 (1975) *with* Pub. L. No. 93-638, § 202, 88 Stat. 2212 (Jan. 4, 1975) and 25 C.F.R. § 33.3 (1975), now § 273.16, 40 Fed. Reg. 51303 (Nov. 4, 1975). The IEA parent committee may include teachers, students, and at least 50 per cent Indian parents who are selected by procedures arranged by the local school district, while the JOM committee consists of persons elected by Indian parents.

154. The importance of the parent participation and control provisions to Indian communities and the difficulty of legislating workable guidelines on a nationwide basis should not be underestimated. In many communities control of the JOM and Title IV budget may amount to considerable political and economic power. In some instances this power may be used to force local school districts to become more responsive to the Indian community, and in others it may be used to challenge the authority of the tribal council or to advance other interests. The Parent Advisory Councils of the 1970s should be viewed as having almost the same capacity for changing the status quo on Indian reservations as the OEO programs of the late 1960s.

The present JOM and Title IV regulations providing for separate committees but authorizing consolidation of the two in the discretion of the tribal council appear flexible enough to accommodate the diverse conditions found in Indian communities throughout the nation. A legislative requirement that there be only one PAC within a school or school district might appear more efficient, but may impose an unintended and undesirable alteration in the balance of power within Indian communities.

155. *Cf. FY 1976 House Appropriations Hearings* 310.

dination of the parent committees at the local level, and, as an ever increasing percentage of JOM monies are contracted directly with Indian corporations[156] and expended outside the public school system, the need for coordination at the federal level is reduced.[157]

J. New Amendments

The Indian Self-Determination and Education Assistance Act added three new sections to the Johnson-O'Malley Act.[158] Section four requires that prospective JOM contractors submit for advance approval a "plan of educational objectives."[159] Section five makes parent committees from the local community a statutory requirement[160] and section six authorizes the Secretary of Interior to reimburse local school districts for the cost of educating Indian children

---

156. At present tribal groups administer the entire JOM program in Wisconsin, South Dakota, North Dakota, Florida, Alaska, Utah, Nebraska, and in approximately half of New Mexico. BIA data in *FY 1976 House Appropriations Hearings* 63. This represents more than one third of the entire JOM appropriations.

157. A major breakthrough in inter-agency coordination could be achieved simply by redesigning the Title IV and JOM application forms so that they would indicate the programs and projects for which funding has been received or is being sought in the district.

158. 25 U.S.C. § 455 (1975).

159.
> The Secretary of the Interior shall not enter into any contract for the education of Indians unless the prospective contractor has submitted to, and has had approved by the Secretary of the Interior, an education plan, which plan, in the determination of the Secretary, contains educational objectives which adequately address the educational needs of the Indian students who are to be beneficiaries of the contract and assures that the contract is capable of meeting such objectives.

Id.

160.
> (a) Whenever a school district affected by a contract or contracts for the education of Indians pursuant to the Act has a local school board not composed of a majority of Indians, the parents of the Indian children enrolled in the school or schools affected by such contract or contracts shall elect a local committee from among their number.

Id. § 456. The section goes on to provide that the Secretary shall prescribe by regulation the duties and structure of the local committees. *See* § 273.16, 40 Fed. Reg. 51303 (Nov. 4, 1975). Section 456 also contains the provision authorizing the use of the Title IV board in place of a new JOM committee in the discretion of the tribal council. *See* text accompanying notes 152-54 *supra*.

The statutory language quoted above exempts school boards composed of a majority of Indians from the parent committee provisions. Since most school board members—both white and Indian—tend to be employed full time in endeavors other than education, it would seem that the views of Indian parents should be just as helpful to Indian school board members as to non-Indian school board members. An Indian controlled school board failed to detect and correct a pervasive pattern of racial discrimination in the Gallup-McKinley school district. *See* Natonabah v. Board of Educ., 355 F. Supp. at 716. And an Indian controlled school board in the Shiprock, New Mexico district failed to require the district to provide a bilingual education program adequate for the needs of Indian children in the district. *See* Denetclarence v. Independent Dist. No. 22, Civil No. 8872 (D.N.M., filed Feb. 14, 1974). This provision appears to be based on the dubious assumption that Indian school board members have substantially more time to delve into the day to day operations of a school district than do non-Indian school board members. In many instances, moreover, the background of a person—Indian or non-Indian—who has the time and money to run for public office may differ significantly from that of the parents of edu-

from other states who reside in federal dormitories.[161] One portion of the Act, however, appears to be a serious congressional error. Section four contains the following proviso: *"Provided,* that where students other than Indian students participate in such programs, money expended under such contract shall be prorated to cover the participation of only the Indian students."[162] This provision addresses two troubling and persistent problems which arise in connection with JOM. In predominantly Indian schools or classes it seems unfair to exclude on the grounds of race a handful of non-Indian children from JOM funded programs such as an excursion to the state capitol or remedial reading.[163] Secondly, many school districts are unable to support programs such as kindergarten that are desirable for all students without the use of JOM monies. Since JOM monies are appropriated "for Indians," at first glance it appears reasonable to permit non-Indian participation in JOM funded activities on the condition that unrestricted funds be used to support the non-Indian portion of the program.

On closer examination, however, it seems clear that to the extent the provision is utilized, it converts a supplemental program into basic support, thereby vitiating one of the most significant recent reforms in the JOM program. If, for example, a school district offers a kindergarten program for all children and prorates the cost between JOM and state and local monies in proportion to the ratio of Indian to non-Indian children, the JOM funds supplant the other monies.[164] In the case of *Denetclarence v. Board of Education*

---

cationally deprived children, and it is this latter group that needs a greater voice in education decisions.

161. In New Mexico, Arizona, South Dakota, and Alaska the Bureau of Indian Affairs operates dormitories for Indian students living in remote areas not readily accessible to public schools. Through the so-called "bordertown" domitory program, Indian students attend public school in districts reasonably close to their home communities. In the past, the BIA paid full tuition to the public school district for each Indian child, but in 1970 the Comptroller General issued a report criticizing the BIA for this practice. The Comptroller General's Report noted that the education of Indians is the responsibility of the states, that in addition to BIA tuition payments, the local school districts also collected P.L. 874 payments and state A.D.A. payments for each Indian child which resulted in a financial windfall to the local school districts. This section authorizes the Secretary of Interior to make full tuition payments to local school districts only when the Indian children attending school reside in a state other than the one in which the school is located.

Payments under this section should be scruntinized carefully. It is possible, for example, that Indian children will be shipped from North to South Dakota or from Arizona to New Mexico not because schools are unavailable in their home state, but because extra federal monies can be generated by crossing state lines. Indeed, the bordertown dormitory program is something of an anachronism. As more roads are built every year on the reservations, the number of children living away from home in federal dormitories should decline steadily.

162. Pub. L. No. 93-638, tit. II, § 202, 88 Stat. 2213 (Jan. 4, 1975).

163. An analysis of the relationship between Indian law and civil rights law is contained in Rosenfelt, *supra* note 5, at 530-50. Briefly, that article suggests that the seemingly conflicting constitutional policies against racial classifications but in favor of Indian tribal sovereignty can be reconciled.

164. The term "supplanting" refers to the use of federal categorical aid to replace state and local support for an educational program available to all students. *See, e.g.,* 45 C.F.R. § 116.17(h) (1975).

of Independent School District No. 22, the Secretary of Interior and the Secretary of Health, Education and Welfare voluntarily bound themselves to a federal court judgment which specifically identified this practice as constituting a misuse of JOM funds.[165] While Congress has the power to make this major change in the law, there is no indication—apart from the statutory language—that it intended to do so. The provision did not appear in the drafts of the bill which were circulated to Indian people, and it is not mentioned in the committee reports.[166]

Even more serious, the proration provision, in effect, purports to authorize racial discrimination against Indian children—a result which Congress obviously did not intend.[167] Where state or local funds are used to provide educational services for non-Indians, the services must also be provided for Indian children on the same terms and conditions and to the same extent.[168] This goes to the very essence of equal educational opportunity. Providing identical educational services from separate funding sources may appear unobjectionable, but it is not far removed from the provision of identical services in separate facilities and, ultimately, the provision of unequal services. Where such distinctions are based solely on race, the Constitution is offended.

If Congress wishes to authorize non-Indian participation in JOM programs where such participation would not dilute the effectiveness of the project, it should do so directly.[169] In order to protect the integrity of the project,

---

165. Civil No. 8872 (D.N.M., filed Feb. 14, 1974) incorporating Agreement of Parties dated Dec. 14, 1973. Paragraph 14 of the Agreement of Parties includes the following:
> All children located in district schools not on the reservation were eligible to attend kindergarten at Ruth N. Bond Elementary School in Kirtland. The kindergarten program at the Bond school was funded partially by operational funds and partially by Johnson-O'Malley funds on a prorata basis. The Johnson-O'Malley contribution to the kindergarten at Bond Elementary School was approximately equal to the percentage of Navajo students who attended the kindergarten there. The provision of such services from Title 1 and Johnson-O'Malley funds constituted supplanting of state and local funds by federal categorical aid.

166. H.R. REP. No. 1600, 93d Cong., 2d Sess. (1974); S. REP. No. 762, 93d Cong., 2d Sess. (1974).

167. Section 205 of the same Indian Education Assistance Act expressly requires school districts receiving JOM funds to provide "the quality and standard of education . . . for Indian students . . . at least equal to that provided all other students from resources . . . available to the local school district." Pub. L. No. 93-638, tit. II, § 205, 88 Stat. 2213 (Jan. 4, 1975). It appears impossible to reconcile the proration provision with this stricture.

168. Natonabah v. Board of Educ., 355 F. Supp. 716; Hobson v. Hansen, 269 F. Supp. 401 (D.D.C. 1967), *aff'd en banc sub nom.* Smuck v. Hobson, 408 F.2d 175 (D.C. Cir. 1969); Hobson v. Hansen, 327 F. Supp. 844 (D.D.C. 1971); *cf.* Brown v. Board of Educ., 347 U.S. 483, 493 (1954). *See also* 42 U.S.C. § 2000d (1970); 43 C.F.R. §§ 17.1, 17.2, 17.3(b); United States v. Jefferson County Bd. of Educ., 372 F.2d 836, 899-900 (5th Cir. 1966), *aff'd per curiam on rehearing en banc*, 380 F.2d 385 (5th Cir.), *cert. denied*, 389 U.S. 840 (1967).

169. Title I regulation 45 C.F.R. § 116.17(a) (1975) permits the participation of educationally deprived children who live outside the project area "if such a participation will not dilute the effectiveness of the project with respect to children residing in the project area." The analogy to JOM is not a true one, however, because in the Title I example all participants will be "educationally deprived children" who are within the class of beneficiaries designed by Congress. For

however, any non-Indian participation should be expressly approved by the local Indian parent committee and a minimum ratio of Indians to non-Indians should be prescribed.[170] In all events, the proration proviso should be repealed.

Conclusion

During the last half decade the Indian Education Act, the Indian Self-Determination and Education Assistance Act, the revised Johnson-O'Malley regulations, and the improved administration of Title I have created a statutory and administrative framework which makes it possible for Indian communities to shape educational programs in a more flexible, relevant, and responsive manner. Equally important, the nationwide recognition of the inequities resulting from a school finance system based largely on local real property taxation and the movement for increased state funding and equalization of local school budgets provide further assistance for the education of Indian children. In order to achieve greater equity in the allocation of resources and to improve the efficiency and responsiveness of educational agencies at all levels of government, further legislative refinements, such as those suggested here, are needed. In general, federal financial assistance to the states must be coupled with federal insistence that the states discharge their responsibility to provide an adequate basic education program in a non-discriminatory manner. The major federally funded compensatory education programs serving Indians are basically sound. With the development of rational funding priorities and the adoption of specific, minor amendments, the efficacy, efficiency, and equity of the compensatory programs will be immeasurably enhanced.

JOM, however, the class of beneficiaries is limited to "Indians." 25 U.S.C. § 452 (1970). It should be noted that neither the Indian Education Act nor its regulations addresses this issue. If Congress considers the question of non-Indian participation in JOM, it should do the same with the IEA.

170. It must be noted that large numbers of Indian people feel strongly that JOM benefits should be limited exclusively to Indians and that activities suitable for all students should be funded by operational monies. If Congress were to authorize the expenditure of JOM monies for non-Indians even under the restrictive provisions suggested above, Indian parent committees might perceive pressure from school administrators and their non-Indian neighbors which would induce them to give a high priority to the preservation of racial harmony in place of the educational needs of their children. In this instance, then, the consequences of a broad delegation of authority to local Indian parent committees should be considered most carefully.